The University of the Future

Editors

Dan Remenyi
Kenneth A. Grant
Shawren Singh

The University of the Future

Eds. Dan Remenyi, Kenneth A. Grant and Shawren Singh

First edition, December 2019

Copyright © 2019 the Authors

All rights reserved. No part of this publication may be reproduced in any material form (including photocopying or storing in any medium by electronic means and whether or not transiently or incidentally to some other use of this publication) without the written permission of the copyright holder except in accordance with the provisions of the Copyright Designs and Patents Act 1988, or under the terms of a licence issued by the Copyright Licensing Agency Ltd, Saffron House, 6-10 Kirby Street, London EC1N 8TS. Applications for the copyright holder's written permission to reproduce any part of this publication should be addressed to the publishers.

Disclaimer: While every effort has been made by the editor, authors and the publishers to ensure that all the material in this book is accurate and correct at the time of going to press, any error made by readers as a result of any of the material, or other information in this book is the sole responsibility of the reader. Readers should be aware that the URLs quoted in the book may change or be damaged by malware between the time of publishing and accessing by readers.

ISBN: 978-1-912764-51-8

Published by: ACPIL, Reading, RG4 9SJ, United Kingdom, info@academic-conferences.org Available from www.academic-bookshop.com

Contents

	Contents	i
	Acknowledgements	iii
	The Editors	iv
	Contributing Authors	v
	Introduction	vii
1	**Common Sense and the Future Proofed University**	1
	Gabriel Donleavy	
2	**The Education Continuum: A Journey of Reinvention**	15
	Madelyn Blair and Denise Lee	
3	**The 21st Century University: Quo Vadis?**	29
	Mandla Stanley Makhanya	
4	**The University: Current Perspectives and Views for the Future**	45
	Ivy Adwowa Efiefi Ekem	
5	**Smart Learning and Smart University Campuses**	55
	Niyi Awofeso and Adi Arida	
6	**What is this Slippery Thing called *Education*?**	65
	Dan Remenyi	
7	**Teaching and Learning in the 21st Century University**	91
	Kenneth A. Grant and Steven A. Gedeon	
8	**Higher Learning in the Age of Data**	105
	Andrew D. Banasiewicz	
9	**Ethics, Sustainability and 95 Theses for Higher Education Reform**	121
	Christopher J Moon	
10	**Popular Media and Ethical Business Schools of the Future**	141
	Lakshmi Balachandran Nair	
11	**Knowledge and Skills for Postgraduate Business Students of the Future**	151
	Peter Sharp	
12	**Bildung and the Digital Revolution**	165
	Emanuela Marchetti	
13	**Learning Designs and Systems in the University of the Future**	183
	Anthony 'Skip' Basiel	
14	**Future-Proofing a Region's Knowledge Economy**	201
	Gareth Huw Davies, Naomi Joyce and David Bolton	

15 **Knowledge Gaps: Future of Universities in Low and Middle Income Countries** 219
Cees Th. Smit Sibinga, Maruff Oladejo, Isaac Kajja and Arwa Z. Al-Riyami

16 **Decarbonisation Roadmap for Universities of the Future** 229
William Horan, Rachel Shawe, Richard Moles and Bernadette O'Regan

17 **Higher Education in a Post-Conflict Society** 241
Dima Moain Dayoub

Epilogue 255
Index 259

Acknowledgements

This book is on the face of it the product of 28 authors from 15 countries. But this is in fact an underestimate of the number of people and the different sources of ideas which are represented here. Academics talk continuously about their profession and about how their universities are performing. They regularly have ideas as to how to improve performance both at the individual and organisational level. It is this on-going conversation among hundreds of academics which this book has tapped into, in a small way. It was realised that no one book could represent anything more than a micro-slice of what is currently being discussed about the future of the university and it was never the purpose of this exercise to try to forecast what would happen to universities. There are far too many universities of different types to make such an exercise valuable.

By this acknowledgement the editors wish to offer thanks to all those with whom they have discussed this subject over many years and from whose input their ideas have developed.

The success of this book will be measured by the extent that it facilitates discussion and reflection by academics and others on how the university system works and how individuals and organisations might contribute to the future evolution of the university as an important institution in our society.

The Editors

After completing an MBA **Dan Remenyi** spent 15 years in business as an ICT consultant before undertaking a PhD. Since obtaining his doctorate he has held a variety of visiting professorships in the United Kingdom, the Republic of Ireland and South Africa. He originally researched and taught in the ICT management field, but for the past two decades he has increasingly focussed on research methodology and the sociology of research. He has had some 30 textbooks published. Some of his books have been translated into Chinese, Japanese and Romanian. He is the Academic Director of Academic Conferences and Publishing International Ltd (ACPIL) and also an Extraordinary Professor and the University of the Western Cape in South Africa. He holds a BSocSc MBA and PhD.

Ken Grant is the Chair of the Department of Entrepreneurship and Strategy in the Ted Rogers School of Management at Ryerson University. He is a frequent visiting professor in the UK, Europe and Asia. His research interests include entrepreneurship, strategy, knowledge management and innovation, and pedagogy and he is an active coach and supporter of student entrepreneur activity across Ryerson and internationally. Prior to joining Ryerson, Ken had an extensive career as a management consultant and industry executive in Canada and the UK, leading global consulting practices in several major firms. He holds a BA degree from the Open University, an MBA from the Schulich School of Business and a DBA from Henley Business School and is a Certified Management Consultant.

Shawren Singh holds a B Com, B Tech, MSc and PhD is an Associate Professor in the School of Computing at the University of South Africa, the largest university on the African continent. He has spent more than 20 years teaching and researching in the Information Systems space. In 2014 he obtained his PhD, based on research into eGovernment in South Africa, from the University of the Witwatersrand. His current research has focused on digital scholarship and e-Government. He is currently the chair of the Information Systems research committee in the School as well as serving on the Employment Equity Committee of the College of Science, Engineering and Technology of UNISA.

Contributing Authors

Author Name	Affiliation
Arwa Z. Al-Riyam	Department of Haematology, Sultan Qaboos University Hospital, Muscat, Oman
Adi Arida	School of Health and Environmental Studies, Hamdan Bin Mohammed Smart University, Dubai, United Arab Emirates
Niyi Awofeso	School of Health and Environmental Studies, Hamdan Bin Mohammed Smart University, Dubai, United Arab Emirates
Lakshmi Balachandran	Faculty of Social & Behavioural Sciences, Utrecht University, Netherlands
Andrew D. Banasiewicz	Merrimack College, North Andover, MA, USA
Anthony 'Skip' Basiel	Queen Mary University of London, UK
Madelyn Blair	Pelerei, LLC, Washington DC, USA
David Bolton	School of Management, Swansea University, Wales, UK
Gareth Huw Davies	School of Management, Swansea University, Wales, UK
Dima Moain Dayoub	The Higher Institute of Languages, Tishreen University, Syria
Gabriel Donleavy	UNE Business School, University of New England, NSW, Australia
Ivy Adwowa Efiefi Ekem	School of Medical Sciences, University of Cape Coast, Cape Coast, Ghana
Steven A. Gedeon	Ted Rogers School of Management, Ryerson University, Toronto, Canada
Kenneth A. Grant	Ted Rogers School of Management, Ryerson University, Toronto, Canada
William Horan	School of Natural Sciences, University of Limerick, Ireland

Naomi Joyce	School of Medicine, Swansea University, Wales, UK
Isaac Kajja	Makerere University, Kampala, Uganda
Denise Lee	PwC, Washington DC, USA
Emanuela Marchetti	Department for the Study of Culture, Media Studies, University of Southern Denmark, Odense, Denmark
Professor Mandla Stanley Makhanya	Principal and Vice Chancellor, University of South Africa, Pretoria/Tshwane, South Africa
Richard Moles	Centre for Environmental Research, University of Limerick, Ireland
Christopher J. Moon	Middlesex University, London, UK
Maruff Oladejo	University of Lagos, Nigeria
Bernadette O'Regan	School of Natural Sciences, University of Limerick, Ireland
Dan Remenyi	ACPIL UK and University of the Western Cape, South Africa
Peter Sharp	Regents University London, UK
Rachel Shawe	Centre for Environmental Research, University of Limerick, Ireland
Cees Th. Smit Sibinga	IQM Consulting, Zuidhorn & University of Groningen, Netherlands

Introduction

There is a potential problem deeply embedded in the title of this book. By using the words "The University" it is possible to believe there is a suggestion that there will be only one type of university in the future or that there will be a "best" model for a university in the future. Clearly such a suggestion would be nonsense. As there are today, there will continue to be many different types of universities[1] in the future with multiple objectives, values, types of students, funding sources, facilities and faculties. There will be many ways of delivering and assessing university education. However, this is not to imply that the word university will become a descriptor for a vague and ill-defined concept or organisation[2]. Universities will continue to attract those who wish to pursue learning. The issue is perhaps how this learning will be structured and how it will be delivered, which will look quite different to what we know now. Further, whereas it may be said that there is a dozen or more different types of university today perhaps in the future there will be dozens of different types of universities. The kaleidoscope effect which will be produced by the increase in the number of universities will be intensified by the fact that until recent years universities in many, if not most countries, were typically modelled more or less on an approach to higher education originally developed and slowly evolved for centuries. An important aspect of the original model of the university was the fact that universities were perceived as *public service not-for-profit institutions*. Today this mind set has changed and there are now universities created with the intention of profit making. Furthermore, with traditional sources of funding becoming more difficult, there has been a general change in attitude towards finance with concepts like the bottom line being introduced in many of the established universities.

How the book was produced

It was for this reason that it was suggested that this book, produced by inviting contributions from academics and other interested parties from around the world, might be able to capture some of the diversity which will be increasingly present in universities as the years go by. Thus, the book is a collection of ideas from a wide range of individuals from four continents. Most contributing authors are practicing academics, but there are also contributions from others who have a particular interest in and have an interesting opinion about how universities may develop in the future.

To bring these ideas together a call for chapters was issued and some 50 individuals responded showing interest in contributing to this work. This

---

[1] The word university should no longer conjures up one image. Like the word aeroplane which can be used to describe anything from a single engine Cessna to an Air Bus A380 the word University can now describe a wide variety of different institutions all with different capacities, capabilities and potential.
[2] There is a suggestion in some quarters that this has already begun to happen due to the many different types of institutions which now call themselves universities.

eventually led to 23 submissions being received and of these 17 chapters make up the book.

In total there are 28 authors involved in the production of these chapters and these authors come from 15 different countries; Australia, Canada, Denmark, England, Ghana, Ireland, Netherlands, Nigeria, Oman, South Africa, Syria, Uganda, United Arab Emirates, USA and Wales.

Each chapter in the book offers a different perspective on one or more of the many different dimensions involved in the operation of a university. These chapters have been inspected by the editors who have endeavoured to retain, as fully as possible, the voice of the authors. Consequently, very few changes have been made to the original text provided. Clearly, the views expressed in each chapter are those of the author/s and are not necessarily endorsed by the editors.

We have not attempted to standardise the English used by the different authors. Thus some of the papers have been produced using vocabulary and the spell checker for North American English and some papers have used other varieties of the language.

Each author or group of authors were asked to write a short statement which articulates the main thrust of their chapter. These are provided below and it is hoped that they will be of assistance to readers in deciding which chapters are most interesting for them to study in some detail.

This book does not attempt in any way to forecast what will happen to universities in the future. It is the purpose of the book to point out the many complex issues which constitute the fabric of a modern university and to make some suggestions as to how universities might be conceptualised in the future in order to deliver the maximum benefit to all the various stakeholders.

The book has also been produced in the expectation that it may be of value to prospective students who are considering enrolling at a University and are not quite sure what a university education can deliver and how to choose the most appropriate university for their purposes.

A short statement relating to each chapter

ONE
Common Sense and the Future Proofed University
Gabriel Donleavy
UNE Business School, University of New England, NSW, Australia

The transition from elite higher education to mass higher education is a process that is still unfinished. While massification has had benefits for people previously unable to access higher education, it has been accompanied by costs to teachers, taxpayers and to the quality of the educational experience. In the chapter, the history of massification is summarised in part one and the costs are discussed. In part two the further expansion of university education over the course of the next decade is considered. The rise of online education to dominance in the near future is argued. The nature and consequences of increasingly sharp competition for students and between students is addressed and some survival strategies for a university caught up in these pressures are discussed. The need for cultivating adaptability to the unforeseen is explained as a key survival strategy that in turn requires rethinking both university governance and the courses offered. Courses that have savoir faire and the ability to use common sense are argued to be essential and the nature of such future courses is briefly adumbrated. In part three predictions are made about university evolution for the 2030s of which the most important is the implosion when the expansion hits natural barriers of graduate unemployment, replacement of skilled mental labour by Artificial Intelligence (AI) and by the steep decline in birth rates from the peaks that had fuelled university expansion. Attention is drawn to the adaptability of the public library as a learning centre that universities could merge with as part of the their strategy to compete effectively. Finally it is argued that a return to the enlightenment values of elite education and the collegiality and parity of esteem within the academy that was involved is of itself a recipe for success after the implosion kills off the notion that university success and competing against all others as if a university were a soccer team dies its overdue death.

TWO
The Education Continuum: A Journey of Reinvention
Madelyn Blair[1] and Denise Lee[2]
[1] Pelerei, LLC, Washington DC, USA
[2] PwC, Washington DC, USA

In the global workforce individual mobility, set in a fast-paced and changing marketplace, requires today's workers to build a strong adaptable skillset. A formal university degree is now just the beginning of the story. Workers in the future will change careers more times than their parents changed job titles. The ability to work for one organization and then retire is gone. Not only is job security becoming obsolete in the workplace, but the increasing pace of technology and automation, through AI and robotics, is moving beyond the replacement of repeatable tasks to affecting white collar jobs, such as accounting. Discussed in this chapter is the role of universities in the future and how they must evolve to be relevant with the myriad of forces at play including technology, structures, and the needs of the student of tomorrow.

THREE
The 21st Century University: Quo Vadis?
Professor Mandla Stanley Makhanya
Principal and Vice Chancellor, University of South Africa, Pretoria/Tshwane, South Africa

21st Century higher education is sailing into a future that is being driven substantially by seismic and accretive shifts in technology and attendant forces that are calling into question the notion, role and purpose of education and with it, the role of the university. Key drivers of the current disequilibrium and disruption in higher education include: accelerated technological innovation; concerns around sustainability, social justice and equity; a borderless yet increasingly divided and fragmented world influenced increasingly by changing demographics; and a plethora of "actors" or stakeholders whose aims and objectives differ substantially from those which are currently assumed or provided for. The collective impact of these forces on society and institutions of higher learning is impelling leaders and management, staff and students of all ages to "unlearn" and re-learn (or learn anew) if they are to prevail and remain relevant in future. This chapter will provide some thoughts and insights on the future of the university in this fluid context.

FOUR
The University: Current Perspectives and Views for the Future
Ivy Adwowa Efiefi Ekem
School of Medical Sciences, University of Cape Coast, Ghana

The current university is separated from the community physically, mentally and socially. Knowledge acquired is second-hand. Topics in research often have no bearing on the society and findings are often not of value to policy makers and implementers. The link with the community and everyday living is absent. True citadels of learning must through their activities and products, help make communities and the world at large better places, both in terms of human development, justice for all and environmental wholesomeness. This chapter considers these issues and suggests how education in the university of the future needs to fully integrate problem-based learning and community engagement.

FIVE
Smart Learning in University Education: Benefits, Potentials and Challenges
Niyi Awofeso and Adi Arida
School of Health and Environmental Studies, Hamdan Bin Mohammed Smart University, Dubai, United Arab Emirates

The University of the Future will, at its core, retain its phylogenic roots as a community of facilitators and learners advancing knowledge within defined settings (*universitas magistrorum et scholarium*). Its ontogeny will, however, continue to change to align the aspirations, skills and competencies of its graduates with society's workforce requirements. This chapter reviews how technologies are being utilized to advance the mission of Universities of the Future. Context-aware ubiquitous learning (i.e. smart learning) is an approach that enables students to learn from the real world with support from learning management systems using mobile, wireless communication and sensing technologies.

SIX
What is this Slippery Thing called *Education*?
Dan Remenyi
ACPIL, UK and University of the Western Cape, South Africa

Everyone knows what education is. Or do they? Politicians endlessly talk about the importance of education and the population listens attentively. But in fact, the concept of education is rather nuanced and not that well understood. This chapter explores how education functions and what can be expected of it. It particular the chapter looks at the university as an educator, student engagement, how examinations are conducted and how to assess today's university performance. The idea of "work-ready" and internships are addressed and a new expression, work-savvy is coin. Then the difficult debate concerning the decolonisation of education is explored. Last but not least the issue of the future is addressed, which leads to "A tale of two educations".

SEVEN
Teaching and Learning in the 21st Century University
Kenneth A. Grant and Steven A. Gedeon
Ted Rogers School of Management, Ryerson University, Toronto, Canada

Universities and their professoriates need to reconsider how to address their teaching responsibilities. Despite innovative efforts across the world, most university courses are delivered in an ineffective lecture-based manner by research-focussed faculty who have often received little or no education and training in pedagogy. Student-centric learning pedagogies such as active and experiential learning are recognised as key tools in student engagement, yet their use is not systemic. Professors should be trained on how students learn and how to achieve competency-based learning outcomes through a range of pedagogical techniques. Universities should provide improved teaching support for these pedagogies through new technologies and more effective learning spaces. This chapter discusses these issues and makes some suggestions for improvement.

EIGHT
Higher Learning in the Age of Data
Andrew D. Banasiewicz
Merrimack College North Andover, MA, USA

In this chapter, university-based teaching and learning is examined from the perspective of rapid maturation and proliferation of advanced self-functioning technologies, broadly referred to as artificial intelligence (AI). Offering an expanded conception of what it means to 'learn' and to 'know', one that expressly differentiates between reason-based and technology-based learning modalities encompassing human and machine learning, the author argues that AI technologies are reshaping the very mission of institutions of higher learning. By expressly addressing the interaction between higher learning and advanced information technologies, this chapter makes an important contribution to the University of the Future body of work.

NINE
Ethics, Sustainability and 95 Theses for the Reform of Higher Education
Christopher J. Moon
Middlesex University, London, UK

This chapter charts the historical development of universities and their mission, the rise of Higher Education Institutions (HEIs), and the challenges faced by HEIs in adapting to current issues faced by society. According to Yong-Hak (2019) universities today are considered as focal points for achieving the United Nations Sustainable Development Goals (SDGs). Yet, only a minority of universities have committed to achieving the SDGs; and those that have made a commitment tend to focus only on SDG#4 Education (Moon et al, 2018). This chapter, therefore, critically discusses the power of academic institutions to look ahead, to mobilise knowledge and to be truth-seekers in the age of sustainable development. The chapter includes research on the take up of the UN Higher Education Sustainability Initiative (HESI) from over 300 HEIs globally, recognises challenges faced by HEIs, and provides recommendations for changes in governance, curriculum and pedagogy.

TEN
Popular Media and Ethical Business Schools of the Future
Lakshmi Balachandran
Faculty of Social & Behavioural Sciences, Utrecht University, Netherlands

This chapter discusses the use of popular media (short clips from movies or TV shows, short novels or story excerpts, games etc.) as tools for sustainability-oriented business and management education. The sustainability issues experienced by our fast-changing society cannot be fully captured by academic articles, long lectures, or case studies alone. Popular media is an efficient way of reaching the 21st century student who has limited attention span and is more visually (rather than textually) oriented. The author discusses some examples of such popular media and subsequently examines how student audiences responded to their use in two Bachelor programs.

ELEVEN
Knowledge and Skills for Postgraduate Business Students for the Future
Peter Sharp
Regents University London, UK

This chapter identifies challenges Higher Education Institutions (HEIs) face in the 21st century in the context of training postgraduate business and management students in appropriate knowledge and skills for the future. These challenges include understanding what future employers will need from employees, who should be responsible for training students, what methods should be used, and the level of emphasis on work placements. The chapter explains why the greater emphasis on training business and management students to be employable is likely to continue in the future and discusses trends from literature and learning experiences of international business students from work placements. Recommendations are given for what HEIs need to do in the future: they should take time nurturing business students up to and through work placements; and, generally, should emphasise training that instils confidence, communication skills and self-understanding so that future postgraduates are able to adapt to change well and keep learning in their roles.

TWELVE
Bildung and the Digital Turn
Emanuela Marchetti
Department for the Study of Culture, Media Studies, University of Southern Denmark, Odense, Denmark

The *digital turn* has brought radical transformations in society. The advent of online learning is threatening the educational role of universities, while the increasing need of digital skills has forced humanists to stretch beyond their core competences. In this chapter, the author aims to show policy makers that universities and the humanities are living institutions, able to face societal changes. Hence, she argues for higher investments in qualified research-based teaching, which is a driving force for introducing innovation in education and for fostering the individual development of students as future citizens, able to contribute to society in its complex.

THIRTEEN
Learning Designs and Systems in the University of the Future
Anthony 'Skip' Basiel
Queen Mary University of London, UK

This chapter explores trends in society and higher education to inform possible future university models, features and technologies. The argument is presented in two parts. First, an analysis of higher education futurists provides insight into possible ways to 'deschool' society. Variations of informal learning designs and supporting technology are offered. Changes in the economy and the skills needed to move from our current model to a future knowledge economy are discussed. Sample case studies illustrate drivers for new higher education curriculum and instructional design. Next, the use of interactive immersive webinar design as a future blended learning solution is critically reviewed. Webinar pedagogy is examined to provide insight into selecting appropriate blended learning elements in the future higher education context.

FOURTEEN
Future Proofing a University in a Region's Knowledge Economy
Gareth Huw Davies[1], Naomi Joyce[2], David Bolton[1]
[1]School of Management, Swansea University, Wales, UK
[2]School of Medicine, Swansea University, Wales, UK

This chapter explores the case of Swansea University through *infrastructure* and *activity* initiatives, identifying learning of potential benefit to other post-industrial regions. These initiatives emphasise the diverse interactions across ecosystems, and the timescales involved in supporting knowledge-based regional economic development. Universities evolve over periods measured in decades and generations, though with increasing focus upon Research Excellence and Knowledge Exchange Frameworks providing added impetus to demonstrating societal relevance of university activity. This chapter demonstrates how, despite enormous contextual changes, a university role has remained one of enlarging the world of knowledge to the benefit of the community it serves.

FIFTEEN
Knowledge Gaps: The Future of Universities in Low and Middle Income Countries
Cees Th. Smit Sibinga[1], Maruff Oladejo[2], Isaac Kajja[3], Arwa Z. Al-Riyam[4]
[1]IQM Consulting, Zuidhorn & University of Groningen, Netherlands
[2]University of Lagos, Nigeria
[3]Makerere University, Kampala, Uganda
[4]Sultan Qaboos University Hospital, Muscat, Oman

In general, the level of education and knowledge in a society depends largely on family environment, primary and secondary school teaching and level of education at vocational and academic institutes. The higher the degree of final education the more important is the baseline education and knowledge acquisition at high schools and colleges. One of the indices of the UNDP Human Development Index (HDI) system is education and in particular the years per individual spent in education, and percentage of youngsters in age categories for elementary, secondary and tertiary education. The higher the HDI, the more years spent in education and the larger the percentage of youngsters exposed to higher education. This chapter considers the knowledge gap in individuals living in newly independent post-colonial countries and suggests some approaches to close this gap.

SIXTEEN
Decarbonisation Roadmap for Universities of the Future
William Horan, Rachel Shawe, Richard Moles and Bernadette O'Regan
University of Limerick, Ireland

In facilitating societal transitions towards environmental sustainability, university campuses have been identified as ideal locations to focus resources, in terms of deployment and experimentation of decarbonisation technologies, due to their ability to demonstrate best practice for further replication within the wider society. This chapter outlines a roadmap to inform how universities can reduce their carbon emissions, with illustrative application to Ireland's growing higher education sector. Given projected global growth of student numbers and the associated increase in material throughput, university campuses serve as a useful testing ground to inform carbon reduction strategies for similarly growing community populations nationally.

SEVENTEEN
Higher Education Context in a Post-Conflict Society
Dima Moain Dayoub
The Higher Institute of languages, Tishreen University, Syria

At the turn of this century, fast-paced technological advances have been a catalyst for change across various sectors, including higher education. On the horizon lie unprecedented technology-enabled opportunities of access, inclusion and infrastructure capacity expansion. However, enormous challenges to academic integrity and future employability loom. Diversified higher education modes of delivery that are adaptable to learners' unique circumstances will overwrite the image of universities as bricks-and-mortar sources of one-way knowledge transfer for the elite and high-achieving. Universities will be platforms of multimodal nodes of knowledge, and access to these platforms will be largely virtual. The notion of attendance will be expanded to mean commitment and interaction with learning resources outside fixed classroom timings. Promising future directions involve not only broadening access to higher education, but also the horizons of students' experiences by harnessing the powers of immersive technologies and international digital open-source content, and by upgrading the skills of students and faculty alike. Finally, tomorrow's universities will need to assert their online presence through digital content production; otherwise, they run the risk of remaining invisible. The contribution of this chapter lies in casting light on the relative notion of the future in the case of universities rising from years of conflict-imposed disruptions and striving to fulfil human, societal and economic reconstruction on one hand, and to advance towards future objectives on the other.

1

Common Sense and the Future Proofed University

Gabriel Donleavy
UNE Business School, University of New England, NSW, Australia

Introduction

A common mood among academics throughout the first world is nostalgia for the golden age of elite education (Trowler 1997, Holm-Nielsen 2018). Forty years ago, classes were small, heads and deans were friendly and collegial team leaders support staff supported academic activity, research was undertaken for its own sake and also for its social utility; but never just to get a publication to help keep one's job. It was usually safe to hold tutorials with members of the opposite gender without the need of a chaperone or surveillance. Tests, quizzes, essays and examinations were marked solely with reference to the academic performance of the candidate. It was assumed students enrolled onto a course in order to acquire a body of knowledge and a set of cognitive skills that would serve them well with whatever they chose to do after graduation. It was widely accepted that universities prepared tomorrow's leaders, tomorrow's citizens and tomorrow's professional for a life of service to the public good (Stoer 2006, Holford 2016). It was obvious then that university education was an utterly different process from job apprenticeships and technical training. Training was, by definition, about learning to do properly tasks intrinsic to a particular job, trade or business. To the educational idealists of the fifties and sixties, this fine academic life did not need to remain the possession of the aristocracy, the affluent bourgeoisie and the *unusually* gifted proletarian. The idealist saw universities as potentially making society less class ridden and more egalitarian. The assumption was that if more teenagers were admitted to universities, class barriers would be more permeable, the nation would be wiser hence richer and that society itself would reflect the leavening and levelling that university expansion would entail (Altbach 1999). Oxford, Cambridge and the top Redbrick universities in the UK in the period from the mid-sixties to the early eighties were places of great diversity of regional accent and worldwide ethnic diversity. It seemed as if the move from elite higher education to mass higher education was a great success for all involved.

The ascendancy of neoliberalism with the installation in office of Margaret Thatcher entailed a value for money framing of state investment in higher education in England (Trow 1998, Longden 2000). It was quite new and quite discomfiting to find that value meant market value and it was argued that the main beneficiary of a higher education was the graduating student. Accordingly, free education privileged graduates against the rest of society. Student fees and loans replaced state subsidised education and fees were steadily increased. At the same time, public money flowing from the taxpayer to universities was repeatedly cut. To ensure private sector business disciplines were adopted by universities, funding councils replaced grants committees. This meant that the pressures of the free market were sharply and steadily directed at the universities not through the student market directly but through a government bureaucracy of funding councils and quality assurance agencies (Trow 2006, Kromydes 2017). To expand university numbers, polytechnics were renamed universities, caps on enrolments were removed and staff student ratios were allowed to rise to a level where seminars or tutorials with any meaningful interaction between student and staff became impossible. Student Staff Ratios (SSRs) of over 25 were almost universal outside of Oxbridge by the late nineties when the New Labour government first introduced student fees (Trow 2006).

Numbers were further increased in England by renaming colleges as universities subject to jumping hurdles imposed by the Quality Assurance Agency and the Higher Education Funding Council. Overseas recruitment at full cost fee levels increased numbers too but the main effect of the international recruitment acceleration was to confirm higher education as an industry like any other and to promote mercantilist competition with other Anglo countries in the race to recruit students from Asia (Kromydes 2017). This in turn gave rise to an increased salience for university league tables, as a proxy for signifying "value" (Donleavy and Chen 2019). The triumph of competition over co-operation was not confined to teaching, but was, if anything, even more Social Darwinist in research. University disciplines were all graded in the Research Assessment Exercise (RAE) with government block grants for research going only to the disciplines able to convince the inspectors their research was at international level, preferably so called 'world class". Again, the rationale was the free market, but the reality was tight state control.

Finally, universities were allowed to reorganise as business corporations, following the Eversheds (2009) report to the Cameron government. The distinction between a business company and a university had become a difference only of product line and of access to state cash. There was no substantial difference as regards corporate culture, hierarchical organization, management of "human resources", or managerial prerogative.

The last source of new numbers was the internet. This enabled students to take degrees online, not only from the national open universities, but soon from most regular universities too. In Australia, a significant number of universities have far more students enrolled online than on campus. In the wake of online higher education, 2008 saw the emergence of Massive Open Online Courses (MOOCs) that offered entirely free course units, until a student anted a credential at which point cash was required. The MOOCs had attrition rates often over 90% but the main providers have asserted the indirect payoff in marketing and PR was underpinned by enough income from the credentialing process to make it all worthwhile. It is still general that online courses have higher attrition rates than on campus equivalent courses (Rohs and Granz 2015, Henebery 2016, Costa et al 2018). Perhaps this is because it is a matter of easy come, easy go.

Another feature of the transition from elite to mass education is the emergence of well-funded private provider groups in vocationally oriented courses like accounting, rather less in the higher cost fields such as medicine and astrophysics.

Allied to the expansion of student numbers and new designated universities has been the emergence of vocational degrees in trades such as tourism, nutrition and even hairdressing. There are still apprenticeships and there are still successful technical colleges, but many have sought parity of esteem with traditional universities by turning apprenticeships into work based learning and higher diplomas into baccalaureate degrees.

Students in the age of mass education are no longer pupils, no longer patients to be cured of the disease of ignorance, but are enthroned as consumers, albeit consumers whose consumer sovereignty is conditional on being willing to assume decades of debt servitude like the bonded labourers of the pre-Victorian age.

The university of the near future

Defining the near future as the next decade, we can assume the trends outlined above will continue to gain momentum within a social, economic and regulatory structure that we would continue to recognise from today's perspective. In contrast to all these assumptions about the relative stability of human and state policies and structures, it is reasonable to assume there will continue to be technological advances, scientific discoveries and robotic or AI progress, that will have an essentially disruptive effect and in one or two cases, remake the way we communicate and learn as thoroughly, and as unpredictably, as the smart phone and tablet did in the previous decade. Because these breakthroughs are inherently unpredictable, it behoves a university not to waste resources planning for the unplannable, but rather to invest resources in becoming more rapidly and more appropriately adaptable to anything. That is, universities must monitor institutional and cultural sclerosis as part of their annual risk management review, as adaptability to the unforeseen is likely to increase significantly as a critical success factor in the increasingly competitive and cut-throat world of higher education, going forward.

Not all universities are yet significantly shaped by the presence of online students, but by the end of the decade, there will surely be only a few very specialist universities where the dominant mode of instruction and learning will be in person rather than online. Yet, no university is yet offering courses to prepare tomorrow's university teachers to acquire excellence in this demanding and nuanced way of managing learning. The need is obvious and early movers on this could expect great financial and status gains from offering such courses. The wider impact on academics of the coming dominance of online tuition over face to face is the need for them to adapt to a potential 24/7 availability with their students. One thing certain to make an online learning customer dissatisfied is the teacher who responds too little, too late or not at all to queries, even if the query was put on a closed form on the learning platform rather than in a bilateral communication to the teacher. Online students are more demanding than face to face ones because they have no lecture theatre, no classroom and no student union or café infrastructure to assure them that they belong to a community. They require the extra assurance of prompt and personalised attention to partially compensate for this. They are apt to be more conscious of value for money than face to face students are, precisely because online students do not receive the infrastructure and positive externalities that face to face students do. Some universities are still publicly declaring that the experience of taking their courses online is not significantly different, and especially not at all inferior, to taking the same courses face to face in person. This claim is simply invalid. The two learning experiences are so different that it is better to say one cannot be compared to the other than to claim they are effectively the same. Any academic teaching both modes can attest to this. In due course, university management and professional staff may conceivably also come to this realisation.

The successes of western universities in recruiting offshore full fee paying students in the last decade has prompted other countries to begin to fish in the same seas. This in turn has started to induce China and India to raise their "quality" in the usual western sense so as to retain a larger proportion of their compatriots inside the university system in their native land. The top universities in China have begun to copy the like of Monash, Warwick and INSEAD in establishing branch campuses offshore. It is likely that international competition in higher education will only intensify in the next decade. This means universities will become even more like large business corporations, and some will go one step beyond to become more like military units in their culture and operations. Such 'spearhead" universities will be very high ranked, will be driven by performance metrics, and will compete with fee inducements and giveaways (such as free laptops to all new enrolees). They will pressure academic staff to teach more subjects, to pass a greater proportion of borderline students, to do only research that attracts big grant financing, and to acknowledge as valid research results only those articles that get published in the very top ranking journals whose acceptance rates are below 5%. Perhaps the comparison with a military outfit is a little premature. Perhaps a better fitting metaphor is the soccer club struggling to keep its best players, struggling to rise in or out of its league and whose fortunes are driven more and more by the cash its tycoon patron makes available to the club. The courting of tycoons to finance competitive universities will see whole universities named, or more often renamed, after the saviour tycoon. This is not very different from how Harvard, Stanford or Bond universities began. Just as London came very late to skyscrapers last century, so we can expect England to catch up soon with the US in endowing "tycooniversities". Entrepreneurs with long periods of public exposure on such TV programmes as Dragons' Den in the UK or Shark Tank in Australia, could well see a university as both a good investment and a low risk ticket to immortality. Conversely universities will not confine their naming patronage to buildings, departments or campuses any longer but will be happy to rebadge the entire institution if the price is right. As was said by someone in response to Walpole's quip that every man has his price; not everyone can be bought, but everyone has a bait they cannot resist swallowing. All of this is congruent with, arguably derivative from, the increasing role of market forces to shape the nature of higher education.

The deskilling of the university teaching academic is blamed by some writers on massification and commodification of the educational process and the greatly increased power of management and of the professional staff who were once called support staff (for example:- Trowler 1997, Chomsky 2014, Melhuish 2018). IT is still widely feared for its possible replacement of people by machines by way of increasing technological unemployment. It is the experience of most university academics, however, that the number of staff needed to run an IT system tends to increase over time. Similarly, although continuing university expansion has been afforded partly through a decline in the student unit cost of teaching and the matching rise in staff student ratios, there has arisen within the university a feudal style court surrounding the office of "Executive" Dean. Originally there were Heads of Department that reported to Deans and academics were organised in disciplines, one or two disciplines for each department. Now, we seem to need a Deputy Dean, an Associate Dean Teaching and Learning, an Associate Dean Research, an Associate Dean International, a Faculty Academic Manager, a Faculty General Manager, etc. Appointing accountants, hedge fund managers and people of that type to a university council may well ensure the university cuts its payroll and electricity bills, extends its teaching period as near to 24/7 as it can manage with its penumbra of casual teachers. It is not likely to be the most effective source of building the adaptability and competitive effectiveness that universities need ever more pressingly as competition gets more deadly in an institutional survival sense. Retired generals and admirals such as used to fill the boards of British business firms for the decade after World War Two might be better attuned to the realities of the present university environment than accountants and hedge fund managers. I speak as an accountant myself.

The Ukraine elected a comedian to run the country in 2019. Some would say certain Anglophone countries have done the same. Elections do not usually produce the most expert, the most qualified or the most relevantly experienced people to run things. They do, however, produce the people able to command the most trust and goodwill, at least until actions and omissions destroy those endowments. Public corporations have annual general meetings where the executive and the CEO could be sacked if shareholders are dissatisfied enough to vote them out. In the old days of elite education, senior posts were elected. In the large modern university, elections to internal committees occur but elections to senior positions are almost wholly extinct. Is it surprising therefore that university staff are alienated from, and often contemptuous of, their executive seniors? Is it surprising that the professoriate and the general body of university employees are fearful and unhappy? Universities are even more like private governments than any public business corporation. It is hard to gather convincing empirical evidence that unaccountable dictatorship creates value, enhances excellence or increases the rate of scientific innovation This does not mean the conditions are ripe for a revolution in the university sector. It does suggest that the survival needs of better faster adaptation are not helped at all by present sclerotic governance cultures.

When an email is addressed to a student by name but has been composed to be sent to every student in a big cohort, it may alienate some recipients by its inauthenticity in pretended familiarity. If it is admitted that small tutorial class sizes were a major factor in the academic successes of elite higher education, such successes cannot be duplicated in mass higher education with much larger SSRs and predominantly online modes of learning. It is however possible to recreate over 50% of the old elite experience, by having peer mentors and small study groups for on campus enrolees together with a portfolio of forums, Skype and Zoom sessions for online students. It is not the size of the whole organisation that affects the student experience but the size of the groups in which s/he is a member. The adaptive university will seek to optimise the range and depth of the different teams in which their students will experience the university. Most universities still underestimate the salience to students of social and relationship capital building, even as they cast aspersions on the top universities as being more attuned to having the children of the elite meet other children of the elite than to acquiring knowledge. It is an Anglo deficiency not shared by Europeans to have only one word for "to know": whereas French, for example, takes connaître to be just as much knowing as savoir. Indeed, for some savoir faire – knowing how to do – is impossible without a great deal of connaître to accompany and underpin it. The adaptive university will realize this and seek to improve its students' social and networking skills. The non-adaptive university will treat such skills as non-academic and to be dealt with by the student choosing which societies and clubs they will belong to their "spare time". And spare time is a concept with little content or salience left to it as the internet age evolves.

Lastly, the intensification of competition does make it important to form and nurture alliances. A good alliance is one that is reliable, relevant and robust. Negotiating an alliance involves compromise, but not to the point where one party feels ever after that they were pressured to sign an unequal treaty. A large and rich enough university can set up subsidiary campuses to compete in other countries for on campus students. However, that is expensive, carries political risk (e.g. expropriation under a hostile future government as was a factor in the exit of Central European University from Hungary) and only works if the university already has high brand recognition among the target population and its parents in the new country. A joint venture between a rich high brand western university and a middle to high level local university shares the market risks, reduces the expropriation risk and should reduce the expense too. For a university high in the most widely recognised league tables such as the Shanghai Xiaotong or the Times Higher, the choice of potential negotiating partner and ally is virtually unlimited. The western university gains enrolments and market penetration; the local one gains international prestige, local income and access to international grants that would not have been possible without access to top academics with the kind of track records grant bodies like to see leading the projects they fund. The middle and lower ranked universities in the West cannot approach the acquisition of allies and partners in the same way. They need not, however, be confined to forming partnerships on a one discipline, one project or one entry pathway basis, as so many have been up to now.

Let us take Wessex Poly University, a fictitious ex technical college near Cirencester England with a total enrolment of 16,000 students of whom 12,000 are online. It has only six ongoing institutional partnerships at home and internationally and all of them are discipline specific. It wants to raise its numbers and its ranked performance by wider scope partnerships in the near future within its five-year strategic plan. It has identified its strongest selling points and its competitive threats, so it has already taken the first step to designing an effective alliance building strategy. Its next step is to identify other universities with similar competitive threats but with different competitive strengths with a view to offering students at the two universities the opportunity to do part of their studies at one university and part at the other - across the board if practically possible. Joint degrees, preferably awarded in two certificates, full double degrees, and two plus two or three plus one study years are all competitive strategies not possible without a partner but are attractive to many students. The more geographically separated the universities are, the more attractive is the joint experience to some kinds of student. On that logic one would have expected to see almost every British university partnered with almost every Australian and New Zealand university, but that scenario has not eventuated. Monash and Warwick have a quite similar arrangement, but both these are already high ranked in their own countries. The two sides of the world have yet to see the other side as a source of alliance rather than a source of competition; but increasing competition from European, American and Asian universities will change this perception over the next decade.

Over the last decade the main pond that western universities have fished in has been the Peoples' Republic of China (PRC) but the PRC is just beginning to start its own academic fishing industry. India, on the other hand, has been neglected on the grounds that few of its students can afford full fee places or online enrolments and few of its universities can afford, or need to attract foreign students. That too is beginning to change as India becomes more developed, implements its space race ambitions and pursues a determined strategy to raise its international academic profile. Accordingly, a middle ranking western university should be looking for good Indian partners now while India is more prepared than it will be in a few years' time to approve partnerships with western universities that transfer know how and enable western learning channels to become available to Indian students at affordable rates. For the western partner, the need to ensure that any joint study programmes are affordable will probably entail the active involvement of a financing agent, perhaps a large Indian business, bank or family trust, to endow the Indian students with the funds to pay the western partner's fee levels, which should nevertheless be below their normal international full fee levels or else why would the Indian partner even consider such a partnership in the first place.

Next consider a regional or small town university in the west. Most of the sons and daughters of local residents who are of university age and have the requisite entry scores, leave home to study as they want to have big city life opportunities. The small town university can sustain viability to some extent by acquiring a good online reputation, but it also wants to attract enough on campus students to provide a full student experience. Such a university needs to consider turning what are disadvantages to domestic students into advantages for international ones. Parents in much of Asia and beyond value the quiet, safety and lack of decadent distractions small town universities can be perceived to offer. The university should seek pathway partners in the countries where this cultural view is most pronounced, and seek alliances with universities in such countries to negotiate student exchanges, twinning arrangements and joint research especially in the science, technology, engineering and medical fields which have access to a greater range of large international research grants than do other disciplines. Such an alliance may need to recruit star academics near the end of their careers in contracts to bid for grants where a star with a relevant track record is a near necessity for submitting a successful bid.

Other commonalities can drive university alliances to deal with international competition for students and resources. Universities in their countries' capital cities have distinct issues that do not trouble provincial universities. Universities in towns that border neighbouring countries of a less friendly character have issues in common, as do universities in coastal areas specialising in maritime life, naval defence or high profile seasonally patterned tourism. Universities in different countries with similar names form the natural basis for international strategic alliances. Consider the number of universities round the English speaking world with Victoria in their name for example. The USA's University of New England is twinnable with Australia's university of the same name. Just as in warfare or business, so in academic competition, coalitions are an effective way of defending against competition from larger better resourced single rivals.

After 2030

Looking beyond the next decade, competition between universities around the world, having intensified through the twenties is set to implode in the thirties as falling funds, falling cohorts of school leavers and the widespread availability of alternative paths to credentials all take their toll. It is already clear in 2019 that there are more graduates than there are jobs in many countries of the world (Bankston 2011, Eremia 2015). It is clear too that the effect of university massification on social and economic barriers and hierarchies of esteem has not just been negligible but possibly negative (Ansell and Gingrich 2017, Tsiplakides 2018). The old divisions of elite society were supposed to be ameliorated by expanding universities creating hitherto unavailable equality of opportunity. Few people expected that instead the universities would themselves internalise the existing status divisions in society, thereby providing a legitimacy for inequality that was not so much there before. The difference between a top ten university degree and one from a recently emergent private provider or converted college of technology operates to keep graduates of the latter out of employment opportunities available to the former. This is especially acute in England which has had class barriers encrusted on the body of the nation for a thousand years. It applies to some extent though in every country, and it is in many respects the fruit of the 'search for excellence', which is the uncontroversial objective of university learning and research. Because knowledge involves connaître as well as savoir, it is inherent in the concept, calibration and communication of scholastic excellence that it will dovetail with social privilege, plutocratic elites and the beneficiaries of inherited privilege of any material kind. Expecting institutions dedicated to pursuing any kind of competitive 'excellence' to generate more equality as a result is contrary to common sense, a quality that has been conspicuous by its absence from higher education thought and policy in the last half century. It is contended with deadly seriousness that the reacquisition of common sense is an essential ingredient of long-term university survival and of institutional adaptation to the inevitable unexpected.

Common sense is a solution-oriented combination of recognition of facts, scepticism towards unevidenced opinions and prudence in assessing what is

Common Sense and the Future Proofed University

possible with the people and institutions available. It is realism without the implicit approval and support for the status quo that the notion of realism too often involves. Common sense will have to be taught in future as it will not be absorbed by osmosis in the nuclear family or in schools which are understaffed, under policed and narrowly credential focused. I have placed its return beyond 2030 as I think it will take that long for society, university boards, employers and carer minded students to realise both its usefulness and its teachability. Many universities have critical thinking explicitly listed as one of the attributes they seek to produce in all their graduates. Few universities have courses directly aimed at enhancing the ability to practise critical thinking. Out of our present age of massive information overload, of fake news accusations and of the postmodernist corruption of the possibility of universal values such as truth, some universities could lead the return to the Enlightenment project via the pathway of critical thinking and common sense. Employers may not want recruits to go too far in "critical" thinking, but they never say there needs to be a limit to common sense. What is centrally addressed by common sense is the ability to distinguish fact from opinion, to develop good judgment grounded in unflinching realism that is evidence based, and to avoid over generalisations.

Common sense discerns the extreme improbability of transiting from elite education to mass education with insufficient funding to continue the virtues (such as small SSRs) and expecting the benefits of massification to remain miraculously undiluted. Just as reading newspapers and magazines got rebadged as media studies, so critical thinking and common-sense studies would probably acquire a new name on their first outing from university launching pads, perhaps something like 'applied cognition' or 'higher heuristical studies'. Whatever the badge turns out to be, it is contended that these skills will be essential to be supplied by the adaptable and competitive university in the 2030s. If this assertion is correct, we should expect the first mover universities to espouse it much earlier, certainly by 2025.

As unbundling of units from courses and subjects from programmes becomes more general, so the acquisition of taught degrees could come to resemble more and the acquisition of badges (literal ones) in the boy scouts and girl guides. Badges would be awarded for units, bigger ones for hopefully coherent clusters of units constituting whole courses (after a target number of credits have been earned). The fully integrated course with few electives would be in the minority but would retain a substantial market among the professions. Such unbundling and badging would make it easier to credentialise each and every one of the soft skills and character traits many employers have long complained to be lacking in current graduates. Communication, presentation, negotiation and analytical thinking, creative thinking, interpersonal skills in general and becoming a more affable and less of a Type A[1] person are examples of what future students will learn and employers will appreciate. This would go some way towards rectifying the

---

[1] Type A behaviour is trusted in managerial psychology with type B. The former shows drive, need for achievement, excitability and taut nerves. Type B is laid back, prefers harmony to run on the board and is not easily excited or stressed. Type A was thought to be typical management behaviour which carried a high risk of stroke or heart attack and associated smoking to calm the nerves. Fortune and other wide circulation business magazines still use these terms.

imbalance between savoir knowledge and connaître knowledge. The rest of the missing connaître skills require the active engagement of alumni, mentors, friends and other non-intimate human contacts to help a student learn influencing skills and getting along with others well enough to have a tolerably happy working life. This will be of especial importance to those students identified early as introverted, nerdy and afraid of too many or too frequent everyday face to face social contact. The more time students spend on the net mediating all their human interactions through a screen, the more they will need these kinds of connaître courses.

Another consequence of increasing worldwide competition is that the universities who are at or above average in the competition will want to see rating agencies evolve into, or be supplanted by, global regulatory agencies. Quality assurance already has such a global federation in The International Network for Quality Assurance Agencies in Higher Education (INQAAHA). The universities doing well will say that their quality needs to be defended by global regulatory agencies that demand certain minimum standards to allow membership. This pathway is well trodden by business schools for whom, for example, accreditation by AMBA (the Association of MBAs, based in England) is regarded by some to less sought after than accreditation by EQUIS (European Quality Improvement System, based in France) which in turn is seeking to gain parity of esteem, in the eyes of some, with the American AACSB. AACSB was once the American Association of Collegiate Business Schools but renamed itself in the last decade as the Association to Advance Collegiate Business Schools in order to demonstrate its global acclaim to pre-eminence. Top and second tier business schools now have all three accreditations and say they are 'triple crowned accredited'. Non accredited schools still pick up domestic students but the international students they attract comprise largely people who could not get into triple crown schools. It is easy to predict other disciplines will follow the business school path and that whole universities will go beyond their present practice of designating national elite cliques to progress to continental ones, thence to global ones. Any global regulation that results from that would be by consent of the universities who set up the authority in the first place. It would have to wait for world government for such authority to lay down the law to a university in any one country, but the accounting profession has shown that this does not matter if the national regulatory agencies sign up to membership of the global body and implement its standards – saving them considerable time and effort in the process.

The public library has adapted well to the challenges of the publishing revolution and the digital replacement of hard copy books by equipping itself with databases, internet notebooks and DVDs to supplement and partially replace its book stocks. This adaptability could see the learning centre of the future be sited in public libraries great and small. Universities could close under-subscribed campuses and partner with public libraries to dedicate timetabled hours in the week and dedicated links on the library floor to the students taking units with the university. The university saves property maintenance costs while the library enhances its usefulness to the community and its income too. Some big universities and some cross-university alliances may take over libraries to make them exclusive, but the regulatory authorities may need to be consenting to this appropriation first and not all will do so. If the library provides, or more likely franchises, a small café adjoining its main premises, then the student would have many of the essential ingredients of the old on campus experience. Libraries as the retail outlets for many university supplies seems a good bet for the 2030s right across the world, since the complementarity between the new university and the old public library is clearly there to be exploited

More important than any other development anticipated in this paper and more inevitable too is the implosion of universities as the ultimate result of increasingly bitter competition for shrinking cohorts and shrinking reservoirs of funds. Graduate unemployment will rise as more students become qualified for jobs that do not exist. Jobs for which a degree needed in the teens and twenties of this century, but which did not have degrees as entry tickets in the 1980s, will find that market forces have made their degrees useless. Not only hairdressing, motor maintenance and media studies are vulnerable here but also accounting, financial advising, banking and paramedic careers are threatened. To practise in these professions the only reason for getting a degree at the time of writing this article is because the country's professional body insists upon it and does so for prosocial esteem and to demonstrate parity with the old learned professions of law and medicine. What we can predict about competition between professional bodies domestically and internationally is that some will compete on price and will not insist on a degree, preferring to credentialise through their own qualification and perhaps through a degree equivalent acquired through units earned through piecemeal courses provided by many different tertiary education providers by way of acquiring "scout" type badges. This development could occur is such a clustered away in space and in such a short period of time that it triggers the implosion. Just as stock market crashes and commodity crashes are triggered when supply continues so long as to exceed effective demand, so the expansion without limit of massified universities cannot continue without a dramatic correction one day. The modern university is a business supplying credentials for paid employment, but employment is continuing to lose stability, the numbers of people joining the precariat is rising and the big growth spots in the advanced economy are in AI, electrification of vehicles, green energy and commercialisation of space – not one of which is labour intensive. Even the service industries of the world are not infinite in their capacity to absorb clerks, waiters, cleaners, cooks and salespersons - few of which require degree level credentials anyway. Self-employment, entrepreneurship and the search for innovation are no way out for the many, only for the lucky and gifted few, very few indeed. The birth rate in all countries with a mature economy and a large civilian middle class is falling while the ageing part of the population is increasing. However, neither baby boomers now nor Generation X by the 2030s provide a large enough population of (optimistically) life-long learners to save the universities from the falling birth rate. Why would the aged of the future want to pay enormous tuition fees for what they could largely obtain at a tenth of the price online through learning centres and bargain basement private providers? Maybe some of them still might want the cachet of being associated with an elite university like Harvard, Stanford, Oxford, Cambridge, the Sorbonne, Moscow State, Renmin, Tsinghua or Fudan. They will be able to satisfy that desire with an intensive stint at their would-be alma mater or by an online course validated by the elite university but taught by a sub-sub-sub-contractor (as

Tsinghua already does inside China, for example). The university industry all round the world is utterly unprepared for the Implosion and present day university board members and executives will be long retired by the time it eventuates. It will be unprecedented in the history of higher education and will go down in history's Hall of Infamy to sit alongside the Wall Street Crash, the Black Death or Passchendaele. The institutional carnage will be comparable to those disasters, even though the deaths through mental illness, suicide and poverty that follow the Implosion will not be so great. The universities have never had a mass catastrophe before. It will be the ultimate result of unabated massification that lacks the common sense to cut its supply coat to fit its demand cloth.

After the Implosion, universities we have never yet heard of will buy up the carcases of the dead and wounded for bargain prices, somewhat as China's Lenovo bought the PC from IBM and a succession of Asian owners bought the Singer sewing machine licences and brand name. China and India may well be the main countries with university groups able to thrive after the Implosion and a century of reverse colonialism may follow; but the most robust, sustainable and adaptable western universities would also survive and do some buying of their own. Thus would begin a new cycle of expansion that may soon forget the lessons of the first generation of massified expansion.

One force may mitigate the effects of the Implosion and that is a dialectical swing against neoliberalism and unlimited salience of market forces such that in one or two countries communitarian or socialist governments are elected. I do not mean social democratic parties, but socialist ones that will take control if not ownership of natural monopolies like electricity and whose commitment to universal education means they abolish tuition fees and loans as a burden to students but puts them back on the shoulders of the general taxpayer.

Conclusion
Enlightenment at the end of the dark tunnel?

This chapter has done nothing to dispel the gloom and demoralisation of much of the professoriate in so many universities. That is because it has only looked at the present and near-term future of universities. If we look even further into the future, we can say that the demeaning of academic labour as human livestock to be factory farmed as intensely as possible cannot continue indefinitely. Possibly before Implosion in some celestially blessed quarters, and after it in many other seats of learning, collegiality and love of learning for its own sake may quietly re-emerge. The academic equivalent of pre-Raphaelites, or perhaps more appositely, the Renaissance people of the future rediscover the now extinct academic virtues that made life so agreeable for the elite educators of the past. These communities of scholars may initially be like medieval monasteries, quarantined and isolated from the lay community and having to sacrifice personal wealth and personal vanities in exchange for such protection, perhaps the next mutation of think tanks could be like that. Such neo-monastic communities will need a powerful neo-feudal protector. The neo-monastic academic community would research for him rather than offer prayer for his soul. However, sooner or later, the wider community would want to participate in this cloistered grove of academy. A new massification would get under way but perhaps next time, it could be done while collegiality and love of learning for its own sake are somehow preserved. It would be like turning the Garden of Eden into the Central Park of Eden – not necessarily impossible but extremely difficult. Perhaps we should remember what JFK said in 1961 about going to the moon within the decade: "*We choose to do these things not because they are easy but because they are hard*". Indeed.

References

Altbach P G (1999), "The Logic of Mass Higher Education", *Tertiary Education and Management* 5(2) 105-122.

Ansell B and Gingrich J (2017), "Mismatch: - University education and labor market institutions" *Political Science and Politics* 50(2), 423-425, DOI 10.1017/S1049096516002948.

Bankston C L I (2011), "The mass production of credentials: subsidies and the rise of the higher education industry", *The Independent Review* 15(3) 325-349.

Chomsky N (2014), "The Death of America Universities", *Jacobin* <online https://jacobinmag.com/2014/03/the-death-of-american-universities>, Accessed 12 June 2019

Costa, C; Teixeira, L; and Alvelos, H (2018); "Exploring the Usage of MOOCs in Higher Education Institutions: Characterization of the Most Used Platforms", *International Journal of Information and Communication Technology Education* 14(4), 1-17.

Donleavy G D and Chen K C (2019), "Recent Trends in East and West University Governance: Two Kinds of Hollowness," Chapter 5, pp 88-109 in S G Redding (ed) Handbook of Comparative Higher Education Systems and University Management, Oxford: Oxford University Press. DOI 10.1093/oxfordhb/978019882905.013.5

Eremia D (2015), "Changes in an Age of Mass Higher Education", *Journal of Community Positive Practices* 15(3) 70-81

Eversheds (2009), *Developing Future University Structures: New Funding and Legal Models*, London: UniversitiesUK <http://www.universitiesuk.ac.uk/highereducation/Docments/2009/FutureUniversity Structures.pdf> Acessed 16 June 2019

Henebery B (2016), "The rise, fall and future of MOOCs", L&D online, 25 Oct 2016. Access through https://www.ldphub.com/general-news/the-rise-fall-and-future-of-moocs-225531.aspx

Holford J (2016), "The misuses of sustainability: Adult education, citizenship and the dead hanof neoliberalism", *International review of education* 62(5) 541-561, Doi 10.1007/s11159-016-9591-4

Holm-Nielsen L (2018), "Universities: From local institutions to global systems? Implications for students, staff and institutions", *European Review* 26, S124 – S148, Doi 10.1017/S1062798717000606

Kromydas T (2017), "Rethinking higher education and its relationship with social inequalities: Past knowledge, present state and future potential", *Palgrave Communications* 3(1), Doi 10.1057/s41599-017-0001-8

Longden B (2000), "Elitism to inclusion – some developmental tension", *Educational Studies* 26(4),455-474.

Melhuish G (2018), "The Machiavellian Takeover of Australian Universities", *Quadrant* 62(1-2), 66-74.

Rohs, M and Ganz M (2015), "MOOCSs and the Claim of Education for All: A Disillusion by Empirical Data" *International Review of Research in Open and Distributed Learning*. 16(6), 1-19, November.

Stoer S (2006), "New forms of citizenship, European construction and the reconfiguration of the university", *Higher Education Policy* 19(3) 299-318. DOI 10.1057/palgrave.hep.800126,

Trow M (1998), "American perspectives on British higher education under Thatcher and Major", *Oxford Review of Education"* 24(1) 111-129

Trow M (2006), "Decline of diversity, autonomy and trust in British education", *Society* 43(6) 77-86, DOI 10.1007/BF02698490

Trowler P (1997), "Beyond the Robbins trap: Reconceptualising academic responses to change in higher education (or Quiet Flows the Don", *Studies in Higher Education* 22(3) 301-318

Tsiplakides I (2018), "Differentiation in higher education", *Social Science* 7(2) 28. DOI 10.3390/socsci7020028

Gabriel Donleavy has four decades of university teaching and managerial experience in Australia, England and the Far East. He is currently at Australia's University of New England in Brisbane as Professor of Accounting and President of the Union branch there.

2

The Education Continuum: A Journey of Reinvention

Madelyn Blair[1] and Denise Lee[2]
[1]Pelerei, LLC, Washington DC, USA
[2]PwC, Washington DC, USA

Individual mobility in the global workplace

Stability has never been more ephemeral than it is today. Just at the moment we feel we have things under control, the world changes, and moves on, disrupts itself. All the careful preparation becomes just the beginning of the learning called for in the next step. In other words, we discover that we must build on what we know and at times we must build starting from scratch. Often what we must learn is not yet in books, and experts, who can be called upon, do not yet exist. It is a very different world.

The average lifespan of a company was 67 years in the 1920s. Today, it is 15 years, an average of 50 fewer years. Changes in corporate viability makes jobs less secure even when the company ends because it has been acquired by another larger firm. There are no guarantees with M&A (Mergers and Acquisitions) that the jobs will continue as they had in the past. When the change hits, your satisfaction is replaced with a sense of genuine confusion and concern with your level of knowledge or capability. With this warning sign of dissatisfaction, you would find yourself becoming flummoxed, obsolete, or dysfunctional. In the past, you called upon a teacher, friend or a colleague to help you understand. That is still true but, you must also become your own teacher, when you must think through situations without feeling incompetent, when you must become an avid learner, ready to explore the unknown and chart your path forward.

Let's look at some of the factors that are in play. Two great minds have spoken on the impact of disruption. Carl Sagan said, "Extinction is the rule. Survival is the exception." Charles Darwin said, "It is not the strongest of the species that survives, nor the most intelligent. It is the one that is the most adaptable to change." The message is clear. We must adapt or become extinct. The good news is that humans are remarkably adaptable, and we are strongly committed to survive. Now, place these points in line with the enormous disruptions that are occurring every day.

The rate of change is rising at a frightening pace. Forests covered 5.9 billion hectares in pre-industrial time. Today, it is just over 4 billion hectares or 30% less. A simple statistic about forests affects us. Aside from the impact on the replacement of carbon dioxide with life-giving oxygen, the price of wood is now much higher forcing the creation of new building products for homes and other structures. Carpentry skills must change to reflect this. Architecture skills must now accommodate these new materials. We see that university programs are having to reflect these changes. For example, a degree in architecture must take into account the change global forces that fundamentally change how this skill is applied in the marketplace.

Over the last century, the human population has grown from 2 billion to almost 8 billion, 4 times larger. A greater population places demands on food production. Agricultural techniques change with almost every season. Consider the recent challenge to the soybean plant. A major agrochemical company developed a special type of soybean that allows it to handle a specially designed herbicide. Use of the herbicide is fine on the new soybeans but quite devastating on other (original) soybeans. Even when it is not applied, the fumes drift to other fields and has become a particular problem for farmers in the American mid-west. A solution that was introduced now confounds long-term techniques. Where are universities in this conversation? How are universities tapping into trends that will impact the knowledge that is shared in the classroom? What mechanisms are being put in place to update curriculum that may have been written years ago?

In 1920, there were about 600,000 telephones in the world. Today there are almost 9 billion cell phones alone. That's 15,000 times more. This is only one technological change that has impacted both jobs and even cultures. We live differently as a result. That's a big change. The ability for students to connect today across the world has never been greater. Universities can tap into a student pool that is global. These digital natives are seeking knowledge and universities need to challenge themselves on how to design programs that tap into this connectivity and capability. Global economy changes the rules. We live in a truly global economy. Globalization is considered one of the top 10 challenges facing businesses today including universities. Recent trade tensions have altered specific situations yet have not altered this reality.[1] Even as we try to separate from the globalization we find we are intractably linked.

This linkage is demonstrated through the flows of capital, people, and trade that have increased exponentially since 2001. However, these are eclipsed by the explosion of information and knowledge at our fingertips. In attempts to 'handle' it all, we have compromised our attention spans, finding it more and more difficult to focus. Not to mention people's obsession with digital technology. Information overload is an understatement. Knowledge grows when populations grow. There are simply more minds exploring. When that is combined with interconnection between and among these minds, the synergies produce still more understanding and knowledge. With data capture technologies, information that was never recorded before is now available for access and analysis. The flow of information and the access to this flow is 'inhuman.' Everyday quintillions[2] of bytes are shared

---

[1] The State of Globalization in 2019, and What It Means for Strategists, HBR, February 6, 2019

[2] A million bytes has 6 zeros. In the USA, a quintillion has 18 zeros.

over the Internet. Quintillions? It's a number you can't even comprehend. With access has come exposure – both of ourselves and of ideas. Distinguishing between information and opinion becomes an additional challenge, especially for the careful reader. For universities this is a content overload issue. Not only from the point of being cognizant of this overload, but through the selection of what to teach and how to research.

Technology brings more than efficiency. Technology is often seen as the solution, yet new technologies give no attention to the social impacts. Displacing skilled work is the obvious, but the shifts in cultural norms aren't even considered sufficiently to think about unintended consequences. The obsession with digital technology leads to both positive and negative outcomes. A dimension of our privacy has been lost. Mobile phones allow children's locations to be monitored while parents see even very young children become affixed to the screen. Sharing family information even with videos allow far-flung members to stay connected. At the same time, the technology opens children to those who would prey on them. Young people struggle to determine the best major to take in their studies as they watch the swift, unmistakable changes in their world mutate future career possibilities.

Culture shifts place new demands on our lives. We tend to see technology as advancement. Less often do we examine the 'advances' or changes to human culture. Technology has changed our cultures, but so too has increased understanding. The more we learn, the more insight we can obtain about life, our relationships, and our society. Two very different technological events describe how wide the range of demands are. When human kind viewed earth-rise over the horizon of the moon, the perilous nature of our world gained greater understanding. It was a step for mankind along with Neil Armstrong. When an earthquake deep in the ocean became a tidal wave that swept through the Fukushima Daiichi Nuclear Power Plant, the examination of nuclear power came under increased review. Each had impact on our cultures as well as our industries and our educational system overall. They altered our individual lives in subtly, but real ways and universities need to have a response.

Formal degrees are just the beginning

Students often believe that once they have finished their classes and obtained their degrees, they no longer need to study. They have proven that they have obtained the lessons required for work and life. Nothing could be further from the truth. If those students think about the new technologies that have entered their lives, they may recall they had to study how to use the technology and, more importantly, how to bring the new capabilities and the resultant benefits into their lives. They don't see this as 'study', because they see the benefits to themselves from the beginning, and this alone motivates them to engage in study and learning – again.

But technology changes are only one dimension of change in today's environment. Change is occurring across all dimensions of a person's life. People's lives are full of changes. After spending four years in one company, you recognize that you are bored, and it is time to shift from your career to another. You find yourself economically self-sufficient so that pursuing another area of interest is possible. You take a sabbatical. You decide it's time to have a child. On the other hand, AI (Artificial Intelligence) has replaced your work, and you are let go. Outsourcing has diminished your responsibilities. You have reached retirement age and simply are not ready to retire.

Even the person who is fortunate enough to have a long career in a company (an occurrence that is on the endangered list) discovers that with every promotion, she has had to work her way up the learning curve of the new job. The irony is that if the company you work for is not teaching the right learning then you may be going up the wrong learning curve and suddenly be obsolete. On the other hand, with the right learning curve you are enlivened. Promotion is sought for the benefits of money and power, yet the deeper benefit is that it offers personal growth. Personal growth builds confidence and a capacity to handle disruption, the time when innovation is essential.

Drucker has said that all business is the business of innovation. Innovation depends on knowledge and creativity spurned on by curiosity. In a disruptive world, the ability to innovate is essential for survival. Thus, businesses should be concerned that employees are self-starters so that when opportunities for learning are offered through promotion, lateral transfers, exciting projects, or support for additional education, employees will respond. *"Nearly every human being is on the lookout for growth opportunities. If a person can't grow with a company, they will grow away from it."*[3]

Stuck in work that never presents a challenge or opportunity, can quickly destroy initiative and verve. In these cases, business gets less and less productivity from them. More than this, business sets itself up for not being able to innovate when disruption occurs. It's a closed system. Discourage staff from learning and create a business incapable of surviving disruption.

The careful observer of life discovers that learning is never over. Those who step away from learning often become bored, disengaged, and eventually dysfunctional. Students need to discover this reality, but so too must educational institutions.

Faculty see themselves as experts who must convey content to the student like a massive information transfer. Teaching that sees content as the reason for education needs to shift. Content transfer (the lecture) is only the start as any great university will tell you. However, teaching the content should be done in a manner that acts as a door being opened to the broader content beyond what is being taught. Educational institutions that do this offer a great service that goes well beyond the content and even the degrees. Students need to learn new content, but that content should bring them to where they understand enough to ask questions of the topic.

Interestingly enough, digital books were seen as the solution to the expense of textbooks. Recent research (Barrett, 2019) shows *"We are finding that even though undergraduates prefer to read digitally, these preferences aren't actually showing positive or even equalness in terms of effect on comprehension,"* says Lauren Singer Trakhman, who studies reading comprehension at the University of Maryland's Disciplined and Learning Research Laboratory. *"When it comes to*

---

[3] Johnson, Whitney. (2018) Build an A Team, Harvard Business Review Press, P. 17

things like pulling details, key facts, numbers, and figures, participants are doing a lot better after reading in print." Not only do students retain less when reading digitally, Trakhman says, "*they're more likely to overestimate how well they comprehended the material.*"

Questions are a reflection of both understanding and desire to understand more. Eager, capable employees tackling new challenges are a key driver of innovation within an organization. Author Alex Haley once said, "*When an old person dies it's like a library burning.*" When employees leave a firm, books burn: we lose a wealth of vital institutional knowledge and expertise. Let's not be the innovation book burners in our organizations. This leads to cognitive flexibility and curiosity. These need to be nurtured into action in students. Curiosity is the reason that humankind has survived with such voracity about knowing what is around the next corner. Education should be the place where this skill is awakened, enhanced, and honed.

The elusiveness of career planning

Workers today can anticipate that they will change careers more times than their parents changed job titles. The days of committing to one employer, just out of high school or college, and then working their way up the ladder is increasingly becoming an unlikely career path. Industries, and the jobs they support, are changing so fast that it is forecasted that 40% of jobs today will not exist, or will have been significantly modified, in just 10 years. This massive amount of change in the job market and how people plan, not only their formal education, but their careers is creating a tremendous amount of stress and uncertainty.

In 2018 in the World Economic Forum Report it was stated that, "The emerging contours of the new world of work in the Fourth Industrial Revolution are rapidly becoming a lived reality for millions of workers and companies around the world. The inherent opportunities for economic prosperity, societal progress and individual flourishing in this new world of work are enormous, yet depend crucially on the ability of all concerned stakeholders to instigate reform in education and training systems, labour market policies, business approaches to developing skills, employment arrangements and existing social contracts." People that would normally look for security and identity in their careers are struggling to understand how to plan a path forward. The Fourth Industrial Revolution is commonly defined as the current and developing marketplace in which disruptive technologies and trends such as the Internet of Things (IoT), robotics, virtual reality (VR) and artificial intelligence (AI) are changing the way we live and work. It is clear that the defining influencer of this generation is the digital experience and the impact of the Internet on all aspects of our lives.

How do we plan for constant change? "*it is also clear that the Fourth Industrial Revolution's wave of technological advancement is set to reduce the number of workers required for certain work tasks*" (World Economic Forum Report, 2018). There will be much change and not only a reduction in the recognized careers of today, but new careers emerging that are not yet defined. In the past people looked to their career and formal education to guide their path forward and establish stability in their lives. A student would select a university degree that would give them the credentials to pursue a career in that discipline, sometimes following family traditions. For example, if the father was an engineer, the son may follow in his footsteps. But in today's digital world, heavily influenced by globalization, students are exposed to so many options they become confused. Many students admit they don't know what to study or what they want to do for a career.

The different forces that are impacting the workforce of the future are frequently discussed in the corporate boardroom. The question is - how is information about workforce trends being communicated to today's students to help them make decisions? With the cost of education on the rise and student debt at crisis levels, selecting the wrong path can have critical ramifications. In fact, the mindset shift required of today's students is increasingly one of flexibility and mobility. We have to be prepared for the fact that jobs and careers will continue to evolve. This is especially important for universities as they design programs that matrix different disciplines and meet the needs of the current workforce.

Working in one discipline or for one company is moving into the past. The future is shifting towards a reality that your current job will be used to not only earn a living but to gain more knowledge, build a broader network and improve your position for the next opportunity. This mindset shift dilutes the loyalty to the organizations we work for and starts to place the focus squarely on what is best for the individual. This is difficult for organizations trying to attract and retain talent. The messages from the organizations are that they have excellent benefit packages, the opportunity to work in cohesive teams, great chances to learn etc., but the tension is there that the worker may leave for a better opportunity or the organization may layoff the worker due to a change in business strategy. This leads to no security and an increase in stress for both the worker and the company.

It is impossible to ignore that while organizations are indicating to the worker that we want you to stay - there is an increase in off-shoring whole departments or companies overseas to countries with lower wages. Organizations are making investments in technologies, such as automation and artificial intelligence that will increasingly make jobs currently on their payroll obsolete. In fact, technology has destroyed far more jobs than trade deals with other countries, such as in the auto industry. There are constant acquisitions and divestitures that are combining groups of workers that inevitably lead to layoffs. Finally, with the increase in the right to work laws and the reduction of the power of unions in the workplace that would advocate for the worker, the stability of the job is reduced and the focus again turns to the individual.

The fact that the individual worker must plan a solid path forward from the choice of formal education through the organizations they choose to join leads to the need to embrace lifelong learning. With the increasing changes in the marketplace, the skills that people have today will need to be upgraded continuously over their lifetime. It is important for students today to understand they are starting on a lifetime journey that will not end in four or eight years. Students must be prepared to understand that their careers will continue to evolve.

Understanding the gig economy

Have you heard about the gig economy? In fact, more and more people are participating in the flexibility of the gig economy worldwide. What is the gig economy? It is a labor market characterized by the prevalence of short-term contracts or freelance work as opposed to permanent jobs (Google Dictionary). The gig economy enables workers to control their work, their time and where they live. These workers have made the mindset shift that they control their own employment.

Not all workers in the gig economy do it by choice. There are some that take on temporary work to make extra money to feed their families and others that have been laid off from permanent work and not been able to find another job. These workers are in the transition to the gig economy, not by choice, but by necessity. For example, ride-share drivers could be considered part of the gig economy. Many workers that have advanced degrees work for ride-share companies for extra money. On the other hand, some gig workers make their jobs full time such as a ride-share driver, because, for instance, they like the independence or they have lower levels of education that do not enable them to get more high paying positions.

Other workers have embraced the gig economy as a lifestyle. They have advanced degrees. They are digital natives defined as a person born or brought up during the age of digital technology and therefore familiar with computers and the Internet from an early age. These digital natives have strong technology skills that enable them to work worldwide. There are workers that travel the world and are connected to their employers through the Internet and a laptop. Geography no longer determines where and when we can work. There are workers that live in Asia but have customers in the US. The popularity of the gig economy is on the rise, and it focuses on the individual worker and the skills they have been able to acquire through both formal education and work experience. This is requiring individuals to be more entrepreneurial and expand their skillsets continuously. Again, the focus is on lifelong learning.

In addition, technology firms are stepping into the gig economy. Different apps such as TaskRabbit, Freelancer and Fiverr enable workers to connect to jobs and even manage the payment structures. This enables a seamless connection between the work and the talent and enables the workers to have no connection to the brick and mortar organizations of the past. Apps are popping up frequently with jobs ranging from technical editors to dog walkers as well as advanced technical capabilities such as software development and business consulting. In addition, large consulting firms, such as PwC, have also produced an external talent tool called the Talent Exchange. The Talent Exchange encourages independent consultants to fill out a profile and be staffed on consulting engagements across the US on a temporary basis.

All positions in the gig economy represent a risk to the worker and a risk to the employer. There are usually no benefits provided through jobs in the gig economy. No healthcare, no vacation time, no sick time and no retirement plan. In the US, there is an increased focus on discussing portable benefits. Portable benefits would follow the worker, and both the worker and the employer would pay into a government program that would provide these benefits. This is an interesting idea, but still fairly far off in the future. The risk to the employer is that the talent can walk out the door at any minute. There are no controlling factors such as loyalty to the organization or being connected to the culture. This fluidity creates both an opportunity to not have to payroll the talent but a risk in the loss of the ability to build corporate knowledge into the workforce.

Another side to this story is demonstrated by the recent bill introduced into the State of California legislature. This *"new bill moving through the California legislature this summer (2019) could upend this business model. Known as AB 5 (the "AB" is for "Assembly Bill"), the law would create a test for classifying independent contractors, making it more difficult for gig economy giants and other low wage industries—such as domestic work, trucking, and construction—to exploit the contractor loophole"* (The New Republic). California is taking the lead in looking at how companies are taking advantage of workers in the gig economy. *"The state estimates it loses $7 billion in payroll tax annually due to companies misclassifying employees as independent contractors"* (The Intercept). This trend to enact laws to offset the abuses of the gig economy will probably increase in the next few years as other governments look at the relationship between the status of independent contractor and the ability for organizations to pay no benefits or exploit the workers.

As mentioned previously, some workers enter into the workforce as independent contractors willingly and knowingly while others that are trying to make a living work for giants such as the major ride-share companies and are not always aware of what is happening with their rights. For example, "Like other gig economy companies, ride-share companies' profit margins may sometimes rely on skirting basic federal and state labor protections—such as those denied by classifying drivers as independent contractors instead of as employees. This business model has allowed gig-employment apps to rapidly expand over the past decade into multibillion-dollar global enterprises. Meanwhile, the workers whose undercompensated labor helped build those companies are not eligible to form unions. (The New Republic). Increasingly, the conversation is turning from the benefits of the gig economy to the darker side of how these companies are not pro-worker but pro-profit.

Many students take advantage of the gig economy to make money on the side to pay for housing, tuition, books etc. The need for universities to educate their students on the advantages and disadvantages of these types of employment is increasingly more important. As students struggle to handle the ever increasing cost of education, there is a responsibility of the universities to enter into the conversation of the gig economy and how it will effect students while they are in school and after they graduate.

Impact of Artificial Intelligence (AI) and robotics

AI is seen as the savior by providing capabilities that augment humans, increase productivity, and even improve accuracy. When AI is employed in this manner, it will most often replace talent.

Historically, automation and other technologies were being designed that created *new* work which employed people. The insertion of technology that employed more people represented a competitive advantage. For example, the agricultural mechanization in the 19th century introduced jobs in manufacturing, sales, and more. "*Employment and wage growth have been disappointing over the last two decades partly because productivity growth has been weak, and even more importantly because new tasks have failed to materialize. The future of work will be much brighter if we can mobilize more of the technologies that increase labor demand and ensure vigorous productivity growth.*" (Acemoglu and Restrepo, 2019) But is this even realistic?

With today's AI introductions, the productivity gained will be at the loss of economic social value. Acemoglu argues that we are walking down the path of developing the wrong kinds of AI. We should be developing AI with attention to how it will *create* work for humans. An example of technologies that may increase labor demand is where AI is employed to give predictions that inform decisions made by people and, thus, improve them or even make them possible because of predictions previously not possible (Agrawal et al 2019).

This scenario demands examination and creativity.

Table 1: The World Economic Forum has identified the Top 10 Skills

in 2020	in 2015
Complex Problem Solving	Complex Problem solving
Critical thinking	Coordinating with Others
Creativity	People Management
People Management	Critical Thinking
Coordinating with Others	Negotiation
Emotional Intelligence	Quality Control
Judgment and Decision Making	Service Orientation
Service Orientation	Judgment and Decision Making
Negotiation	Active Listening
Cognitive Flexibility	Creativity

Source: Future of Jobs Report, World Economic Forum

What kind of skills should people be developing? Some of them have been called soft skills, referenced in the table for 2020. They are also called 'durable skills' by Jeremy Auger, a co-founder and chief strategy officer of training company D2L. "*We refer to them as 'power skills', because without them, people's technical skills aren't running on all cylinders*," says Heide Abelli, Sr VP for Product Development, Skillsoft. Regardless of the name, these are skills that never get obsolete and can move from company to company (Fisher 2019). The skills transcend degrees, yet education can be used to development them.

Robotics have been designed primarily to do tasks previously done by manufacturing workers. It is a clear substitution of resource, eliminating human work. When used in manufacturing, robots are often cordoned off for safety reasons making the resource shift explicit. Robots are able to work with precision. When the precision needed for a task is beyond human capability, e.g., speed of response, the labor is eliminated from the task. In other words, with robotics, productivity of workers is not increased. Workers are eliminated. The end result is a loss of work opportunities. Participation rates fall especially among men with less than a college education (Binder and Bound, 2019). According to Atak et al, (2019).

> *"The extent to which the disruptive effects of the mechanization of the past serves as a prologue to the technologies of the present or future, or whether the modern technologies of robotics and artificial intelligence are fundamentally different in some way, remains an open question."*

The impact of global forces

Global workforce trends are requiring people to keep reinventing themselves and redefining their professional identities. The foundation of these identities is formed with the choices that are made with decisions of what degrees to pursue and what university to attend. These identities are formed at the beginning of people's careers. They define who we think we are and what our place is in the world.

When global forces such as climate change, technology, automation, urbanization, and globalization start impacting industries and the jobs they represent, people's identities are impacted. Automation is transforming our relationship to the workforce. If a worker starts their career as an accountant and finds security and pride in their profession but that profession is changed through automation and their job is eliminated, it effects their entire life. Workers that do not monitor global trends that are moving jobs to our cities, to other countries or eliminating them altogether are at risk. The question is not whether, but how we are going to adapt, or we will be left behind.

Many universities have seen this need and offer virtual education at all degree levels from bachelors, masters, to PhD. Solid education is offered by such institutions as Walden University, Drexel, Johns Hopkins, Columbia University School of Professional Studies and others. Some of these schools have adapted beyond virtual lectures to include student driven decisions that build learning capacity beyond absorption of content to include meaning making. One such program is the PhD in Management program at the College of Management and Technology at Walden University. Designed explicitly to keep the student in the driver's seat of learning and promote self-directed learning within a context, this program integrates scaffolded research skills into the curriculum where students are expected to delve into the content literature of their designated specializations. Through a themed based approach students identify current topics and trends to create research-based projects. The role of the faculty is to demonstrate content expertise, facilitate the process and coach the students as they develop into self-directed scholar practitioners.

Stepping into this void is the predatory for-profit educators. Under the President Obama Administration there were regulations to try to control these types of universities. They promise a degree in a very short period of time and that a job is just around the corner. In reality these organizations used the US Department of Education student loan program as a type of predatory lending. It is clear that *"There is a student loan crisis in the United States. The massive amount of debt held by students is now the second leading cause of indebtedness in the country. The effect of this debt on the economy at large, as well as on the people who hold it, has been widely discussed and is overwhelmingly negative."*

(Hendricks, 2019). At the same time as this increase in student debt, there is a reality that even a secretarial job now requires a bachelor's degree. People at varying points in their careers think that if they go back to school maybe they can make more money and have a better life. These people sometimes don't have time to take four years out of their lives to do this but are a susceptible to the getting into debt for programs that are not priced at instate tuition levels. Returning military veterans are also a target audience of these organizations.

These learning opportunities take advantage of the US Department of Education loan programs and lead to students signing up for massive amounts of debt. The degrees in some of these universities are not worth the paper they are written on. In addition, some of them have then filed bankruptcy and gone out of business. Increasingly, the US Government is moving to give these students some relief, but the risk is still very real. In fact, *"Following the collapse of for-profit Corinthian Colleges Inc. in 2015 and ITT Technical Institute in 2016, which were accused of predatory practices, thousands of students were left with a massive amounts of student debt. Under the borrower defense rule, borrowers can petition the Education Department for federal student loan discharges if they can prove that their school defrauded them under state law."* (Powell 2019) The catch is that the students have to prove the fraud. For many students this is a very difficult thing to have to do. They are not lawyers. It is clear that universities that provide high quality degrees must be willing to step up and provide opportunities for the target audiences of these students that are looking for a more efficient way to get additional education.

There is clearly a need for individuals at different points in their lives to get a degree without having to go through a four-year program. Respected universities must tailor their programs to meet this need with a more competitive approach. Universities today need to move to a stronger awareness of the marketplace and what students are looking for in order to better their lives.

Key learnings and the implications on the future of education

The many issues and topics discussed in this chapter are summarized in Table 2 and include the main points on the implications of the future of education.

Table 2: Key learnings and implications of the future of education

Key Learnings	Implications of the Future of Education
Individual mobility in the global workplace	
• Change is a feature of life. • Change can be beneficial when it builds greater knowledge or greater understanding of the consequences of the change. • Change can cause disruption in individual lives, communities, nations, and globally.	Today's students and workers must continue to learn as much as they can continuously throughout their lives. The changes today and on the horizon do not give us the roadmap of what to learn when. Therefore, one must continue to stay abreast of changing trends in both technology and the marketplace and navigate with eyes wide open and a mind towards lifelong learning.

The University of the Future

Key Learnings	Implications of the Future of Education
Formal degrees are just the beginning	
<ul><li>When individuals see the benefit of learning, they learn on their own whether they are being taught or are teaching themselves.</li><li>To survive disruption, business needs both capacity and habit to innovate.</li><li>Knowledge, creativity, and curiosity are essential for innovation.</li><li>Students need to learn more than content.</li><li>In addition to the knowledge gained for degrees, students need to learn the value of curiosity to stimulate learning and creativity.</li></ul>	Educational institutions must recognize that teaching content is only a part of their mission. Encouraging and even nurturing curiosity needs to be more than an assumption of education and become a conscious choice to design and act to do so. Nurturing curiosity is done by opening exercises that depend on students asking questions followed by allowing time for these questions. Further it demands that faculty or instructors respect the questions of students.
The elusiveness of career planning	
<ul><li>Today's career profile reflects movement across companies and even across industries.</li><li>Jobs have transformed with many disappearing, with others coming into being that were never before seen or even imagined.</li><li>Planning a career with reliability is impossible.</li><li>The digital experience is the defining influence of Millennials and future generations.</li><li>Formal education is no longer the key to career stability.</li><li>Lifelong learning is essential for readiness in this economy.</li></ul>	The constant transformation and emergence of new jobs or even careers places an emphasis on developing a deep desire to learn for its own sake. This is best done when content is placed into a wider perspective, encouraging students to see how knowledge builds on previous understanding, thus, teaching both the content and how to discover meaning. Putting students into the role of teacher (as in a seminar) deepens learning further and how to apply it to their career path.
Understanding the gig economy	
<ul><li>Business has capitalized on the benefits to itself of the gig economy, e.g., flexible workforce, focus on specific talent matched to specific task.</li><li>Creating unions is more difficult for workers within the gig economy.</li><li>In the gig economy, assuring a sufficient revenue can require multiple tasks or jobs be held simultaneously by workers.</li><li>Job security is obsolete.</li></ul>	The gig economy demands a shift to an entrepreneurial mindset where the individual has more control but must assume responsibility for ongoing learning and the implications of risk-taking that comes with that control. Educational institutions can build into its teaching methods means for building entrepreneurial skills into programs experientially so that students are prepared for the gig economy so different from historical versions.

Key Learnings	Implications of the Future of Education
impact of AI and robotics	
• Current AI and robotics are ones that replace people. The primary reason of this augmentation was to enhance productivity and has become replacement of people. • The top 10 skills of today are ones that are often denigrated as soft skills yet are the power skills that transfer to any job/industry. • The top ten skills cannot be 'taught'. They must be learned through foundational content plus an experiential environment that encourages and nurtures the right mindset and behaviors that support those skills.	AI and robotics are designed to replace people. So if you want to prepare people for the technological change that is coming you must focus people's education on what people do best. This is the "soft" or "power" skills. In the model discussed earlier, the top ten skills are needed by all workers to the greatest extent possible. Students should attend learning events and identify opportunities to use these skills both in work and in the classroom, for example by using explicit exercises designed to aid them in developing their own 'top-ten' skills experientially.
The impact of global forces	
• People must reinvent themselves throughout their careers. • Identity tied to work is severely threatened. • Many profit educators have abused the privilege by going after the vulnerable, poor, or ignorant while providing useless degrees. • Public policy in the US has supported this abuse. • Models of effective profit education exist. • Jobs historically not needing a degree now demand it because of availability of 'degreed' individuals. • Extreme focus on productivity at work rarely leaves time to set aside two years let alone four for a degree. • Acquisition of any degree can be done through alternative means. • Education needs to recognize marketplace forces that students face.	Educational institutions must expand on the options for students. Especially options that can be done part time, virtually, and in shorter time periods than 4 years. Certifications are legitimate ways to prepare students for specializations that build on foundational knowledge, preparing the student for certain career options in a relatively short, more cost-effective manner. When students are self-learners, the options for educational institutions must shift to respect the position of the students and consciously build on it.

References

Acemoglu, Daron and Restrepo, Pascual. (2019) *The Wrong Kind of AI? Artificial Intelligence and the Future of Labor Demand.* https://economics.mit.edu/files/16819

Agrawal, Ajay, Gans, Joshua S., Goldfarb, Avi. (2019) Artificial Intelligence: The Ambiguous Labor Market Impact of Automating Prediction, *Journal of Economic Perspectives*, Vol 33, Number 2, Spring 2019, pages 31-50.

Atack, Jeremy, Margo, Robert A., Rhode, Paul W. (2019) Automation of Manufacturing in the Late Nineteenth Century: The Hand and Machine Labor Study, Journal of Economic Perspectives, Vol 33, No 2, Spring 2019, pages 51-70.

The University of the Future

Barrett Brian (2019) "Transformation of the Text Book"
 https://www.wired.com/story/digital-textbooks-radical-transformation/
Binder, Ariel J., and Bound, John. (2019) The Declining Labor Market Prospects of Less-Educated Men, Journal of Economic Perspectives, Vol 33, #2, Spring 2019, pages 163-190.
Fisher, Anne. These are the most important skills you need to be successful in the modern workplace. *World Economic Forum* in collaboration with *Fortune*. May 15, 2019 https://www.weforum.org/agenda/2019/05/soft-skills-are-hard-to-measure-and-in-demand-can-they-be-taught
Gurley, Lauren (2019) "California Looks to Give Gig Economy Workers Their Due" The New Republic https://newrepublic.com/article/154517/california-ab5-gig-workers-employees
Cohen, Rachel (2019) "A California Bill Could Transform the Lives of Gig Workers. Silicon Valley Wants Labor's Help To Stop It" The Intercept: https://theintercept.com/2019/07/18/uber-lyft-california-gig-economy-labor-unions/
Hendricks, Scotty (2019), "Predatory Loans and the Schools that get Students to Take Them", Big Think https://bigthink.com/politics-current-affairs/predatory-student-loans
Powell, Farran (2019) "What defrauded student loan borrowers need to know", US News https://www.usnews.com/education/best-colleges/paying-for-college/articles/2018-10-18/what-defrauded-student-loan-borrowers-need-to-know
World Economic Forum "The Future Of Jobs Report 2018",
 http://www3.weforum.org/docs/WEF_Future_of_Jobs_2018.pdf

Denise Lee is a Director at PwC with clients in the public and private sectors. Her projects focus on the development of knowledge strategies that enable effective and efficient sharing of knowledge. Ms. Lee has taught at Johns Hopkins University, University of Maryland and Kent State University in the US.

Madelyn Blair is a business owner and faculty member specializing in unlocking resilience for individuals and work teams. Dr. Blair is faculty at Columbia University, blogger on Psychology Today, author of five books including her new book Unlocked. She holds a PhD from the University of Tilburg.

3

The 21st Century University: Quo Vadis?

Mandla Stanley Makhanya
Principal and Vice Chancellor, University of South Africa, Pretoria/Tshwane. South Africa

Background

A convergence of transformational global and national trends that extend beyond the traditional remit of higher education are impelling a fundamental rethink of global higher education and calling into question the global assertion of universities as 'seats of learning' and generators of new knowledge, and more recently, incubators of students who will acquire the skills and competencies needed to flourish in the workplace, and thus contribute to the socio-economic development of the societies that they serve. (Abowitz, 2008; Brighouse & Dungy, 2012; Levine, 2014; Mcpherson, 2015; Shapiro, 2005).

Prevailing global higher education policy reveals that education is regarded as a "fundamental human right", and that education *per se,* is regarded as a primary driver and catalyst of socio-economic development. The Education 2030 Incheon Declaration and Framework for Action Towards Inclusive and Equitable Quality Education and Life-long learning for all (2016) asserts: *"We reaffirm that education is a public good, a fundamental human right and a basis for guaranteeing the realization of other rights. It is essential for peace, tolerance, human fulfilment and sustainable development. We recognize education as key to achieving full employment and poverty eradication"* (p.7). The UNESCO Position Paper on Education Post (2015) addresses emerging considerations in the remit of responsibilities ascribed to universities and higher education. These include a social and sustainability transformative dimension of teaching and learning that focuses on the wellbeing of people and their right to an improved quality of life through quality education, as well as the notion of 'responsible (global) citizenship' (p4). We thus note a strong focus on the sustainability, social justice, inclusivity and equity aspects of higher education, as well as a growing emphasis on the responsibility of ordinary citizens to participate actively in their own development, that of their communities, and the spaces that they inhabit. This signals a shift from education that is tasked to develop a critical citizenry, to education that will ensure that the critical citizenry will simultaneously be developed as responsible *global* citizens by incorporating the ethical stewardship of our planet and a commitment to the sustainability of its ecosystems. Perhaps

Sustainable Development Goal (SDG) 4 best encapsulates the preceding policy trajectory and intent when it states that in the 21st century, the intention is to: *"Ensure inclusive and equitable quality education and provide life-long opportunities for all by 2030."* (UNESCO 2015)

While efforts towards achieving Education for All (EFA) have yielded some progress (UNESCO Jomtien Statement, 2011), more recent data indicate that progress has come to a standstill and that it is virtually certain that the EFA and Millennium Development Goal (MDG) education agendas will not be realised by the envisaged dates (Montoya & Mundy, 2018). There is thus a need to revisit education agendas within the prevailing contexts, so as to deliver agreements and actions that will resurrect the momentum for both EFA and MDG 4 (UNICEF/UNESCO, 2008).

The current societal dynamics and challenges require higher education solutions which are flexible, integrated and holistic and which should not only include transdisciplinarity and engagement with professional bodies, business and industry in the development of courseware and teaching practice, but also an openness to different modes of assessment and credentialising to meet different societal requirements. Furthermore, higher education institutions should be open to fundamental restructuring (including administrative) to ensure the responsiveness and agility that is required to ensure ongoing relevance. This is particularly true in the current global context of massive socio-economic inequality, where in OECD countries for example,

> *"...the richest 10% of the population earn 9.6 times the income of the poorest 10%. In the 1980s, this ratio stood at 7:1 rising to 8:1 in the 1990s and 9:1 in the 2000s... while there is always a gap in education outcomes across individuals with different socio-economic backgrounds, the gap widens in high-inequality countries as people in disadvantaged households struggle to access quality education. This implies large amounts of wasted potential and lower social mobility... In many countries, younger workers, especially those with only temporary work contracts have a lower chance of moving on to a more stable, career job... Women have made substantial progress in narrowing the participation, pay and career gap with men and this has put a brake on rising inequality. But they are still about 16% less likely to be in paid work and earn about 15% less than men. (OECD, 2015).*

It is from this platform of inequality (or abundance) that rapid, ongoing and accretive advances in technology are propelling societies forward in virtually every sphere of endeavour and inducing higher education institutions to provide a level and quality of education and student experience and support that equips students for relevance in the workplace and which simultaneously inculcates responsible and critical global citizenship for the sustainability of the planet. (Barnett, 2000; Castells, 2009; Oblinger, 2003). 21st Century graduates need to be contextually relevant, socially mobile, ethical, critical, responsible, adaptable and appropriately equipped to navigate an opaque future.

Poverty is often scaffolded on pre-existing socio-economic inequality, and this is directly linked to a lack of digital equity, which entails ensuring that everyone has equal opportunities to use the tools and resources needed to fully participate as a citizen in today's digitally-powered world. (ISTE, 2006). To date, the affordances of the digital revolution, when it comes to access to a quality and affordable education have not been realized to the extent that it could be claimed to have made a measurable impact on the lives of those who need it most (Bennet & Kent, 2017; Kalman, 2016).

In addition, higher education is now confronting a number of nascent factors and forces, including technological advancements, socio-economic and political dynamics, concerns around sustainability and an increasingly borderless world, which at best, will hamper and delay the achievement of EFA and SDG 4, and at worst, will severely inhibit its attainment by 2030 if they are not highlighted, discussed and integrated into thinking around higher education practice in the future. This will be an enormous setback to sustainability, social justice and equity and as such, it calls for a broader, more nuanced contemplation of higher education futures in a state of transformation.

Higher education in transition

Higher education is at once responsive to, and a driver of, change in the extent that higher education institutions could be seen as microcosms of, or even proxies for, their State and their national developmental aspirations. Seen through the lens of this symbiotic transformational relationship with the State, broader society and global membership, it could be suggested that many of the current challenges faced by universities had their genesis in the advent of the internet (in 1991) and subsequent digitisation, which contributed to and facilitated burgeoning globalization and the massification of higher education, which has continued unabated. The demand for higher education is predicted to expand from 97 million students in 2000 to over 262 million students by 2025 (UNESCO, 2009:10) this from a base of 68 million in 1991(UNESCO, 2006: 21). Most, if not all universities, especially those in developing nations, have therefore experienced rapid growth in student numbers and ongoing demands for access. In terms of leadership, management and operations, there is a growing focus on business and governance principles, drivers and nomenclature, which many academics now claim have diluted and diminished more traditional understandings and exercise of scholarship, not to mention pedagogy and didactics. Evidently, both public (and private) universities now find themselves in a position of having to prove constantly their value and worth in contemporary society (Bok, 2003; Suspitsyna, 2012).

One thus discerns a move from the more traditional understanding that higher education institutions exist to educate students for lives of public service, to advance knowledge through research, and to develop a critical citizenry and leadership, to one where universities are increasingly pressured to prepare graduates with the requisite knowledge and skills and the ethical and social responsibility to meet the very dynamic and transient workforce needs arising from what is increasingly being dubbed 'the 4th Industrial Revolution (4IR)'. Key drivers of this transformation include:
- rapid, accretive technological innovation and advancement that is influencing global society in a revolutionary manner;

- Changing global demographics, growing concerns around the sustainability of the planet and the development of a global citizenry;
- a co-dependent, yet conflicted and profoundly unequal world; and
- a complex array of higher education stakeholders and role players who are reshaping our understanding and practice of education in fundamental ways, often via digital instruments, platforms and communication.

Filippakou & Williams (2014) and Pusser (2006) argue that these profound changes have shifted higher education worldwide from what was once a public good to a private benefit, while Gumport, 2000; Kerr, 1994 and Thompson, 2014 assert that colleges and universities have begun to operate as a corporate industry with predominant economic goals and market-oriented values, which, according to Bylsma (2015), has reduced higher education to a transactional process rather than maintaining its transformative potential.

This dual role has resulted in the rise of the new industrial model of privatization, commercialization, and corporatization and has altered higher education's traditional mission, and increased the mission differentiation in higher education systems in preparing all graduates for democratic participation, active citizenship, and personal development (Kezar, 2004; Lambert, 2014). In other words, we note quite fundamental mission drift. Institutions of higher learning are not only under pressure to promote access, affordability, and graduation in today's uncertain future, but also enhance individuals' core competencies and dispositions (i.e., "noneconomic" benefits) such as: the ability to think logically, the capacity to challenge the status quo, and the desire to develop sophisticated values for entry into the highly competitive global labour market (Brennan, Durazii, & Sene, 2013; Selingo, 2016; Tilak, 2008; Washburn, 2005). Technological innovation and digitisation continue to play a fundamental role in this transformation trajectory.

Accelerated technological innovation and influence

The World Economic Forum (2109) sums up the 4th Industrial Revolution as follows:

> *"The Fourth Industrial Revolution represents a fundamental change in the way we live, work and relate to one another. It is a new chapter in human development, enabled by extraordinary technology advances commensurate with those of the first, second and third industrial revolutions. These advances are merging the physical, digital and biological worlds in ways that create both huge promise and potential peril. The speed, breadth and depth of this revolution is forcing us to rethink how countries develop, how organisations create value and even what it means to be human. The Fourth Industrial Revolution is about more than just technology-driven change; it is an opportunity to help everyone, including leaders, policy-makers and people from all income groups and nations, to harness converging technologies to create an inclusive, human-centred future. The real opportunity is to look beyond technology and find ways to give the greatest number of people the ability to positively impact their families, organisations and communities" (p.1).*

Quo Vadis?

For Higher Education institutions in developing societies, the aspects of both 'peril' and 'promise' hold true. On one hand, most are struggling to navigate an unparalleled nexus of complex and (potentially) destructive socio-economic and political forces, while on the other, the potential and promise of 4IR offer a platform from which to transition into a more equitable, relevant future. Furthermore, even as institutions of higher learning in developing societies grapple with their contextual realities *vis a vis* 4IR (and technological innovation *per se)* they are obliged to deal with the fundamental institutional change that will be required to derive benefit from its affordances, and the disruptive impact that this will have regarding institutional leadership and management, and the need for staff (academic, professional and administrative) and students of all ages to unlearn and relearn for a future that holds little certainty.

There is a view that those higher education institutions that are not willing or able to make the necessary changes are likely to suffer a decline in relevance and impact. However, at the same time, there is a growing voice that is questioning the relevance of 4IR for their countries and the purported benefits for societies in real terms. Concerns include perceptions of elitism and hegemony, the entrenching of race and gender imbalances (including the ongoing dominance of white males and males in general) and the legitimisation of behaviours and agendas which might be contrary to the genuine wellbeing of citizens, especially those in developing nations (Unwin, 2019; Poole, 2017; Overton, 1996; Gillwald, 2019; Sello 2019).

Many institutions are responding to these forces by exerting greater administrative control in line with business administration and governance practices, which are arguably antithetical to traditional understanding of higher education practice and perhaps more pertinently, the empowerment of staff to create, innovate and transform meaningfully, while developing professionally in their disciplines. This stressful state of disruption and disequilibrium is taking place at a time when the role of higher education institutions has never been more critical in equipping and preparing societies for the new world which they will inhabit. It is sobering to contemplate that the appositeness of their response will in large measure determine and shape their own relevance and by extension, that of their higher education sectors.

In a report titled *The Future of Jobs: Skills stability* the World Economic Forum (2016) predicts [that] *"On average, by 2020, more than a third of the desired core skill sets of most occupations will be comprised of skills that are not yet considered crucial to the job today, according to our respondents"* (p.13). As growing numbers of articles attest to massive job losses and redundancies, it is unsurprising that questions are being asked about the purpose and relevance of education? Who, and what, are we educating for?

Current societal dynamics and challenges require higher education solutions which are flexible, integrated and holistic and which should not only include transdisciplinarity and engagement with professional bodies, business and industry in the development of courseware and teaching practice, but also an openness to different modes of student support, assessment and credentialing to meet different societal requirements and student expectations. There is a growing emphasis on the Recognition of Prior Learning as a means of drawing more experienced yet non credentialised students onto the system, and acknowledgement that concerted attention should be given to the upskilling of mature learners as a means of ensure their ongoing employability in the transforming world of work. Furthermore, as already mentioned, higher education institutions need to be open to fundamental restructuring (including administrative) to ensure the responsiveness and agility that is required to ensure ongoing relevance. This is particularly true in the current global context of massive socio-economic inequality and poverty gaps.

21st Century higher education institutions will therefore need a different kind of leadership (perhaps a much younger leadership) that truly understands and is able to navigate the complexity and pressures of the prevailing contexts. This is evidently a context that extends beyond that for which they have traditionally been responsible, and includes but is not limited to the influence of the socio-economic and political forces globally, continentally and nationally on the academic and the administrative functions and mandate of the institution; an ever-increasing community of role players and stakeholders all of whom will have their own agendas, which may be in competition with those of the university; and crucially, delivering a relevance and quality of pedagogy that will ensure the relevance of graduates into the future. Such leadership will need to be comfortable with pushing the boundaries of transformation and driving the mindset change that is required for a productive workforce and an agile, efficient and effective institution.

Key to achieving this, is an invested academe, which is currently not the case in many institutions. Reports from across the globe attest to disgruntled, depressed and even suicidal academics. (Farber, 2018; Oswald, 2019; Orozco *et al,* 2018; Pitt, 2018; Richardson, 2019). Even where an institution has the most inspiring vision and leaders and an irrefutable rationale for change and transformation, dealing with resistance to change remains a sticking point in many institutions. In the academe, change is often rebutted as an assault on academic freedoms and institutional autonomy, but equally often, rebuttals are grounded in legitimate concerns around excessive workloads and administrative demands over and above academic responsibilities. Excessive workloads are deemed to be the result of the rampant corporatisation of the university. For many academics this has simply become intolerable (Kember& Leung, 2006; Rahim et al, 2016; Rea, 2012; Thompson et al, 2006.). Many mature and experienced academics who were trained, and who grew their careers and reputations in a different era (a seemingly gentler more leisurely era), are now immersed in a fast-paced, highly prescriptive and in their view, intellectually superficial and bereft dynamic, which is rendering them powerless and even, increasingly obsolete. While undoubtedly an inevitable consequence of the current global dynamics, academics are sometimes expected to 'let go' much of what informs their personal and professional worth and esteem and to relearn, re-create and reinvent, often at an advanced age when academic careers almost spent. Given the longevity of academic life in many countries, this is a serious issue that merits at least the same amount of attention as that which is devoted to administrative efficiency and financial profit.

Quo Vadis?

A borderless, unequal world influenced by changing demographics

Historically most of those who have been, and continue to be, excluded from education opportunities (and social justice, equity and access), come from emerging nations and economies. Many reside in the so-called 'Global South'. However, entrenched globalisation facilitated by technological and digital advances are driving an increasingly 'borderless' world in which private, public and for-profit providers are changing the entire notion and concept of education. (Miyoshi, 1993; Middlehurst, 2003; Cunningham 2000.). The impact of this *borderlessness* is summed up succinctly by Diarra (2004):

> *"Globalization does not render the world a space with clearly delineated borders, but rather a mosaic of zones of prosperity and zones of poverty which fragment and intermingle in perpetuity. The geographic distribution of poverty is complex yet is particularly strong in Africa... children from this region are born into debt and begin their lives disadvantaged by the lack of economic development suffered by the African continent and its crushing burden of debt"* (p. 122).

This pervasive truth is echoed and confirmed in the OECD report: "In It Together: Why Less Inequality Benefits All", quoted above.

The statistics and information below have been selected to emphasise the disparities that exist across key population groupings and how these will impact on higher education delivery and individual and national futures. Perhaps the most sobering statistics are the mean age and the percentage of people under the age of 25 years in key influential countries/continents.

Table 1: Mean age and percentage of people under 25 in selected countries/continents (Desjardin: 2019)

COUNTRY	MEAN AGE (2019)	MEAN AGE BY 2050	% PEOPLE UNDER 25
USA	37.8	50	32%
EUROPE	41.8	46.6	33%
INDIA	27	37.5	50% +
CHINA	37.3	48	12.78 %
AFRICA	19.4	24.8	60 % +

Populations in North America and Europe are growing older and fewer young people are coming into higher education. Efforts to attract foreign student are not realizing the success that was envisaged with countries such as China evidencing a decline in international enrolments (Barnes, 2018; Fischer, 2019; Magnier & Bases. 2019). The volatile socio economic and political contestations playing out in this hemisphere are possibly contributing to the state of flux in higher education, making it exceedingly difficult to predict or plan with any certainty, education futures and needs. This is contributing to the fragmentation of global higher education into regional and national enclaves, which are more contextually focused, and needs driven. This trend is finding its echoes across the world as financial constraints are shaping higher education agendas to an increasing degree. The adage *charity begins at home* is finding wide resonance as funding for higher education continues decreasing and change and impact are being affected by individuals, businesses and NGOs 'on the ground' rather than by governments or ministries of education.

If one looks at the Continent of Africa, a worrying picture emerges. 41% of the African Population is under the age of 15 and the mean age of the continent is only 18 (some put it at 19) (World Population review 2019a). In less than a decade, all these young people will be eligible to access higher education. The active working age population (25-64 years) has grown more rapidly than any other age group, from 123.7 million (33.3 per cent) in 1980 to 425.7 million (36.2 per cent) in 2015, and unemployment is the norm, rather than the exception (des Jardin, 2019).

"The population of Africa is currently projected to quadruple in just 90 years, with a growth rate that will make Africa more important than ever to the global economy... Many consider Africa's population growth a bit frightening, with predictions placing the continent's population at 2.4 billion by 2050. By 2100, more than half of the world's growth is expected to come from Africa, reaching 4.1 billion people by 2100 to claim over 1/3 of the world's population" (World Population Review, 2019b).

These data highlight some serious implications for the fulfilment of SDG 4 and the provision of a quality education and higher education on the African continent. There is no doubt that currently, Open Distance e-Learning (ODeL), together with a dedicated focus on collaborations that include the sharing and leveraging of facilities and capacities, will be the most viable means of managing what is likely to be a crisis of education provision, as early as the next decade.

Thus, two certainties emerge. Firstly, at present, the only viable means of accommodating the millions of students nationally and on the continent (an in other similarly impacted developing contexts), is ODeL, and it is going to have to be hugely innovative and efficient ODeL if it is to produce graduates of substance and stature who are informed and equipped to become tomorrow's leaders, administrators and entrepreneurs, as well as the responsible and critical citizenry envisaged by the SDGs.

Secondly, given that there is limited financing available for the establishment of additional institutions, individual institutions will not be able to service such student numbers on their own, and there is even less of a chance of producing the kinds of research needed to realise the vison of SDG 4. This means a concerted focus on collaboration and the leveraging of our collective resources on the one hand, as well as the harnessing of our collective knowledges and research capabilities and capacities across the globe on the other. This much has been recognised by key global higher education players. At the recent *U7* Alliance of World Universities Summit held on 9 & 10 July 2019, the U7+ Alliance members voted and adopted six principles to address five major challenges of the multilateral agenda: The challenges identified comprised:

- Universities as key actors in a global world
- Climate and energy transition

Quo Vadis?

- Inequality and polarized societies
- Technological transformation
- Community engagement and impact

It is evident that there is consonance amongst global leaders regarding all the factors that have been identified and discussed in this chapter. These challenges will be supported by six principles and 245 related actions, some of which are linked to specific institutions. The six principles (which have actions embedded), include:

1. Pursue joint action through the U7+, including meeting each year in the context of the G7 process, "so that our actions can weigh in the discussions and contribute to making positive change a reality".
2. Recognise universities' distinctive responsibility to train and nurture responsible and active citizens who will contribute to society, from the local to the global level.
3. Recognise that "our universities have a major role to play in addressing the environmental issues and challenges to sustainability such as climate change, biodiversity and energy transition. This should include leading by example on our own campuses."
4. Recognise that universities have a distinctive and leading role to play regarding equality and inclusiveness in the world, and in combating polarisation in society.
5. To engage with stakeholders and solve complex issues of global relevance that universities must promote interdisciplinary research and learning, in particular bridging in research and teaching between social sciences, humanities, the life sciences and STEM disciplines (science, technology, engineering and mathematics).
6. Recognise that the U7+ "has the power to serve as a lab to consolidate best practices that can be shared both within our network and more broadly with universities and similar institutions worldwide for inspiration" (Marshall & O'Malley, 2019).

In similar vein, the PCF 9 Edinburgh Statement (2) was released subsequent to the recent Pan Commonwealth Forum 9 (PCF 9), held in Edinburgh in September 2019, and it also voiced its intention to mobilise members to: achieve accomplishment at scale; impart skills for productive lives; create new digital dividends; harness teachers as skilled agents of change; positively disrupt higher education; and challenge assessment. PCF undertakes to do this by mobilizing all stakeholders and actors, galvanizing political will by collaborating with critical thinkers, innovators and practitioners, sustaining the momentum and building an active network of learning, support and action, starting now (PCF 9: 2019).

There is no gainsaying that there is a global awareness of the challenges that are being faced in higher education, as well as a deep determination to address these constructively and with urgency.

Conclusion

Globally, higher education is becoming increasingly fragmented and polarised and the notion of education is being reshaped in line with technological advancements and the entry into higher education of an avalanche of for-profit providers eager to leverage the affordance of technology for financial gain. Traditional higher education providers, both in the distance education and face-to-face contexts have entered the fray, with varying degrees of success and influence.

More than a decade down the line, it is clear that that despite the hype around the potential of technology, digitisation and its application in higher education practice and delivery at scale, it is now increasingly, albeit tacitly, acknowledged that providing quality education to masses of students who were previously denied it because of personal circumstance, is simply not achievable or affordable. The staggering complexity and expense of adapting existing systems, business models, institutional operations and cultures has more often than not (in a number of high-profile cases and institutions) ended in failure from which it has been difficult to recover. Also, there is growing evidence that students themselves are not entirely satisfied with the notion of no or low levels of contact with lecturers. What we see emerging is yet another divide, between the digitally endowed who have choices and the digitally needy who have fewer choices and options when it comes to a quality education.

Open Education Resources (OERs) are gaining traction as a means of offsetting the cost of courseware development and textbooks in particular, but its widespread uptake and successful application and implementation have yet to be fully accepted, tested and measured, given the challenges around, for example, knowledge hegemony and contextual demands, including licencing and resistance from academics who mostly prefer to develop their own courseware. One also notes a move into online education, which is defined differently depending on the location and context, as well as public or private and for-profit entities, but again, it is fragmented, with little research on its general implementation and success. However, the importance of these initiatives becomes quite stark when one considers the picture of population demographics for the emerging nations, and the implications that these have for the provision of higher education and the achievements of the SDGs.

Coupled with the need for technical and digital upskilling of the existing workforce, educators must look at strategies and business models that ensure national continuity and medium to long-term sustainability. This picture differs from continent to continent and nation to nation, but there is no gainsaying that a clear understanding of national population demographics, coupled with the reality of the socio-economic and political contexts are reshaping higher education in fundamental ways. In this understanding nuanced student demographic and student profiling is critical.

Finally, universities that wish to survive and thrive have no other option than to reinvent themselves through a futures-centric mindset that includes a multi-stakeholder, broadly participative leadership and management, collaborative business models, a fundamental commitment to sustainability through ethical stewardship of the institutional and the planet's resources, a genuine appreciation of the people who comprise the university community, and quality, relevant courseware, assessment practices and student support, that will prepare graduates for an uncertain future and provide a foundation for future flourishing.

References

Abowitz, K. A. (2008). On the public and civic purposes of education. *Educational Theory*, 58(3), 357–376.

Barnes, J. (2018), Is the Golden Age of Chinese Studying Abroad at an End? Political headwinds could deter Chinese students from universities in the U.S., Australia, and the U.K. *The Diplomat.* Retrieved from: https://thediplomat.com/2018/10/is-the-golden-age-of-chinese-studying-abroad-at-an-end/

Barnett, R. (2000). Thinking the University, again. *Education Philosophy and Theory, 32 (3).* 319-326.
https://doi.org/10.1111/j.1469-5812.2000.tb00457.x

Bennet, R. & Kent, M. (2017). Massive Open Online Courses and higher education: what went right, what went wrong and where to next. New York. Routledge, Taylor &Francis.

Bok, D. C. (2013). *Higher education in America.* Princeton, NJ: Princeton University Press.

Brennan, J., Durazzi, N., & Sene, T. (2013). *Things we know and don't know about the Wider Benefits of Higher Education: A review of the recent literature.* London, UK: London School of Economics and Political Science (LSE).

Brighouse, H., & Mcpherson, M. (2015). *The aims of higher education: Problems of morality and justice.* Chicago, IL: University of Chicago Press.

Bylsma, P. E. (2015). The teleological effect of neoliberalism on American higher education. *College Student Affairs Leadership,* 2(2), Article 3. Retrieved from: http://scholarworks.gvsu.edu/csal/vol2/iss2/3 Cassuto

Castells, M. (2009). *Communication power.* Oxford: Oxford University Press.

Cunningham, S., Ryan, Y., et al. (2000). *The business of borderless education, Evaluations and Investigations Programme no. 00/3*, Department of Education, Training and Youth Affairs, [Canberra]. Retrieved from:
https://www.voced.edu.au/content/ngv%3A36322

Desjardin, D. (2019). Mapped: *The median age of the population on every continent.* Visual Capitalist. Retrieved from:https://www.visualcapitalist.com/mapped-the-median-age-of-every-continent/?utm_source=email&utm_medium=social&utm_campaign=SocialWarfare

Diarra, F.D. (2004). IV. *Towards new and re-emerging forms of discrimination? human rights literacy for the twenty-first century* (Translated from Paul Robert, L'Atlas géopolitique et culturel du Petit Robert des noms propres (Paris, 2000:108) in Universal Forms of Cultures – Barcelona 2004. New Ignorances, New Literacies. Learning to Live Together in a Globalising World. United Nations Educational, Scientific and Cultural Organisation. 2005. Paris.

Dungy, G. (2012). Connecting and Collaborating to Further the Intellectual, Civic, and Moral Purposes of Higher Education. *Journal of College and Character*, 13(3), 1-12. DOI: 10.1515/jcc-2012-1917

Farer, T. (2018). *UCT sets up inquiry into Bongani Mayosi's suicide.* 03 August 2018 - 13:38. Sunday Times, Times Live. Retrieved from:
https://www.timeslive.co.za/news/south-africa/2018-08-03-uct-sets-up-inquiry-into-bongani-mayosis-suicide/

Filippakou, O., & Williams, G. (2014). *Higher education as a public good: A critical perspective.* New York, NY: Peter Lang Publisher.

Fischer, K (2019) How International Education's Golden Age lost its sheen. *The Chronicle of Higher Education.* Retrieved from:
https://www.chronicle.com/interactives/2019-03-28-golden-age

Gillwald, A. 2019. *South Africa is caught in the global hype of the fourth industrial revolution.* Retrieved from: https://mg.co.za/article/2019-08-26-south-africa-is-caught-in-the-global-hype-of-the-fourth-industrial-revolution

Gumport, P. (2000). Academic restructuring: Organizational change and institutional imperatives. *Higher Education,* 39, 67-91. https://doi.org/10.1023/A:1003859026301

Kalman, Y.M. (2016). Cutting through the hype: evaluating the innovative potential of new educational technologies through business model analysis. Open Learning: The Journal of Open, Distance and e-Learning, 1(31), 64 – 75. https://doi.org/10.1080/02680513.2016.1164592

Kember, D., & Leung, D.YP. (2006) Characterising a teaching and learning environment conducive to making demands on students while not making their workload excessive. *Studies in Higher Education,* 31(2), 185-198, DOI: 0.1080/03075070600572074

Kerr, C. (1994). *Troubled times for American higher education: The 1990s and beyond.* Albany, NY: State University of New York Press.

Kezar, A. (2004). Obtaining integrity? Reviewing and examining the charter between higher education and society. *The Review of Higher Education,* 27(4), 429-459. http://dx.doi.org/10.1353/rhe.2004.0013

International Society for Technology in Education (ISTE) (2006). *Digital Equity Toolkit – Working Draft.* Retrieved from: http://www.laurelfelt.org/digital-equity/

Lambert, M. T. (2014). *Privatization and the public good.* Cambridge, MA: Harvard University Education Press

Levine, P. (2014). A defense of higher education and its civic mission. *Journal of General Education,* 63(1), 47-56.

Magnier, M., Bases, D. (2019). South China Morning Post. US universities brace for decline in Chinese students after Beijing warning. American academia becomes newest front in US-China friction. As tensions mount and distrust expands the two sides face off in new areas. Retrieved from: www.scmp.com/news/china/diplomacy/article/3012997/us-universities-brace-decline-chinese-students-after-beijing

Marshall, J., and O'Malley. B. (2019, 8 June). *G7 university presidents to tackle global challenges.* Retrieved from: https://www.universityworldnews.com › post › story=20190608063131641

Middlehurst, R. (2001). University Challenges: Borderless Higher Education, Today and Tomorrow. *Minerva,* 39, (3-26). 10.1023/A:1010343517872.

Miyoshi, M. (1993) A Borderless World? From Colonialism to Transnationalism and the Decline of the Nation-State. *Critical Inquiry,* 19 (4), 726-751. https://doi.org/10.1086/448695

Oblinger, D. (2003). Boomers, Gen-Xers & Millennials: Understanding the New Students. *EDUCAUSE Review.* July/August (pp37-47).

OECD. (2015). *In It Together: Why Less Inequality Benefits All.* OECD Publishing, Paris. http://dx.doi.org/10.1787/9789264235120-en

Orozco, R., Benjet, C., Borges, G., Moneta Arce, M. F., Fregoso Ito, D., Fleiz, C., & Villatoro, J. A. (2018). Association between attempted suicide and academic performance indicators among middle and high school students in Mexico: results from a national survey. *Child and adolescent psychiatry and mental health,* 12 (9). doi:10.1186/s13034-018-0215-6

Oswald, A. (2019). *Middle aged academics are at greater suicide risk than students.* Times Higher Education. Retrieved from: https://www.timeshighereducation.com/opinion/middle-aged-academics-are-greater-suicide-risk-students

Overton, M. (1996). Agricultural Revolution in England: The Transformation of the Agrarian Economy 1500–1850. *Cambridge Studies in Historical Geography.* Cambridge: Cambridge University Press. doi:10.1017/CBO9780511607967

Pitt, C. (2018). News 24. *UCT must take responsibility for Prof Mayosi's death* – former Fees Must Fall leader
News 24. 2018-07-31 14:03. Retrieved from: https://www.news24.com/SouthAfrica/News/uct-must-take-responsibility-for-prof-mayosis-death-former-fees-must-fall-leader-20180731
Poole, S. 2017. *The Fourth Industrial Revolution review – adapt to new technology or perish.* Retrieved from https://www.theguardian.com/books/2017/jan/06/the-fourth-industrial-revolution-by-klaus-schwab-review
Pusser, B. (2006). Reconsidering higher education and the public good. In W. Tierney (Ed.), *Governance and the public good* (pp. 11–28). Albany: SUNY Press.
Rahim, M.S.A., Saat, N.Z.M., Siti Aishah, H., Arshad, S.A., Aziz, N.A.A., Zakaria, N.N., Kaur, K., Kamaruddin, M.M. and Suhaimi, N.H.F. (2016). Relationship between Academic Workload and Stress Level among Biomedical Science Students in Kuala Lumpur. *Journal of Applied Sciences,* 16: 108-112. DOI: 10.3923/jas.2016.108.112 URL: https://scialert.net/abstract/?doi=jas.2016.108.112
Rea, J. (2012) Key academic claim: Control workloads and create new jobs [online]. Advocate: *Journal of the National Tertiary Education Union,* Vol. 19 (2), 19-20. Retrieved from: https://search.informit.com.au/documentSummary;dn=617784404270631;res=IELBUS> ISSN: 1329-7295.
Richardson, H. (2019). University counselling services 'inundated by stressed academics'. Retrieved from: https://www.bbc.com/news/education-48353331
Sciences Pro. (2019). U7+ ALLIANCE: A UNIVERSITY ALLIANCE TO WEIGH IN ON THE G7 AGENDA. O710 2019. Retrieved from: https://www.sciencespo.fr/en/news/news/u7-alliance-47-universities-commit-to-tackle-global-issues/4248 PCF9 Edinburgh Statement. (2019) Retrieved from: https://comosaconnect.org/wp-content/uploads/2017/05/pcf9-the-edinburgh-statement-20.pdf
Selingo, J. (2013). College unbound: The future of higher education, and what it means for students. New York, NY: New Harvest
Sello, L. (2019). *4IR and Africa. Promise or peril?* Investec. Available at: https://www.investec.com/en_za/focus/innovation/4ir-and-africa-a-digital-divide.html?medium=referral&source=daily-maverick&campaign=gm-sa-partner&term=4ir-in-africa&content=&position=&adgroup=&keyword=&matchtype=
Shapiro, H. T. (2005). *A larger sense of purpose: Higher education and society.* Princeton, NJ: Princeton University Press.
Suspitsyna, T. (2012). Higher education for economic advancement and engaged citizenship: An analysis of the U.S. Department of Education Discourse. Journal of Higher Education, 83(1), 49-72.
Tierney (Ed.), *Governance and the public good* (pp.11–28), Albany, NY: State University of New York Press.
Tilak, J. (2008). Higher education: A public good or a commodity for trade? *Prospects,* 38, 449-466.
Thomsen, J.L., Jarbøl, D., Søndergaard, J. (2006). Excessive workload, uncertain career opportunities and lack of funding are important barriers to recruiting and retaining primary care medical researchers: a qualitative interview study, *Family Practice,* 23 (5) 545–549, https://doi.org/10.1093/fampra/cml034
Thompson, R. J. (2014). Beyond reason and tolerance: The purpose and practice of higher education. New York, NY: Oxford University Press.
UNESCO. (1998). World Declaration on Higher Education for the Twenty-First Century: Vision and Action. Retrieved from:

http://www.unesco.org/education/educprog/wche/declaration_eng.htm#world%20declaration

UNESCO. (2006). *Global Education Digest. Comparing Education Statistics around the World*. UNESCO Institute for Statistics. Montreal. (pp 76-79).

UNESCO/UNICEF. (2007). A Human Rights-Based Approach to EDUCATION FOR ALL. A framework for the realization of children's right to education and rights within education. *A Human Rights-Based Approach to Education* © United Nations Children's Fund/ United Nations Educational, Scientific and Cultural Organization. Retrieved from: https://www.unicef.org/publications/files/A_Human_Rights_Based_Approach_to_Education_for_All.pdf

UNESCO. (2009). The 2009 World Conference on Higher Education: reacting to new dynamics. Retrieved from: http://unesdoc.unesco.org/images/0018/001832/183274e.pdf. (p.10)

UNESCO. (2015). Sustainable Development Goals. Available at: http://www.un.org/sustainabledevelopment/sustainable-development-goals/. Accessed: 2016/04/20

UNESCO. (2015). Position Paper on Education Post-2015. ED-14/EFA/POST- 2015/1. Retrieved from: https://unesdoc.unesco.org/ark:/48223/pf0000227336 (p 4)

UNESCO (2016). Education 2030. Incheon Declaration and Framework for Action Towards Inclusive and Equitable Quality Education and Life- long learning for all. ED-2016/ws/2. Available at http://en.unesco.org/ world-education-forum-2015/incheon-declaration.

UNESCO. (2018). Summary of Progress towards Education for All. Working document prepared by UNESCO for the Tenth High-Level Group Meeting on Education for All. Retrieved from: zttp://www.unesco.org/new/fileadmin/MULTIMEDIA/HQ/ED/ED_new/pdf/Summary%20of%20progress%20towards%20EFA-colors.pdf

UNESCO. (2018). Data for Sustainable development. *Time to Get Serious About Education for All, with Progress at a Standstill.* Posted on February 28, 2018 by UIS Data Blog. Data for Sustainable Development. UNESCO Institute for Statistics Blog. By Silvia Montoya, Director of the UNESCO Institute for Statistics (UIS) and Karen Mundy, Chief Technical Officer, Global Partnership for Education (GPE). Retrieved from: https://sdg.uis.unesco.org/2018/02/28/time-to-get-serious-about-education-for-all-with-progress-at-a-standstill/

Unwin, T. (2019, March 23). 5 Problems with 4th Industrial Revolution – Your Weekend Long *Read*s. Retrieved from: https://www.ictworks.org/problems-fourth-industrial-revolution/#.XWZJWSgzaxo

Washburn, J. (2005). University Inc.: The corporate corruption of American higher education. New York, NY: Basic Books

World Economic Forum. (2016). *The Future of Jobs: Skills stability.* Retrieved from: http://reports.weforum.org/future-of-jobs-2016/skills-stability/

World Economic Forum. (2019). *Fourth Industrial Revolution.* Retrieved from: https://www.weforum.org/focus/fourth-industrial-revolution..

World Population Review. (2019). *Africa Population 2019.* Retrieved from: http://worldpopulationreview.com/continents/africa-population/

Quo Vadis?

 **Mandla Stanley Makhanya** is Vice Chancellor of the University of South Africa and is a prominent proponent of higher education leadership and advocacy, nationally, continentally and globally, more especially as it pertains to Open, Distance and eLearning.

4

The University: Current Perspectives and Views for the Future

Ivy Adwowa Efiefi Ekem
School of Medical Sciences, University of Cape Coast, Ghana

Introduction

The first definition of university I came across as I started this article stated, "*a high-level educational institution in which students' study for degrees and where academic research is done*". This definition clearly stops at the process. The product is missing. Is it time to modify the definition of a university? Should it rather read "a high-level educational institution which forms a confident human being through teaching, outreach and research"? In both definitions - given and proposed - universities are educational institutions. What then is education? "*Education is the process of facilitating learning or the acquisition of knowledge, skills, values, beliefs, and habits. Educational methods include storytelling, discussion, teaching, training and directed research*".

Peter Ustinov (1977) in "Dear Me" says "*After all, what is education but a process by which a person begins to learn how to learn?*" What is education meant for? What is the objective? I'd like to look at excerpts from *Arthur W Foshay, "The Curriculum Matrix: Transcendence and Mathematics" Journal of Curriculum and Supervision, 1991;* He says amongst other things, that the purpose of education is to bring people to as full a realization as possible of what it is to be a human being; develop the intellect, serve social needs, contribute to the economy.

For university education to be fit for purpose, the concept from Foshay would be worth following. Universities should not only develop the intellectual capabilities of individuals but the university should be of service to society; thus, contributing to the economies of nations and the total human interaction. These should serve as bedrocks of the various programmes that are offered. Such efforts would help position universities as proper higher educational institutions that would move us closer to what we should all desire - a better world.

This can be achieved through different means by different communities with different philosophies and backgrounds while making sure that the salient features are still maintained. A university that is deemed the best should be the one that has the capacity to train any human being irrespective of their IQ or circumstance. This view is supported by UNESCO in its inclusive education policy which states:

> *"a process of addressing and responding to the diversity of needs of all learners through increasing participation in learning, cultures and communities, and reducing exclusion from education and from within education"* (unesco.org.pk/education/icfe/resources/res41.pdf)

The individual who emerges as a product of such training should be equipped enough to fit a niche in society waiting to be dynamically occupied.

By engaging qualified human resources in appropriate environments with regards physical and soft structures, coupled with the use of the right instructional methods, research and outreach, potentially every human being can be developed to meet the right standards – that is being human, serving the society and contributing to the expansion of any economy. It should however be acknowledged that none of these can be achieved without adequate financial support.

The human resource

A closer look at the composition of faculty members at the various universities in my country reveals that the entry qualification to teach at the university is the possession of a doctorate degree (Ph.D.) or a level 8 qualification as stated in the UNESCO educational document (ISCED 2011). The question is, is a PhD sine qua non the qualification needed for training and nurturing another individual to be able to reason and be a life-long learner of value to society? Can an "illiterate" person assist in any way in producing the functional human being we all desire? And why should one be less capable in the training of a fellow human being in the arts and sciences of life when they are above 60 – 70 years depending on the jurisdiction?

The University of the Future I envisage would have what it takes to engage faculty without the restrictive barriers of background and age.

Take the level of students; although I reckon there must be an entry qualification for any educational venture, the criteria and standards currently set do not encompass all who truly qualify. The boundaries are set taking into consideration physical issues such as space and facilities, which is not a true reflection of the situation on the ground. The implication and repercussion of this is that many students are denied the opportunity to develop their intellect and personalities, which in turn means society is deprived of their possible contribution. To make it worse, many who do qualify may never be able to get in because they can neither fund their education nor get access to loan facilities for that purpose.

The University of the Future needs to expand in order to build enough capacity to give room to all who qualify as well as have sub-levels where non-qualifying but genuinely interested candidates could be given the requisite training to meet the desired attainments for a university education. And this expansion need not be physical; it can be virtual. Advancement in technology makes this a high possibility in every way.

The appropriate physical environment

What is available for teaching and practical training in and outside the classroom? What is the living environment of staff and students? Are all utilities including internet access assured? What is the surrounding natural environment like? Does it foster the development of the human being? Are universities with very limited structures by way of physical buildings appropriate? Are universities located within busy cities with no greenery good for learning? What should a good university's physical infrastructure look like? Are there guidelines? Should the guidelines differ from country to country? In my search I found one guideline for the setting up of new universities for Pakistan. Can UNESCO have something similar? My suggestion would be for UNESCO to present a minimal standard and a framework to assist all societies in setting up any new university. This would ensure a basic standard for all universities including their physical environments. This is important if it is accepted that the ultimate aim of university education is to have a functioning human being who will be of benefit to society. And to ensure fairness and equity, all societies ought to be brought along to realize that the basic tenets of life are the same for all. In this way, universities can truly contribute their quota to the agenda for a better world.

The appropriate soft structures

What is the organizational structure of the university? What are its statutes? Who determines who leads? What is the age cut-off and why? Is money the motivation for mounting new courses? How can the poor have access to quality education like anyone else? Who is qualified to access university education? How are the members of the university work force incentivized? Does that affect output? Universities naturally aim at excellence and would want to remain competitive. Well laid down protocols and policies modified at regulated intervals to suit the developing age would help not only governance but staff motivation and retention. This is most important in the selection of leaders, promotion of staff and staff conditions of service. Universities would have to actively seek endowments for various activities, especially student scholarship schemes if talent is to be harnessed for the betterment of society.

Finances

Should a university depend on the government for subvention, on itself or on student fees? The bottom line is that there should be sound financial support for the university to be able to run its programmes without compromise on account of poor financial inflows. Public funding would appear to be insufficient at all times. Universities should also create programmes aimed at bringing in money by way of student fees. This should not be done without serious consideration for the resources needed for the programmes – both human and otherwise. On the other hand, universities, being places with a concentration of intellect and skill should probably harness this more than has previously been done and in collaboration with industry bring in much needed funds on a regular basis. For example, it should be possible for a university with an agriculture department, a nutrition unit and food processing unit to feed not only the students but also staff and members of the local community for a fee. This should be placed in context where staff conditions of service are realistic and motivating.

The role of endowments and student loan schemes should be pursued and made more visible. Student loans which render a graduate a pauper for years should also not be encouraged. The development of anyone is eventually not to the benefit of the individual alone but to his/her community, the country and the world at large. The fortunate in society by way of financial resources should be encouraged to support universities to the benefit of all.

The Product – The Graduate

Sun Kwok says, and I agree, that

"A good university education should train a student as a person, to broaden their mind and horizons, to allow them to see the relationships of apparently disparate phenomena, to acquire knowledge independently and to develop the confidence to challenge authority or dogma. These are the qualities that will make them leaders of the future. Such training requires a very different set-up from the current discipline-specific, narrowly focused subject learning that was popular in the old days of the British Empire or the Soviet Union".

Developing such a person as described here means providing the student with fundamental skills and helping them learn on their own and adapt to evolving circumstances. The skill set is led by effective communication and language skills. Quantitative skills, such as the ability to analyse a problem, see hidden patterns, identify relevant variables and formulate solutions, are crucial to many jobs in society as well as success in everyday interaction and living. Open-mindedness and fairness are qualities that would be expected in such a trained individual. The product should be a confident energetic individual with an enquiring mind, able to function in a niche and generally enhance societal values.

To function as a unit, a community, like all functioning units will have diverse elements but acts with the single aim of surviving. This means that diversity is not only necessary and unavoidable but desirable. This diversity is in all areas including individual interest and passion regardless of gender. Up until the present there are still gender sensitive statements. There exist opinionated views on various university programmes. Some programmes are seen as more important and thus better to be studied and pursued than others. Students are made to feel that certain subjects would not advance their progress in life. This mindset is quite pervasive in some jurisdictions.

I know of names of courses being modified just to sound good in the ears of the prospective student – so for example, 'Sanitation' is named 'Environmental Technology', to make it more appealing. Agriculture is read as a subject, but then often not practiced because it is looked down upon. This is what I refer to as a missing link. In our jurisdiction, these two examples are areas where as a nation we can make our greatest impact if health and food sufficiency are to be achieved. A young female who chooses to read a programme in the (performing) arts, such as drawing or music and dance could incur the displeasure of her parents. They would feel she had set herself on a path to fail in life because such a course of study offers no guarantee of success. A Ghanaian who chooses to read Ghanaian Languages at a university in Ghana is questioned as to why they did not choose a better subject, and if languages, why not French or Spanish or Chinese. A man chooses to read Food Science or Nursing and eyebrows get raised.

Sun Kwok (2015) says that university education is not just about enhancing one's career prospects but rather it broadens students' minds and horizons, allowing them to discern connections and analyse problems, thus empowering them to change the world. The critical query then is, how do we get such an all-rounded graduate? I would suggest that it is down to how the university delivers its curriculum. This is clearly stated in a press release in 2017 by the Association of American Colleges and Universities. It is titled and I quote, *"Employers Judge Recent Graduates Ill-Prepared for Today's Workplace, Endorse Broad and Project-Based Learning as Best Preparation for Career Opportunity and Long-Term Success"* (Tritelli 2017).

The recommended instructional methods to deliver a curriculum

No subject should be seen to be of greater value than another, once the instructional methods to develop the intellect of the individual studying it are assured. At the university, it is expected that the interest and inclination of the student is harnessed to the fullest through discourse, reasoning and research. The university should unearth potential and imbue creativity in the student for the enhancement of both the individual and for society.

Problem Based Learning (PBL)

Problem Based Learning is a well-established educational methodology. It is not as well employed as would be desired for a world that is lacking in problem solving skills. Problem based learning is a form of delivering a curriculum based on real practical issues. These practical issues / problems are formulated as scenarios and discussed using a prescribed method. This method encourages independent learning and gives students practical skills in tackling puzzling situations and defining their own gaps in understanding the context of relevant problems, making it more likely that they will be able to apply the knowledge when needed. It is a way of learning which encourages a deeper understanding of the material rather than superficial coverage.

As part of the delivery, students are put in smaller groups that are maintained throughout the programme. These small tutorial groups give the students a chance to discuss a problem (scenario) in detail. Everyone's opinion is respected. Time is also given away from the discussion group for independent study of the problem at hand. This gives the students a chance to be responsible for their own learning. The few hours of lectures they may have are aimed at helping with this independent research. When the group meet again they harness the information from each other and with the direction of a facilitator, acquire the right knowledge.

STEAM education

"STEAM is an educational approach to learning that uses Science, Technology, Engineering, the Arts and Mathematics as access points for guiding student inquiry, dialogue and critical thinking. The end results are

students who take thoughtful risks, engage in experiential learning, persist in problem-solving, embrace collaboration, and work through the creative process. These are the innovators, educators, leaders, and learners of the 21st century!" (https://educationcloset.com/steam/what-is-steam/ accessed 24th July 2019).

STEAM education aims to take over the traditional acquisition of information for a single "pure" subject. This mode of education invariably has students participate in their own acquisition of knowledge rather than sit as assumed passive vessels to fill with the teachers' garnered knowledge. It inculcates enquiry, dialogue and thus team building and community living. The student is encouraged to think globally as a number of different angles to any one topic are examined in theory and practice.

The individual subject areas mentioned are thus simply different angles of looking at the same concept as a way of guiding the student as she/he searches for information. This is best done using teacher-facilitated but student-led modes of delivery in its various forms – individual study, group learning, hands-on and community based as it occurs within a problem based learning curriculum.

In the real world and in everyday living, rarely does one subject dominate a role unless in combination with others. For example, the business woman is not only artistic in attracting customers but uses engineering, technology and mathematics to get the business on a sound footing. The role of a mother is even more daunting – balancing pregnancy, childcare, finances, emotional support, homemaking etc. Everything is integrated and this should apply to the methodology of teaching, otherwise we would end up raising engineers who cannot build anything or agricultural students who cannot cultivate anything and doctors who have no empathy towards their patients.

As a tool for integrated teaching and learning, STEAM education encourages the intentional connection between different curricula and their learning objectives. This means that for teachers it should also reflect in the way students are assessed. To do STEAM education properly, teaching staff would have to come together and redesign their curricula and discuss the best ways to implement it. Avenues and facilities for small group discussions are necessary parts of the infrastructure of the institution.

The benefits of STEAM education are that students can think independently of others, be able to express themselves with no right or wrong way to come to correct solutions, get hands-on learning, be responsible for their own learning, acquire team-building skills and understand how different disciplines connect with each other. This would also engender creativity – a quality necessary for living.

Outreach

There cannot be any meaningful development without outreach. In an outreach scenario, the faculty together with the student try to engage with the community and share the knowledge acquired and the findings of research from within the university to the doorsteps of the community. The university and the community should be collaborators.

Students of institutions of higher learning are to be "Important contributors to society and nations - the 'civic and community engagement' theory" (Richard Lerner et al, 2014). This is achieved through outreach. For any activity to be recognized as a tool for educating a student and qualify as Outreach, there should be involvement by faculty, the students and community or industry. The activity itself should lead to learning by students; improvement in industry / community practice; improvement in teaching and scholarship by faculty and finally publication. When choosing an outreach activity, it is important to ensure that it is in line with the University's vision and mission and that it will seek to enhance the image of the university and the industry/community. Universities should be seen to be actively supporting outreach by taking active role where necessary in the university-community engagement. Ultimately, outreach should bring desired development to communities and industry as well as serve as an learning platform for students and also facilitate the improvement of teaching and scholarship skills of faculty.

Research

What informs the research agenda? Is it relevant to the community? Is it well funded? Are the results used for the benefit of society? The research question must be relevant; it should identify an output which can have utility value. All the players who may have a stake in the output should be encouraged to support the research so that they will benefit from the findings and be ready to implement them. In this way much more research would be used in real time and not remain on shelves.

Epilogue

It is important to bear in mind that education cannot exist independently of the community. The entire community must be an integral part of the classroom and contribute as well as be a source of learning for students. The ambience around student hostels, student classrooms, lecturers and heads of departments, all play critical and crucial roles in student learning and development.

Students are encouraged to use the opportunities made available to them from so many people; the government, parents, siblings and friends to study effectively and not to waste time on inappropriate information often found on social media. Students should spend time reading wide outside their domain of study so as to broaden their horizon and perspective.

Lecturers should pour out their hearts and teach/train to harness the intellect and creativity of their students. The objective of every lecturer should be to bring out the best in every student whilst being mindful that each of them have different strengths and capabilities waiting to be nurtured. The aim of every lecturer should be a determination to contribute to the moulding of each student so that they will better able to contribute meaningfully to society. The classroom and other places of learning should be places the students love and yearn to go to, and not places that they go with trepidation.

The role of other necessities of life has taken the background in a number of universities in Ghana. Proper nutrition is not considered and university-led eateries are virtually absent. Meanwhile a poorly nourished individual is unlikely to achieve their potential. Universities should make it part of their core business to ensure that students are able to feed themselves well by providing an affordable nourishing menu. I cannot stress this enough. As a haematologist I know for a fact that good nutrition provides a good level of haemoglobin which is absolutely necessary for learning and critical thinking and this really should be insisted upon from childhood. Nations should prioritize nutrition. A poorly fed individual cannot study, and not only that, even when their haemoglobin is corrected in later life their thinking processes would have been affected for life.

Everyone should play their role. The business of university education is in the long run for the development and enhancement of our world. The golden rule says "Do unto others what you'd like them to do unto you" in other words "Love your neighbour as yourself". If you have been assigned a duty, do it diligently knowing that your own poor performance will affect others negatively and vice versa. Let us all re-educate ourselves holistically by reckoning that none is better than the other because of what he/she chose to study or where they happen to be born. We are all equally important in the big picture of life and our attitudes affect us and others both positively and negatively. So let us play our roles to the best of our abilities for the good of all.

There should be mutual respect for one another irrespective of age, gender, society or anything else as we all have roles to play as our contributions to the betterment of the society. Whoever we may be – be it organists, dressmakers, cleaners, farmers, labourers, messengers, doctors, housewives, lawyers etc. – all are necessary. Let us all do our work well and with love and dedication knowing that we all depend on one another with no individual being more superior than the other. Good education will make us all more human.

God helps us to learn to be independent thinkers from childhood as we are assisted by parents, teachers etc, and that we will be willing to sacrifice and critically think and proffer as well as seek solutions in all spheres to move our nation and our world forward.

Conclusion

The University of the Future is one that is not independent of the community; one that is dynamic and with products readily available to solve the community's problems. This university will be one that is so well funded by all stakeholders that attendance will not only be for the rich but for all. It would be one whose research agenda is such that results are applicable to solve ongoing and pressing problems and seek to modernize in an environmentally wholesome way, the lives of every living thing. Ultimately the University of the Future will have no boundaries between it and the community.

References

Foshay, Arthur W (1991) "The Curriculum Matrix: Transcendence and Mathematics" Journal of Curriculum and Supervision, 1991

Interview with the UNESCO-IBE Director, Clementina Acedo
unesco.org.pk/education/icfe/resources/res41.pdf retrieved 20th July 2019

Kwok Sun (2015). What is the purpose of University Education. Opinion.
https://www.scmp.com/comment/insight-opinion/article/1889686/what-purpose-university-education Accessed 24th July 2019

The University: Current Perspectives and Views for the Future

Lerner Richard M, Wang Jun, Champine Robey B, Warren Daniel J.A and Erickson Karl (2014) "Development of civic engagement: Theoretical and methodological issues", International Journal of Developmental Sciences 8(3):69-79 doi: 10.3233/dev-14130

Tritelli, David (2017) Employers Judge Recent Graduates Ill-Prepared for Today's Workplace, Endorse Broad and Project-Based Learning as Best Preparation for Career Opportunity and Long-Term Success" 2015 *(Press release). Washington, DC: Association of American Colleges and Universities. 20 January 2015.* Retrieved 11 April 2017.

Ustinov, Peter. Dear Me. London, Heinemann. 1977. ISBN 0-434-81711-2

What is STEAM (2019) https://educationcloset.com/steam/what-is-steam/ accessed 24th July 2019

 **Ivy Ekem** (MB ChB, FWACP) is an associate professor of Haematology and the current Dean of the School of Medical Sciences, University of Cape Coast, Ghana. She has 22 years' experience as a University Lecturer.

5

Smart Learning and Smart University Campuses

Niyi Awofeso and Adi Arida
School of Health and Environmental Studies, Hamdan Bin Mohammed Smart University, Dubai, United Arab Emirates

Background

The word university is derived from the Latin *universitas magistrorum et scholarium*, which broadly translates as a community of teachers and scholars whose corporate existence had been recognized and sanctioned by civil or religious authority or by both. Antecedents of modern universities may be traced to Plato's academy of Athens, founded in 427 BCE and lasted until 86 BCE. Plato inherited the land on which the Academy was eventually built, and began holding informal gatherings there to discuss philosophical issues with some of his friends, eventually receiving civil recognition as a formal academy advancing knowledge in astronomy, mathematics, politics, philosophy and physics in 385 BC (Kampouris, 2018). Institutions similar to the Academy of Athens, such as Morocco's University of al-Qarawiyyin founded 859 ACE, originated in the Middle East and North Africa region (Lulat, 2005). However, the history of bricks and mortar universities such as the University of Paris, which evolved in 1150 from the cathedral school of Notre Dame, may be traced to medieval Christian traditions in Europe during which monks and nuns taught classes within walled and sectioned monasteries. Pope Gregory VII's 1079 Papal Decree played a key role in the development of modern European Universities as it ordered the regulated establishment of cathedral schools that transformed themselves into the first European universities (Olaf, 1997).

In modern parlance, a university is an institution of higher education offering tuition in vocational and non-vocational subjects, and typically having the power to confer degrees. As at 2018, there were about 24,000 universities globally, with 3944 in India, 3257 in the United States, and 2208 in China (Statista, 2019). John Newman (1862) viewed the role of a university as a place for the communication and circulation of thought, by means of personal intercourse, in which the intellect may safely range and speculate. He viewed universities as a setting where inquiry is pushed forward, discoveries verified and perfected, and error exposed. In 1810, Wilhelm von Humboldt, who advocated for the creation of the University of Berlin, proposed a university based on several core principles: unity of research and teaching, freedom of teaching and academic self-governance (Stanford Encyclopedia of Philosophy, 2016). Most of the raison d'etre for universities highlighted by Newman and Humboldt are under increasing pressure in the 21st century, due in part to a need for universities to be accountable to stakeholders, changing skill-set requirements in the employment market, globalisation, the requirement for universities to provide lifelong learning experience, commodification of university education, and rapid technological change. Also emerging are new university ideological concepts such as the ecological (green) university - a university that's deeply networked to the society around it, makes its knowledge resources freely available, and engages actively to bring about a better world through innovation and entrepreneurship, advocating for equity and sustainability thinking (Barnett, 2011).

One of the important attributes that contemporary universities need to imbibe is enhanced efficiency and effectiveness in teaching, research and community/industry partnerships. The European University Association, together with its partners, initiated a project called Universities for Strategic, Autonomous and Efficient Management in 2014 to address this issue. In the United Kingdom for example, the university sector delivers great value for society and the economy, performing 75% of publicly funded research and development, support for innovation, engagement in global and local collaboration, and serves as the second top destination for international students worldwide. However, financial pressure on the sector is growing due to an increasing teaching workforce and costly teaching technologies, significant cuts in capital funding, real time decline in public research funding, and uncertainty around tuition fees and international student enrolments (Estermann and Kupriyanova, 2018).

The use of a wide array of technologies to improve efficiency at operational level, to enhance quality and access to higher education, to improve the quality of research and to optimise communication and collaborations with stakeholder communities and industries creates unique opportunities and formidable challenges. For various reasons the use of technology to improve higher education is unequal from region to region, from countries within a region, and institutions within a country. Thus, while recognizing and pursuing the important potential of technological tools to improve the quality of university education and to enhance learners' access, the segmented use of higher education technology tools carries a risk of exacerbating existing inequalities as it requires financial means, necessary infrastructure and human skills to harness the potential of technology in higher education. The University of the Future needs to use technologies creatively and selectively in order to create value for money. The concept of value for money combines the achievements of the economy (reducing the costs of inputs), efficiency (getting more output for the same or less input) and effectiveness (getting better at what universities set out to do). The emerging concept of the Smart University – one which enhances the education, research, and work experience of stakeholders by incorporating digital, innovative, and internet-based technologies for the betterment of the society at-large – embodies the concept of using technology to create value for money in the governance of universities and the achievement of quality learning outcomes.

Smart Learning and Smart University Campuses

Domains of the smart campus and smart learning

The concept of a smart university campus is an extension of the concept of smart cities. As described by the University of Glasgow which works closely with the city of Glasgow's Future Cities Catapult project to develop the Smart Campus concept, *The Smart Campus actively learns from and adapts to the needs of its people and place, unlocking the potential of e-technology and enabling world-changing learning and research* (Future Cities Catapult, 2018). Unlike large cities, however, the leaders of smart university campuses have greater control over their assets and can therefore introduce technologies selectively to optimise their operations. Smart campuses and smart learning are emerging together with rapidly growing university design concepts that represent an integration of smart and intelligent systems, smart objects and smart environments, smart technologies, various branches of computer science and computer engineering, state-of-the-art smart educational software and/or hardware systems, agents and tools, and innovative pedagogy and advanced technology-based teaching strategies and learning methodologies. With regards to smart university campuses, the United States is leading the way, with on-campus innovations around energy (e.g. the University of Texas at Austin has a fully independent grid that provides all its energy), transport (e.g. the University of Michigan has introduced a self-driving shuttle system) and information (e.g. the University of Minnesota has installed 300 digital signage boards, updated with real-time data). At the United Arab Emirates' Hamdan Bin Mohammed Smart University (HBMSU), a partnership with Phillips enabled the development of state-of the-art connected LED lighting controlled by its Interact Office system. The technology enables faculty staff to control and personalize light settings using a smartphone app, while students can be guided to rooms using lighting-based indoor positioning technology (Phillips lighting, 2018). In Australia, Deakin University implemented an artificial intelligence system named Genie. It's a digital assistant, in the form of a Siri-style voice-activated smartphone app, with information on assignments, timetables, and referencing. Because it runs on machine learning principles, it grows more useful the more it is used (IBM, 2017).

The adjective 'smart' in smart learning involves some similar characteristics to the ones attributed to a person or technology equipment that is regarded as being 'smart'. Being 'smart' is attributed to an action or decision that involves careful planning, cleverness, innovation, and/or a desirable outcome. In the words of the chancellor of HBMSU, Mansoor Al Awar, *"smart learning is a broad term for education in today's digital age. It reflects how advanced technologies are enabling learners to digest knowledge and skills more effectively, efficiently and conveniently. Smart learning comprises transformations in four components of tertiary education: the learner becomes a proactive leader rather than a static follower of the educational process; academic faculty focus on being a mentor and a coach rather than just being a teacher; the curriculum is overhauled to better reflect how knowledge is evolving both in form and delivery, and; the learning environment is expanded to consider new realities, such as the dominance of mobility, which has opened vast opportunities for mobile learning"* (Al Awar, 2017). The adaptation of smart environments for learning at university level, together with new technologies and approaches such as ubiquitous learning and mobile learning, are integral to smart learning. Smart learning aligns with the perspective of Chatti et al (2010) that the University of the Future should promote learning which is essentially personal, social, distributed, ubiquitous, flexible, dynamic and complex in nature. The interactive technologies typically used in smart learning are sensitive, manageable, adaptable, responsive and timely to educators' pedagogical strategies and learners' educational and social needs. Personalized learning environments enable university learners to create custom learning mashups using a wide variety of digital media and data.

Smart learning entails the fusion of pedagogy and technology for facilitating a transformation of the curriculum, teaching behavior, programme administration as well as best practices of infusion and piloting of new ideas. At HBMSU, seven rounds of brainstorming retreats referred to as 'innovation lab for the future of smart learning' produced dozens of innovative teaching and learning initiatives, most of which have been successfully implemented at HBMSU and shared with academic peers internationally (HBMSU, 2017). Core attributes of smart learning environments include; (a) context-awareness, implying that the system is able to provide learning support based on the learner's online and real-world status; (b) adaptive and prompt support to learners, using analytics-based assessment of the needs of individual learners from different perspectives (e.g., learning performance, learning behaviors, profiles, personal factors); (c) adaptable user-interface, the ways of presenting information and the subject contents to meet the personal factors (e.g., learning styles and preferences) and learning status (e.g., learning performance) of individual learners. Learners in smart universities can interact with the learning environment via mobile devices (e.g., smartphones or tablet computers), or wearable devices (e.g., Google Glass or a digital wristwatch). At HBMSU, the state of the art virtual learning environment – Smart Campus – is available in major app stores for use by stakeholders with required log in credentials (Albawaba, 2016), and acknowledged by the United Nations Educational, Scientific and Cultural Organization (UNESCO) as a best practice virtual learning environment (UNESCO, 2017).

The learner domain

The smart learning concept comprises learners who are proactive in accessing and utilising ubiquitous, predominantly digital learning objects, and in experiencing personalized and seamless learning. Smart learning is focused on learners and content more than on devices. Features of smart learning include formal and informal learning, stimulation of intellectual curiosity, learning on demand, use of technology and multimedia to make learning a fun experience, social and collaborative learning, personalized and situated learning, and application and content focussed. Personal and smart technologies make learners engage in their learning and increase their independence and proactiveness in more open, connected and augmented ways by personally richer contexts (Zhu et al, 2016). Smart learning seeks to mould students into 'smarter learners', who can integrate smart learning environments and customised learning objects into their knowledge and skills development, so as to develop contemporary skill sets such as critical thinking, entrepreneurship, communication, collaboration, and innovation. A smart learning approach aims to provide learners with practical and personalized opportunities to acquire information, manage knowledge, interact and collaborate with peers and instructors, so that students can apply their knowledge and skills to solve problems and achieve goals According to Duran-Sanchez et al. (2017, p2); *"the objective of smart learning is to improve the learning quality and student outcomes throughout the student's educational process; it focuses on contextual, personalized and transparent learning capable of encouraging the emergence of students' intelligence and facilitating their ability to solve problems in real environments; students are provided with personalized education where they can learn flexibly, in any place and at any time, and work collaboratively"*. To optimally benefit from smart learning settings, learners are required to develop above average technology skills and to acquire personal technology devices that interoperate with university virtual learning environments. The affordability and availability of technology in the form of small, handheld computers like smartphones and tablets, in addition to the software these devices use, have created opportunities to expand what students can learn and how they can learn it. Bring-your-own-device technologies in smart learning contexts eliminate the barriers to learning of time and space but may be limited by cost (e.g. of internet data), learners' digital literacy skills, and ability to innovate.

The academic faculty domain

Academic staff are key to the successful implementation of smart learning initiatives in higher education. A precondition for academic faculty to contribute optimally to smart learning environments is for such staff to be ahead of the curve with regards to smart learning technologies, smart learning curriculum design, smart learning objects, and smart learning environments. Such orientation is particularly important since most senior academic staff studied and worked at traditional universities and may therefore be inadequately exposed to smart learning prerequisites. At HBMSU, it is mandatory for all teaching staff to undertake a university funded, customised certificate course in online curriculum and instruction. Feedback from HBMSU lecturers who undertook this training program attest to its usefulness in preparing academic faculty for teaching roles to facilitate smart learning. Technological tools embedded in e-learning platforms such as Moodle assist faculty to monitor progress with smart learning activities (Bdiwi et al, 2019). Teaching presence refers to the methods that an instructor utilizes to promote a quality online environment and facilitate an effective community of inquiry. It is composed of design and organization, facilitating discourse, and direct instruction (Swan et al., 2008). Anderson et. al. (2001) describe the design and organization aspect of teaching presence as the planning and design of the structure, process, interaction and evaluation aspects of the online course. They viewed facilitating discourse as the means by which students are engaged in interacting about and building upon the information provided in the course instructional materials. Direct instruction is contextualized as the instructor providing intellectual and scholarly leadership in part by sharing their subject matter knowledge with the students. An important shift in the role of academic staff in smart learning settings is the evolution in their roles from teachers to mentors and coaches. Coaching is akin to a continued dialogue or conversation between the coach and the coached in which the coach instructs, counsels and tutors another in how to improve his or her performance in a specific area. The benefit of effective coaching goes beyond mere improvement in performance. It increases personal satisfaction, inspires a commitment to excellence, builds trust and fosters the individual's development for achieving the highest potential that a learner is capable of. Coaching positions the power and accountability for learning with the learner, thus preparing a solid academic foundation for lasting success in learners' personal and professional pursuits. Mentoring is initiated when someone offers just the right kind of support, well-suited to the emerging needs of the person they are mentoring because they deeply understand that person and have an extensive repertoire of possible practices/responses which they can draw on, tweak and adapt according to circumstances and needs. Mentoring is largely egalitarian, and equates the learner (or junior academic faculty) to a colleague.

The curriculum domain

The smart learning curriculum is continually overhauled to better reflect how knowledge is evolving both in form and delivery. Smart learning raises key pedagogical issues related to course content, technology integration, learning and assessment strategies, learning performance evaluation, and learning behavior and pattern analysis. Smart learning curricula require redefinition to promote deeper, challenging, motivating learning tasks, moving away from content memorisation towards authentic, situated, real-world application. Learning objectives need to be carefully crafted to reflect core knowledge, skills, and roles in real life contexts. Mapping is required to link course learning objectives to program learning objectives, as well as to assessment tasks. An important component of smart learning forms is digitization of learning objects – digital resources that may be reused to support learning. Because many learning objects are non-textual (e.g., digitized slides, animations, or video clips), locating learning objects within a digital library can be a daunting task without the help of metadata. At HBMSU, the library department as well as the technology support department utilize the virtual learning environment (including Ellucian's Banner system for curriculum integration and learner information) to develop metadata and make them easily accessible to users. HBMSU is currently an accredited Banner training centre for the Middle East region (HBMSU, 2016). Preferred smart learning assessment modes include e-assessments, adaptive testing, and feedback methods that are personalized, automated, real-time, evidenced-based, and data-driven. Assessment and course activity technology scaffolds may further assist learners to track their training progress.

The learning environment domain

A smart learning environment, then is one that is effective, efficient and engaging. Key features of smart learning environments include: location-awareness, context-awareness, social awareness, interoperability, seamless connection, adaptability, ubiquitousness, multimodal interaction, and high engagement (Zhu et al, 2016). Ubiquitous learning, a key feature of a smart learning environment – is one that is supported by mobile and embedded computers and wireless networks to facilitate learning in real time and real world locations within the context of the learner. Ubiquitous learning facilitates learning anytime, anywhere, thus minimising the encumbrances of time, location and environment on learning opportunities, while providing learning guidance, hints, and supportive tools the right time and form.

Emerging adaptive learning environments include adaptive, intelligent tutoring systems, and ambient intelligent environments (Augusto, Nakashima, and Aghajan 2010). At HBMSU, the smart campus is an internationally acknowledged technology-rich on-stop shop for learners as well as teaching and administrative staff. The smart campus is complemented by a Cloud Campus, a social smart learning initiative which provides high quality life-long learning services using social media channels (Edarabia, 2017). Another important feature of learning environments is the university's physical facilities such as temperature regulation of buildings, recreation and dining facilities, classroom design, and lighting. In October 2018, HBMSU launched the first smart campus building in Dubai (Emirates News Agency, 2018).

Conclusion

The University of the Future needs to be smart in terms of its general infrastructure (smart campus) as well as the stakeholders devoted to optimal tertiary educational outcomes (smart learning). A smart campus links devices, applications, and people to deliver two key value propositions: enabling new experiences and improving operational efficiency. When enrolled learners, academic and administrative faculty on physical and virtual campuses share a common technology infrastructure, they can interact with each other to enable experiences and efficiencies that weren't hitherto possible. An important component of smart campus is fast internet Wi-Fi connectivity with ease of access. The smartness of smart campuses should be evident in learner advising, payments, course registrations, interoperability of varied technological appliances to the virtual learning environment. Sustainability thinking should permeate smart campus development, with intelligent lighting and water systems to reduce waste and promote low carbon-climate resilience development strategies and environmental sustainability.

A smart learning framework improves on traditional on-campus approaches to education by requiring learners to be motivated, technologically adept, and self-paced in their learning activities. Academic staff, apart from developing core competencies in their field, are also expected to be skilled in online course design and instruction. In addition, the role of academic faculty is refined from lecturer to coach and mentor. Smart universities are implicitly committed to overhauling their course curricula such as to better reflect real world challenges, and to assure that the delivery and assessment of courses is appropriately enhanced with technology to facilitate optimal learning and retention. The learning environment is expanded to consider new realities, such as the dominance of mobility, which has opened vast opportunities for mobile learning. Finally, smart universities need to provide smart learning environments characterized by efficiency, effectiveness and continuing engagement. Using appropriate technologies and data analytics, smart learning environments are able to exploit teachable moments, identify the characteristics of learners, provide appropriate learning resources and convenient interactive tools, monitor and evaluate learning process and outcomes in order to promote effective learning. Hamdan Bin Mohammed Smart University is recognised by the United Nations Educational, Scientific and Cultural Organization for its pioneering role in the smart university and smart learning concepts implementation globally.

References

Albawaba. (2016). 'HBMSU's 'Smart Campus' wins first place in Middle East Regional Awards category of 2015 Wharton-QS Stars Reimagine Education Awards'. URL: https://www.albawaba.com/business/pr/hbmsu's-'smart-campus'-wins-first-place-middle-east-regional-awards-category-2015-wharto

Al Awar. (2017). 'Pioneering smart learning'. Ellucian. URL: https://www.ellucian.com/emea-ap/insights/pioneering-smart-learning Accessed 30 April 2019.

Anderson, T., Rourke, L., Garrison, R., & Archer, W. (2001). 'Assessing teaching presence in a computer conferencing context', *Journal of Asynchronous Learning Networks*, 5(2). URL: https://auspace.athabascau.ca/bitstream/handle/2149/725/assessing_teaching_presence.pdf;jsessionid=20295CBD91B05F1B21964132E80E803C?sequence=1 Accessed 10 June 2019.

Augusto, J. C., Nakashima, H., and Aghajan, H. (2010) 'Ambient Intelligence and Smart Environments: A State of the Art'. In: Nakashima H., Aghajan H., Augusto J.C. (eds) *Handbook of Ambient Intelligence and Smart Environments*. Springer, Boston, MA, doi: https://doi.org/10.1007/978-0-387-93808-0_1

Barnett, R. (2011). The coming of the ecological university. *Oxford Review of Education*, 37, 439-455, doi: 10.1080/03054985.2011.595550

Bdiwi, R., B., de Runz, C., Sami, F., and Cherif, A., A. 'Smart Learning Environment: Teacher's Role in Assessing Classroom Attention'. *Research in Learning Technology*, 27, doi: https://doi.org/10.25304/rlt.v27.2072

Chatti, M. A., Agustiawan, M. R., Jarke, M., & Specht, M. (2010). 'Toward a Personal Learning Environment Framework'. *International Journal of Virtual and Personal Learning Environments*, 1(4), 66-85. doi:10.4018/jvple.2010100105

Duran-Sanchez, A., Alvarez-Garcia, J., Del Rio-Rama, M., and Sarango-Lalangui. O. (2017). Analysis of the scientific literature published on smart learning. *Espacios*, 39(10). URL: http://www.revistaespacios.com/a18v39n10/18391007.html Accessed 10 June 2019.

Edarabia. (2017). 'Toyota refers to Hamdan Bin Mohammed Smart University's experience in education'. URL: https://www.edarabia.com/132830/toyota-refers-to-hamdan-bin-mohammed-smart-universitys-experience-in-education/ Accessed 10 June 2019.

Emirates News Agency. (2018). 'HBMSU launches first Smart Building'. URL: http://wam.ae/en/details/1395302712487 Accessed 11 June 2019.

Estermann, T., and Kupriyanova, V. (2018). *Efficiency, Effectiveness and Value for Money: Insights from the UK and other countries* – A USTREAM Report. URL: https://www.eua.eu/downloads/publications/ustream%20efficiency%20effectiveness%20and%20value%20for%20money%20uk%20and%20others.pdf Accessed 9/6/19.

Future Cities Catapult. (2018). 'Smart Campus - University of Glasgow'. URL: https://futurecities.catapult.org.uk/project/smart-campus-university-of-glasgow/ Accessed 10 June 2019.

HBMSU. (2017). 'HBMSUs 7th Innovation Lab highlights role of technological innovation in education and knowledge'. URL: https://www.hbmsu.ac.ae/news/hbmsus-7th-innovation-lab-highlights-role-of-technological-innovation-education-and-knowledge Accessed 8 June 2019.

HBMSU. (2016). 'HBMSU kicks off training sessions at the Banner Training Center'. URL: https://www.hbmsu.ac.ae/news/hbmsu-kicks-off-training-sessions-at-banner-training-center Accessed 10 June 2019.

IBM. (2017). 'Reimagining the University at Deakin: An IBM Watson automation journey'. The outsourcing unit working research paper series, paper 17/04. URL: http://www.umsl.edu/~lacitym/LSEOUWP1704.pdf Accessed 10 June 2019.

Kampouris, N. (2018). 'The Platonic academy of Athens: the world's first university'. Greek Reporter, November 12. URL: https://greece.greekreporter.com/2018/11/12/the-platonic-academy-of-athens-the-worlds-first-university/ Accessed 9 June 2019.

Lulat, Y.G.M. (2005). *A History of African Higher Education From Antiquity To The Present: A Critical Synthesis*, Greenwood Publishing Group, 2005, ISBN 978-0-313-32061-3, pp. 154–157.

Newman, J.H. (1852). *The idea of the University*. Notre Dame University Press.

Olaf, P. (1997). The First Universities: Studium Generale and the Origins of University Education in Europe. Cambridge: Cambridge Univ. Press. ISBN 978-0-521-59431-8, 17 – 19.

Statista (2019). Estimated number of universities worldwide as of July 2018, by country. URL: https://www.statista.com/statistics/918403/number-of-universities-worldwide-by-country/ Accessed 9 June 2019.

Phillips lighting. (2018). 'University goes to the top of the class with new connected lighting technology'. URL: https://www.signify.com/global/our-company/news/press-release-archive/2018/20180319-state-of-the-art-lighting-controlled-by-interact-office-at-hbsmu Accessed 11 June 2019.

Stanford Encyclopedia of Philosophy (2016). *Wilhelm von Humboldt*. URL: https://plato.stanford.edu/entries/wilhelm-humboldt/ Accessed 9 June 2019.

Swan, K., Shea, P., Richardson, J. C., Ice, P., Garrison, D. R., Cleveland-Innes, M., & Arbaugh, J.B. (2008). Validating a measurement tool of presence in online communities of inquiry. *E-mentor, 2*(24), 1–12. URL: http://www.irrodl.org/index.php/irrodl/article/view/2379/3685 Accessed 10 June 2019.

UNESCO. (2017). In Pursuit of Smart Learning Environments for the 21st Century. In-Progress Reflection No. 12 on Current and Critical Issues in Curriculum, Learning and Assessment. URL: https://unesdoc.unesco.org/ark:/48223/pf0000252335 Accessed 11 June 2019.

Zhu, Z., P. Yu, M., and Riezebos, P. (2016). A research framework of smart education. *Smart Learning Environments*, 3: 4. Doi: 10.1186/s40561-016-0026-2

Zhu, Z., Sun, Y., Riezebos, P. (2016). Introducing the smart education framework: Core elements for successful learning in a digital world. *International Journal of Smart Technology and Learning*, 1, 53 – 66, doi: https://doi.org/10.1504/ijsmarttl.2016.078159

Niyi Awofeso is currently a Professor at the School of Health and Environmental Studies Hamdan Bin Mohammed Smart University (HBMSU), Dubai. He holds postgraduate qualifications in infectious diseases medicine, public health, business administration and health administration.

Adi Arida is Professor and Dean of School of Health and Environmental Studies, HBMSU, UAE. He is actively involved in the management of smart learning initiatives such as curriculum design and content development of online courses.

6

What is this Slippery Thing called *Education*?

Dan Remenyi
ACPIL, UK and University of the Western Cape, South Africa

The best gift that a parent can give a child

In recent years there has been a tendency to think that attendance at the university is the primary if not the only route to higher education. This is not true. There have always been highly educated individuals who have had little or no formal attendance at the school or any other institution of learning. Self-teaching or autodidacticism has been the way that the vast majority of individuals have improved their knowledge over the millennia[1] and it is important to note that at the end of any university degree programme one of the hoped-for outcomes is that the individual will be inspired to continue with his own intellectual development, perhaps without reference to any other institution.

In thinking about education, it has to be understood that this concept means many different things to just about everyone. It is difficult to generalise about what education really is and how it functions in society. In the 1980s British Telecom created an advertisement which amusingly revealed one small dimension of society's complex attitude to education which is still memorable nearly 40 years later. It was called "You've got an Ology!²"

In most societies the provision of education is seen as a special duty every generation has toward the young and its primary objective is to provide the next generation with the know how required to live a satisfactory life. Dewey (2008) described this as the process of renewal. It is sometimes considered as the best gift that a parent can give a child as it has the highest rate of return of all possible investments. In general, education is perceived as being the key to success. However too much is often expected of education. Being educated does not guarantee being successful. Even with access to the best schools and universities an individual can fail to achieve what is regarded by society as even moderate success. It is perhaps useful to think of an education as being a special tool which if not used correctly will produce no useful result and may perhaps even result in failure. But education is not a tool in the same sense that a skill or a training course

---

[1] Until relatively modern times schools were very rare institutions and only attended by the most privileged sections of society.
[2] See: Maureen Lipman video at https://www.youtube.com/watch?v=vEfKEzX9QLE produced as an advertisement for British Telecoms, 2006.

might be perceived to be. Education transcends skills and training by providing a broad contextual understanding of any topic and the environment in which the topic is being considered.

Although it has been argued that education begins in the womb and it is clear that the early years are vitally important, here the only focus is on post-school higher education.

Understanding education

For centuries the sole purpose of the university was to educate a small number of the most privileged men in society. In the early days of the university quite young individuals were often admitted as students and consequently a more accurate description might be that the universities educated the most privileged boys in society. Fortunately, over the years our society has changed this description dramatically. Despite the introduction of fees and the need to meet a basic standard of earlier school performance, the university education system is now open to the vast majority of individuals at least in the Western world.

But before the question of what education might mean in the future can be answered it is necessary to ask and answer what does education mean today?

Education is spoken about all the time. Politicians in particular believe that education is a major concern to society and former United Kingdom Prime Minister Tony Blair is famous or perhaps infamous for his battle cry "*education, education, education*". This comment was made at the Labour Party conference in 1996 when Blair stated, "*Ask me for my three top priorities for government and I will tell you: education, education and education*". Regrettably, in the end the Blair government did not make many positive adjustments to the education system in the United Kingdom.

Politicians and education

When politicians speak of education they are mostly concerned with the early stages from kindergarten or nursery to primary and secondary school education[3]. Education during the early stages of life is of great importance as it prepares individuals for all the challenges which lie ahead of them. If these early years are not utilised appropriately it may severely curtail an individual's opportunities of being able to achieve any degree of excellence in post-school education[4]. There is much controversy in society about how these early years should be organised and funded and the debate is often fierce with different political parties proclaiming that they have the best possible solution. Those commentators who perceive education as an important part of a democratic society argue that these early years are often not well enough focused to develop critical consciousness in the young (Giroux 2011).

---

[3] Obviously tertiary education is also of importance to politicians but there are far greater numbers involved and much larger amounts of funding required in the early years of education.

[4] Of course, there are many examples of individuals who had little or no formal schooling but who have excelled in all sorts of aspects of later life. Informal self-education is difficult but it can produce excellent results.

What is this Slippery Thing called Education?

A possible definition

Despite the apparent importance attributed to education by the politicians and the population there is not much understanding of its nature. The term education can be confused with training or as Smith (2015)[5] points out education is confused with schooling which he suggests is often based on drill or rote learning. This is the process of preparing someone to undertake a task such as learning to pass an arithmetic test, to drive a car or bake a cake, to mention only three examples, and is therefore particular in its possible outcome. In contrast to rote learning, Dewey (1916) pointed out that education is a social process which is about developing a person's potential. An on-line dictionary definition of education is partially instructive as it states that education is, *"the act or process of imparting or acquiring general knowledge, developing the powers of reasoning and judgment, and generally of preparing oneself or others intellectually for mature life".*[6] But there are shortcomings in this definition one of which is the fact that it refers to "general knowledge" and this needs clarification. The second issue here is that education is not only an "act or process" but also it is what the receiver of the education possesses when the act or process is completed. On the question of general knowledge, being educated certainly implies an understanding of more than one particular topic hence the word general, but there is danger in the term general knowledge as it may be taken to mean a rather superficial acquaintance with a subject and superficiality is contrary to what is implied in the description of being educated.

A description of education

Defining education is like defining an elephant. It is much easier to describe than define education. Education is about developing an individual's cognitive ability/capacity for knowledge, self-awareness, reflection and ability to locate ideas in an overarching framework of understanding. It is informative to ask why education is regarded as important in so many different societies. It seems to be a fundamental desire of humanity to give the next generation some help in understanding the environment into which they have been born and to give them some tools with which to cope with the challenges which lie ahead. The provision of education is therefore, in a sense, an act of faith that we can improve our society through the transmission of appropriate knowledge to the next generation. Appropriate education also plays some role in transmitting society's values, although it may be argued that deep values are mostly learnt by the young observing the behaviour of role models.

The purpose of education seems to be to provide a fuller life experience for individuals while at the same time producing more rounded and therefore more useful members of the community. And it is most important to understand that education may be acquired in various ways. Oscar Wilde (1891) famously pointed out,

---

[5] Smith S, Infed, http://infed.org/mobi/what-is-education-a-definition-and-discussion
[6] https://www.dictionary.com/browse/education

"Education is an admirable thing, but it is well to remember from time to time that nothing that is worth knowing can be taught."

This facetious comment of Wilde's brings to our attention the aphorism that experience is the best teacher, the origin of which is attributed to Roman luminaries such as Julius Caesar[7]. However, it has also been argued that experience alone does not achieve anything. Rather it is the active reflection on experience which has the potential to improve human understanding and therefore knowledge.

There has often been a suggestion that education could increase the moral tone in society and this may be true in certain circumstances but the idea of associating education with morality has been brought into question by the fact that regimes such as Nazi Germany received the backing and active support from many highly educated individuals[8]. Furthermore, the Nazis corrupted the whole concept of education during their short period in power.

Education is time specific in that what would be considered a satisfactory education in one period of time would be woefully inadequate in another. It is also location specific.

Education is about cultivating an attitude which creates an interest in learning but not just facts and figures. Those who participate in TV quiz programmes may be knowledgeable, but would not necessarily be considered educated[9]. Education is rather about many facets of life including the importance of a desire to learn and to understand that learning is of most value when it is used within society and is usually best employed to solve problems. Learning in isolation delivers relatively few benefits. Cultivating this desire to learn according to Illeris (2002) is "*a cognitive and emotional and societal activity*" and thus needs to be understood at the broadest level. On the other hand, education which is not directly informed by detailed, specific, in-depth information which is of direct benefit to individuals will at best be rather hollow. Education, a word which almost everyone will claim to understand, is a slippery concept and this was well demonstrated by John Searle (1990) when he wrote *"As with taxation and relations between the sexes, higher education is essentially a continuously contested territory"*.

Processes of education

In the above description of education, the idea that the processes of education prepare someone for mature life is of some importance. It is expected that an educated person will be capable of some degree of reflection and self-criticism and that he or she will be prepared to respect the thinking of others. Collini (2015) refers to this as the process of broadening. The issues embedded in the concepts of argument, reasoning, judgement and respect are highly complex and furthermore, how they are understood is often thought of as intensely subjective or personal. Therefore, the accolade of declaring an individual to be educated is typically sparely given. The opposite is perhaps more common whereby an individual may be declared to be ignorant and this term often implies much more than a lack of

---

[7] https://www.phrases.org.uk/bulletin_board/21/messages/1174.html

[8] An example of this is the fact that Josef Mengele was a doctoral graduate of the University of Munich and Heinrich Himmler was a graduate of the Technical University of Munich.

[9] Certainly the IBM computer which beat the human contestant could not be considered educated.

knowledge and has connotations of insensitivity, crassness and even lack of respect. It is certainly an insult to be declared ignorant.

In any description of education, it is important to state that the educational level achieved by any individual is a direct result of that individual's motivation to make him or herself educated. It is not possible to educate anyone. The best that can be achieved is for a school or a university to create an environment in which the individual wants to develop him or herself by achieving a significant level of knowledge. This can be encouraged if the right facilities are available and the right methods of tutoring, coaching or mentoring are applied. But at the end of the day the overwhelmingly most important issue is the individual's own motivation.

Finally, it is important to point out that the above description of education has primarily dealt with the circumstances of the young. In this respect this description is incomplete. Any individual in society can at any time accept the challenge of developing his or her own level of education. It is by no means the prerogative of the young and there are many examples of individuals who only became literate in their mature years, achieving admirable levels of education. Modern universities have generally accepted some mature students and in fact, at least in some cases, welcome them. Universities have developed degree courses aimed at midcareer individuals which turned out to be highly successful both from the universities' point of view and also for the career development of the individuals who completed these courses of study.

The Two Cultures

A perennial issue which arose in many discussions of tertiary education related to how knowledge may be classified. Traditionally it has been said that there are two great fields of learning and these are addressed by studying the *World and its Forces*, this is a reference to science both pure and applied, and by studying *Man and his Ways* and this refers to studying the humanities[10]. This statement is problematic not only because of its insensitive gender reference but also due to the fact that it does not address the great body of knowledge which could be understood as lying between the sciences and the humanities which is, of course, social science. But ignoring social science for a moment, the dichotomy between original science and the humanities has been referred to as the Two Cultures (Snow 1959)[11] and it has been suggested that the study of these represent two largely incompatible ways in which we can obtain an understanding of the world. Although the distinction between these two bodies of knowledge was generally well accepted there were a few dissenting voices concerning Snow's interpretation (Leavis 2013). The issue of the Two Cultures does not receive much attention

---

[10] Collini (2012) seems to think that the Two Cultures argument is rather passé but nonetheless offers an interesting definition of the humanities. He suggests that the "humanities" is now taken to embrace that collection of disciplines which attempt to understand, across barriers of time and culture, the actions and creations of other human beings considered as bearers of meaning, where the emphasis tends to fall on matters to do with individual cultural distinctiveness and not on matters which are primarily susceptible to characterisation in purely statistical or biological terms.

[11] The term Two Cultures came into use as a result of a lecture delivered by the Cambridge academic, Sir Charles Snow. The lecture entitled *"The two cultures and the scientific revolution"* was delivered as the Read lecture at Cambridge University in May 1959.

today although there are still those who believe that social science is in some way not entirely legitimate in that the application of scientific methods to the study of human beings is not quite appropriate. However, experienced educators tend to find more in common in examining the methods of scholars of all fields of study than is normally suggested. Scholars in all fields tend to focus on careful consideration and definition of the issues to be studied, traditions of scholarship in the field, self-awareness of their approach, the availability of evidence, the ability to be reflective, the significance of their contribution and where their studies will eventually lead.

As a result of seeing knowledge in terms of the Two Cultures a question arose as to which of these cultures produced the better educated person. Those who studied the humanities often argued that scientists were, at the end of the day, mere technicians and, to those who made this argument the people who worked in the applied areas of engineering were regarded as even less educated. On the other hand, those who had studied science argued that their education was much more rounded in that there would be few university educated scientists who were not aware that Shakespeare was regarded as the all-time best playwright and that Milton, Keats and Shelley were amongst the best poets who ever lived. On the other hand, very few of those who had studied the humanities would be able to state the second law of thermodynamics or knew what the specific gravity of water was. Although these arguments were interesting enough, they were generally not regarded with any great degree of seriousness by those who thought carefully about the subject of education.

How education is delivered

There are many ways in which education may be delivered or attained and these range from formal events to personal encounters. These events can be large scale or on a one-to-one private encounter basis. The event can involve humans or animals or simply an encounter or experience with a machine. It is not possible to prescribe how education should or could be delivered. But in general individuals do not learn from experiences alone but rather, experiences trigger a process of reflection which results in learning. The classical way of describing this combination of experience and reflection is referred to as the dialectic.

The dialectic process[12] is often understood to be composed of different minds[13] exchanging ideas and usually consists of at least three steps. In the first place an individual makes a statement which is heard by another or others. This statement is referred to as a *thesis*. Then, one or more of the listeners on reflection declare that the statement can be improved by applying some additional information or concepts or argument[14]. This is referred to as an *antithesis*. The original person hears this argument and reflects on it. The final step is when the original individual changes his or her statement as a result of this further reflection on the suggestion made by the listeners. This is referred to as a *synthesis*. This three step process

---

[12] The dialectic is attributed to Socrates (it is sometimes referred to as the Socratic method) who is said to have developed it while arguing with people he met in the streets and markets of ancient Athens.

[13] The dialectic process can of course occur within the mind of one single person with his or her own ideas interacting with each other.

[14] The additional information may be contrary to what was being said before.

What is this Slippery Thing called Education?

describes one cycle of a dialectical argument/discussion which could consist of many cycles. In each cycle of the discourse the participants are actually involved in discovery which is at the heart of the learning process.

This form of learning is what can be delivered by conversation between individuals who wish to further their knowledge rather than engage in confrontational argument. This process clearly requires both reasoning and judgement and this is sometimes regarded as being at the heart of what is referred to by Dewey (1916) as a social process.

There are two classical skills which are implied in the dialectic which are communication and critical thinking. Without the ability to formulate a clear expression of the original idea or the changed (synthesised) idea the dialectic simply will not work. When it comes to concepts and arguments the individuals engaging in dialectic exchanges will have to have a fine ability with words. Communication and critical thinking are sometimes referred to in academe as transferable skills. The key to a successful dialectic encounter between the individuals involved is clear thinking and the ability to pick out nuances in the arguments which will typically flow to and fro in a dialectic exchange.

As can be seen from this description of the dialectic it is an enormously labour-intensive process and therefore it has limitations when it comes to the massification of education. Not many universities can afford this approach which is seen by some as being outmoded and elitist[15]. However, the ancient or elite universities tend to favour the use of dialectic type experiences as the main strategy for stimulating their students to learn.

Dialectical learning is not compatible with the massification of education which relies on ideas, in the form of printed or electronic material being distributed and/or broadcast in some form to large numbers of learners. This is commonly achieved by lecturing and in some cases there can be many hundreds of students present at a single lecture. Lectures are known to have a low educational value other than that they permit the transfer of some information to a large group. There is a well-known description of a lecture which states "*a lecture is the process by which the notes of the lecturer are transferred to the notebook of the student without going through the mind of either party!*" This has been attributed to a number of different commentators including Mark Twain[16].

It has been argued that students are unable to retain any degree of attention in a lecture situation for more than a short period of time; 10 to 15 minutes is often cited. In actual fact the situation can be understood from another perspective in that it is difficult to deliver a truly engaging lecture and few members of any university faculty are capable of delivering material to students which will capture their attention for a full 45 or 50 minute lecture[17]. University faculty are not instructed in the art of delivering engaging lectures and thus this lack of skill can hardly be

---

[15] Greene's Education Oxford, The History of the Tutorial, See : https://www.greenes.org.uk/greenes-education/our-history/the-history-of-the-tutorial/

[16] Quote Investigator, See: https://quoteinvestigator.com/2012/08/17/lecture-minds/

[17] The inadequate level of lecturing skills is one of the best kept secrets of the academy.

surprising. It is unfortunate that the lecture itself rather than the lecturer is so frequently criticised and even ridiculed.

There is another crucial flaw involved in the way that universities attempt to transmit knowledge through lectures. When the lecturer faces a large group of students and sometimes this can be as much a several hundred students in a lecture theatre, it is difficult if not impossible to pitch the lecture so that it will be satisfactory all those who were present. Some of the students will be more knowledgeable and motivated than others and some of the students will be attending a lecture only because it is in some way compulsory. The result of this is that the lecturer often attempts to deliver a presentation which will not lose those students who are not too knowledgeable and will entertain those who may find the whole business tedious. This can be referred to as lecturing-to-the-average and it is possible that there may be no one in the lecture theatre who is anywhere near "the average".

There is another issue which is to do with the fact that if students are adequately motivated they may even find poor lecturing engaging. Learning is ultimately initiated as a result of internal attitudes within the student and sometimes the student's desire to learn is sufficiently strong that it can be surprising just how much can be learnt even with the most inappropriate pedagogical techniques. This is the basis for Oscar Wilde's cryptic comment about the challenge of teaching.

Large groups tend to be more impersonal and students invariably find that their motivation levels are highly influenced by relationships they build with faculty and within groups that are established to provide learning support. Massification has tended to reduce faculty contact and as a consequence there is little student faculty interaction in some modern universities.

The university as an educator

Thinking about how one might describe undergraduate education Collini (2012) provided the following:

> *"Undergraduate education involves exposing students for a while to the experience of enquiry into something in particular, which has no general goal other than improving the understanding of that subject matter. One rough and ready distinction between university education and professional training is an education relativizes and constantly calls into question the information which training simply transmits."*

This would seem to be a statement of aspiration rather than a description of what actually happens in the classrooms and the tutorials, as the amount of material which needs to be covered in many undergraduate programmes is such that there is not much time available for the sort of reflection which is implied by the description, "*constantly calls into question*". The other part of this definition which is important to consider is the meaning of the words "*experience of enquiry*". It is not at all clear what this might mean but surely it implies something more than the presentation of material through the process of a lecture.

Reflecting on this it is clear that there are basic pedagogical issues with regard to how universities facilitate the learning processes of students and it is worth

What is this Slippery Thing called Education?

pointing out that with regard to the qualifications of university lecturers they are typically appointed without any reference to their knowledge of pedagogy or as mentioned above their ability to lecture or teach. Junior faculty appointments are made on the basis of examination results at either the Bachelor or Master's level. Senior faculty appointments require individuals to have been published in suitable academic journals. They are not expected to have published in the field of pedagogy but rather in the topic of the department or school in which they will be working. There is seldom any suggestion that newly appointed faculty need to be acquainted with some of the ethical challenges which they may face as academic teachers. In some respects, this is curious especially when it is compared to how those who are involved in primary or secondary education are selected for their posts. On the other hand, the message implicit in this policy is that anyone competent in their subject should be capable of guiding university students to learn and maybe this is true, especially if we do not confine our interest in their competence as a lecturer but expand it to the function of a coach or mentor.

Teaching approaches

The way that universities are structured is not always helpful in producing rounded individuals. Although the nomenclature varies from place to place universities are structured in terms of faculties, departments and schools. The purpose of this is to group together fields of study that have some sort of commonality or subjects which would enhance student and faculty understanding of a particular topic. Thus in a Business School it is possible to have a Department of Marketing, the Department of Operations Management, the Department of Finance etc. Sometimes these groupings can be helpful but in our increasingly complex society we are often looking for learning which needs to draw on different elements from within different groups. Therefore, the idea of multidisciplinary or cross disciplinary studies is becoming more important. Not all academics are comfortable with this combining of different disciplines and this can be an obstacle in the development of well-rounded students. Some universities have tried to rename departments and subjects to better reflect how the learning offered through these groupings can be used in society.

Another important point in this discussion is that many syllabi aimed at most subjects are jam-packed with information[18]. Whether in the sciences, the humanities or with the social scientists there is simply an awful lot of material to be covered during the relatively short periods that most universities regard as terms or semesters[19]. The volume of material which has to be absorbed by the student often results in them attempting to learn it by rote or by the use of some other memory device. Most universities will supplement their lectures with tutorials but it is sometimes remarkable how difficult it is to engage students in open discussion during these events. Some students will fear that their comments may be regarded as stupid; fear of the stupid question is prevalent in many circumstances.

---

[18] Students can sometimes regard the information supplied in lectures to be irrelevant to them. And this may indeed be the case. Sometimes lecturers teach their favourite topics without much consideration as to how this material might fit into the overall scheme of the topic.

[19] A number of universities have quite short teaching years some of which are as few as 26 weeks.

Other students will say that they perceive the situation as being one whereby the intention is that the lecturer should pour the information into their heads. The argument is sometimes made that the student is there to receive information whereas many faculty would perceive that the student needs to work at developing him or herself into an educated person. The situation whereby the student acts as a passive recipient does not exist in all universities nor in all subjects and it certainly is not one which should be encouraged.

Nonetheless it has to be admitted that before students can engage in a dialectic type conversation it is really important for them to have acquired a substantial body of information about the topic which will be discussed. There is probably no shortcut in acquiring this information and the reality of the need to start the learning process by something that might in some ways resemble either drill or rote learning, needs to be faced. After all, before a pupil can make any progress with reading it is necessary for him or her to learn the alphabet and this is normally achieved through the teaching of songs which are learned off by heart. Similarly, mathematics is built on some knowledge of arithmetic which in turn relies on knowing the *times tables* which are also often learnt by rote. In this respect we are not looking for the equivalent of *Mr Memory* from *The 39 Steps* but rather an accumulation of an adequate[20] number of facts and figures to be able to make sense of the situation to be discussed.

Sometimes the term "deep learning" (Rushton 2005) was used to describe students acquiring a more comprehensive or mature understanding of the material which is being presented to them. In this context deep learning was not well defined but it implied learning accompanied by some level of reflection. However, artificial intelligence now incorporates a number of techniques one of which is referred to as deep learning and it is unlikely that this notion will continue to be used to describe human experiences in the field of education.

But there are those who argue that these debates do not arrive at the heart of the matter. Learning occurs much more effectively by doing than by listening or even discussing. Action learning has been on the agenda in a relatively small way for a very long time. Today, it is being taken much more seriously and universities are looking for opportunities to integrate exercises and projects into the underpinning structure of their degrees. This produces much more effective learning than any of the other methods available. It is however not easy to find suitable projects nor is it necessarily easy to monitor and control them. Consequently, this is a major challenge which universities face in the future.

Gamification

In recent years a considerable effort has been made to increase student engagement in the learning process through the development of game-based learning. Much of this activity has involved the application of computer technology to learning events in such a way that the student is entertained while at the same time being educationally developed. This technology has implications for many fields of study and can be used from elementary courses to advanced topics. Those who are involved in this believe that it will open up a large array of new opportunities to

---

[20] Clearly there is no simple answer as to what might constitute an adequate number of facts.

enhance the learning experience and that it will become a significant part of how tertiary educational events are delivered.

However, although there is some evidence to support this assertion, in this regard the jury is still out.

The student's direct involvement

Once the student is sufficiently informed to be able to structure an argument his or her direct involvement in the education process changes. But now another difficult issue sometimes raises its head. Some students have said that they are reluctant to develop their own arguments if they are contrary to the known opinion of the faculty. It is hard to find students, certainly at the undergraduate level, who do not believe that there is a right and a wrong answer to most if not all questions addressed in their subject. And there is a self-preservation streak in most students which would suggest that taking a contrary view to the faculty need not necessarily lead to success. Therefore, it is sometimes quite difficult to establish any meaningful dialogue with a group of undergraduate students. This situation can be relieved, at least to some extent, by encouraging formal debates among students themselves and also between students and members of staff. However, the art of debate is seldom if ever taught in the modern university[21]. Mostly students are allowed to discover this on their own. The art of debate is not a naturally acquired skill and thus students' achievements in this respect are rather mixed.

Engagement is in the psyche of the beholder

The degree of engagement which students experience with the material they are being taught is directly related to how individuals perceive its utility. The principle of academic freedom by which each faculty member could decide what to teach, how to teach it, and how it should be examined has partly survived into the 21st century and sometimes there is a disconnect between how teacher and student perceive utility. In fact, there are often big differences between how the relevance of course content is presented to the students. Sometimes this issue is not addressed at all. Faculty will simply dive into the academic material and pursue it without the slightest consideration for how its context could be understood by students. Some members of faculty are conscious of the need to select material which will have direct utility to the student in career endeavours. In general, it is very mixed as to whether a student is in a position to be able to connect his or her studies with future opportunities. This will often lead to students not becoming engaged with the course material.

Examinations

Examinations at the end of courses and modules are also a mixed affair. In fact, a student's performance is not always assessed by means of an examination. Sometimes assignments are used instead to show the student's competence. The use of an assignment is an important pedagogical strategy but there is considerable doubt as to whether it should be used as the only means of assessing a student's

---

[21] In some respects, this is rather surprising as in former times universities had departments and faculties of rhetoric which amounts to the same thing as argument. The teaching of how to argue used to be central to a university education.

performance. Where invigilated examinations are conducted sometimes examination questions simply ask for the regurgitation of material which has been presented in the classroom. It may be interesting to know how much of the information presented during the course has been retained by the student but this should hardly be a primary way by which the student's success should be assessed.

Another well-known shortcoming of traditional examinations is the fact that the same questions are regularly asked again and again. This presents a difficult problem in the sense that the questions which are repeated annually are normally those of the greatest import to assess an understanding of the subject matter. On the other hand, by repeating the same question or a very similar question in each examination it gives the students the opportunity to "spot" thus reducing the need to have a command of all the material which was presented during the course. There are other ways of setting examinations, but they tend to be considerably more labour-intensive on the part of the faculty.

A particularly unsatisfactory method of testing retained information is sometimes used with undergraduates which involves their being examined through the process of multiple choice tests[22]. It is true that these can be constructed in creative ways and that imaginative schemes for reading or marking can be designed; nonetheless it would seem to suggest that acquiring a level of education necessitates a more engaging way of examination. But the massification of education has put an enormous strain on university resources and it has been argued that when there are substantially large numbers involved multiple choice testing is virtually inevitable.

On some degree courses especially where the student numbers are low, assessment of student performance has been made on the basis of class participation. Students are not always pleased with this as it is often thought to be a highly subjective measure.

In order to produce a closer alignment with practical skills universities are looking towards the use of student involvement in real projects as a means of assessing his or her performance in the degree. It is clearly much better to test a student's ability to apply what has been learnt by observing how he or she can apply the knowledge in a real situation. To operationalise such an approach presents numerous challenges. In the first place it is not necessarily easy for the university to find real projects. Where it does have the necessary connections in business or industry or government it can be quite difficult to match students to the type of work that is really required in the real life situation. Then, there is the question of evaluating students' performance. All of these issues are challenging both from an academic and a practical point of view and it is especially difficult to organise these types of educational events when one is looking at anything other than really quite small groups.

Evaluating education

The evaluation of education is an extremely thorny issue. Every country has its more prestigious universities which are regarded as being better educators. At the

---

[22] These multiple choice tests are sometimes referred to as quizzes.

same time within any given university there are better and worse educators (using this word as a synonym for teacher) and it is difficult to evaluate their performance.

From an external point of view performance in examinations has been seen, at least in some cases, as an indication of a "good" education but this has also to be seen in the context of the prestige of the particular university.

Overall the question of evaluating education involves more than just examinations. Comments made by Daniel Coit Gilman (cited by Menand et al. 2017) in the latter part of the 19th century are interesting in demonstrating how much was expected of a university graduate. According to Gilman the answers to the following questions indicate whether a university has performed satisfactorily with regard to delivering a sound education to its students;

1. Are the youth who are trained within its walls honest lovers of the truth?
2. Are they learned, are they ready, are they trustworthy?
3. When they leave the academic classes, do they soon find a demand for their services?
4. Do they rise in professional life?
5. Are they sought for as teachers?
6. Do they show aptitude for mercantile, administrative or editorial life?
7. Do they equip themselves with credit in the public service?
8. Do the books they write find publishers?
9. Do they win repute amongst those who have added to the sum of human knowledge?

These are but a few of the suggested criteria for evaluating whether an appropriate education has been delivered. This list looks dated to the modern eye and in the 21st century point number 3 would certainly be the first item on such a list closely followed by number 4. Or perhaps number 6.

The type of thinking demonstrated by Gilman here is a more effective way of evaluating education than any examination can offer. But it clearly has the problem of not being able to deliver a quick result and it can be argued that such an assessment would not be objective. Furthermore, it is perhaps reasonable to suggest that too much was being asked of a university.

The concept of "work-ready"

As previously mentioned, in recent years universities have grown to believe that employers have not found their graduates sufficiently "work-ready" to play the role expected of them as graduate employees. This criticism was fair especially when universities were snubbing the idea of developing skills for their graduates. The idea that there was a chasm between education and training was at its best flawed.

Ensuring that graduates are "work-ready" is a different issue which needs to be addressed specifically. Typically, academics have different responses to the accusation that the graduates are not "work-ready" or adequately "work-ready". Very few academics will declare these days that it is generally not the function of a university to prepare its graduates for work. It is now generally admitted that even from the earliest days of universities there has always been some aspect of education which either explicitly or implicitly implied that the university experience led to some degree of "work-readiness". Thinking of the ancient universities and their original mission it is clear that they were set up to deliver the necessary qualifications for the professions of their day.

But in modern times where the university prepares students for careers in law or medicine or engineering or accounting, the graduates are not necessarily in a position to practise their profession immediately. There are a number of reasons for this and taking the example of law, the most obvious is that there are different house rules from one firm of lawyers to another. There may also be regional differences with regard to how the courts work. Different firms will have different attitudes towards how work is done and how their staff should handle specific clients. There are striking differences with regard to the management style within organisations. Some firms will be run relatively democratically and other firms will have a tyrant as a boss. All of these directly affect how an individual will present him or herself for work and how they will fit into the organisation. Furthermore, in the case of law there will normally be further exams to be taken before the graduate becomes a member of the appropriate society to practice his or her profession. Thus the term "work-ready" is not always that helpful.

When it comes to degrees which do not directly lead to a professional qualification such as a BA in a modern language or in a subject such as history or mathematics, academics regard their task as preparing their students with skills of critical thinking and communication so that they will be able to choose from a number of different positions and different types of organisations and to be able to play with relative ease some productive role in the organisation. In the 21st century under the heading of communication it is common to find not only the skills of writing and presentation but also those related to the use of a computer and appropriate business software.

Internships

The call for being "work-ready" does not only come from employers. Some graduates have found it quite difficult to obtain suitable employment and they demand more attention to be given to the issues related to their post-university life especially with regards to employment. In this respect there are stark differences between the ancient or elite universities and the more modern ones. There are often queues of employers waiting to interview graduates from the best universities while on the other hand graduates from the less prestigious institutions struggle to obtain interviews, never mind actually acquire paid employment. Some universities have responded to this by advocating internships and the record of universities in this respect is quite patchy. Interns report that sometimes they are simply used as cheap labour. Interns are either not paid or they receive very small remuneration. Sometimes their travel expenses are paid and sometimes they are not. They are not always given much coaching or mentoring. Sometimes after a period of internship when they enquire as to whether a paid position might be available interns are informed that they could have a second period of internship.

It is difficult to imagine how a university would be able to easily find an adequate number of internships for all the students who might require them. Furthermore, there is a high burden of administration associated with maintaining the type of contact with employers which is necessary if large-scale temporary employment opportunities are to be created.

However, at the end of the day the criticism of not being "work-ready" is reminiscent of the accusation that academics, both faculty and students, do not live in "the real world". It is difficult to know quite what this term means. Academics and students continually face issues of success and failure. Like everyone else they have expenses to meet and they need to find the necessary funding to live and/or pay the fees etc. There is really nothing unreal about the life of an academic or for that matter student.

Work-Savvy

Perhaps the term "work-savvy" would be a better one to describe how universities might be able to prepare graduates for life within an organisation. What may be really important under the heading of "work-savvy" is that the graduate is of a mature frame of mind. The graduate needs to be sensible with regard to his or her capabilities; he or she needs to know at least to some extent what should properly be regarded as his or her strengths and weaknesses. In the workplace it is most important to be emotionally intelligent which involves inter alia being able to distinguish between short-term satisfaction and strategies for long-term improvement. It is critical that new graduates do not attempt to appear superior or in any way be arrogant towards co-workers. There is also the question of developing skills in communication and critical thinking without which much of what else has been learnt during the degree will not be employable.

Some of the characteristics of an employee described here have been recognised by universities and are now sometimes addressed under the heading of transferable skills which have been included in the curriculum of some courses.

Competence and confidence

Older individuals when asked what the most important thing was they learnt during their time as a university student will sometimes reply that it was both competence and confidence. The issue of competence is relatively clear in that if the degree courses have been structured well and delivered effectively the recipients should have gained some considerable amount of knowledge which if applied correctly would result in their being regarded as competent in their field. Thus, competence directly relates to formal education.

Confidence is quite a different issue and it comes from students being able to hold their own in conversation with both the faculty and their peers. It is here that the dialectic can be of great importance. But it is not only the skills of argument that produce a confident person. Confidence is acquired through a very wide range of social contacts and thus the facilities and the opportunities which the university offers in this respect are of considerable importance. Both sports and cultural activities fall into the category of social interaction. High performance in sporting activities leads to higher levels of confidence and those who achieve distinction in activities such as the Students' Representative Council or debating societies will also benefit substantially. It should also be noticed that students taking libations (alcoholic or non-alcoholic) together can lead to the development of important relationships which result in improved social competence and confidence.

Networking with others and discovering that their challenges and issues are similar is also an important way to develop confidence and social software can possibly play an important role in this respect.

An individual's confidence is more directly related to informal education acquired outside of a classroom and this confidence may be seen as a type of self-empowerment to stake a claim that they have an opinion which is worthy of consideration.

Is there a downside to education?

Besides the comment made by Oscar Wilde and quoted above i.e. *Nothing worthwhile knowing can be taught"*, there are perhaps two other issues which need to be raised in order to temper enthusiasm for education. The first is that in certain situations some individuals have been regarded as being too educated. This would normally only apply to the skills dimension of education. There can be situations where there are no vacancies for a particular skill level but plenty of jobs for juniors in that field. Employers which have advertised for a range of jobs can argue to someone who has missed one of the better positions and who is prepared to compromise and take a more junior position, *"That such a proposal is unacceptable because such a post will make you bored in no time!"* or *"I can't offer you that job because it carries a salary of a grade 5 and your qualifications would normally entitle you to a grade 8"*. There seems to be a general mistrust of engaging anyone who is overqualified for a position.

This lack of suitable work may simply be the result of some difficulties in the employment market but it can be very frustrating to the individuals concerned and they may even regret having pursued their education to the level they have attained.

In addition, in a more direct way it has been said that the acquisition of a doctorate can render an individual unemployable in a number of jobs which he or she may have been able to access before with a lesser degree such as a Master's. The possession of a doctorate has been used to suggest that an individual might not be adequately "practical" or be too academic in their orientation towards the particular job. This argument may be entirely untrue but nonetheless it has been used and is still being used.

The second issue refers to the way in which education can and usually does change individuals' outlooks and life chances. It often creates a new mindset or worldview in an individual and this can open up many more opportunities than were available before. This has an impact on the individual's social mobility and those who originated in working-class families may often find themselves, as a result of their education and the work they consequently undertake, de facto members of the middle class. In many cases this will not be a problem but for some individuals they can feel disconnected from their basic culture or their friends or even their family. At the same time they may not feel entirely comfortable being part of the stratum of society they have arrived at. This can be disrupting to both the individual and his or her family. On a much more personal level the acquisition of education by a child can trigger emotions of jealousy from parents or even siblings who did not have this opportunity and may feel "left behind". One of the complexities which arise in this situation is that there is often an assumption that social mobility is always beneficial. In fact, this is sometimes not the case. Moving away from one's roots can be an exceptionally challenging endeavour and needs to be undertaken with considerable concern for the consequences.

These downsides to education are clearly outweighed by the benefits available and it has been argued that the money spent on education is normally the best investment anyone can ever make.

Finally, it is worth pointing out that the word education is sometimes hijacked in certain societies and what is presented as education can be nothing more than propaganda. This has been common practice in many authoritarian regimes through the world since time immemorial.

e-Learning as a facilitator of education

Any discussion of education would be incomplete without addressing the changes which have been brought about by e-Learning. Much is said about this elsewhere in this book and therefore in this chapter all that remains to be said is that the precursor to e-Learning which was usually described as computer aided learning was perceived as facilitating training and the development of low-level skills. This has now changed and various forms of e-Learning including Massive Open Online Courses (MOOCs) are now considered to be appropriate to facilitate university level education. However, there are still a material number of commentators who believe that the best education is to be acquired from the modern day equivalent of "sitting at the feet of the masters". One may recall that Dewey (1916) said education was a "social process" and many educationalists remain committed to this notion.

Those who promote e-Learning point out that social media are able to produce what they claim to be the equivalent of social contact across the Internet. However, there are those who believe that electronic contact through modern technology is not a proper substitute for getting to know and working with individuals who are in the same room. Furthermore, Collins (1975) points out that there are certain tasks which can only be learned by working alongside a skilled practitioner. Until the technology can reproduce humanoid holograms this type of educational experience is beyond our capability.

Education through the Looking Glass

An issue has been raised related to the potential that there is a Eurocentric bias built into university education. The argument which is mostly advanced by those who are concerned with indigenous people in Africa, the Americas, Australia and New Zealand etc. points out that there is very little if any recognition given to the knowledge developed over eons by people who were not part of the established academic tradition. This argument goes on to claim that education can never be neutral and thus always has an agenda behind it. Writing in the preface of Freire's (1970) book, Richard Shaull states that:

> *"There is no such thing as a neutral education process. Education either functions as an instrument which is used to facilitate the integration of generations into the logic of the present system and bring about conformity to it, or it becomes the 'practice of freedom', the means by which men and*

women deal critically with reality and discover how to participate in the transformation of their world."

As a result of this attitude there has been a call for the decolonisation of education. It is not easy to appreciate exactly how education can be de-colonised but this call for change in our approach to education appears to be requesting a recognition of several things including:
1. societies in Africa, the Americas, Australia and New Zealand etc. developed distinctive cultures which resulted in satisfactory ways of life which sustained substantial numbers of people over considerable periods of time;
2. these societies had their own methods of learning and disseminating the knowledge they required for their prosperity;
3. although they were entirely different to the European approach these methods of learning should be recognised and credited with having delivered success;
4. universities have sometimes exhibited racist attitudes towards indigenous knowledge and learning;
5. the current Eurocentric attitude towards education and the life for which it prepares individuals is not the only way in which societies can be arranged.

It is argued by those seeking the decolonisation of education that the acceptance of the above will lead to a new way of organising universities including the establishment of non-traditional approaches to developing learning objectives, methods of teaching/learning, curriculum development and evaluation. There are also implications regarding admission to university as well as the funding of education at all levels.

These critics refer to the lecture as the banking model for education. They understand a lecture as being the process by which an attempt is made to deposit knowledge in the head of the learner. They rightly argue that much more is to be gained by encouraging learner discussion and then thinking for him or herself (Freier 1970)[23].

Paulo Freire, a Brazilian philosopher of education, emphasises the following:
1. It is through dialogue which respectfully engages with ideas that educational progress is made.
2. Progress is ultimately made through action and dialogue is part of this action in that it leads to a new type of consciousness and from there to new lived experiences.

Couched in these terms one can see the influence of a wide variety of philosophers on Freier's thinking ranging from Plato to the Pragmatists (Menand 2002, and Freire is only one of many who argue for the radical reform of education labelled critical pedagogy (Breuing 2011) which is now an established school of thought.

---

[23] Infed http://infed.org/mobi/paulo-freire-dialogue-praxis-and-education/

Although the argument concerning decolonisation of education was originally limited to indigenous people in the areas mentioned above, there is now a view that university education may have been hijacked by the neoliberal agenda and that it is being used as a mainstay to sustain a philosophical outlook that allows societies to be driven by the principles of the market economy. This neoliberal agenda has been described as seeing the human condition as being bounded by capital, markets and free enterprise and is said to be driving both managerialism and marketization within universities and by so doing limiting the opportunity for any real debate about the improvement of society. This view (McLean 2019) which is similar to that expressed by Giroux (2011) has not yet been taken up by any substantial number of scholars but it does pose many important questions which deserve to be answered by the many academics who support the traditions to which we have grown accustomed.

There is much more to the issue of the decolonisation of education and to many established academics this topic appears to belong to a different dimension similar to the world which Alice entered when she moved through the Looking Glass. Nonetheless it is important to recognise that the suggestion of the decolonisation of education is not a whimsical fad but an interesting challenge to traditional educational thinkers which may lead to a need to make serious changes to our general attitude towards pedagogy.

Assessment of today's university performance

When it comes to today's employment market it is clear that employers award a considerable amount of credit to an individual who has a university degree. Specialised knowledge apart, this is primarily because a degree is a strong indication of the individual's desire for self-improvement and it also shows that he or she has been able to sustain his or her intellectual focus for a non-trivial period of three or more years. It is also possible, although it is definitely not guaranteed, that an individual with a degree will have some skills with regard to communication of their ideas and their ability to be able to critically comment on the ideas of others. It is probably the case that these skills are more likely to be possessed by graduates from the ancient or elite universities than those from the more modern institutions.

There is no doubt that it is necessary to recognise a sustained and considerable level of achievement on the part of the university system in the education and the development of society.

On the other hand, it is clear that today there is a definite concern about how various aspects of strategy within the university are managed. There are many issues to be addressed here but universities are concerned about the fact that older models of learning have not been as effective as they should have been. There is a realisation that *talk and chalk* is not the way forward and that the traditional *sage on the stage* has severe limitations. The idea that lecturing is an effective way of transmitting knowledge and that the student should see the lecturer as the primary source of knowledge is now quite outmoded. There is also the issue of tutorials especially when these are conducted by teaching assistants who may not have much experience in any aspect of pedagogy.

In terms of an assessment of how well universities deliver education in today's environment it can be said that there is clearly a range of success. This is reflected in the demand for places in universities as well as the demand for graduates when the university degree is completed. Evaluating a university's performance is complicated by the many different types of students ranging from some of the most gifted people in the world to those who find it a challenge to understand and to learn what is presented to them. Different types of universities suit different individuals and it is important that the right type of university is chosen for any particular person. There are mixed views as to how well the universities perform.

The university league tables may be a useful way for individuals to select which institution they should attempt to gain access to. But these tables should only be considered as one way of learning about a prospective university. There is nothing to beat visiting the university and obtaining information from current students or those who have recently been a student. But even with this personal approach it is still quite difficult to obtain a realistic picture of the quality of the dedication to deliver a "good" education on offer.

The increasing financial pressures on universities have generally not helped in improving the quality of the student experience. There is no doubt that well delivered education is expensive and there is little expectation that costs will not continue to increase. It is interesting that some private universities which have been set up for the sole purpose of making a profit have been able to launch degrees for which they are charging a lower fee than the established institutions. This suggests that some of the established institutions are not working cost effectively.

Education in the future

It would seem that human curiosity is deeply rooted in our DNA. Our desire to learn is one of the most distinguishing features of the human psyche. The demand for tertiary education will continue to grow and this will produce an increasing number of suppliers with offerings ranging from the "best-in-the-world" to shoddy and even fraudulent experiences (Clifton et al. 2018). There have been bogus degrees[24] for many years and this phenomenon is likely to grow. There will always be a need for strict government control of education.

For those who obtain a degree from a reputable university, what Kevin Carey (2015) said about his degree will probably apply, "... *everything important that subsequently happened in my life depended on that piece of paper*".

There are at least two entirely different ways of thinking about how our society will cope with higher education in the future and what it will mean to our society. The first of these, which we may call *steady as she goes*, is to accept that although imperfect the current manner in which universities function is essentially on the correct track and that incremental improvements will be made to deliver more effective education. The second is to admit that with the improvement in circumstances of many individuals throughout the world the demand for education will skyrocket to the point where our old approach and institutions will simply

---

[24] See : https://www.nidirect.gov.uk/articles/avoiding-bogus-degrees

become irrelevant. This scenario could be called the *brave new world*. If this actually occurs, then education will have to be rethought from the ground upwards.

In terms of the *steady as she goes* scenario universities will continue to research pedagogy in an effort to find better ways of assisting and encouraging their students to learn. There will always be a gap between research findings and what will be implemented in the universities. It will be down to the quality of leadership in the university to change the old attitudes and introduce new pedagogical regimes. This can be a slow process but sooner or later more action-orientated learning models of education will be generated with a greater focus on achievement rather than on being able to reproduce in written or in verbal argument the facts and figures of the situation. Where appropriate, university courses will be assessed through project work which will where possible have some clear benefits for both the learner and society.

In general universities will continue to look outwards for opportunities to engage with their societies. The age of the acceptability of the remote Ivory Tower has long since passed. The university is expected to be a vibrant part of our society delivering the benefits to those who are looking to improve their knowledge and how to apply it.

There are a number of key issues which will directly influence how university education will develop in the future and these are costs, size of classes, and academic integrity.

It was probably inevitable that the massification[25] of university education would result in the introduction of fees. While the total bill for university education was relatively small the state was prepared to fund the university system. Now that there are very much greater numbers at university the student has to find a considerable sum to fund his or her degree. It is now estimated that on average a degree will cost somewhere between £50,000 and £60,000[26]. This high cost has triggered a great concern for the ability of graduates to find appropriate employment so that the debt can be repaid. This is partly the reason why the "work-ready" issue has become so vocalised. There are some who argue that the high cost will limit student growth but in reality it is probably more likely to sharpen students' ability to discern the most appropriate degree course for themselves. And like the recent lawsuit taken against a university for misrepresenting the employment opportunities available on acquiring one of its degrees, if the university does not live up to its promises there are likely to be consequences.

Universities will argue that there is more to being a student than simply obtaining factual information. One of the functions of a university degree which is not often mentioned is that the university provides the opportunity for the student

---

[25] It is not appropriate to argue against massification in a democracy. Everyone should be allowed to pursue their education as far as it benefits them. However, massfiication brings with it a considerable cost which does not seem to have been properly understood or for that matter taken into account.
[26] There is little doubt that these costs will continue to escalate. The fees in the UK have been maintained at approximately £9,000 for about 10 years despite inflation running at somewhere around 2% to 3% per annum. In some countries the national total of student fee debt is enormous. It is estimated at US $3 trillion in the USA.

to develop emotionally. This applies both to the younger traditional student and also to mid-career individuals. Being partly removed from day-to-day responsibilities can enable an individual to reflect on his or her circumstances, potential, and opportunities. This can be an effective way of establishing a personal focus for the future which is required by almost everyone in society.

Large classes of students increase the pressure on faculty. It is more difficult to lecture to large numbers and as a result some universities insist on splitting their large classes into three or even four and having the lecture presented multiple times. The lecturing load associated with these classes is considerable as is the work involved in the class assessment in examinations. Some academics believe that artificial intelligence will come to their aid and that this technology will be able to lighten their academic and administrative burdens. It has been suggested that every student will have a robot tutor and helper. This may indeed come to pass although at the present stage, at the end of the second decade of the 21st century, artificial intelligence is still in a rather immature form and this optimistic vision of the future may well be some decades away.

Social software which is already playing some role in many universities will grow in importance. As mentioned earlier, education has an important social dimension and social software may be used as a key facilitator of relationships. It is now highly unlikely that anyone who is not a smart phone user will not have problems in fulfilling the requirements of a degree course at a university.

Academic integrity is under serious attack and it is important that universities make sure that there is no question of any inappropriate behaviour on the part of students or member of faculty. Where integrity is jeopardised it is important to rectify the situation immediately and to take punitive action against those concerned.

A tale of two educations

With regard to the *brave new world* scenario the world demand for higher education is likely to be approximately half a billion people in the next 20 years. At this time the world population will probably be in the order of 8.5 or 9 billion people. There will not be sufficient resources in terms of organisations, venues or faculty to accommodate the level of education demanded by this population. Universities will have to take drastic action. Under these circumstances there are two possible outcomes. The first is that universities will return to their former ways and become increasingly elitist with very difficult entry requirements and fee levels which will only be affordable by the wealthiest segment of the population[27]. In fact, there is little doubt that this will happen with regard to the elite universities in the first and second worlds. However, in parallel with this there will be a continuing development of large-scale distance learning universities such as we see in India and China which will increasingly rely on information and communications technology to be the delivery mechanism for their educational programmes. The quality of these institutions will be quite mixed. These universities will become more and more focused on the skills required in the

---

[27] In this scenario the number of students attending universities will either remain relatively constant or may decline.

workplace although they will make every effort not to allow their offerings to be confused with simple training programmes.

On the one hand, this will amount to the continuous development of mega-universities such as we are seeing in India and China today whose *raison d'être* will be the delivery of more practical and often technical education with the emphasis on skill development. At the same time there will be a demand for specialised universities such as the Dyson Institute of Engineering and Technology which is a boutique operation. Traditionalists find the intense specialisation offered through these institutions to be counter to the original spirit of a university and refer to them in derogatory terms[28]. However, this does not matter much to many people in society. The graduates of these institutions will probably find perfectly adequate career paths.

Mega-universities can be highly profitable and this will attract private sector investment. It should be expected that there will be an increasing number of distance learning institutions.

There is much debate as to how far computer technology will be able to take on the task of educating the world. Those who are enthusiastic about this technology believe that we are on the cusp of developing artificial intelligence to the point that it will be used extensively throughout the educational process. These people believe that if artificial intelligence is used properly it will completely revolutionise our approach to education. The argument is that these systems will tirelessly provide the full gamut of educational processes and will through the system's interaction with the student be in the position to deliver much better advice, instruction, monitoring, and attention to detail than any human instructor could possibly do. This is a highly utopian point of view and there are those who argue that this will not happen and even if it does, there will be unfortunate and unintended consequences. There is little consensus as to how beneficial the impact of artificial intelligence will be on our society.

Clearly the jury is out on this issue. Information and communications technology has completely changed many aspects of our lives and even if full artificial intelligence is never achieved there is no doubt that computer-based technology will continue to improve and that humanity will find more and more applications where it will be beneficial to our lives.

It is interesting to speculate that one day in the future a graduate might be asked the question, in much the same way as one is asked today "Which university did you attend?": "Which suite of artificial intelligence software directed/facilitated your university education processes?"

But there are several other factors which will affect the future of education besides the ones which have been discussed in this chapter. The most important of these are the changing demographics especially of Europe and the USA.

---

[28] Degree mills or sausage factories will be the sort of language used here by some academics. In fact, specialist universities with strong industry connects may well become an important way to produce work-savvy individuals, provided a reasonable range of subjects is included in their curricula and that a broad perspective is taken to the material presented.

It has become a tiresome cliché to talk about the rapid rate of change and it is not appropriate to indulge in that type of refrain again here. What is worth pointing out is that on top of all the other aspects of our lives that are changing we are faced with the conviction of many people in the developing world that they should move towards Europe or North America. In the medium term this redistribution of population is probably unstoppable and with it will come the increasing demand for more educational facilities. If we look at just Europe we find hundreds of thousands of people from the Middle East, Africa and other parts of the world wanting to take up residence and make new lives for themselves on this continent. It may be possible to slow down this movement, but it is certainly not possible to stop it. Most of the people arriving are in dire need of education, if they are going to play a reasonable role in the new societies to which they have arrived. These people will totally change the demand for education and although this demand will probably never be fully satisfied, the only way that developed societies are going to be able to cope with the new levels of population and their demand for education is through the application of the most innovative applications of technology.

This will be enormously expensive and may well produce financial crises.

It will not become easier to acquire education. It will require both perseverance and sacrifice as well as some considerable prior learning. Hopefully universities will become more sensitive to the students' requirements and will draw on pedagogical research and the use of the latest technology to improve the processes with which they facilitate student learning. Universities are likely to attempt to get closer to prospective employers for their students and it is hoped that this will not unduly influence the content of their syllabi. The notion of "work-ready" is problematic but what this term signals is that there is concern about how to improve students' orientation towards how they will be able to contribute to any organisation which might invite them to become a member of their staff. It is also important that students become emotionally intelligent[29] with regard to how they might be able to progress in their chosen career. It may well be better to use the term "work-savvy" in the sense in which it has been described in this chapter.

There will be no shortages of challenges to both the universities and to their students in the forthcoming years.

It is unlikely that the challenges described here will be solved in the lifetime of anyone who is reading this book.

References

Alam M, 2017, The Abuse of Unpaid Interns, Virginia Commonwealth University, May 31, 2017

Breuing M, 2011, Problematizing Critical Pedagogy, International Journal of Critical Pedagogy, Vol 3 (3) pp 2-23

Cary K, 2015, The End of College, Riverhead Books, New York.

Clifton H, M Chapman and S Cox, 2019, 'Staggering' trade in fake degrees revealed, BBC, 16 January 2018, London.

Collini S, 2012, What are universities for? Penguin, London.

---

[29] See : https://www.inc.com/justin-bariso/13-things-emotionally-intelligent-people-do.html

What is this Slippery Thing called Education?

Collins H, 1975, The Seven Sexes: A Study in the Sociology of a Phenomenon, or the Replication of Experiments in Physics, Sociology, Sage, London.
Dewey, J. (1916/1980). Democracy and education: An introduction to philosophy of education. In J. A. Boydston (Ed.), The middle works: 1899–1924, volume 9, 1916 (pp. 1–370). https://www.gutenberg.org/files/852/852-h/852-h.htm#link2HCH0001
Dewey J, 1916, Democracy and Education. An introduction to the philosophy of education (1966 edn.). New York: Free Press.
Freire P, 1970, Pedagogy of the oppressed, Continuum, New York.
Gilman D, Cited by Menand L, P Reitter and C Wellmon, 2017, The Rise of the Research University, The University of Chicago Press, Chicago.
Giroux H, 2011, On Critical pedagogy, Bloomsbury, London.
Illeris K, 2003, Three Dimensions of Learning: Contemporary learning theory in the tension field between the cognitive, the emotional and the social, Malabar, Florida.
Leavis F, 2013, two cultures? – The significance of CP Snow, Cambridge University Press, Cambridge.
McLean J, M Graham, S Suchet-Pearson, H Simon J Salt, A Parashar, 2019, Decolonising strategies and neoliberal dilemmas in a tertiary institution: nurturing care-ful approaches in a blended learning environment, Elsevier, https://www.sciencedirect.com/science/article/pii/S0016718519300703#!
Menand L, 2002, The Metaphysical Club: A Story of Ideas in America, Flamingo, London.
Menand L, P Reitter and C Wellmon, 2017, The Rise of the Research University, The University of Chicago Press, Chicago.
Rushton A, 2005, Formative assessment: a key to deep learning? Vol 27, Is 6, Medical Teacher.
Searle J, 1990, The storm over the university, The New York Review of books, December 6
Wilde O, spoken by Gilbert, in The Critic as Artist, pt. 1 (first published in Intentions, 1891).

Dan Remenyi has worked at 10 different universities over the past 30 years as a visiting professor where his main interest has been in the sociology of research. He has also acquired an interest in how universities function as both educational and research organisations.

7
Teaching and Learning in the 21st Century University

Kenneth A. Grant and Steven A. Gedeon
Ted Rogers School of Management, Ryerson University, Toronto, Canada

Introduction

To be fit for purpose, the 21st century university and its professoriate must reassess how they handle their teaching responsibilities. Participation in tertiary education is approaching 50% in many developed countries with students, parents and government expecting universities to prepare the student for their future career and funding models are frequently linked to admission numbers and retention. This continued increase in the future, combined with reduced government funding, will put pressure on university class sizes and student to professor ratios which will make teaching even more challenging in the future (Lee, 2009). However, at many institutions, teaching is seen as less important than research, with a professoriate whose professional development is focused on research, with little or no attention paid to mastering the art of teaching. Much is known about how to deliver better education, with a minority of passionate faculty investigating, experimenting and delivering innovative and effective classroom experiences, possibly with detrimental effects on their careers. This paper discusses the research/teaching conundrum, briefly reviews what has been learned about effective teaching and makes some suggestions for change.

The western university model

Universities have always had two key roles, to create knowledge and to transfer knowledge. Finding an appropriate balance between these roles in the 21st century is perhaps the most significant question affecting the lives of individual professors within each university. There are three primary university models from the 19th Century that make up the foundation of most Western Universities – the English (largely Oxbridge) general education model, the Scottish applied knowledge model and the German research model. However, as universities became widespread in the 20th century, the development of a professional professoriate became largely focused on the German model, with research having the dominant role in virtually all decisions that affect professors from hiring to tenure, promotion, salary and access to funding. The mandatory entrance ticket for a faculty position is a doctorate and in gaining that doctorate, candidates can spend up to 10 years to gain their three degrees (Becher, 1989). During all that time they gain knowledge and discover new knowledge, developing their research skills. Performance is primarily assessed through refereed publications and books. During that time, they are likely to spend little or no time learning about teaching – the skills needed to transfer knowledge and develop students' competencies and attitudes. This is in contrast to school teachers who, typically, need to gain at least one teaching qualification to add to their academic degrees, before they are permitted to teach (as well as potentially requiring certification or licensing in some jurisdictions).

When university study was for the select few, this might have been acceptable, although even then the role of the "professional" disciplines (for example, medicine and law for manly years, accounting, nursing and business more recently) were anomalous. Indeed, some of the professoriate have argued that such applied disciplines have no place in a "real" university. In some countries there were institutions of higher education that were seen as less prestigious and more focused on practical applied education, often called community colleges, applied colleges, fachhochschule or polytechnic universities, but even these, at least in such countries as the UK and Canada, have aspired toward status closer to that of traditional universities, awarding degrees rather than diplomas and increasingly looking for doctoral level faculty. These trends are encouraged by governments, seeing this as a cheaper delivery model.

The 21st Century challenge

Over the last 50 years or so something has changed. The proportion of young people attending university has exploded, for example, in the UK, from about 5% in 1960 to about 35% in 2000 with similar growth being observed in most developed countries (Mayhew, et al., 2004). Many governments have set targets of having 50% or more of their youth gaining higher education qualifications. These policies are based on two fundamental beliefs – a more educated population improves economic growth and a university degree improves the employment and career earnings of their graduates. While it might have been true that the privileged few who attended university in the early to mid 20th century were motivated by the pursuit of knowledge, most of today's students, especially at the undergraduate level, are doing this to improve their career prospects, and their funding is increasingly coming from parents and by them taking on significant personal debt.

While the growth of students has been dramatic, this has not been matched by the investment in faculty. Growth rates of faculty have been less than half of the growth rate of students across the developed world, with a further push, especially in the United States, to hire a very high proportion of temporary faculty, both full and part-time, who are paid significantly less, have little job security and whose work is focused on teaching. This has created a paradox, a professoriate that has been trained as researchers, who often view teaching as a necessary evil, especially at top research universities conflicting with an increasing need to teach more classes each of which contains more students.

Our students are also becoming increasingly challenging to teach. Some suggest that students are customers or consumers, a claim that others argue vehemently against. And, whether consumer or not, many of these students complain about their university experience. They are often not happy about the quality of teaching, the relevance of what they are being taught, and they drop out at significantly high rates -- in Europe and Canada, degree completion rates are in the 70-75% range with the US, likely below 60%. Also, as has been frequently reported, today's young person is very different from the student of the past. They are technically literate (far more than most of their professors), adept at social media use and with a short attention span. Few read books or newspapers, relying on pushed knowledge through their online sources and from their friends. In addition, they are likely working part or even full-time to support their studies.

The workload and faculty development conundrum

Whenever professors talk about their jobs the conversation often turns to "workload" – the expectations of the relative contribution expectations across their various roles. Almost universally, this is split into the categories of research, teaching and service, sometimes with efforts to develop formulas for each. A commonly quoted ratio is 40:40:20, the suggestion that approximately equal effort is spent on research and teaching with a lesser amount on service. In reality, these ratios vary enormously, with faculty at elite research universities spending a much lower proportion of time on teaching while those at the majority of universities will likely have the reverse situation, especially those with large undergraduate populations.

The typical qualification for a permanent (i.e. tenured) faculty position is a terminal degree in the appropriate subject, most often recognized by the award of a PhD, although other designations are possible, more generally described as a doctorate. While most often the PhD term refers to a research doctorate there are also a range of professional doctorates, including MD, JD, DBA and DPM, where advanced study is combined with significant practical field experience.

Research doctorates are the primary career route for academic appointments. Depending on the system, an individual might spend 6 to 8 years following their undergraduate degree to gain their doctorate. Throughout this process the focus is on developing research skills to investigate a specific body of knowledge, normally within an identifiable academic discipline, with the final qualification being a successfully defended thesis. Thus, the individual is well prepared for the research element of their career workload. However, in the vast majority of PhD programs, there is no content related to pedagogy or teaching. The PhD candidate may be required to carry out some teaching as part of their doctoral journey, but they are not expected to gain any formal understanding of teaching theory and pedagogy. A few jurisdictions, such as Switzerland, and some individual universities may require new faculty hires to undergo a short period of teacher training, but such behaviour is not widespread. Thus, the new faculty member has likely received very little formal training in what may be the largest part of their job responsibility. And the typical new hire into a tenure stream role is expected to further develop their research capacity and output to gain tenure. Further, a wide variety of research has demonstrated that applied disciplines aspire towards purer and more rigorous research, with tenure and promotion decisions tending to focus more on research achievements than teaching. Indeed, even non-research intensive universities also aspire to progress towards the more research focused model.

The conundrum is clear. Our professoriate has been developed with a research focus, but, increasingly, likely in the majority of cases, is expected to carry out teaching as their core responsibility. Little, if any, evidence exists that being a good researcher is linked to being a good teacher, especially at the undergraduate level (Hattie and Marsh, 1996). There is evidence that as faculty become more research focused, they tend to view teaching as a lesser responsibility (Braxton and Bayer, 1999). Despite the reification of research as the most important role for a professor, a sizable body of the professoriate does see teaching as an important and perhaps the most important part of their job, however, in many universities this is also seen as a career limiting move (Boyer, 1990). It is also paradoxical that, in many universities, academic freedom is used as an argument that tenured faculty should never be reviewed in their classrooms, yet their other core responsibility, that of research, is constantly reviewed by their peers (Braxton and Bayer, 1999).

What do we know about effective teaching?

The National Academy of Education (NAE) Committee on Teacher Education has identified a framework for effective teaching that includes knowledge of the learners and how they learn; understanding of curriculum content and goals; and understanding of and skills for teaching (Darling-Hammond, 2006). We know that teachers should accommodate the individual learning styles of the learners (Cassidy, 2004). We know that educators should focus on achieving competency-based learning outcomes that fit into an integrated and relevant curriculum (Gonczi, 1999). And we know that professors should be skilled at a range of pedagogical techniques. This means that the 21st century university and professor need to change.

Lectures don't work very well!

Despite knowing all these things about effective teaching, over the centuries, the lecture continues to be the primary method of knowledge transfer in a university setting. Unfortunately, most lectures do a lousy job at all three elements of good teaching. The famous painting of Henry of Germany giving a lecture at the

University of Bologna in the 14th century is frequently used to demonstrate that this is not a new problem, showing that a significant proportion of the students in the classroom are sleeping, talking, reading and not listening to the lecture. The scene will be familiar to a 21st century student. Henry stands at the front of the class, behind a podium and students sit in a tiered seating arrangement facing him. Not much has changed in seven centuries, except that instead of some 20 to 30 students, the room may contain several hundred! Likely the only difference will be that at Bologna, there was no projection screen upon which PowerPoint slides are shown.

Literally hundreds of studies have demonstrated the ineffectiveness of lectures, examples of typical findings include:
- Students frequently retain less than 25% of what is being taught
- Student attention falls off significantly after 15 to 20 minutes

- Good students likely read about 50% of assigned readings
- Students taught in the traditional way are more likely to fail than those in more active classes

The lecture has traditionally been seen as a low-cost content delivery method with increasingly large class sizes. However, technology will eventually replace most elements of this expensive out-dated delivery model with on-line videos, distance education, artificial intelligence and telepresence advancements in the 21st century. Lectures also don't follow the NAE framework that takes into account the learning styles of students, delivers competency-based learning outcomes demanded by employers, and uses multiple pedagogical techniques. Lectures are based on a teacher-centric teaching model instead of a student-centric learning model.

Teaching or learning?

In many disciplines, the most common 20th century approach to course delivery likely included the selection of an appropriate textbook, usefully segmented into chapters that may correspond to a week's study, complemented by PowerPoint slides developed by the author of the book. The course description and structure were based around the knowledge, or content, that the professor wished to transfer to the student. Students were assigned readings, and perhaps assignments to be done outside of class time and attend lectures, typically from one to three hours in length. In some disciplines, this may be complemented by laboratory or workshop activities. The course ran over a period of 12-14 weeks. Assessment was often based on memory retention of this knowledge. In essence, the professor was "teaching about" the topic. Students were passive recipients. This form of education is called the teacher-centric teaching model, often described as the "sage on the stage" approach, with the assumption being that the professor holds the knowledge which is being transferred (taught) to the student. Lectures, assigned readings, and examinations are all pedagogical techniques based on this educational model of transferring knowledge.

The contrasting student-centric learning approach increasingly adopted by faculty wanting to improve their teaching is a focus on the student's "learning outcomes" – what the student is able to do after the course is over rather than what they remember from the course content. Rather than passing a test, students demonstrate the attainment of learning outcomes through enacted mastery and demonstration of competencies.

Students are more likely to achieve these learning outcomes if they are engaged with the learning process. Although frequently studied, student engagement can be a somewhat "murky" concept with many interpretations (Parsons and Taylor, 2011), with Kahu (2013) identifying four distinct research perspectives – behavioural, psychological, sociocultural and holistic. Trowler and Trowler provide a useful definition:

> *Student engagement is the investment of time, effort and other relevant resources by both students and their institutions intended to optimise the student experience and enhance the learning outcomes and development of students, and the performance and reputation of the institution (Trowler and Trowler, 2010, p2).*

Thus, this can extend all the way from enhancing the students learning in class to their wider participation in the whole of the University and its activities. Trowler and Trowler also make the point that student engagement is not the same thing as student satisfaction, but that both are frequently of interest to government and policymakers in considering the performance of universities, with another important insight from their work being the recognition that successful projects to improve student engagement require significant institutional commitment to support individual faculty and students. Learning outcomes are often structured at increasing levels of attainment, such as Bloom's Taxonomy, with its six levels of achievement, with "remembering" at the lowest level and "creating" as the highest level. (Armstrong, 2019)

At a more practical level, engaging students to achieve learning outcomes is best done by active and experiential learning. In this student-centric approach, the student is at the centre of the experience, learning knowledge, skills and attitudes through the guidance of the professor through a variety of experiences, (which still may include some lecture components). Achievement is demonstrated by what the student can do by the end of the course, with multiple approaches to assessment of learning outcomes. This is sometimes described as the "guide on the side" approach. Courses designed for active learning are learner centred, and involve engaging activities that allow frequent practice, feedback, reinforcement of course concepts and attainment of learning outcomes. Expensive face-to-face in-class time periods are primarily used for groupwork and coaching with any lecturing components normally being short, perhaps only 10 to 15 minutes for each element. To be done effectively, students need individualised assistance in their learning community, possibly from peer groups, assessment happens frequently but with low-risk assignments and an evolution of the experiences so they can build their competencies during the course (National Center for Academic Transformation, 2005). Many studies have shown how active learning improves student performance and engagement (e.g. Freeman et al., 2014).

For this to happen, the 21st century university should implement improved curriculum design (Valliere, Gedeon and Wise, 2014) and the professor needs to be familiar with the principles and practice of good course design (Nomme and Birol, 2014) and be willing to play a number of different roles – course designer, teacher, facilitator, coach, mentor and motivator. Without professional pedagogical development, institutional support and a reasonably balanced workload, this is a challenging task. The literature includes a wide range of pedagogical techniques that are all considered student-centric to varying degrees. Table 1 gives the reader a take-away set of pedagogies and references that categorize, summarize and condense the key techniques discussed in the remainder of the chapter. The goal is to show at a glance the many different student-centric learning pedagogies that can augment and/or replace the traditional teacher-centric teaching pedagogies of lecture, textbook readings and exams. We have categorized them by how they might fit into a classroom or outside the classroom and whether they involve technology or new spaces.

Teaching and Learning in the 21st Century University

Table 1: Student-Centric Learning Pedagogies

Pedagogical Technique	Sample References	Guide to Use
Role Playing, Simulations, Game Playing	Stumpf et al., 1991; Low, et al., 1994; Hindel, 2002	In-class use or distance education, good for developing skills in a risk-free learning environment.
Extra-Curricular Activities, Student Clubs, Startup Incubators	Haensly, 1985; Ollis, 2012	Used primarily to enhance the overall student experience, can also be integrated into the curriculum for project-based courses
Case Studies, Living Cases	Learned, 1991; Katz, 1995	In-class use, good for theory integration and problem-based learning
Project-Based Learning, Experiential Learning, Service Learning	Bringle & Hatcher, 1996; Kolb, et al., 2001; Beard & Wilson, 2002; Gedeon, 2014	The deepest level of student-centric learning, good for skill and attitudinal learning outcomes.
Field Experience, Internships, Co-Op Programs	Marchioro, et al., 2014;	Good for tying student jobs to their education. Good for learning skills and gaining relevant experience.
On-Line Videos, Flipped Classroom, Micro-Certification, MOOCs	Tucker, 2012; Gilboy, et al., 2015; Gedeon, 2019	Integrative capstone courses, good for tying extra-curricular activities into course credit.
Interviews, Life Stories, Field Trips, Journals, Self-Reflection Assignments	Solomon et al., 1994; Rae and Carswell, 2000; Mitchell and Chesteen, 1995	Good for introductory courses and to provide students with role models and motivation. Good for learning values, expert scripts and principles.

Experiential learning goes beyond active learning. In applied disciplines, such as nursing, this has been standard practice for many years. However, its incorporation into a broader range of academic disciplines is more recent. Simply explained, students learn by doing, applying knowledge in a real-world context to develop skills, attitudes and new ways of thinking (Lewis and Williams, 1994). This can be field-based experience, whether in projects, practicums, placements or internships or as a classroom activity, including role-playing, case studies and simulations. Field-based experiences can place significantly greater demands on the institution and the faculty member and require careful design of assessment activities. In addition, this can be expanded to co-curricular and extra-curricular activities, both mandatory and voluntary, in which the student takes part outside of their course and assessment work. A key element to active and experiential learning is the act of self-reflection. Including specific self-reflection activities is likely to "yield deeper levels of reflection with improved learning" (Moon, 2004).

Another key element of engagement and active learning is students playing a role in their own education and the education of others. Properly structured group activities and projects, peer assessments and feedback, helping students form learning communities within classes and programs, having students present workshops to one another to help develop specific skills and knowledge areas, are all used successfully to enhance the student experience and learning.

In summary, student-centric learning experience and achievement is enhanced when faculty demonstrate commitment and authenticity in how they run their classes, where students care about what they are doing and their experience is tied to their values and their social environment. Their influence and interaction with their peer group is key to enhancing these learning environments and experiences.

As Einstein is reported to have said, "*I never teach my pupils, I only attempt to provide the conditions in which they can learn.*"

The role of technology

There is no doubt that the 21st century will see an increase in the use and usefulness of information and communications technology in the curriculum, with distance learning, broadcast lectures, use of computers for a variety of simulation and other activities being common. More recently, the concept of hybrid or blended learning course delivery has emerged, where students experience a variety of interactions while taking a class, which might include viewing lecture -type content electronically, either synchronously or asynchronously, students taking part in group and class activities, with some students physically in the room and others attending remotely using technology. One form of this is the "flipped classroom", where students watch recorded lectures, videos and other structured activities between the classes and, when they attend the class, the focus is on active, often group based, activities building on the material viewed outside the class with the instructor, who may be faculty or some form of teaching assistant providing structure and guidance.

Most universities have learning management systems which can be used for course administration, content sharing, knowledge delivery, student interaction and assessment. These are often used as the foundation for the delivery of online courses, with varied levels of success. A range of studies have shown online courses tend often to be replicas of in-class, lecture-based delivery with limited student interaction in other words, repeating the errors of the traditional lecture format. On the other hand, non-traditional distance-based universities such as the U.K.'s Open University and Canada's Athabasca University have demonstrated for decades that undergraduate and graduate degrees can be delivered successfully without the use of the lecture method and, initially, with creative use of information technologies.

The last decade has seen the emergence of MOOCs (massive open online courses), presented as a breakthrough technology for education, providing widespread access at low cost. This was obviously very attractive to some institutions, since physical infrastructure was not needed. Despite the hype, success is not obvious (Gedeon, 2019). While millions of students have signed up for such courses, dropout rates are very high, often above 90% (Murray, 2019). Amongst the key reasons cited for these dropout rates is the passive delivery format of most of the early offerings, replicating in-class lectures, with "talking heads". Observers are reporting recent efforts to provide more active and experiential learning in efforts to improve completion rates (Leonard, 2019).

One of the most disruptive impacts of ICT is the massive growth in the use of mobile devices and social media. In many ways, today's students' lives revolve around this technology, with computers becoming a much less popular method of accessing knowledge. These devices and technologies are frequently described as distractions and problems, yet there have been a few efforts to date to use them to improve student engagement in the classroom with pop-quizzes, surveys, polls and chat features. In this case the knowledge gap may be reversed, with the student often being much more knowledgeable than the professor.

A 2014 report on undergraduate use of ICT prepared by EDUCAUSE, emphasises that the issue is no longer whether to use ICT in the University, but rather "how to use technology in ways that are consonant with institutional culture and identity to help students succeed in individual courses, in their college experience, and in their educational objectives" (Dahlstrom and Bichsel, 2014). The study indicated that students expected anytime, anywhere access to their course material, with few instructors using the technology and most considering it to be distracting.

Spaces for learning

Another change required of the 21st century university is the need for new innovative flexible learning spaces. As mentioned earlier in this paper, the most common environment for the delivery of a university education is the lecture theatre. For university administrators and planners this is a highly efficient concept, allowing the delivery of classes to varying numbers of students with an efficient use of space, given the high student density in the room. In certain programs, there are additional learning facilities, such as computer rooms, science labs and, for some arts and creative programs, studio space. When first introduced, lecture theatres were, in essence, a new technology innovation that allowed the students to clearly see their lecturer and, possibly, watch demonstrations being carried out at the front of the theatre. Indeed, it has been suggested that the first uses of this concept were for anatomy classes in mediaeval Italy. Harvard University, initially in its law faculty and later in its business school introduced the "case room" design which is a horseshoe or U-shaped room that allows the professor to move into the centre of the room and for students to see and speak with one another during the class (Osigweh, 1987).

However, the adoption of active learning approaches dramatically changes the expectations for the teaching environment, with a greater need for flexibility and the ability to easily rearrange the room for different learning purposes. At its simplest, this implies easily movable desks and chairs, but much more is possible. The basic need is often for groups to be able to work together and for the faculty members to circulate between groups to facilitate their work. Movable partitions, multiple whiteboards and flat screens allowing students to connect their own electronic devices and collaborate on their work are often needed. External, small group meeting spaces are also helpful. Sometimes, individuals and groups need space to store project materials. Many universities are piloting new forms of learning space often focused around the concept of collaboration. By addressing space, pedagogy and technology together, new approaches to active learning can be developed. It is also possible to design large-scale collaborative spaces that include pod-type structures that allow student groups to be brought together in small groups and take place in combined classroom activities. Successful pilots of such spaces have demonstrated the benefits of this type of approach (Martin-Clement, 2019).

One area that has seen dramatic change in many universities is the library. University libraries still provide a vast range of physical books and other materials, but they have adapted to provide access to a wide range of electronic databases and have become lenders of many more things than books. Some provide loans of computers, others include specific resources that may be useful to students beyond their classroom activities, for example, 3D printers. In many universities, libraries may provide the only available spaces for students to meet, study or work together outside of class.

So, what to do?

While many innovative teaching initiatives can be found in universities across the world, the institutional barriers to significant change are major. As Abbott has suggested, the behaviour and work of a faculty member is influenced first by their academic discipline, next by their (likely) discipline-based department and then, and only to a limited degree, by their institution (Abbot, 2001). The principles of academic freedom and the constraints of typical faculty union agreements often limit the power of universities to influence what goes on inside the classroom. In addition, given the financial pressures they face, universities aim to maximise the use of their existing resources and often wish to avoid spending significant capital on new technology, space or teaching resources. Despite this, changes can be made.

Doctoral programs should include learning educational methods and practicing pedagogical elements in the development of their doctoral candidates making them better suited to the majority of academic positions available to them. Universities should consider making some form of teaching training available and, perhaps, mandatory, for new hires. Faculty with interest in teaching should be encouraged to conduct pedagogical research and such research should be considered as part of their research against whatever standards are used to measure their performance. Conducting such research will better inform them on how to be effective teachers.

Most universities have some form of learning and teaching centre and efforts should be made to embed them more closely with faculties and departments and to ensure that their offerings are consistent with the University's strategy for technology use to support education.

Universities need to have well-developed and properly funded strategies to use technology to enhance the student experience by encouraging hybrid active learning courses, delivered in non-traditional formats, recognising students' use of mobile technology and social media. Properly done, this makes it much easier for an individual faculty member to innovate in the classroom. The development of new teaching spaces providing capabilities for a variety of active learning experiences is also key.

University faculty career streams should match the needs of the individual institution, giving equivalent and appropriate weight to teaching and research, allowing advancement and recognition for both. This can be enhanced, where appropriate, by wider use of the concept of teaching-focused faculty, often referred to as professors of practice or clinical professors.

In conclusion, universities can become better fitted for the future roles they face by ensuring that their strategies address the teaching challenges discussed above. This need not be presented as an either/or conflict with research as both can be achieved.

References

Abbot, A. 2001. *Chaos of Disciplines,* Chicago, University of Chicago Press.

Armstrong, P. 2019. *Bloom's Taxonomy* [Online]. Center for Teaching, Vanderbilt University. Available: https://cft.vanderbilt.edu/guides-sub-pages/blooms-taxonomy/ [Accessed September 30th, 2019 2019].

Beard, C., & Wilson, J. P. 2002. The Power of Experiential Learning: A Handbook for Trainers and Educators. Stylus Publishing, PO Box 605, Herndon, VA 20172-0605.

Becher, T. 1989. *Academic Tribes and Territories: Intellectual inquiry and the cultures of disciplines,* Milton Keynes, UK, The Society for Research into Higher Education & Open University Pres.

Boyer, E. L. 1990. Scholarship Reconsidered: Priorities of the Professoriate. The Canadian Foundation for the Advancement of Teaching.

Braxton, J. M. & Bayer, A. E. 1999. *Faculty Misconduct in Collegiate Teaching,* Baltimore, Johns Hopkins University Press.

Bringle, R. G., & Hatcher, J. A. 1996. Implementing service learning in higher education. *The Journal of Higher Education,* 67(2), 221-239.

Cassidy, S. 2004. Learning styles: An overview of theories, models, and measures. *Educational psychology,* 24(4), 419-444.

Dahlstrom, E. & Bichsel, J. 2014. ECAR Study of Undergraduate Students and Information Technology. Louisville, CO: EDUCAUSE.

Darling-Hammond, L. 2006. Constructing 21st-century teacher education. *Journal of teacher education,* 57(3), 300-314.

Freeman, S., Eddy, S., Mcdonough, M., Smith, M., Okoroafor, N., Jordt, H. & Wenderoth, M. 2014. Active learning increases student performance in science, engineering, and mathematics. *Proceedings of the National Academy of Sciences,* 111, 3410-3415.

Gedeon, S.A. 2014. Application of Best Practices in University Entrepreneurship Education: Designing a New MBA Program, *European Journal of Training and Development,* Vol 38, No. 3, pp. 231-253

Gedeon, S.A. 2019. Theory-Based Design of an Entrepreneurship Micro-Credentialing and Modularisation System within a Large University Eco-System *Entrepreneurship Education and Pedagogy,* Special Issue on Modularisation and Micro-Credentialing of Entrepreneurship Education, manuscript accepted for publication, available online at https://doi.org/10.1177/2515127419856612.

Gilboy, M. B., Heinerichs, S., & Pazzaglia, G. 2015. Enhancing student engagement using the flipped classroom. *Journal of nutrition education and behavior,* 47(1), 109-114.

Gonczi, A. 1999. 12 Competency-based learning. Understanding learning at work, 180.

Hattie, J., & March, H. W. 1996. The relationship between research and teaching: A meta-analysis. *Review of educational research,* 66(4), 507-542.

Haensly, P. A., Lupkowski, A. E., & Edlind, E. P. 1985. The role of extracurricular activities in education. *The High School Journal,* 69(2), 110-119.

Hindel, K.(2002). A grounded theory for teaching entrepreneurship using simulation games, *Simulation and Gaming*, Vol 33 No 2, pp. 236-241.

Kahu, E. R. 2013. Framing student engagement in higher education. *Studies in Higher Education*, 38, 758-773.

Katz, J.A. 1995. Managing practitioners in the entrepreneurship class", *Simulation and Gaming*, Vol 26 No 3, pp. 361-375.

Kolb, D. A., Boyatzis, R. E., & Mainemelis, C. 2001. Experiential learning theory: Previous research and new directions. *Perspectives on thinking, learning, and cognitive styles*, 1(8), 227-247.

Learned, K.E. 1991. The use of living cases in teaching business policy, *Journal of Management Education*, Vol 15 No 1, pp. 113-120.

Leonard, W. 2019. So why did MOOCs fail to live up to the hype? *University World News*, February 8, 2019.

Lewis, L. H. & Williams, C. J. 1994. Experiential Learning: A New Approach. *In:* Jackson, L. & Caffarella, R. S. (eds.). San Francisco: Jossey-Bass.

Low, M., Venkataraman, S., And Srivatsan, V. 1994. Developing an entrepreneurship game for teaching and research, *Simulation and Gaming*, Vol 25 No 3, pp. 383-401.

Marchioro, G., Ryan, M. M., & Perkins, T. 2014. Implementing an interdisciplinary student centric approach to work-integrated learning. *Asia-Pacific Journal of Cooperative Education*, 15(4), 359-368.

Martin-Clement, N. M. 2019. The Use and Impact of the Collaborative Lecture Theatres: Digging up the foundations of the Lecture Theatre. Leeds Institute for Teaching Excellence.

Mayhew, K., Deer, C. & Dua, M. 2004. The Move to Mass Higher Education in the UK: many questions and some answers. *Oxford Review of Education*, 30, 65-82.

Mitchell, R.K. And Chesteen, S.A. 1995. Enhancing entrepreneurial expertise: experiential pedagogy and the new venture expert script, *Simulation and Gaming*, Vol 26 No 3, pp. 288-306.

Moon, J. A. 2004. A Handbook of Reflective and Experiential Learning: Theory and Practice, New York, RoutledgeFalmer.

Murray, S. 2019. Moocs Struggle to lift rock-bottom completion rates. *Financial Times*, March 3rd, 2019.

National Center For Academic Transformation. 2005. *Five Principles of Successful Course Redesign* [Online]. Available: http://www.thencat.org/PlanRes/R2R_PrinCR.htm [Accessed October 10th, 2019 2019].

Nomme, K. & Birol, G. L. 2014. Course Redesign: An Evidence- Based Approach. *The Canadian Journal for the Scholarship of Teaching and Learning*, 5.

Ollis, T. 2012. A critical pedagogy of embodied education. In A Critical Pedagogy of Embodied Education (pp. 209-225). Palgrave Macmillan, New York.

Osigweh, C. 1987. The Case Approach in Management Training. *Journal of Management Education*, 120-133.

Parsons, J. & Taylor, L. 2011. Student Engagement: What do we know and what should we do? Alberta: University of Alberta.

Rae, D. And CarswelL, M. 2000. Using a life-story approach in researching entrepreneurial learning: the development of a conceptual model and its implications in the design of learning experiences, *Education and Training*, Vol 42 No 4/5, pp. 220-228.

Solomon, G.T., Weaver, K.M. & Fernald, L.W. Jr. 1994. Pedagogical methods of teaching entrepreneurship: an historical perspective, *Gaming and Simulation*, Vol 25 No 3, pp. 67-79.

Stump, S., Dunbar, L. And Mullen, T.P. 1991, "Simulations in entrepreneurship education: oxymoron or untapped opportunity?", *Frontiers of Entrepreneurship Research*, Babson College, Wellesley, MA.

Trowler, V. & Trowler, P. 2010. Frameworks for Action I: Enhancing Student Engagement at the Institutional Level. York: The Higher Education Academy.
Tucker, B. 2012. The flipped classroom. *Education next*, 12(1), 82-83.
Valliere, D., Gedeon, S.A., & Wise, S. 2014. A Comprehensive Framework for Entrepreneurship Education Special Issue on Entrepreneurial Education in the *Journal of Business and Entrepreneurship*, Vol 26, No 1, pp. 89-120.

Kenneth A, Grant is the Chair of the Department of Entrepreneurship & Strategy in the Ted Rogers School of Management at Ryerson University. He was the School's first Faculty Teaching Chair and was a partner in two major consulting firms before joining Ryerson.

Steven A. Gedeon is Chair of the Ryerson Entrepreneur Institute and Associate Professor of Entrepreneurship & Strategy at Ryerson University. He has designed and delivered entrepreneurship curricula and courses throughout North America and Europe

8
Higher Learning in the Age of Data

Andrew D Banasiewicz,
Merrimack College, North Andover, MA, USA

Introduction

In the world that moves and changes at an ever-faster pace, institutions of higher learning, most notably colleges and universities, are often seen as bastions of steadiness. On the surface that would indeed appear to be so, but those institutions are also being remolded, albeit slowly, by a myriad of socio-politico-economic forces including changing demographic trends, disruptive technologies, and globalization. Perhaps the clearest manifestation of the transformative effect of those change agents has been the heightening of universities' self-interest, which can be seen as a direct consequence of growing competitive pressures. The race to offer customized, on-demand, multi-modal (on-campus, online and blended) education that fits-in with students' work and lifestyles can be seen as one manifestation of that trend, while the ever more frequent and ambitious fundraising campaigns offer another obvious example. All and all, efforts to adapt to changing social, political and economic realities can be characterized as structural self-re-engineering, an important step toward modernizing decades or even centuries-old educational institutions. Receiving considerably less attention, however, is the impact of some of the same technological and competitive forces on the essence of *teaching* and *learning*, and the very idea of what it means *to know*.

Implicit in the traditional conception of higher education is human centricity since formal education is essentially structured transfer of knowledge from (human) teachers onto (human) learners. And while new technologies have been widely adapted as facilitators that transfer, the essence of teaching and learning continues to be framed in the context of human-to-human exchanges. But the emergence and rapid maturation of advanced self-functioning technologies, broadly referred to as *artificial intelligence* (AI), and more specifically *machine learning* (ML) applications, underscores the need to re-think what it means to learn. An analyst using ML algorithms to sift through large volumes of raw data learns, but in a manner that is quite different from the same analyst reading a textbook or listening to a lecture. Moreover – and that is the real difference-maker – it is not just the analyst who learns. By continuously updating networked patterns and associations it derives from data, the ML application also learns. In a more general sense, a growing array of manmade electronic systems are now capable of learning autonomously, that is, without human input, as illustrated by widely used technologies including spam filters or electronic personal assistant such as Apple's Siri or Amazon's Alexa. All considered, if learning is now shared between humans and human-developed artificial agents, what does it mean to 'known' and to 'learn'? And by extension, will, and if so how, the evolving conception of knowing and learning reshape the centuries-old institution of higher learning?

It is likely that the manner in which institutions of higher learning adapt to changes brought about by the onslaught of intelligent automation will play a major role in shaping the future of higher education. But questions remain. Will future universities emphasize training of the mind, which, as discussed in the next section was the original goal of higher education, or will they focus even more on endowing students with defined skill sets, which is commonly the goal of professional education? What elements comprising the traditional pillars of a university – competent faculty, capable students and learning resources – will need to change, and how? Finding sound answers to such complex and enduring questions is a journey that begins with shared understanding of the genesis of higher learning as a formal, institutionalized pursuit.

The institution of higher learning

The origins of contemporary western universities can be traced back to the emergence of democracy in ancient Greek city-states, most notably Athens, and the concurrent idea of liberal education. Derived from the Latin word 'liberalis', or 'appropriate for free men', ancient Greek democracies regarded the study of grammar, rhetoric and logic as an essential enabler of free citizens' participation in civic life. And while feudal societies that followed in their wake were in many regards less erudite, clergy and nobility carried forth the core ideals of liberal education, eventually even adding mathematics, music and astronomy to what was considered proper education for the then ruling classes. During the same time period, education of first slaves and later commoners was limited to specific, typically servitude related skills, now broadly characterized as vocational training. Thus in the more general sense, the original focus and, more importantly, intent of higher learning was to develop the whole human being to their full potential, which is something that to this day remains the goal liberal arts education, though not necessarily the dominant goal of more broadly defined higher education.

That is because starting in the latter part of the 19th century universities began to steadily expand their initially general education-minded focus by offering more and more vocational training, delivered through growing arrays of professional schools, as exemplified by law, engineering, education, medicine or business. That educational scope-expanding trend has been so transformational that nowadays the general perception of university education is far more closely aligned with advanced vocational training than with the comparatively vague notion of 'developing the whole human being'…So, in the course of nearly two and a half millennia since Plato's Academy and Aristotle's Lyceum, the needs and values of societies slowly but systematically built, defined, and then re-defined what constitutes higher learning. And while numerous factors contributed to that evolution, the onset of the Industrial Revolution exerted perhaps the most profound influence.

Changing needs – changing focus

A widely embraced conceptualization of industrial progress depicts the underlying process through several distinct stages, briefly summarized in Figure 1 below.

The development of commercially viable steam engine in the early 18th century is commonly believed to have been the spark that eventually ignited the 1st Industrial Revolution, which was further fuelled (no pun intended) by the subsequent discovery of oil, and the resultant large-scale mechanization. Significantly more complex to build, operate and maintain than the comparatively simple hand tools used earlier, the growing array of industrial machinery required properly trained engineers and managers to design and utilize those progressively more complex tools. The subsequent invention of electricity, widely credited with sparking the 2nd Industrial Revolution, further expanded the need for advanced technical training, a trend that continued with the rise of electronics and computing that ushered the 3rd Industrial Revolution.

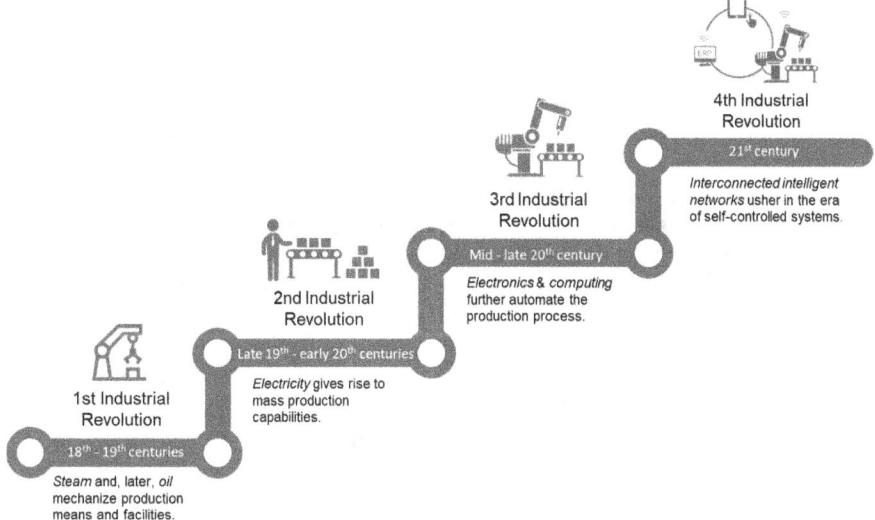

Figure 1: A summary of industrial progress

The relatively recent proliferation of data-driven interconnected intelligent networks, widely taken to signal the 4th Industrial Revolution, gave rise to data science as a new and distinct field of academic training, a yet another point adding to the trend of vocationalization of higher education.

Somewhat hidden in that high-level view of the march of industrialization is the emergence and gradual maturation of machine-centric learning. Commonly referred to as *computer* or *digital revolution*, this chapter in the book of industrial transformations is graphically summarized in Figure 2.

The University of the Future

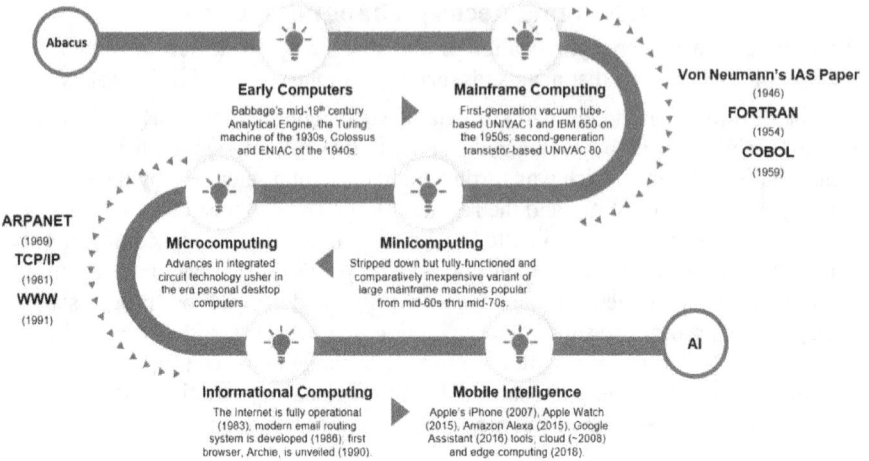

Figure 2: From abacus to AI

At least notionally, the abacus can be considered to be the original computer, although perhaps the most direct predecessor of modern computer was Babbage's Analytical Engine, first described in 1837. However, it wasn't until about a century later that the pioneering ideas of Alan Turing and John von Neumann laid the conceptual foundations that soon after gave rise to modern computing, with commercial systems in the form of large, complex and expensive mainframe machines entering the marketplace in the 1950s. In the years that followed, numerous hardware and processing related innovations inspired, first, minicomputers, which offered comparable (to the much larger mainframes) computing capabilities at about a tenth of the cost, and eventually microcomputers, now known as personal computers, which leveraged advances in integrated circuit design to pack unprecedented computing power into small, portable devices. The coming together of electronic computing and communication technologies then gave rise to the Internet and the era of informational computing, characterized by the use of computing devices to share and create information. The subsequent addition of wireless transmission of data, voice and video, and progressively more autonomous self-learning software applications brought the current era of mobile intelligence, where broadly defined computing systems are not only responding to human directions, but more and more are directing human actions.

When considered within the confines of higher learning, computer revolution can be seen as explosion in the ability to learn from data. Electronic transaction processing and electronic communication systems and platforms generate now famously vast quantities of data, while the progressively more autonomous data processing mechanisms and agents offer increasingly more evolved data utilization capabilities. More and more, learning from data is becoming as important as learning from books or experience.

Learning from data

How do we know that we know? From the somewhat abstract epistemological perspective, *knowledge* can come from one's own experience, information obtained from others, and inferences of logic. Those who feel that knowledge comes primarily, or even exclusively, from sensory experiences are often labeled as empiricists. As a philosophical stance, *empiricism* treats knowledge as probabilistic and subject to continued, evidence-based revision, and the empiricist reasoning is a fundamental part of the scientific method which posits that any knowledge claim must be tested against objective data, rather than resting solely on logic or intuition. Although the philosophical roots of empiricism can be traced back to the work of Aristotle and other Hellenic thinkers, as currently framed it is a relatively modern doctrine largely shaped in the Age of Reason. Manifesting itself in the departure from the mysticism and superstition of the Middle Ages, it brought about a fundamental shift in the way mankind viewed itself and pursued knowledge, resulting in great changes in scientific thought and exploration, all of which ultimately gave universities their current empirical orientation.

More on point, empiricism is a perfect companion to the Age of Data. The ever-expanding digitization of all manners of business and social interactions yields vast arrays of objective data, which in turn creates previously unimaginable opportunities for empirical learning. However, technological progress (see Figure 2) also continues to affect what it means to 'learn from data'. Consider Figure 3.

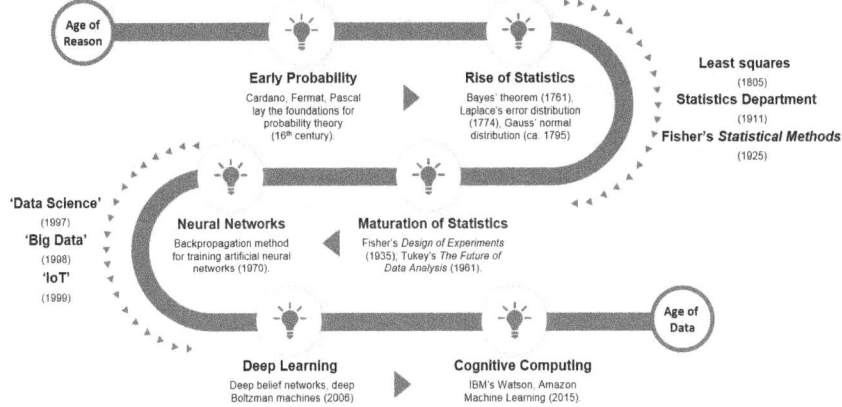

Figure 3: The evolution of data learning

The opening of human mind that characterized the Age of Reason resulted in numerous societal and scientific advances, including formal, i.e., mathematically based, study of chance, which in turn gave rise to the emergence of a new branch of applied mathematics known as statistics. The ensuing popularization of the notion of *statistical inference* then lent support to the hypothetico-deductive application of the scientific method, which then framed knowledge creation as a process of statistically testing falsifiable claims (i.e., hypotheses) using data derived from observation or experimentation. The later emergence and rapid maturation of electronic computing eventually produced machine learning, which marked the beginning of a new era, one in which not just mankind, but manmade devices are able to learn from data. And while early machine learning applications were limited to identification of simple recurrence-based patterns hidden in relatively homogeneous data, rapidly accelerating computing capabilities (summarized in Figure 2), coupled with advances in computer and neural sciences led to the development of progressively more capable and autonomous machine learning technologies. Now commonly referred to as AI, those systems exhibit increasingly human-like functioning, best illustrated by the now common deep learning and cognitive computing applications, and soon to become common self-driving vehicles.

And so the learning journey that began with the opening of the human mind in the Age of Reason is now taking us into the new world of blurring distinction between 'man' and 'manmade'. It is easy to see why, at least some, futurists see signs of oncoming singularity, or the merging of human and artificial intelligence. But it is also just as easy to imagine that the seemingly slow but interminably creative human analog (meaning capable of representing any process in terms of infinite values, which implies infinite ability to conceive) brain will continue to innovate in ways that are hard to imagine today, just as our modern innovations would be hard to imagine for our predecessors.

Technological progress and higher education

The currently – i.e., early 21st century – unfolding period, often referred to as the Information Age or the Age of Data is often depicted a yet another step on the continuum of technological progress (first summarized in Figure 1), but perhaps it is more appropriate to think of the current era as a new chapter in the evolution of mankind. Consider Figure 4.

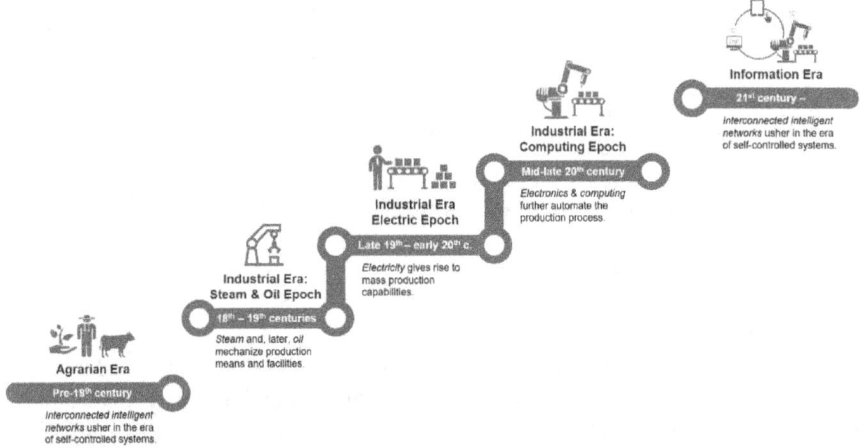

Figure 4: The eras of change

Agriculture-based agrarian societies were (and still are, in few isolated parts of the world) organized around producing and maintaining of crops. Those societies existed as far back as 10,000 years and can be thought of as the foundational era of human socio-economic development, lasting many centuries, until the onset of the 1st Industrial Revolution in the early eighteen-hundreds. The purpose of higher learning in agrarian societies was, as discussed earlier, to enable the ruling classes – initially the free citizens of Greece and Rome, and later feudal nobility and clergy – to *govern*. Any vocational training required by the working classes to produce goods and perform services necessitated only comparatively basic practical training, given the simple techniques and tools used during that period.

The emergence and rapid proliferation of initially steam- and later oil-powered mechanization effectively brought the agrarian era to an end. The comparatively quick succession of the 1st, 2nd and 3rd industrial revolutions can be seen as successively more advanced industrial development periods, or epochs, each rooted in a distinct disruptive innovation, and jointly comprising the Industrial Era. Underpinning the rise of large-scale mechanization was an exponential increase in the complexity and sophistication of means of production, which in turn gave rise to the emergence of highly trained and skilled classes of professionals. As a result of those and other (e.g., political, legal, etc.) changes, the focus of higher education slowly began to expand to include a growing array of specialized, professional education-oriented programs, and the overall goal of higher learning began shift away from learning to *govern* and toward learning to *make*.

Another key transition period began in the second half of the 20th century. Commercially jump-started in the 1950s, electronic computing first emerged as a limited access, special purpose tool, but the arrival of personal computers in the 1980s transformed computing into everyday utility for nearly everyone. The subsequent emergence of the Internet as a new communication modality, soon after enhanced by the utility offered by the World Wide Web interactivity, and further expanded by the rapid maturation of mobile connectivity and the proliferation of interconnected personal and commercial data capturing devices, laid the foundation for the current Information Era. Characterized by intelligent, meaning automated or even autonomous, interconnected networks, the commercial and personal consequences of the resultant changes are as monumental as those that characterized the agrarian-to-industrial society transformation. Just as steam-, oil- and electricity-powered machines changed how work was done, self-functioning, interconnected systems – perhaps best illustrated by self-driving vehicles – are now again changing not only how work is done, but also how lives are lived. Not surprisingly, the transformational impact of artificial intelligence extends into higher learning as more and more of the 'make' related work is handled by independently functioning systems – as a result, the focus of university learning will begin to shift away from *making* and toward *conceiving*, as graphically summarized in Figure 5 below.

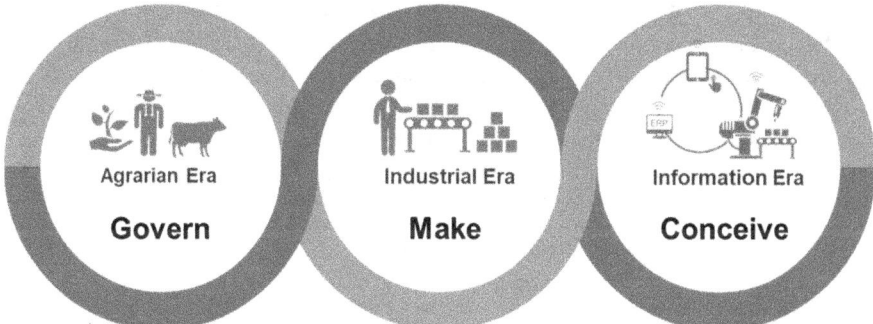

Figure 5: Shifting focus of higher learning

Starting with the purpose of educating of elites during the Agrarian Era, the focus of higher education shifted during the Industrial Era toward training of the new professional class, and it is once again shifting, this time in response to transformative changes brought about by the burgeoning Information Era. Technological progress is gradually alleviating direct physical work, while at the same time generating vast volumes and rich varieties of data, and the combination of those two related but distinct trends is ushering in the age of *information-driven creativity*. New knowledge is created, and ideas are tested not just by mining and analyses of data, but also through AI-driven capabilities to simulate reality in a way that transcends experience and physical existence, perhaps best exemplified by research aiming to describe conditions that existed moments after the Big Bang. In contrast to general creativity, which is rooted in subjective reasoning and/or imagination, information-driven creativity can be described as conception of novel ideas spurred by the use of available data. It entails going beyond what is currently known but in a manner that is guided by insights derived from currently available information.

What does that mean in practice? First and foremost, the traditional teaching model, the core of which changed very little since the days of early universities, ought to be reconsidered. More specifically, rather than being structured (i.e., curriculums comprised of sets of standard courses), largely undifferentiated (i.e., students consuming the same content within the same time period), and oriented more toward assimilation than discovery of knowledge, the new teaching and learning model ought to be more flexible, individualized and exploration minded. Intelligent technologies need to play a more fundamental role in teaching and learning, not just as a mean of different (i.e., online) content delivery, but also as a mean of discovering new knowledge. Making use of augmented, mixed and virtual reality technologies will allow learners to see beyond the boundaries of currently existing reality, making it more likely for more learners to conceive novel ideas that may not have emerged in a more traditional learning setting. As noted earlier, human brain is analogue, which implies potentially unlimited capability to create, It follows that focusing higher learning more on discovery of new, rather than the assimilation of old knowledge, infusing discovery-promoting technologies into the learning process, and individually-tailoring learning pathways will help institutions of higher learning to continue to unlock more and more of human creative genius.

Learning to conceive: Inputs and outcomes

In the most rudimentary sense, learning can be seen as a process of consuming inputs, in the form of various stimuli, with the goal of generating outputs, in the form of knowledge. Broadly defined, learning process inputs can be either episodic, taking the form of ad hoc stimuli, or ongoing, manifesting themselves as recurring stimuli. Learning process outcomes, on the other hand, can take the form of incremental knowledge, or updates to existing knowledge. Consider Figure 6.

Higher Learning in the Age of Data

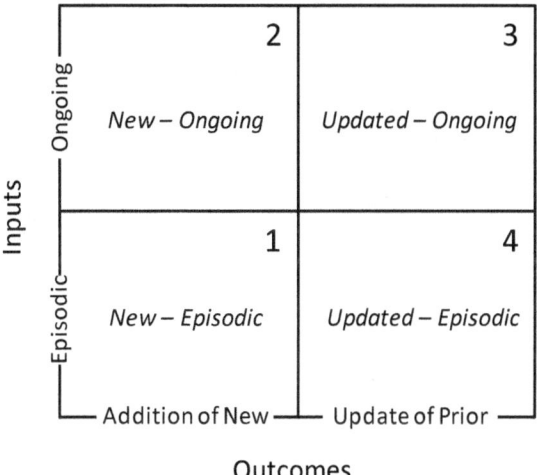

Figure 6: Learning inputs and outcomes

The resultant 2x2 learning input-outcome classification yields four distinct learning scenarios: new knowledge produced episodically (quadrant 1), new knowledge produced on ongoing basis (quadrant 2), ongoing update of prior knowledge (quadrant 3), and episodic update of prior knowledge (quadrant 4). Jointly, those four dimensions of learning capture the 'what' aspect of learning in the form of distinct types of knowledge assets derived from different informational sources and learning modalities, such as theoretical understanding of a new phenomenon of interest derived from the most recent empirical research findings (quadrant 1) or the most recent data-derived frequency of a particular type of insurance claims (quadrant 3). Essential to properly framing and contextualizing those distinct types of knowledge assets is a more in-depth detailing of the 'how' aspect of organizational learning, with particular emphasis on learning modalities.

Learning modalities

The ability to reason, defined as the power of the mind to think and understand by a process of logic, is most emblematic of human learning, while the ability to identify patterns in vast quantities of data is most descriptive of machine learning. It thus follows that the Information Era-fitting conception of learning should encompass, but also expressly differentiate between two meta-categories: reason-based, which embodies individual and collective cognitive and behavioral acquisition of knowledge, and technology-based, which encapsulates the capability of technological agents to translate patterns in data into performance of tasks. Each of the two meta-categories can be further subdivided into more operationally meaningful categories of 'experiential' and 'theoretical' for reason-based learning, and 'computational' and 'simulational' for technology-based learning. Figure 7 below offers a graphical representation of the resultant typology of learning.

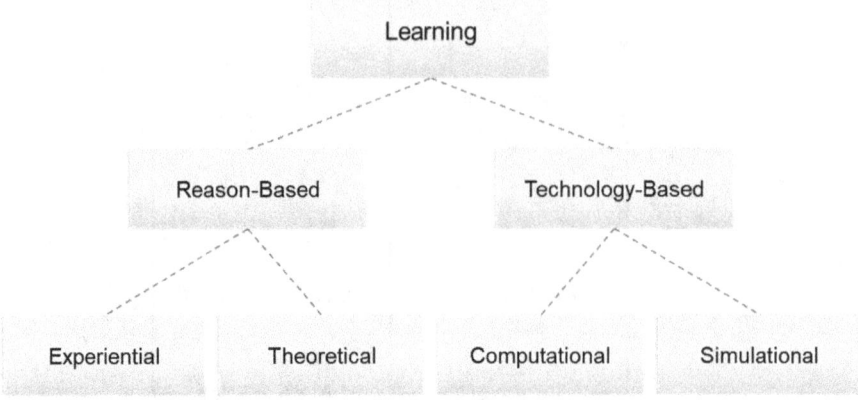

Figure 7: The typology of learning

Although outlined in Figure 6 as four distinct manifestations of learning, experiential, theoretical, computational and simulational modes can also be thought of as progressively more sophisticated means of knowledge creation. From early man gazing at the stars and trying to make sense of natural phenomena (experiential learning), to early philosophers and scientists discerning the underlying laws of nature (theoretical learning), to modern data- and technology-enabled investigators identifying new and testing presumed relationships (computational learning), to the now-emerging means of simulating reality as a mean of learning that transcends experience and physical reality (simulational learning). It is important to note, however, that even though theoretical learning can be deemed more cognitively evolved that experiential learning, and along similar lines simulational learning can be seen as more technologically advanced that computational learning, it is important to think of those four distinct learning modalities as complements, not replacements, in the same way that airplanes, automobiles, bicycles and simply walking all offer complementary means of traversing distance.

Reason-based learning

At an individual level, learning can be broadly characterized as acquisition of new, or reinforcement of existing knowledge. The underlying process begins with awareness-arousing stimulus being encoded into short-term memory in one of two forms: iconic, or visual, and echoic, or auditory. The process of learning is then initiated: It starts with the formation of new neuronal connections, which is followed by consolidation, or strengthening and storing of remembrances as long-term memories, with distinct clusters of neurons being responsible for holding different types of knowledge. Any subsequent retrieval of memories from long-term to active memory brings about re-consolidation, or strengthening of the stored knowledge, often referred to as remembering.

In a more abstract sense, learning can be characterized as adding new or modifying information already stored in memory based on new input or experiences. It is an active process involving sensory input to the brain coupled with extraction of meaning from sensory input; it is also a fluid process, in the sense that each subsequent experience prompts the brain to (subconsciously) reorganize stored information, effectively reconstituting its contents through a repetitive updating procedure known as brain plasticity. Though generally resulting in improvements to existing knowledge, brain plasticity can nonetheless bring about undesirable outcomes, most notably in the form continuous re-casting of memories – in fact, that is one of the reasons eyewitness accounts become less and less reliable with the passage of time. All considered, the widely used characterization of learning as the 'acquisition of knowledge' oversimplifies what actually happens when new information is added into the existing informational mix – rather than being simply 'filed away' and stored in isolation, any newly acquired information is instead integrated into a complex web of existing knowledge.

Within the confines of reason-based learning, the most elementary knowledge acquisition mechanism entails immersion in, or observation of, a process or a phenomenon, commonly referred to as *experiential learning*. Subjective and situational, this mode of learning can be seen as a product of a curious mind driven to understand the nature of a particular experience, and it is built around systematic examination of sensory experiences, particularly those obtained by means of direct observation or hands-on participation. Being entirely shaped by person-specific factors, experiential learning implicitly dismisses existence of innate – i.e., generalizable – ideas, resulting in knowledge that is entirely defined by individual learners. That mode of learning is particularly important in the context of specific tasks, such as underwriting of executive risk or managing of retail customer loyalty programs.

Complementing the experiential learning dimension of reason-based learning is *theoretical learning*, which is focused primarily on common knowledge, or innate ideas that transcend individual experiences. It entails developing an understanding of universally true and commonly accepted abstract formulations and explanations, as exemplified by the axioms and rules of mathematics or the laws of nature. That mode of learning typically plays a very important role in the attainment of professional competence, as evidenced by numerous professional certification requirements.

Plasticity, bias and channel capacity

In a very general sense, knowledge can be thought of as a library – a collection of systematic, procedural and episodic remembrances acquired via explicit and tacit learning. However, as suggested by the notion of brain plasticity, unlike physical libraries, neural networks-stored 'collections' are subject to ongoing re-shaping, triggered by the process of assimilating of new memories. The resultant continuous re-writing of old memories means that an individual-level effective topical knowledge is ever-changing, and that the ongoing interpretation and re-interpretation of knowledge can exert profound impact on individuals' perception and judgment.

While the ongoing re-shaping of knowledge affects the validity and reliability of individuals' knowledge, cognitive bias impacts the manner in which stored information is used. Reasoning distortions such as availability heuristic (a tendency to overestimate the importance of available information) or confirmation bias (favoring of information that confirms one's pre-existing beliefs) attest to the many ways subconscious information processing mechanics can warp the manner in which overtly objective information shapes individual-level sense-making. To make matters worse, unlike machines that 'remember' all information stored in them equally well at all times, the brain's persistent self-rewiring renders older, not sufficiently reinforced memories progressively fuzzier and more difficult to retrieve. As a result, human recall tends to be incomplete and selective.

Moreover, the amount of information human brain can cognitively process in attention at any given time is limited due to a phenomenon known as human channel capacity. Research suggests that, on average, a person can actively consider approximately 7 ± 2 of discrete pieces of information. When coupled with the ongoing reshaping of previous learnings (brain plasticity) and the possibly distorted nature of perception (cognitive bias), channel capacity brings to light cognitively-biological human reasoning limitations.

Emotion, motivation and group dynamics

Looking beyond factors that capture some of the brain mechanics related reasoning limitations, reason-based learning is also impacted by numerous attitudinal factors, most notably those related to emotions and motivation. For instance, more positive experiences tend to manifest themselves in more complete recollections than negative events, and those events that occurred more recently appear to be more significant or thus more likely to recur. Moreover, desire to perform better has been shown to lead to deeper learning, even when time spent on learning, as well as learners' gender and ability were controlled for, highlighting the importance of intrinsic motivation to learning.

It is worth noting that while emotion and motivation usually manifest themselves as individual-level characteristics, those characteristics tend to be, at least partly, group-shaped. More specifically, research in the area of social cognition suggests that individual-level reasoning efficacy is determined by a combination of cognitive (i.e., individual), social (i.e., group), and situational (i.e., individual or group) factors. A somewhat unexpected implication of those findings is the potentially adverse impact of group dynamics on individuals' inclination to 'think out of the box'. A phenomenon known as 'groupthink', which is a dysfunctional pattern of thought and interaction characterized by closed-mindedness, uniformity expectations and biased information search, can coerce adherence to the group's consensus view, effectively muting unique insights of potentially uniquely insightful individuals. Given the popularity of group work, group projects and the generally social setting of traditional higher learning formats, groupthink clearly poses a challenge for how institutions of higher learning can retain their social format, while at the same time promoting individualism that is a necessary ingredient of creative thinking.

Technology-based learning

The growing sophistication and proliferation of self-learning technologies, commonly referred to as artificial intelligence (AI), is beginning to challenge the traditional, human-centric conception of learning. Machine learning, a sub-category of AI that focuses on endowing computers with the ability to learn without being expressly programmed, enables algorithmic systems to discern patterns from available data, accumulate and synthesize the resultant arrays of patterns and use the resultant knowledge as bases for executing specific tasks. In fact, as implied in the term 'artificial intelligence', AI systems are expressly designed to mimic the functioning of the human brain, perhaps best exemplified by neural networks, a family of algorithms modelled after human brain. Unimpeded by human limitations in the form of cognitive bias, fatigue or channel capacity, and taking advantage of practically limitless computational resources, AI is pushing the broadly defined ability to learn beyond the traditional limitations of human-centric information processing. And in some context, most notably when performing routine, repetitive tasks, AI-based decision engines can in fact outperform humans. The primary reason for that is the very non-biological and non-reasoning essence of those systems: Being able to rapidly, tirelessly and nonjudgmentally ingest and summarize the often vast quantities of data enables those systems to systematically and objectively – or more specifically, unemotionally – assess decision alternatives in a way that is extremely difficult, if not outright impossible for human decision-makers.

It is important to emphasize that technology-based learning is a complement, not a replacement for human learning. When decisions are characterized as repetitive and structured and the decision-making context as stable, automated decision engines can make better choices, primarily because of their heightened capabilities to persistently make more exhaustive, expedient and unbiased use of available data. At the same time, however, the same decision engines tend to underperform relative to human reasoning in volatile decision contexts characterized by trend-discontinuity, or where historical data patterns are no longer reliable predictors of future outcomes. However, this somewhat simplistic, one-conclusion-fits-all distinction is beginning to blur, as artificial intelligence is becoming, well, more intelligent.

Though frequently viewed as a singular domain, technology-based learning is comprised of two complementing dimensions: computational and simulational learning. While overtly quite similar in the sense that both modalities are built on the foundation of analyses of typically large volumes of raw data, *computational* learning is focused on the 'what-is' dimension of insight extraction, while *simulational* learning explores the more nuanced and speculative 'what-if' dimension of knowledge, in a manner more befitting of the 'artificial intelligence' label. More concretely, the former encompasses various modes of comparatively simplistic informational summarization and pattern identification, whereas the latter delves, ever more confidently, into systemic epistemology, or theoretical interpretations of observed reality. Together, computation and simulation technologies are slowly emerging as a source of 'new' empirical learning, taking the form of constructed reality-based knowledge creation, or discovery of universal generalizations within artificial representations of the world, broadly referred to as augmented or virtual reality (AR and VR, respectively). It is important to note that technology-, or more specifically AR or VR based learning doesn't merely offer an alternative to traditional reason-based learning – it makes possible generation of previously inaccessible insights, perhaps best exemplified by astrophysical research delving into the birth of our physical universe and conditions that existed shortly after the Big Bang. By simulating impossible to directly experience physical conditions, technology-based learning offers practically limitless what-if inquiry possibilities, which lends further evidence to the impending shift in higher learning, discussed earlier and graphically summarized in Figure 4.

Overabundance

In my recent book, *Evidence-Based Decision-Making: How to Leverage Available Data and Avoid Cognitive Bias*, I argue that making consistently sound decisions is contingent on surmounting of cognitive bias and other reason-warping factors, which in turns calls for commitment to making use of available and pertinent evidence. With that in mind, I frame the notion of 'evidence' with the help of Empirical & Experiential Evidence (3E) typological framework, which systematizes the totality of informational inputs using a 3-tier categorization rooted in the distinction between empirical and experiential sources of knowledge. The ultimate goal and value of the 3E framework, and the supporting operationalizations, is to enable well-informed and unbiased decision-making by leveraging diverse pools of available and pertinent decision-guiding inputs.

A similar problem of input type and volume richness also affects technology-based learning. In the most rudimentary sense, data that power those systems can be conceptualized as a mix of signal, which is potentially informative, and noise, which is generally non-informative. Hence one of the core aspects of data utilization is to separate signal from noise, a task that becomes increasingly more challenging as the volume and variety of available data expand.

While the much talked about staggeringly large quantities of available data are perhaps the most visible manifestation of challenges confronting technology-based learning, it is epistemology, or the essence of validity and reliability of what is considered 'knowledge', that poses an even more formidable challenge. Lacking human reason's face validity, or 'does it make sense' litmus test, AI applications have to rely on generalizable decision heuristics to enable automated algorithms to independently and consistently differentiate between material and spurious patterns. Consider is common scenario: A computer algorithm sifting through data identifies a recurring association between X and Y – once identified, the association is 'learned' and subsequently used as a driver of algorithmic task execution. However, there is often a non-trivial possibility that what manifested itself as a recurring association between X and Y is erroneous, due to both X and Y being influenced by unaccounted for (i.e., not captured in the available data) factor Z, effectively rendering the presumed association illusory. Moreover, even if the X-Y association is unaffected by the unaccounted for factor Z, statistical significance tests commonly used to assess non-spuriousness of associations may produce falsely positive conclusions. One of the key culprits here is the well-known dependence of those tests on sample size – it can be easily shown (by varying the sample size while holding all else constant) that the often large number of records used in analyses can result in magnitudinally trivial effect size being deemed statistically significant, which would be typically interpreted as material.

It is easy to get hung up on limitations, and thus it is crucial to not lose sight of the fact that just as human reasoning has to contend with various inhibitors, such as cognitive bias or brain plasticity, artificial intelligence is subject to vagaries of input data and innerworkings of data processing algorithms. And thus it follows that just as human reasoning cannot be denied its largely self-evident creative brilliance, technology-based learning systems cannot be denied its ability to quickly extract insights out of prohibitively vast, in human manual processing sense, quantities of data.

Andrew Banasiewicz is currently the Director of Data Science & Analytics programs at Merrimack College and the Founder of Erudite Analytics, a consultancy; formerly, he spent more than two decades as a senior level quantitative analyst.

9

Ethics, Sustainability and 95 Theses for Higher Education Reform

Christopher J. Moon
Middlesex University, London, UK

Introduction

Rather than pin my '95 theses' to the glass doors of the university main building (though I now wish I had done this) I emailed my paper (Moon, 2018) to the then Vice Chancellor, Professor Tim Blackman, now VC at the Open University. To his credit the VC later mentioned to me that I had influenced his views and the next Dean to be appointed, in science and technology, would be given a broader remit across the university to influence environmental issues. However, the VC reminded me that sustainability was still not regarded as part of the strategy of the university, and as such the university was still not willing to be a signatory to the UN Higher Education Sustainability Initiative (HESI); and curriculum development was still the domain of individual Deans. This lack of strategic leadership on sustainability had thus far restricted major changes to the curriculum to implement sustainability across the university; despite successive lobbying by staff such as myself, and successive student surveys (NUS, 2018). Why? There is an issue of governance here. The VC's role at universities in general appears to have become more that of business executive than educationalist. The high pay of VCs has been subject to criticism; and some students have started to sue universities for providing what they have perceived to be poor quality education (BBC, 2019). So, what are universities for? Are they businesses which should be evaluated on purely commercial outcomes such as revenue and profit? Or are they educational charities with a 'public service ethos' that have somehow lost their true sense of purpose and mission in society? This chapter addresses some of these issues by drawing on the history of universities and their contemporary challenges.

Background

Universities have a long and controversial history. The original Latin word 'universitas' referred to a community of teachers and scholars; and the oldest university in Europe was founded in Bologna, Italy, in 1088; though various centres of learning existed outside of Europe before then (Britannica, 2019). The initial 'founders' were princes and prelates (e.g. bishops); and as such the main 'rules' were that such places of independent learning should neither be atheistic nor heretical. Thus, by 'instituting' these 'rights' the basis for universities as institutions was born. This distinguished universities from other forms of educational establishments; and we regard degree-awarding institutions today as Higher Education Institutions or HEIs.

In 1988, the 900th anniversary of the University of Bologna, 388 university rectors and heads of universities from Europe and beyond signed the *Magna Charta Universitatum* (Magna Charta, 2019) containing principles of academic freedom and institutional autonomy as a guideline for good governance and self-understanding of universities in the future. As such the *Magna Charta* both celebrates the deepest values of university traditions and encourages universal application. Table 1. outlines a series of 'tensions' such as freedom and autonomy that universities are still tackling today. The items in the table are not in order but are designed to stimulate discussion.

Table 1: Tensions in higher education institutions, (*Source, the author*)

Mission	Culture
Self-regulation	Government policy
Vocational	Non-vocational
Local	Global
Freedom	Autonomy
Research	Teaching
Generalist	Specialist
Innovative	Standardised
Estate	People
Grants	Fees
Diversity	Homogeneity
Silo thinking	Transdisciplinary
Practitioners	Academics
Managerialism	Staff and student centred
Elitism	Liberalism
Public ethos	Private claims
Pure	Applied
Competitive	Collaborative
Copyright	Open source
Physical spaces	Electronic spaces
Sustainability	Complacency
Cynicism	Advocacy
Instrumentalism	Broader societal values

Ethics, Sustainability and 95 Theses for Higher Education Reform

There are now over 20,000 universities globally but only about 1,250 are included in the Times Higher Education world rankings (THE, 2019); and core missions are cited as: teaching, research, knowledge transfer and international outlook. The 'performance indicators' are grouped into five areas: teaching (the learning environment); research (volume, income and reputation); citations (research influence); international outlook (staff, students and research); and industry income (knowledge transfer), see Figure 1. Currently there are 1001 universities in the world ranking; and the top two universities are University of Oxford and University of Cambridge in the United Kingdom.

Probably the most interesting feature of the THE ranking is the place of 'reputation' surveys which account for 33% of the total ranking score. Thus, 50% of the teaching score is apportioned to the 'reputation for teaching' survey and 60% of the research score is apportioned to the 'reputation for research' survey. This means that by far the most significant indication of 'success' in the survey is student satisfaction with teaching and peer satisfaction with research. Research influence accounts for 30% of the total ranking; and international outlook and industry income just 7.5% and 2.5% respectively.

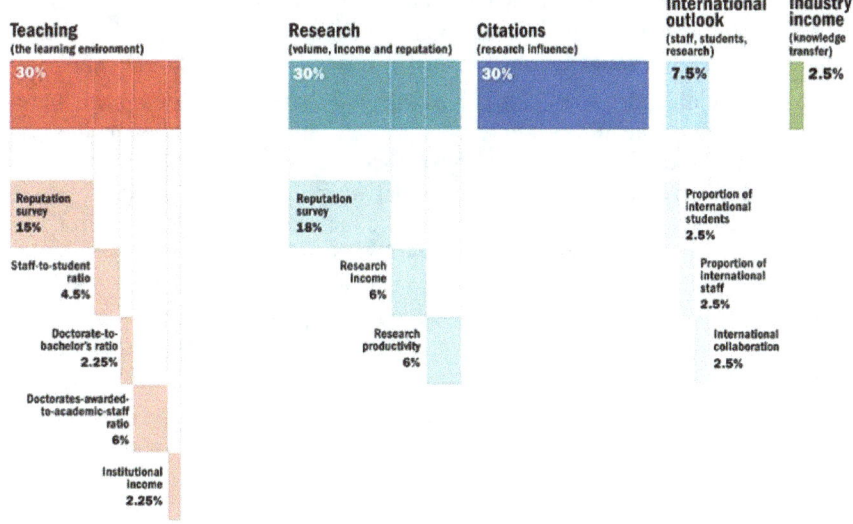

Figure 1: KPIs across five domains, world ranking of universities, (*Source THE, 2019*)

What does this THE ranking reveal about the purpose and mission of universities today? Firstly, it reveals that universities are competing in a world market for students; and league tables could influence student choice as to which universities to attend. The vagaries of league tables though have been highlighted by Moon (2015) who recognised that one of the drawbacks with league tables is that competitors could tend to try and move up the league table by beating their nearest rivals. There is a potential element of 'gaming' here in that universities could be tempted to focus on a few quick wins to improve their ranking vis-à-vis a particular competitor institution. Thus, their improved performance could be driven more by the league table metrics rather than by their overall purpose and mission in society.

The University of the Future

In contrast, there is a new ranking of universities being developed based on commitment to the UN Sustainable Development Goals. Launched in April 2019 at THE's Innovation and Impact Summit in South Korea, data will be collected from September/October 2019. According to THE (2019b) the first edition of the ranking will include metrics based on 11 SDGs, but the long-term goal is to measure performance against all 17 goals. Apparently, the methodology for this ranking is designed to go way beyond current university measures for reputation and research (THE, 2019b). The chief data officer for THE, Duncan Ross, says he is excited by the data submitted from 500 universities thus far; which calls for evidence of SDG policy implementation not just stated intention.

This new method of collecting and analysing data means there is less likely to be any 'gaming' of the ranking system; only genuine efforts to tackle the SDGs will be recorded. On the positive side this should mean that universities re-purpose around the SDGs. However, if only a relatively small sample of universities submit data (at present about 2.5%) then the ranking will not secure global repurposing of university missions. Nevertheless, the introduction of the new measure is regarded as ground-breaking; and asking universities to provide evidence of their social impact is a sign that universities will need to transition from being mere 'machines of knowledge' and league table 'conformers' to being more explicit 'confronters' of the most pressing societal problems such as poverty and climate change.

This potential repurposing of missions suggests that universities that are more 'disruptive' will be the quickest to respond to the challenges identified by the SDGs; and poses questions as to the governance and leadership of HEIs today. Are HEIs with their institutionalised structures, bureaucratic decision-making protocols, and status quo cultures best placed to meet these challenges? Certainly, some VCs are more enlightened than others! Examples of this more enlightened VC mindset include the VC of The Chinese University of Hong Kong, Rocky Tuan, who helped launch the UN Sustainable Development Solutions Network (SDSN) in Hong Kong; and the President of Hult International Business School, Stephen Hodges, with Hult now reporting against all 17 SDGs.

However, the role title itself 'Vice Chancellor' conjures up images of academic or managerial elitism rather than democratic leadership and social reform. To many, the pomp and circumstance of graduation ceremonies with caps and gowns, maces and masters of ceremonies, distinguishes universities from their virtual counterparts, or other types of certification bodies. I recall graduating from one HEI to a royal fanfare followed by a delicious high tea! Other ceremonies have been rather mundane! However, I have also completed a MOOC (Mass On-line Open Course) and received a certificate of completion through the post, without any fanfare! Perhaps the titles and trappings associated with the upper echelon of university life should change with the times!

There is still a place for heritage and history, respecting the values and traditions of the past. And by recognising how universities have changed in their missions, values and practices, helps understand what and how to transform. One question is: are academic ceremonies convened more for traditional PR and marketing or is there a social purpose behind them? Clearly there is a good opportunity to celebrate academic success with friends, parents and colleagues.

However, what exactly is being celebrated? Is it just achieving good knowledge-based exam results? Or is the celebration about becoming a global citizen, contribution to society, tackling specific problems identified by the SDGs? The celebration need not be muted here. However, the emphasis could change with less luxury (ermine, maces, expensive to hire gowns, expensively staged photographs, high tea) to social and ecologically sound events that do not waste resources but actively promote conservation, equality and diversity. Shouldn't all graduation ceremonies be as green and sustainable as possible?

Which values are we asking students and staffs to adhere to? A survey of business school students by the author (Moon, 2015) revealed that the majority had a low interest in the environment and were 'cynical' about studying a green module. The second largest group of respondents were positive on both counts and the author describes these as 'advocates.' They are the students one feels more inclined to put forward for external placements and competitions because of their positive attitude and desire to contribute to social and environmental change. The third and fourth largest group of respondents were roughly equal and described by the author as 'instrumental' and 'complacent' respectively. The instrumental group would study the environment if it helped them gain their degree; the complacent group were interested in the environment but were not actively doing anything about it.

Whilst there are simple pedagogical strategies to cater for all these student mindsets, the findings do reveal a more fundamental problem; HEIs tend to regard all students the same! This 'machine' of knowledge acts like a 'pipe' when we push the students in one end of the pipe and then pipe them out the other end; regardless of their individual learning needs nor in regard to what society really needs. This process has been labelled as 'massification' of higher education; a concern now being raised concerning China (Mok and Jiang, 2016).

The 'age-old' model of universities has changed to a degree. Some universities already report against all 17 SDGs (Ashridge/Hult, for example); and many universities do have innovative pedagogical practices (c.f. CASE, 2018). However, there is concern that some universities are delivering lower quality educational practices e.g. 'Mickey Mouse' degrees or courses (BBC, 2019). Not wanting to disparage Mickey Mouse nor Disney; there are concerns that education has become 'Disneyfied' (Harris, 2005) or 'commodified' (Williams, 2015) in such a way that the degree or 'product' is presented as a glossy marketing image but fundamentally is the same old subject with outdated approaches to teaching and learning. Where is the diversity and innovation needed to tackle the complexity of issues in society? Surely university courses need to tackle universal problems but in ever more sophisticated and locally relevant ways?

Further, how does the university tailor its programmes to specific learning needs? At present we rarely survey students at induction to identify different learning needs; and rely on self-diagnosis of learning needs on application forms or much later when students express extenuating circumstances. Often, language and literacy issues only become apparent when lecturers engage with students in the classroom or after assignments are submitted. One exception is the sustainability literacy test (SULITEST, 2016) now used by over 90,000 candidates in 64 countries. The test - is an online, multiple choice question test available in ten languages; and provides a benchmark in order that providers can then seek to raise literacy across programmes. The mission of SULITEST is to support expanded sustainability knowledge, skills and mindset that motivate individuals to become deeply committed to building a sustainable future and to making informed and effective decisions. Isn't this the kind of mission that all universities should be ascribing to?

Universities of the future

The future of universities is uncertain; as the future is uncertain. 'Universities of the Future' is a Knowledge Alliance Project funded with support from the European Commission. The aim is to generate a paradigmatic change in the way higher education institutions, businesses and public authorities cooperate within the developing framework of Industry 4.0 applications (Artificial Intelligence 'AI', Augmented Reality 'AR', Virtual Reality 'VR', Robotics, etc). Results already include a potential 'blueprint' for the university of the future. The roadmap includes developing a creative and innovative approach for meaningful and fruitful collaboration opportunities within and between members; enrichment of current university courses; toolkits for teachers; and a virtual environment to test ideas. What is lacking though is an emphasis on the UN SDGs. Whereas, competitions such as the 'F Factor' in the UK (F Factor, 2019) or 'Future Factor' relate Industry 4.0 applications specifically to the SDGs; the Enactus competition (2019) ask students to develop real and viable projects to achieve the SDGs. And, organisations such as Sustainia (2019) now map the 100 most innovative entrepreneurial projects across the globe against the SDGs.

Thus, it seems that the 'blueprint' for the university of the future described above is without a social or environmental mission. Yet, as a judge of the 'F Factor', the UKs premier competition for 14-25 year olds, I have found that the focus on the SDGs provides an added incentive for applicants to consider how to use the technology and tools of industry 4.0 to tackle real world problems. Similarly, my approach in HE, facilitating workshops for those wanting to start their own business, has benefited immensely from evidencing Sustainia100 projects related to the SDGs since 2016. Often, I have found students initially unaware of the SDGs, unaware of the hundreds of projects across the globe tackling SDG related problems, including in their own country; and then inspired to make a difference. My own experience as an eco-entrepreneur clearly also helps – as I have the mindset to tackle SDG related problems and the experience in developing several social and eco related projects.

What do we mean by mindset? Sustainability mindset is operationally defined (Moon *et al*, 2019) as: the empathy and compassion necessary to appreciate the plight of other people and in broader terms 'the planet'; and then connecting these to real problems in nature such as climate change. The definition is based on the piloting of a new hybrid measure based on three sub-scales: empathy, compassion and connectedness to nature. Each of these scales is reported in the literature independently of the other. We adapted the scales and tested them as a hybrid measure of sustainability mindset. Results of the pilot provide support for the measure; and implications for how we deliver educational programmes. For example, we need more social entrepreneurs and more eco entrepreneurs. Yet, many enterprise and entrepreneurship programmes in universities tend to regard most, if not all, of their students as traditional entrepreneurs (massification, commodification?) for exploiting rather than conserving resources, and profit maximising rather than having social or environmental goals. By reflecting on their mindset, students have the opportunity to change their aspirations from just wanting to make as much money as possible in the shortest time period and with limited concern for people or the planet.

There is still an important role for universities to provide essential knowledge and skills. However, normally on new lecturer training and development programmes (e.g. PGCHE) the acronym KSA is cited (Knowledge, Skills, Attitudes); yet we appear to have forgotten how to change attitudes. Fundamental knowledge in a subject is still tested in formal assignments, tests and exams. Skills are evaluated in workshops and other practical sessions e.g. presentations, simulations, real world problem-solving. However, attitudes, how do we develop and assess those? Traditional academics can inspire students through their knowledge of a subject. Practitioners or pracademics inspire students based on their real-world experience. Yet, most HEIs still adopt progression and promotion systems based on traditional academic performance i.e. publications and funding bids.

HE policy reform

Universities rarely officially recognise excellent teachers nor inspiring practitioners. There are exceptions, and the recent Teaching Excellence Framework (TEF, 2018) in the UK, following along in the wake of the Research Excellence Framework (REF), provides examples of how TEF 'gold' award winners have introduced systems to recognise and reward Teaching Excellence. The Knowledge Excellence Framework (KEF) similarly aspires to recognise and reward practitioner excellence.

The 'excellence movement' though has a chequered history. Excellence to one can be different from excellence to another. According to Kingston (1986) the "excellence movement" in education places a pronounced emphasis on "rigor," "standards," and a "core" curriculum of "basic" studies. Whilst the paper by Kingston focuses on the American education system, the concerns apply to education more broadly including higher education; basically, anywhere that introduces "excellence" as a key concept. The author suggests that the excellence movement is typified by the introduction of a general curriculum based on core cognitive elements. By having a common curriculum there can be national standards and comparisons between providers.

The downside is that difference, diversity, more creative approaches, new approaches, can all be ironed out; as they do not fit neatly into the common framework. Similarly, with REF, TEF and KEF the intention is to improve standards across the board. However, variation within the frameworks could be limited. Is there space for disruptive, more radical, better approaches by adopting such frameworks too rigorously, if at all? Clearly there is a need for standards. Nevertheless, standardisation should not breed out creativity and innovation; the

The University of the Future

very things we need to tackle the SDGs. The affective and conative is as important as the cognitive.

What evidence is there of the impact of REF, TEF and KEF? Ridley (2018) recognises the UK government purpose of these frameworks as to increase UK productivity; but quotes Jo Johnson, Minister of State for Universities and Science in 2015 as saying: "high-quality publications do not by themselves guarantee impact in the world at large", nor is there "a simple linear relationship between academic excellence and economic growth." Thus, Ridley suggests that REF, TEF and KEF should be abolished and replaced with a 'cradle to cradle' national education service. And Ridley cites the introduction of 'marketisation' under a Tory-led coalition government with David Willetts as Minister of State responsible at the time, 2010-2014; and that Willetts recalled angry students shouting 'we are not consumers' in his memoirs (Willetts, 2017).

The background to the above reforms is usefully reviewed by Ridley (2018) who cites Figure 2. as showing how the impetus behind much of the policy was the desire to increase business-university collaboration (see Review of Business-University Collaboration by Dowling, 2015).

Figure 2: Recent Reviews addressing Business-University Collaboration, Dowling Review 2015

The 'Dowling Review' highlighted the top ten barriers to Business-University collaboration, see Figure 3. And number one on the list of barriers for universities is stated as "University metrics, including the REF, prioritise the production of high-quality publications (p. 27). And the third obstacle highlighted is "Other pressures on academic time (teaching and research) limit resources for collaboration." Thus, it seems there is some support for the view of Ridley (2018) that TEF and REF are not ideal instruments to promote collaboration with business. Will KEF be able to plug the gap? Dowling says that critical to success will be 'strong and trusting personal relationships.'

Rank	Top ten barriers for **business**	Rank	Top ten barriers for **universities**
1	IP and other contract negotiations are difficult to complete, processes difficult to navigate, or take too long	1	University metrics, including the REF, prioritise the production of high-quality publications
2	Business find it difficult to identify academic partners or where academic capability lies	2	IP and other contract negotiations are difficult to complete, processes difficult to navigate, or take too long
3	Business and academia operate to different timescales	3	Other pressures on academic time (teaching and research) limit resources for collaboration
4	Lack of funding	4	Lack of funding
=5	Lack of alignment of objectives: tension between business and university needs or objectives	=5	Collaborative experience not valued as part of academic career progression
=5	Lack of trust or mutual understanding	=5	Lack of time/resource for networking or project development
=7	Businesses focus on the short term, rather than long term R&D	=7	Business and academia operate to different timescales
=7	Other funding issues (for example, SME eligibility, subjects within scope)	=7	Tension between academic desire to publish work, and business concerns about competition
9	Low overall levels of business investment in R&D, including a lack of absorptive capacity	9	Lack of trust or mutual understanding
10	Lack of understanding within business of potential benefits of working with universities	10	Low overall levels of business investment in R&D, including a lack of absorptive capacity

Figure 3: Top ten barriers to Business-University collaboration, (*Source, Dowling Review, 2015*).

Placing renewed emphasis on ethics and sustainability

According to Dowling (2015: 29) the more recent inclusion of 'Impact' has been broadly welcomed as a means of stimulating universities to articulate and ultimately improve the translation of their research into social, environmental or economic benefits. (Is this more than a nod towards triple bottom line evaluation?). Along with the stated need above, to develop strong and trusting personal relationships, the stage is set for a key emphasis on ethics and sustainability. However, Dowling concludes that the stimulation of more positive attitudes by academics towards collaboration with business requires more explicit recognition for staffs who have moved between industry and academia. Especially as there is a perception that "spending time in industry is damaging to an academic career path" (p. 30).

Certainly, the introduction of TEF, REF and now KEF do appear to have created new 'silos' in universities; with staff mapped to new career pathways and forced to choose between Teaching, Research or Practice with concomitant implications for performance appraisal, staff development and career progression. Therefore, the barriers identified by Dowling need to be broken down for more collaborative conditions to exist between colleagues on different pathways and for effective collaboration with external organisations. Without the breaking down of these barriers then 'elitism' can prevail with colleagues on each pathway perceiving that their pathway is more important than another; or deserving more recognition than another.

In fact, in terms of fee income, for most universities the highest revenue earner is teaching not research (50% and 8% respectively, excluding UK government, (Universities UK 2018) see Figure 4. Yet, according to the Guardian (2017) university teaching staff complain they are paid less than researchers and have inferior contracts. This is based on research in 'Russell Group' universities involving interviews of 51 staff, by Bamber *et al* (2017) who found that teaching-only staff felt they were made to feel second-class citizens. In fact, universities in their study were found to offload heavy teaching allocations to teaching-only staff to give researchers more time to publish.

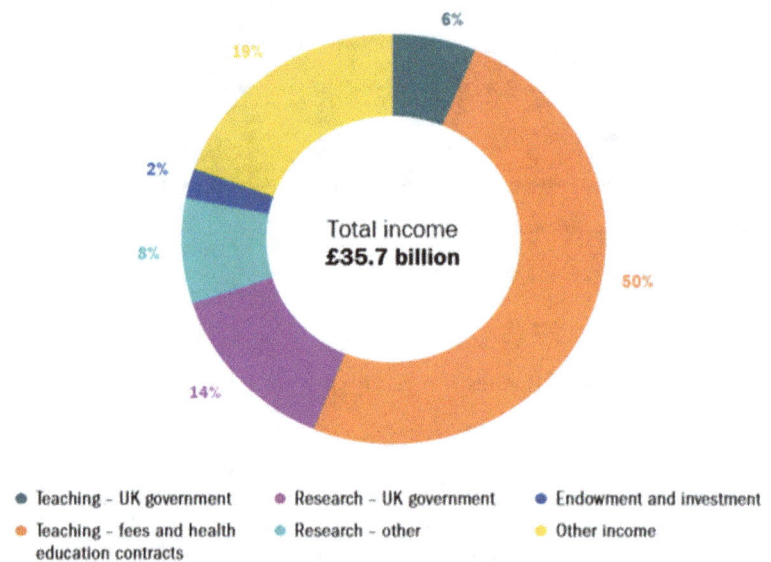

Figure 4: Total income to UK higher education institutions, 2016-2017 (*Source, Universities UK (2018:31)*).

This suggests that the introduction of the new metrics does not appear to have led to culture change in terms of more collaborative and trusting working relationships between colleagues. Whereas, Apostolopoulos *et al* (2018) argue that developing 'the entrepreneurial university' can be an engine for sustainable development. Importantly, they recognise that "the element of staff and students is the internal driver of achieving a sustainable transformation as there is a need for an organisational culture which will be commonly accepted…This highlights the importance of taking a more holistic approach to governance, and the significance of academic-business partnerships and knowledge…'co-creation for sustainability'…with entrepreneurship regarded as a transformative driver towards sustainable development (p.360-361).

Using data underpinning the 2018 SDG Index these authors found a positive correlation in the data between the existence of a strong HE-sector and progress towards the SDGs. However, the correlation is in most cases weak which suggests that more needs to be done by HEIs to focus on sustainable development. The authors conclude: that The SDG index and the data that underpin it are a valuable metric of the road towards entrepreneurial universities and by implication achievement of the UN SDGs (p.367).

The effective governance of HEIs is also highlighted by Moon *et al* (2018) who refer to the IARU (2016) 'Green Guide for Universities' as an example of a call for a more holistic approach to governing sustainable development. The guide includes advise on sustainable campus organisation, campus-wide operations, buildings, laboratories, green purchasing, transport, communication, employee and student engagement. This means that piecemeal or bolt-on approaches to sustainable development in universities are unlikely to provide the comprehensive approach needed to ensure that the entire university is committed to achieving real change in their practices. In fact, there is concern that without such a holistic approach, universities could be subject to legitimacy risks i.e. questioning their very existence if they are not seen to be tackling societal issues and problems (Snelson-Powell *et al.*, 2016).

Yong-Hak (2019) recognises the power of academic institutions to look ahead, to mobilise knowledge and to be truth-seekers in the age of sustainable development. Power though is a double-edged sword. On the one side institutionalised practices are resilient and able to withstand short-term pressures. On the other side, institutions are less flexible and adaptable to change. For example, technical knowledge and skills are needed for employability of graduates today. However, industries can change rapidly; and university programmes can be quickly out of date.

Universities and the green economy

The rise of the 'green economy' is a case in point. According to Eurostat (2018) between 2000 and 2014, employment and value added in the environmental economy across Europe grew considerably faster than employment in the overall economy and gross domestic product (GDP); and the latest figures from ONS (2018) confirm UK low carbon and renewable energy economy grew five per cent in 2016, outpacing the 1.8 per cent growth of the wider economy. This means that the green economy provided more jobs than automotive engineering, IT and Telecoms together. Have universities adapted to these changes? Have they introduced courses on the green economy? What new skills, knowledge and attitudes are being developed in universities to cater for the transition to the green economy? Moon (2015) identified skills needed in the green economy (Table 2.).

Table 2: Skills needed in the green economy

Generic skills	Specific skills
Resource efficiency	• Resource efficient business models • Carbon and natural environment accounting • Eco design and production • Eco project management
Low carbon	• Sustainable engineering and renewables including wind solar and marine • Technicians for retrofitting premises with energy efficiency measures • Operators to reduce vehicle emissions, building emissions, water consumption
Climate resilience	• Modelling and projections of climate change • Risk Management
Skills to manage natural assets	• Accounting for natural environment • Environmental Impact Assessments • Environmental legislation targets • Ecosystem design and management • Land use planning
Sectoral	• Specific skills
All sectors	• Lifecycle analysis/costing, risk analysis and management • Sustainable/carbon procurement
Construction	• Sustainable Architecture, CAD eco design and build, BREEAM, 'Green Deal', insulation and thermal performance
Building Services Engineering, Property Management	• Energy Performance of Buildings, smart metering, renewables
Chemicals and pharma, oil and gas	• Green chemicals, biofuels, additives, etc.
Food and drink manufacturing	• Sustainable farming and food /drink production
Renewables	• Sustainable engineering
Transport	• Eco-designers, sustainable engineering, freight logistics, 'SAFED', green purchasing
Biomass/biofuel/anaerobic digestion	• Green chemical and process engineers
Carbon Capture & Storage	• Sustainable engineering
Waste & Water	• Resource efficiency engineers and technicians
Energy supply and utilities	• Energy conservation and management, micro generation, geologists and engineers concerned about the environment
Automotive Industry	• Ultra-Low Carbon Vehicle design, hybrid/electric, etc.
Land management	• Sustainable land use, flood risk
Other	• FE & HE sustainability and eco lecturers, trainers, etc. Eco-school assessors; sustainability teachers

This is not an exhaustive list but an attempt to indicate that all industries will have to change and adapt to the new skill sets required; including the education industry. At present, business schools in universities are too slow to introduce new programmes that are at the leading edge of these changes; and they tend to focus on the more generic skills needed across industries i.e. skills needed in key functional areas such as law, marketing, accounting, and human resources. These skills will still be needed; but there is little to suggest that the new contexts of the green economy and Industry 4.0 applications are leading to vastly more creative and innovative approaches to pedagogy in all but a few isolated examples.

In fact, Table 2. is rather descriptive in nature and presents a sort of 'shopping list' of skills needed with little basis for policy development other than to include sessions on various sustainability topics within existing educational courses and training programmes. For example, there is a rather confused mix of what could be called 'behavioural' skills and 'cognitive' competences; and little to evidence the lateral thinking, creativity, innovation, compassion and empathy needed by social and ecopreneurs in particular. Yet guidelines to introduce Education for Sustainable Development (ESD) into the curriculum have been around for some time. QAA (2014) calls for integration of sustainability across the curriculum. This does not mean 'deleting' current courses in sustainability but using those courses as catalysts to ensure that all modules include sufficient emphasis on ethics and sustainability.

TEF states that all graduates should be prepared to make a strong contribution to society, economy and the environment (another nod to triple bottom line thinking?). However, REF and KEF appear to be lagging behind in this regard. With TEF there is a call to focus on graduate outcomes; but this does not explicitly include the environment; and with KEF the focus is on economic indicators such as the number of start-ups and not on the socio-economic or non-economic indicators such as the social or the environmental. Yet, Keele University Chancellor since 2012, Sir Jonathon Porritt, presented a lecture in January 2019 highlighting the next ten years as the most critical decade in humankind's short history (Keele University, 2019).

Further, it is also pertinent to note that Porritt's inaugural address as Chancellor in 2012 was entitled: 'Sustainability and The Future of Capitalism!' By implication it seems capitalism per se has not solved the climate crisis thus far. In 2019 the speech of Greta Thunberg in the UK lead to the UK Parliament declaring a climate emergency! This followed months of demonstrations by school children in cities across the globe in support of Greta who had decided to strike from school to lobby the Swedish Parliament; and weeks of climate activism galvanised by those using the 'Extinction Rebellion' logo indicating that time to save the earth is running out.

The IPCC report (2018) strengthened the scientific case for taking action sooner rather than later; and programmes such as Blue Planet I and II with David Attenborough (BBC, 2018) were stark in communicating alarming images of the damaging effects of plastic on marine life. Students too have taken part in climate demonstrations. In Palma, Mallorca, I joined students, school children and families marching through the streets to City Hall one Friday; and then chalked drawings in Place Major on another occasion – witnessing another peaceful protest of kids and their parents. In 2019 I introduced the first two 'plastic free' modules at Middlesex University.

Successive surveys are revealing that students want Universities to do more to tackle climate change with specific student campaigns to disinvest from fossil fuels starting to have an impact; and independent programmes to advise universities how to implement changes are starting to take a foothold (NUS Responsible Futures, 2018). However, only a minority of universities across the globe have signed the UN Higher Education Sustainability Initiative (HESI); and even less have committed to realising more than SDG#4 Education (Moon *et al*, 2018). Thus, universities need to do a great deal more to ensure they are fully committed to achieving the SDGs in full (see Figure 5.).

Figure 5: The UN Sustainable Development Goals

In fact, when Moon *et al* (2018) conducted their survey of over 300 HEIs there wasn't a single university committed to achieving SDG#1 No Poverty. Thus, it seems that ongoing tensions in HE could be hampering the ability of universities to tackle key universal problems (see Table 1.).

In conclusion

Tensions in HEIs prevail. They exist in all organisations. However, this chapter has distinguished HEIs as distinct forms of organisation; with their ability to confer degrees. The 'marketisation' of HE has opened up the label 'university' to a myriad of institutional forms; and the original ethos of the university as an independent centre of learning to promote academic freedom (see Magna Charta, 2019) has been pressured by the adoption of managerialist principles and practices such as those associated with the 'excellence movement'.

These tensions (Table 1.) provide an element of freedom and flexibility for each university to decide how best to organise itself in the educational industry to both survive as independent businesses; and to attract students (customers?) by offering their own brand of degree (product?). However, the tensions identified reveal that there are significant risks in getting this offering right; for both students and staffs. And when the HEI does not get it right then this tension can lead to turmoil.

Ethics, Sustainability and 95 Theses for Higher Education Reform

Whilst the recent trends in the UK have been related to 'neoliberalism' influences (Radice, 2013), the purpose of this paper has not been to focus on political support. Clearly, higher education policy has had a significant influence on the way universities are run. The purpose of this chapter though has been to highlight the critical role that universities can play in sustainable development. In fact, by focussing on the UN Sustainable Development Goals (SDGs) universities have an opportunity to repurpose their missions around tackling the most pressing societal issues and problems; and this requires change from within.

With the rise of 'marketisation' and 'managerialism' universities can lose sight of their true mission and purpose. By acting as businesses universities can lose their distinctive character as places of independent learning. With increasing dependence on the market to attract students' universities can become over reliant on league tables and ratings of excellence. What matters more is that students develop the mindset to tackle poverty, inequality, and environmental degradation.

Government policy can provide the impetus and framework for this to happen. To what extent this should be mandated is an important question that can be addressed when one considers the university as part of a broader ecosystem, see Figure 6. Significantly this places any university as part of society not independent of it. The 'laboratory' becomes a 'living laboratory' wherein control of variables is not the main purpose but a preparatory tool for testing in the real world. Science is thus not the end; it is the beginning. And scientists need to consider the applied nature of their work much more actively than ever before.

According to Mazzarol *et al* (2016) 'the entrepreneurial ecosystem framework (see Figure 6.) provides a helpful structure for analysis of the many factors that contribute to economic growth and development' (citing Isenberg, 2010; ANDE, 2013; WEF, 2013).

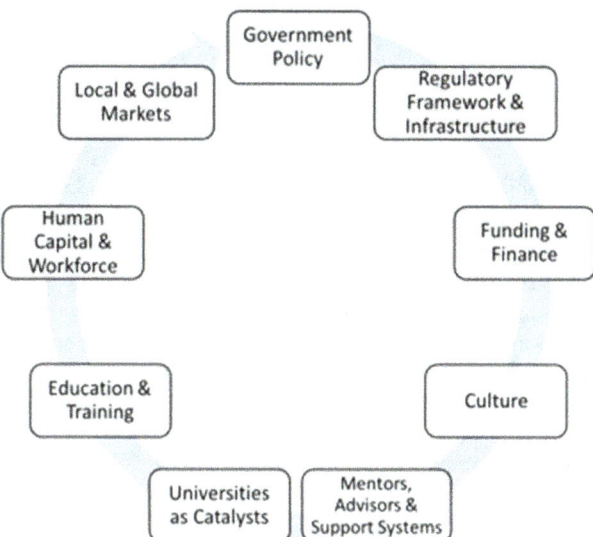

Figure 6: Components of the entrepreneurial ecosystem, (Mazzarol, 2014, adapted from Isenberg 2010, WEF, 2013 in Clark *et al*, 2016)

The University of the Future

The authors use Isenberg's description of the six core domains of the entrepreneurial ecosystem: government policy, the regulatory framework and infrastructure; funding and finance; culture; mentors, advisors and support systems; educational institutions, human capital and workforce as well as local and global markets. However, the main emphasis of their paper is on economic growth and development rather than socio-economic growth and sustainable development; or even de-growth. The authors usefully use data from the Global Innovation Index (GII) to show a country's international performance of their National Innovation Systems (NIS). However, Apostolopoulos *et al* (2018) go further and use data from the Sustainable Development Index (SDI) to show the interconnections between Universities and sustainable development (Figure 9.).

An excellent image of the university as part of a broader societal ecosystem is provided by Ohio State University which aims to become the healthiest university in the world (Figure 7.).

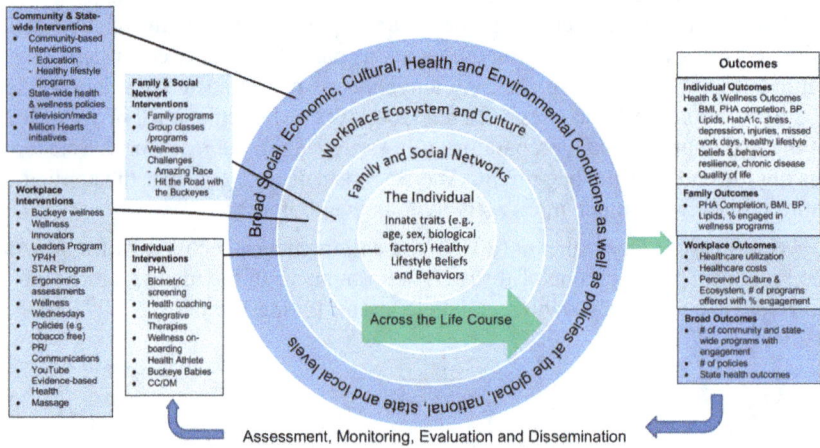

Figure 7: The Ohio State University – The Social-Ecological Framework

Here the centre of the ecosystem is the individual; with broader social, environmental, economic, cultural, health and environmental conditions on the outer rim. An alternative image is provided by Ferdandez (2015) who maps the social innovation ecosystem in the cultural heritage field (see Figure 8.) with universities portrayed as just one part of this broader ecosystem. This image also includes a process diagram in the form of a web which identifies the need for 'new' ways of thinking and practices. What is unique though about the ecosystem model provided by Apostolopoulos *et al* (2018) is that the SDGs are placed at the centre of the nexus of transformation. The informed conceptualisation of the sustainable entrepreneurial university is born (see Figure 9.); placing universities as central catalysts in sustainable development.

Ethics, Sustainability and 95 Theses for Higher Education Reform

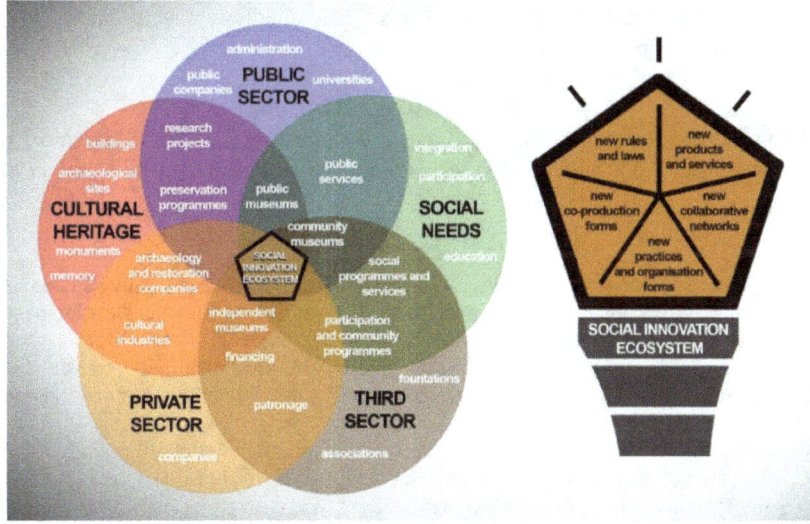

Figure 8: Map of sectors and factors in whose confluence social innovation ecosystem is - in the cultural heritage field, Fernandez, 2015

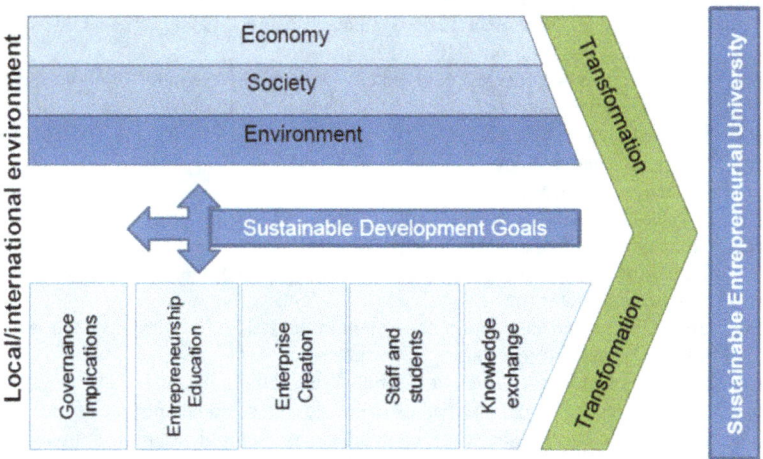

Figure 9: Sustainable Entrepreneurial University Framework, (Apostolopoulos *et al* 2018)

This chapter has reviewed some of the history to the foundation of universities and their contemporary development; and highlighted 'tensions' that universities have to face today. Some universities are breaking free of the mould of outdated institutionalised practices that fail to regard sustainable development as core to their mission and purpose. The repurposing of universities around the UN Sustainable Development Goals (SDGs) provides an opportunity to transform mindsets of staffs, students and practices. The power of universities should be addressed to such goals, generating new knowledge but through more holistic approaches as part of a broader ecosystem wherein they open themselves up to seeking truth in ethical and sustainable ways. This is likely to develop more trusting relationships between all stakeholders.

Acknowledgement

Preliminary research supporting this paper was funded by Enterprise Educators UK and discussed in Moon *et al* (2018), Apostolopoulos *et al* (2018), and Moon *et al* (2019).

References

Apostolopoulos, N., Moon, CJ., Walmsley, A., 2018, The entrepreneurial university as an engine for sustainable development, Int. J. Innovation and Regional Development, Vol. 8, No. 4, 2018: 358-372. https://doi.org/10.1504/IJIRD.2018.097455.

Bamber, M., Allen-Collinson, J., McCormack, J., (2017) Occupational limbo, transitional liminality and permanent liminality: New conceptual distinctions. Human Relations, 70 (12). pp. 1514-1537. ISSN 0018-7267.

BBC, 2018, Blue Planet I and II, https://www.bbc.co.uk/programmes/p04tjbtx

BBC, 2019, Graduate gets £60k payout over 'false advertising' claim, https://www.bbc.co.uk/news/uk-48490572

Britannica, 2019, University, https://www.britannica.com/topic/university.

CASE, 2018, Competencies for sustainable socio-economic development, CASE Knowledge Alliance, https://www.case-ka.eu/

Clark, D., McKeown, T., Battisti, M., (Eds.) 2016, Rhetoric and Reality. Building Vibrant and Sustainable Entrepreneurial Ecosystems, SEAANZ Book Series, Tilde Publishing and Distribution. VIC. Australia.

Dowling, 2015; The Dowling Review of Business-University Research Collaborations, July 2015, https://www.raeng.org.uk/publications/reports/the-dowling-review-of-business-university-research

Enactus; 2019, www.enactusuk.org

Enterprise Educators (2019) www.enterprise.ac.uk

EU., 2019, https://universitiesofthefuture.eu/

Eurostat, 2018, Published Feb 8th, 2018. http://ec.europa.eu/eurostat/statistics-explained/index.php/Environmental_economy_-_employment_and_growth

F Factor, 2019, https://ffactor.me/

Fernandez, JF., 2015. Social innovation ecosystem in the field of cultural heritage: a definition, Hesiod Project Papers, www.hesiod.eu.

Fuster, E., Padilla-Meléndez, A., Lockett, N., del-Águila-Obraa, R., 2019, The emerging role of university spin-off companies in developing regional entrepreneurial university ecosystems: The case of Andalusia, Technological Forecasting and Social Change, Volume 141, April 2019, Pages 219-231.

Guardian, The, 2017, https://www.theguardian.com/education/2017/aug/22/university-teaching-staff-pay-research

Harris, D., 2005, Key Concepts in Leisure Studies, Sage Publications Ltd.

IARU., 2016, Green Guide for Universities. International Association of Research Universities.

IPCC., 2018, https://www.ipcc.ch/2018/10/08/summary-for-policymakers-of-ipcc-special-report-on-global-warming-of-1-5c-approved-by-governments/

Keele University, 2019., Jonathon Poritt, https://www.keele.ac.uk/discover/news/2019/january/special-lecture/jonathon-porritt.php

Kingston, PW; 1986, Theory at risk: Accounting for the excellence movement, Sociological Forum

September 1986, Volume 1, Issue 4, pp 632–656.

Magna Charta, 2019, Observatory Magna Charter Universitatum, http://www.magna-charta.org/

Mazzarol, T; Battisti, M; Clark, D; 2016, The role of universities as catalysts within entrepreneurial ecosystems, in Rhetoric and reality: Building vibrant and sustainable entrepreneurial ecosystems, Publisher: Tilde University Press, Editors: Clark, D., McKeown, T., Battisti, M., 2016. https://www.researchgate.net/publication/307925580_The_role_of_universities_as_catalysts_within_entrepreneurial_ecosystems

Mok, KH., Jiang, J., 2016, Massification of higher education: challenges for admissions and graduate employment in China, Centre for Global Higher Education working paper series, Working paper no. 5 July 2016, ESRC and HEFCE. https://www.researchcghe.org/perch/resources/publications/wp5.pdf

Moon, C.J., 2015, Green Universities and Eco-Friendly Learning: From League Tables to Eco Entrepreneurship Education, European Conference on Innovation & Entrepreneurship 2015. https://www.researchgate.net/profile/Christopher_J_Moon/contributions

Moon, CJ., Walmsley, A., Apostolopoulos, N., 2018, Governance implications of the UN higher education sustainability initiative, Corporate Governance: The International Journal of Business in Society, Vol. 18 Issue: 4, pp.624-634, https://doi.org/10.1108/CG-01-2018-0020

Moon, CJ., 2018, 95 theses for reforming Higher Education Institutions. Are HEIs key to a sustainable society? AdvanceHE, https://www.heacademy.ac.uk/knowledge-hub/95-theses-reforming-higher-education-are-heis-catalysts-sustainable-society.

Moon, CJ., Walmsley, A., Apostolopoulos, N., 2019, The mindset of eco and social entrepreneurs: piloting a new measure of 'sustainability mindset' ECIE 2019. https://www.researchgate.net/profile/Christopher_J_Moon/contributions

NUS, 2018, Responsible Futures, www.nus.org.uk/responsiblefutures.

ONS, 2018, Low carbon and renewable energy economy, UK, 2015 and 2016, Office for National Statistics, UK.

QAA, 2014, Education for Sustainable Development, Guidance for UK higher education providers, June 2014, QAA. https://www.qaa.ac.uk/docs/qaa/quality-code/education-sustainable-development-guidance-june-14.pdf?sfvrsn=1c46f981_8

Radice, H., 2013, How We Got Here: UK Higher Education under Neoliberalism, ACME: An International E-Journal for Critical Geographies, 2013, 12 (3), 407-418.

Ridley, D., 2018, HE Marketisation, https://hemarketisation.wordpress.com/2018/01/16/willetts-the-conqueror-introduction/

Snelson-Powell, A., Grosvold, J., Millington, A., (2016), Business School Legitimacy and the Challenge of

Sustainability: A Fuzzy Set Analysis of Institutional Decoupling, Academy of Management Learning & Education, Vol. 15, No. 4, 703-723.

SULITEST, 2016, https://www.sulitest.org/en/index.html

Sustainia 100. 2019, A Guide to 100 Sustainable Solutions, ISSN: 2246-6479.

TEF, 2018, TEF Outcomes, https://www.officeforstudents.org.uk/advice-and-guidance/teaching/tef-outcomes/#/

THE, 2019a, World University Rankings 2019, https://www.timeshighereducation.com/world-university-rankings/2019/

THE, 2019b, THE developing ranking based on Sustainable Development Goals, https://www.timeshighereducation.com/news/developing-ranking-based-sustainable-development-goals

Universities UK, 2018, Patterns and Trends in UK Higher Education, https://www.universitiesuk.ac.uk/facts-and-stats/data-and-analysis/Documents/patterns-and-trends-in-uk-higher-education-2018.pdf

Willetts, D. 2017, A University Education. Oxford: Oxford University Press
Williams, J., 2015, If higher education has become commodified, what are some of the consequences? https://www.researchgate.net/post/If_higher_education_has_become_commodified_what_are_some_of_the_consequences
Yong-Hak, K., 2019, Welcome address to the Global Engagement & Empowerment Forum on Sustainable Development (GEEF) 2019, President of Yonsei University, South Korea, 2019, https://www.geef-sd.org:446/html/

Chris Moon is Senior Lecturer in eco-entrepreneurship at Middlesex University, London, and visiting Professor at two other universities. In 2019 he was 'F Factor' judge, the UK's premier competition for 14-25-year-olds; lead judge of the international Innovation and Entrepreneurship Teaching Excellence awards; and received an Outstanding Teacher Award 2019 for innovation and entrepreneurship.

10

Popular Media and Ethical Business Schools of the Future

Lakshmi Balachandran Nair
Methodology & Statistics Department, Utrecht University, The Netherlands

Introduction

Rose: What was it you wanted to discuss about my teaching?
Gregory: I have many questions, the first of which is: How do you get them to stay?

The quotation above is from the 1996 movie "*The mirror has two faces*" (Streisand et al., 1996), which portrays the life and romances of two college professors, Gregory and Rose Larkin. The movie shows how Gregory's students are constantly bored or distracted, whereas Rose's students are always shown as engaged and enthusiastic. At two different points in the movie, Gregory asks for advice from Rose regarding his teaching, to which Rose replies "Well, try telling [them] a story". In this chapter, we follow Rose's advice and discuss how telling a story, showing a movie/television clip, or playing a game can enhance the learning experience of students in business schools and prepare them to be change agents for a sustainable and ethical social environment.

The concept of teaching with movies is not new. In fact, most of us might still remember how our elementary school teachers used to play a movie in the classroom. The difference between this traditional use of movies in the classroom and the idea I put forth in this chapter is two-fold. Firstly, I suggest the use of different types of popular media (including, but not limited to movies). Secondly, this use is not just for illustrating a concept but also for familiarizing students with a specific situation and making them critically think of ways to engage in the underlying issue. For example, let us consider the topic of sustainability. Today's generation is very familiar with the concept of sustainability, which is one of the hottest ethical topics of our current society. However, learning to handle sustainability issues hands-on might require more practice than a mere understanding of the involved concepts and the use of popular media is not limited to sustainability-based education alone. However, given that it is a matter of timely relevance in our society, this chapter will predominantly focus on it.

Business schools of the future and sustainability

Our society is fast changing. Many of the problems faced by previous generations have been replaced by new ones. New phenomena and novel ways of handling them are arising every day. Universities and schools have the responsibility to evolve along with the dynamic society and at the same time, ensure that this evolution is contributing to the societal good. One such area of interest is sustainability. As environmental degradation has attained unprecedented magnitude in human history, societies are becoming more and more sensitized about sustainability. This awareness about sustainability in society is reflected in the way people and businesses conduct their day to day functions. Reducing pollution, conserving natural resources, and protecting the environment are hot topics not only for beta scientists, but also for businesses (Schaper, 2002).

Recently, business and management scholars have started researching strategies to ensure ecological sustainability without compromising firm profitability (Daily and Huang, 2001). In parallel, many businesses have started developing strategies for environmental management (Brockhoff et al., 1999). This overzealous pursuit of sustainability has even become a competitive advantage, with companies incorporating sustainability-related responsibilities into several management functions including green operations (Kleindorfer et al., 2005), supply chain management (Srivastava, 2007), and human resource management (Renwick et al., 2008).

As a rejoinder to this demand for a sustainable workforce, business schools have also started integrating sustainability into their teaching and research practices (Ploum et al., 2018). Business schools are researching strategies to ensure ecological sustainability, providing courses and training on environmental management, and promoting green behaviour through rewards. Some business schools are also offering MBA programs which infuse sustainability concepts throughout their curriculum (Gloudeman, 2018). The goal of this sustainability-oriented education is enabling business and management students to acquire information, generate knowledge, develop competencies, and reflect on courses of action in order to ensure long-term sustainable development (Rieckmann, 2012). By doing so, business schools aim to develop student competencies to respond to real-world sustainability problems and opportunities (Dale and Newman, 2005; Ploum et al., 2018).

Challenges encountered business and management education

Educating the managers of the future to think and act in a sustainable manner is not plain sailing. Often times, sustainability-oriented education is too abstract or decontextualized (Delamare Le Deist and Winterton, 2005). This generic approach to sustainability-oriented education does not take into account the specific work environments in which sustainability challenges and tasks occur (Hesselbarth and Schaltegger, 2004). For instance, since the introduction and flourish of platform economies and remote workforces, the business workforce has been changing rapidly. Let us consider gig economies, i.e., the free market systems which started off with Uber. This system was welcomed by both the workers and companies as evidenced by its exponential popularity (Bureau of Labour Statistics, 2014).

Notwithstanding its popularity, a dark side of the gig economy has started to emerge, with companies such as Uber and Foodora being subjected to class action suits for a plethora of human resource management issues ranging from unfair dismissal to underpayment (McEncroe, 2018). The gig economy, it seems, has opened the door to a number of unethical or ethically grey areas. Furthermore, given their different business models and ways of functioning, sustainability activities in such environments might be completely different when compared to traditional companies. In this scenario, how can business schools ensure that their students are learning about the ethical climate involved in gig economies? How can they equip their students to critically think about any sustainability dilemmas and come up with solutions or courses of action? And last but not least, how do they ensure a group of 21st century young adults with short attention spans and a need for constant entertainment comprehend the less obvious nuances of sustainability? It is in this context that popular media can play a role.

Use of popular media in business and management education

In this chapter, I define popular media as the products of various mediums of communication in popular culture; namely stories, novels, movies, television shows, and games (Stack & Kelly, 2006). Popular media can be good at capturing our ever-changing social world and so using this in teaching can help students understand and critically analyze what is actually going on around them. Table 1 provides some examples of popular media which are relevant for ethical and sustainable business and management education.

Table 1: Examples of popular media relevant for ethical and sustainable business and management education

Popular media	Name	Potential topics	References
Stories/novels	Harry Potter	Ethical dilemmas and ethical perspectives in business and management research	Nair, in press -a; Rowling, 2000
Movies	The Circle		Bregman, 2017; Nair, 2019; Speilberg, 2002
	Catch me if you can	Role of reflexivity in business and management research	
TV shows	Crocodile (Black mirror)	Sustainability and its affordability by low-income groups	Netflix, 2017

For example, in the movie 'The circle' (Bregman, 2017) the concept of privacy in the social media domain is discussed. To elaborate, in 'The circle' two different scenes show how the privacy of individuals is disturbed by the users of an app developed by a social media company. In one of the scenes, the individual whose privacy is violated is a convicted felon. In the other scene, it is an innocent citizen. When students watch the movie clips, they might have different ethical perspectives for each one of these situations. By deliberating on these differences and by elaborating on the involved ethical dilemmas in each situation, the teacher can facilitate classroom discussion and learning (Nair, 2019).

Similarly, popular media can also be used as a tool for exposing and familiarizing students with new sustainability-related scenarios which cannot be captured fully by traditional assignments or exam questions. Concurrently, students can be enabled to critically think about different ways of comprehending the involved situation and if relevant, possible courses of action to take. For example, the popular TV show named 'Black Mirror' (Brooker, 2011) portrays a series of dystopian scenarios which are based on real-life technological developments. To be more specific, one of the 'Black Mirror' episodes titled 'Crocodile' exposes a series of murders committed by one successful career woman. However, the episode also has an undertone. It points out how sustainability initiatives in today's world are luxuries affordable to the rich. The lower income groups have other, more immediate matters such as family finances to worry about (Mudede, 2018). By making students discuss this episode, the teacher can familiarize them with the ongoing affordability-sustainability debate. This discussion can also be further extended by deliberating on possible ways of making sustainability affordable and attractive to lower income groups.

Furthermore, popular media portray experiences in narrative forms, which require the students to expend less cognitive effort to understand than traditional instructional techniques (Jonassen and Hernandez-Serrano, 2002), which is a big advantage. Popular media invoke interest and enthusiasm in students. Consequentially, watching a movie clip or reading a short excerpt from a story as part of the course does not appear as exhausting work. This is particularly true for 21st century students, who are visually oriented and have short attention spans. From my own experience I have noticed that the students are more attentive and engaged in a classroom where popular media is used rather than in a classroom where they have to read a long case study or listen to a two-hour lecture. I discuss this student engagement in detail in the section below.

Student engagement

To understand the impact of using popular media in education, I collected data from students in two different Bachelor programs. The pilot test involved collecting data from three students of an international Bachelor program in liberal arts, to develop a few sensitizing concepts (Given, 2008) which would aid the development of a larger sample survey. The students of this particular course had to read a short excerpt from "Harry Potter and the Goblet of Fire" to critically discuss the topics of ethics and reflexivity in research. Afterwards, three random students were asked some semi-structured questions about whether the activity facilitated student engagement (and if so, how). The responses were collected anonymously and confidentially, to ensure the credibility of final results. The summary of responses from the pilot study are in Table 2.

Table 2: Summary of responses from pilot study

Respondent 1	Respondent 2	Respondent 3
• Creative • Practical • Real-life application of the topic • Interactive • Flexible answers • Exciting	• Good value (short excerpt -> detailed description) • Confirm and clarify understanding • Critically think of a situation • Exaggerated example • Fun Application	• Encourages class participation • Clear • Not realistic • Exaggerated example • Fun • Motivation

Adding to the pilot study, I conducted another round of data collection during a course for Bachelor students specializing in education and pedagogy. This sample was different from that of the pilot study in several ways. First of all, unlike the students from the liberal arts program, the students of this program were new to courses conducted in English. Secondly, the capacity of the classroom was also quite big (approximately 100 students on the day of the data collection) compared to the former (approximately 7 students on the day of the data collection). To make the activity even closer to real-life (rather than an "exaggerated" or "not realistic" example as mentioned by the pilot study participants), I chose the two aforementioned excerpts from the movie "The circle" to discuss the topics of ethics and reflexivity (Nair, 2019). Afterwards, I conducted a survey covering 5 main themes, which were developed and iteratively modified based on the responses from the pilot study. The survey responses are illustrated in Figure 1.

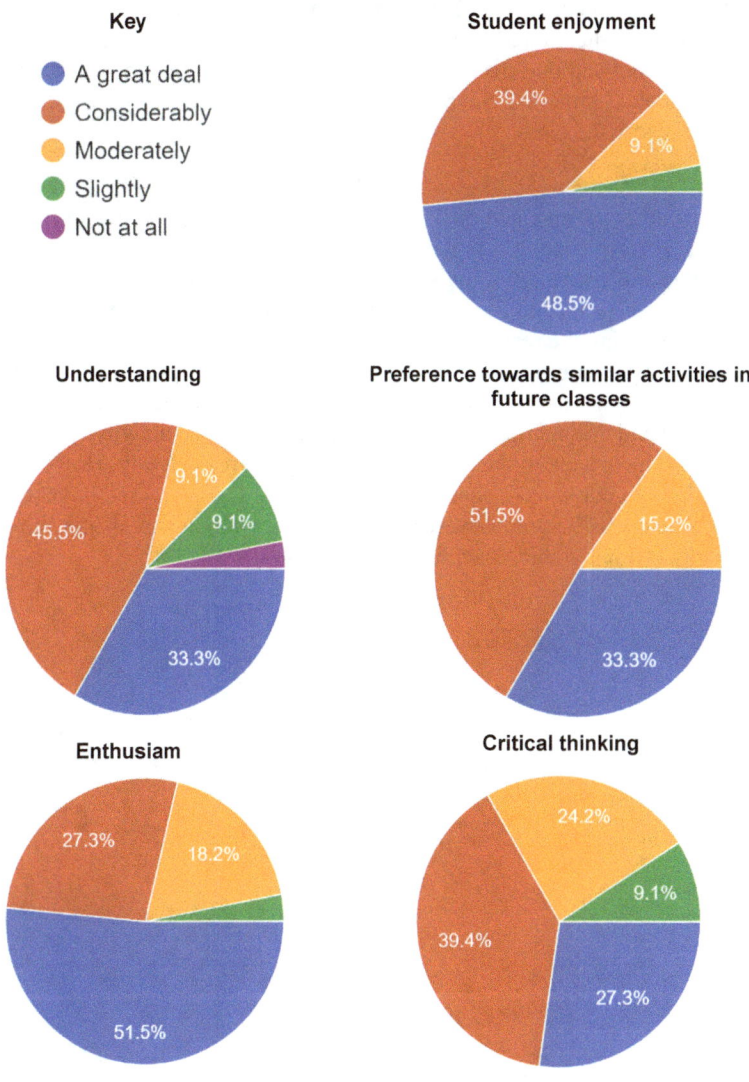

Figure 1: Survey responses

The themes included "enjoyment", "understanding", "critical thinking", "enthusiasm", and "preference towards having similar activities in future classes". For each theme, a five-point scale including the options "a great deal", "considerably", "moderately", "slightly" and "not at all" were provided along with an option to add any further open comments. A total number of 33 students participated in the study. Additionally, I also coded the open responses. These responses revealed that the students liked the activity because it involved a visual element, a comparison element, a concrete situation, a great example, a great movie, clarity of concepts, understandability, a real-life element, and a different take on ethics. The students also found the activity attractive, informative, practical, fun, dramatic, relatable, enthusiasm-invoking, interactive, active, illustrative, and mentioned that they 'just like it'. On a different note, some of the respondents noticed that the length of the movie clips were too long (altogether approximately 7 minutes), the movie was very weird, and that they already knew the topic before the class.

Student grades

To see whether the engagement exhibited by the students was also reflected in their academic performance, it was necessary to examine how well they translated the knowledge and critical thinking accumulated from the activity into their grades. This, however, proved to be difficult to determine rigorously since there was no way of comparing the results longitudinally or cross-sectionally. The students of this course were amongst the first ones in the Bachelor program and hence had no predecessors to use as a benchmark. Furthermore, we did not measure the knowledge and critical thinking of the students before the activity, so it was difficult to make a claim based on the after-activity results only. However, the final grades for the course were checked to see how the students fared in general (see Figure 2 below). The grades were awarded based on their scores in a short-answer type exam (which included application-level questions).

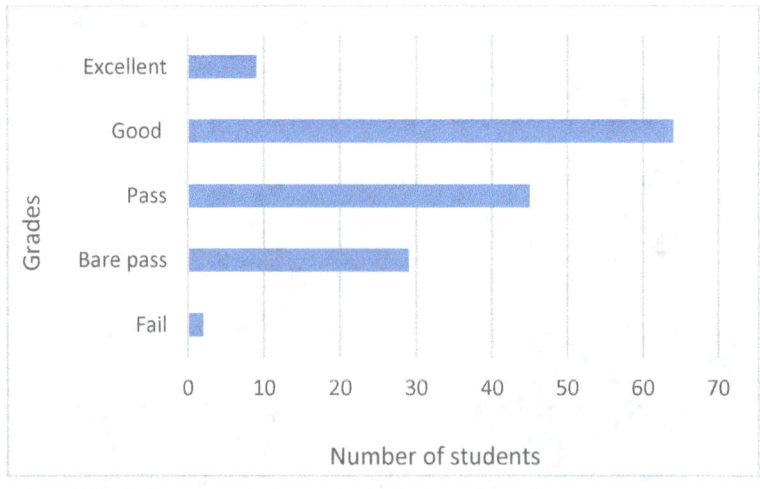

Where, Fail = F; Bare pass = D, Pass = C, Good = B, and Excellent = A

Figure 2: Grades of students from the Education and Pedagogical Sciences Bachelor program

The main limitation of the information provided in Figure 2 is that the data was collected from the Bachelor students of liberal arts as well as education and pedagogy programs rather than from a business school or a sustainability-based program. On the other hand, this data collection allowed us to understand that the use of popular media is well appreciated by students of this particular age group.

Conclusion

Sustainability requires long-term vision and focus. Preparing tomorrow's entrepreneurs and managers to critically think about various aspects of sustainability is one step in this direction. Being sustainable requires constant awareness about the environmental and societal changes going on around us. Sustainability-focused education should therefore focus on continuously developing and amending green practices that cater to the needs of the changing society and environment. As Carney (1845) articulates in her poem 'Little things', it is the little deeds, little grains of sand, and little drops of water that make mighty oceans and beauteous lands. Incorporating popular media of the period into business and management curriculum could be one such little way of developing a sustainable future workforce.

> Little drops of water,
> Little grains of sand,
> Make the mighty ocean
> And the beauteous land.
>
> Little deeds of kindness,
> Little words of love,
> Make our earth an Eden,
> Like the heavens above.
>
> Little seeds of mercy
> Sown by youthful hands,
> Grow to bless the nations
> Far in other lands.
>
> (Julia Abigail Fletcher Carney, 1845)

References

Barlow, S. (2015). Her Story [Interactive movie video game]. Retrieved 09 November 2018 from http://www.herstorygame.com/purchase/

Bregman, A. (Director) (2017). The circle. [Film] United States: Image Nation Abu Dhabi, Playtone, Likely Story, IM Global.

Brockhoff, K., Chakrabarti, A. K., & Kirchgeorg, M. (1999). Corporate strategies in environmental management. Research Technology Management, 42 (4), 26-30.

Brooker, C. (2011). Black mirror [Television series]. United Kingdom: Netflix.

Bureau of Labor Statistics. (2014). Self-employment: What to know to be your own boss. Retrieved from https://www.bls.gov/careeroutlook/2014/article/self-employment-what-to-know-to-be-your-own-boss.htm

Carney, J. (1845). Little Things. Little drops of water, Little grains of sand. Retrieved October 2, 2019, from https://hymnary.org/text/little_drops_of_water_little_grains_of_s.

Daily, B. F., & Huang, S. C. (2001). Achieving sustainability through attention to human resource factors in environmental management. International Journal of Operations & Production Management, 21 (12), 1539-1552.

Dale, A., & Newman, L. (2005). Sustainable development, education and literacy. International Journal of Sustainability in Higher Education, 6(4), 351-362.

Delamare Le Deist, F., & Winterton, J. (2005). What is competence. Human resource development international, 8(1), 27-46.

Given, L. M. (2008). The SAGE encyclopedia of qualitative research methods (Vols. 1-0). Thousand Oaks, CA: SAGE Publications, Inc. doi: 10.4135/9781412963909

Gloudeman, N. (2018, February 22). Is a green MBA worth your time and money? Retrieved from https://www.greenbiz.com/article/green-mba-worth-your-time-and-money.

Hesselbarth, C., & Schaltegger, S. (2014). Educating change agents for sustainability–learnings from the first sustainability management master of business administration. Journal of cleaner production, 62, 24-36.

Jonassen, D. H. & Hernandez-Serrano, J. (2002). Case-based reasoning and instructional design: Using stories to support problem solving. Educational Technology Research and Development, 50, 65-77.

King, R., & King, M. (2009). The good wife [Television series]. United States: CBS.

Kleindorfer, P. R., Singhal, K., & Van Wassenhove, L. N. (2005). Sustainable operations management. Production and operations management, 14(4), 482-492.

McEncroe, R. (2018). Gig Economy Workers Have Rights, Whether Companies like It or Not. Green Left Weekly, 19 Nov. 2018, www.greenleft.org.au/content/gig-economy-workers-have-rights-whether-companies-it-or-not.

Mudede, C. (2018, January 4). Black Mirror's "Crocodile" Savages Modernist Architecture, HALA-like Housing Advocates, and the Anti-Car Urbanist Ethos. Retrieved September 27, 2019, from https://www.thestranger.com/slog/2018/01/04/25678625/black-mirrors-crocodile-savages-modernist-architecture-hala-like-housing-advocates-and-the-anti-car-urbanist-ethos.

Nair L.B. (2019). Beyond fiction and science: Using stories, movies, and games to teach qualitative research. In Innovation in the Teaching of Research Methodology Excellence Awards: An Anthology of Case Histories 2019 (pp. 15-26). United Kingdom: Academic Conferences and Publishing International. ISBN: 978-1-912764-26-6.

Nair, L.B. (In press – a). Mischief unmanaged": Approaching ethics in qualitative business research with Harry Potter. Sage Business Cases.

Nair, L.B. (In press – b). "What is Her Story?": Investigating sexual harassment in modern workplace qualitatively. Sage Business Cases.

Netflix, (2017). Crocodile. Black Mirror.

Ploum, L., Blok, V., Lans, T., & Omta, O. (2018). Toward a validated competence framework for sustainable entrepreneurship. Organization & environment, 31 (2), 113-132.

Renwick, D., Redman, T., & Maguire, S. (2008). Green HRM: A review, process model, and research agenda. University of Sheffield Management School Discussion Paper, 1, 1-46.

Rieckmann, M. (2012). Future-oriented higher education: Which key competencies should be fostered through university teaching and learning? Futures, 44 (2), 127-135.

Rowling, J. K. (2000). Harry Potter and the goblet of fire. New York: Arthur A.

Schaper, M. (2002). The challenge of environmental responsibility and sustainable development: Implications for SME and entrepreneurship academics. Radical changes in the world: Will SMEs soar or crash, 541-553.

Spielberg, S (Director) (2002). Catch me if you can. (2002) [Film] United States: Amblin Entertainment; Parkes/MacDonald Productions.
Srivastava, S. K. (2007). Green supply-chain management: a state-of-the-art literature review. International journal of management reviews, 9(1), 53-80.
Stack, M., & Kelly, D. M. (2006). Popular media, education, and resistance. Canadian Journal of Education/Revue canadienne de l'éducation, 5-26.
Streisand, B. (Director), Streisand, B. (Producer), & LaGravenese, R. (Writer). (1996). The mirror has two faces [Film]. Retrieved August 7, 2019.

 **Lakshmi Balachandran Nair** is Assistant Professor (Senior) at the Methodology and Statistics Department, Utrecht University, Netherlands. Lakshmi's primary areas of expertise are qualitative research methodology and ethics.

11

Knowledge and Skills for Postgraduate Business Students of the Future

Peter Sharp
Regents University London, UK

Insights from other higher education institutions and environments

Broadly speaking, there is an increasing emphasis in higher education to train students to have knowledge and skills that enable them to be effective employees. This emphasis is likely to continue in the future. There are several reasons why this is the case.

In England and Wales, higher education students are now expected to pay for their tuition fees and maintenance. This makes their situation similar to international students studying in the UK who have been in this position for many years[1]. In the past, many students in England and Wales were not expected to pay for tuition fees and /or maintenance if their parents did not satisfy the relevant income threshold. Now that they do, students/parents who pay for their degrees are more likely to want to know whether the cost is worth paying for. For many, this means that students/parents want HEIs to educate students so that they are more employable (Ali, 2016 and Wilton, 2012).

The UK government also puts pressure on HEIs to train students to have relevant knowledge and skills for the world of work (Tymon, 2013). This may be because the Government wants low unemployment and regards HEIs as a vital means of training people to be employable and help make the economy competitive (Wilton, 2012). Also, the HEIs themselves are involved in a highly competitive market for students. HEIs need student numbers to be maintained or increased so that they are financially viable for the future. One of the criteria for demonstrating the value of courses provided is that they make students more employable (Taylor and Hooley, 2014). Also, arguably, in the field of business and management, there are further reasons for HEIs to train students to be employable: the field itself is one that lends itself to direct employability and generation of

---

[1] International students, of course, normally pay a lot more.

business (e.g. entrepreneurship (Garalis and Stazdiene, 2007)). Also, it may be one of the main motivations of HEI staff in the field.

In short, there are many reasons why HEIs are under pressure to train students in knowledge and skills that make them more valuable in the work place. However, some people say that learning knowledge and skills necessary for work may not be done effectively by universities (Tymon, 2013 and Wilton, 2012). In some fields like the British film industry, experts claim that 'learning by doing' in the workplace is the most appropriate way to learn (Schoenfeld, 2018). Although this may be true in some cases, most stakeholders in HEIs, and especially in business and management, would agree that training students to be employable is an important role for an HEI (Taylor and Hooley, 2014). However, what does it mean to be 'employable'? And, what knowledge and skills are required? Although some say that employability is a complex concept and is difficult to define (e.g. Tymon, 2013), it can be defined as:

"...the development of...skills, knowledge, technology and adaptability to enable [students] to enter and remain in employment throughout their working lives." (Ali, 2016, p. 82)

How does this translate into knowledge and skills relevant in the current climate of work which is increasingly technology and knowledge based? Research in a wide variety of Western economies has led to the identification categories of skills and knowledge that are considered important. Table 1 was the result of a literature search that was conducted using key words that included 'knowledge', 'skills' and 'employability'. This generated 30 academic peer reviewed papers. Analysis of the literature in these papers led to the identification of the categories of skills and knowledge in the table.

Table 1: Business Knowledge and Skills Required for Employability

Categories of Knowledge /Skills/ Capabilities	Knowledge, Skills and Capabilities	Place(s)	Author(s)	Notes
Communication Skills and Teamwork	Communication skills, Team work skills, Computer skills, Critical Thinking	Iraq	Ali (2016)	They argue that students should particularly be encouraged to learn these skills by doing extra-curricular activities.
	Different soft skills including teamwork, communication, critical thinking and adaptability are cited	Czech Republic	Myslivcova (2013)	They argue that the issue can be viewed from principles of demand and supply in the employment market
	Employers primarily seek Communication	UK	Tymon (2013)	

Knowledge and Skills for Postgraduate Business Students of the Future

Categories of Knowledge /Skills/ Capabilities	Knowledge, Skills and Capabilities	Place(s)	Author(s)	Notes
	Skills, Teamwork and Integrity			
	Interpersonal, Collaborative and Teamwork	Health workers in Australia	Stone (2010)	She argues that assessments in HEI often do not align with the work skills needed.
	Oral Communication, Problem-solving, and Team working	UK and Australia	Dalton et al. (2018)	They argue entry level students need to learn these skills in education institutions to gain work in industry.
Professional Approach	Professional competences, work experience and soft skills (time management, task completion, verbal and non-verbal communication, teamwork, applying rules/procedures)	Romania	Sumedra and Simona (2016)	They argue that internships improve transition to the labour market.
Global Outlook	Enhanced foreign language skills in addition to high level of communication skills	Asia, Africa and Europe	Dalton et al. (2018)	They cite authors who say business markets seek these skills in particular.
	International experience	Australia	Crossman and Clarke (2010)	They argue that international experience increases employability
	Need for future ready globally aware mind-set	UK	Minocha et al. (2018)	They argue that this should be something HEIs should try to train students to do.
Emotional Intelligence/ Character	Motivation, Emotional Intelligence and Attitudes (and Language and computer skills)	Latvia	Kantane et al. (2015)	
	Self-efficacy based on self-esteem	South Africa	Potgieter (2012)	She argues that universities should

Categories of Knowledge /Skills/ Capabilities	Knowledge, Skills and Capabilities	Place(s)	Author(s)	Notes
	and person's character (e.g. resilience)			help people develop characteristics (e.g. self-esteem) to be more employable.
	Thinking and Personal Qualities	USA	Dalton et al. (2018)	
	Understanding people for acting	UK film industry	Schoenfield (2018)	This paper suggests skills learnt for film industry are best learnt from experience and not in formal education.
Social networking	Social Networking	UK	Coughlan et al. (2012)	They argue social networking increases employability.

Broadly, the literature shows a pattern of a need for communication skills mixed with the ability to work in teams, use technology and have a character that is resilient. Also, future graduates need to be able to adapt to change and keep learning in the role. Also, broadly, most authors consider HEIs as having a role in the enhancement of employability of students but sometimes this could be done in collaboration with other organisations. For example, in extra-curricular activities and/or work placements (Ali, 2016; Sumedra and Simona, 2016). However, it is important to note that in some cases (e.g. UK film industry) formal education for working in the industry may not be considered important (Schoenfield, 2018). These patterns are not likely to change in the future. This is because all these skills, characteristics, abilities and mindsets are relevant for work in the future where continual technological change is juxtaposed with traditional knowledge and skills (Sharp, 2019a).

Context of first-hand insights

Personal background and motivation for mentoring students in industry

Since qualifying as a solicitor and leaving the profession for a Masters in Computing Science, a PhD in Knowledge Management and learning how to help others learn in a Postgraduate Certificate in Higher and Professional Education, I came to London to take up work at an International Postgraduate Business School 14 years ago with a determination to help people cross boundaries between higher education in the 'class room' and 'learning by doing' in the world of work. Part of that determination has meant I have encouraged, and been involved in, nurturing international postgraduate students to find and learn from working in industry for over 10 years. I have helped students train in business and essential life skills and develop life portfolios which apply LIFE (Sharp, 2011). The LIFE concept is an approach I developed to profile people in a relatively short period of time to help identify suitable work roles for an individual (Sharp, 2011). Through this work, I have helped help students build an understanding of themselves to find a suitable match in a work environment to make their next steps in life and flourish (Bolles 2013). This is essential in an environment where there are frequent references to higher education not equipping students sufficiently for the world of work (e.g. Woolcock, 2018).

My role in training and mentoring work placement students

This experience has led me to work with two groups of international postgraduate students; business and management students; and marketing psychology students. My role has been to teach and life coach students to in professional practice and help them get work placements and mentor them through their work roles. As part of the postgraduate programmes, students are encouraged to critically reflect on their learning in professional practice in written reflective reports. This chapter describes and analyses the patterns of learning from students from their experiences on these programmes. These patterns of learning provide a basis for recommending this form of learning for future international students. It also provides insights as to appropriate support structures for HEIs to support this type of learning where students can work in a wide variety of commercial environments.

Reflective approach to learning from student work experiences

I reviewed all the student work experience placements I have been involved in with the international students I have mentored, and I compiled profile information on each of these work placements. Of the 46 postgraduate business and management students, 28 were female and 18 male. Students were from a wide range of continents. All these postgraduate students obtained work placements in companies across the world doing jobs that entailed business and/or management tasks. The types of business ranged considerably and included joint venture companies, travel companies, business consultancies, English language schools, financial services, hotel businesses, digital marketing, helicopter businesses, textiles, construction, metal companies, beauty and cosmetics, flour mills, rubber manufacturing, dental part manufacture, film production, fashion, auction houses, IT and real estate businesses. Of the 13 postgraduate marketing psychology postgraduate students I worked with, 11 were female and two were male. They came from a wide range of continents including the Americas. All the postgraduate students obtained work placements that entailed elements of marketing and psychology and they worked in a wide range of businesses including fashion, fitness, digital marketing, interior design, pharmaceuticals, and luxury branding. I reviewed the learning sections of the professional practice reports of these 59 students to see what students valued from their experiences. The next section reviews the patterns of findings from this research.

Patterns of insights

Patterns of what students said they learnt from their work experience from their Reflective Reports was collated, tabulated and analysed. Almost without exception, students valued their work placement experience as very helpful for their personal learning. Also, a number of broad patterns of the main skills/competencies students learnt from their work placements could be discerned from analysing the patterns. A summary of the most frequently mentioned skills/competencies gained from the experiences of the two groups of postgraduate students is illustrated overleaf (see Figure 1).

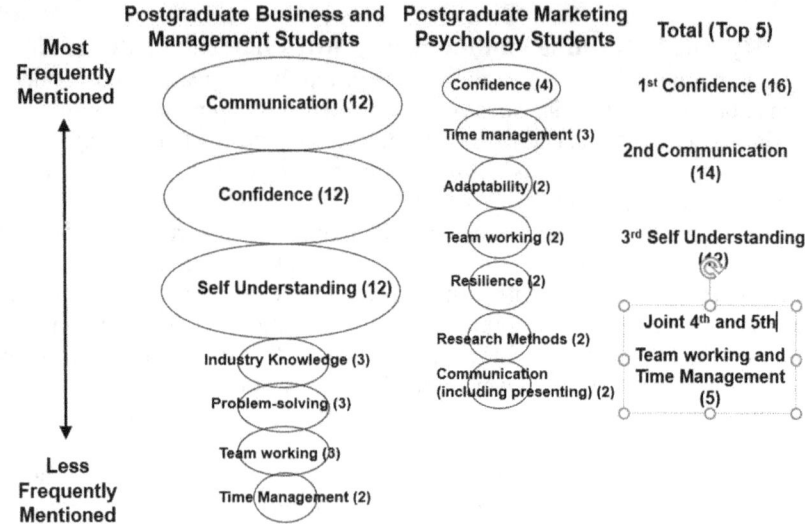

Figure 1: Patterns of skills and competencies learnt

The frequency patterns revealed in Figure 1 illustrate that confidence and communication skills are what postgraduate students most frequently mentioned as valuable things they learnt. Arguably, confidence is more about character and communication more about skills but both can be related. For example, the more skilled a person becomes at communicating the more confident they may become and vice versa. It is interesting to note that although there is much discussion about technology and its impact on our world (e.g. Smith and Tyler, 2011) and the changes related to this in how students interact and learn (e.g. Coughlan et al. 2012), few postgraduate students noted this area as a particularly significant in what they learnt from their work placements. This is the case even though virtually all the students used and learnt new skills that involved information technology.

There are overlaps in the patterns of findings from students on work placement programmes and findings from literature as per Table 1. The literature notes the value of communication skills, ability to work in teams and the value of the need for character traits that bring high levels of motivation and resilience. However, the feedback from the postgraduate students note something else; the significance of developing a greater understanding of themselves (self-understanding). This may be because the postgraduate students completed the LIFE process which is based on understanding yourself well to find a good match with your work placement role and future (Sharp, 2011 and 2019b). It is worth noting that this approach has been very successful from feedback from students and employers over the last 10 years. The approach has ensured that there have been hardly any 'poor matches' of student to organisation and virtually all the experiences of student and organisation has been positive for both parties.

I have considered the broad patterns from literature and international postgraduate students' reflections but this approach can hide the depth of learning and subtleties of experience that students express in individual cases. The next section provides some in-depth case studies to learn more from the experiences of international business, marketing and management postgraduate students.

Individual case examples /stories

Case Examples below trace the story of the 'life' of four students from their postgraduate course through their work placement, to their reflections on their learning. In all four cases, I took the students through the LIFE process (Sharp, 2011) and gave them training in professional practice. Below, are their stories.

Russian student (A) - XYZ

"It is a journey that perhaps has changed me forever. I came from a strict, but happy childhood into a limited existence as a student in London and all of a sudden I have entered the world of international and global politics."
(A)

Student A used her professional practice training to help her obtain a work placement with XYZ Industries (XYZ), a company that works closely with the United Nations and governments to implement joint venture projects. XYZ recruited A as an assistant project manager for 3-month work placement to help establish the production of alternative fuel in a country in northern Africa using a new form of grass. The project involved planning the production of the alternative fuel using 5 million hectares of land and generating employment for over 40,000 people.

A read about the history of the African country and brought together information about the practical economic, geographical, cultural and political implications of the project. She travelled with the project team to countries in Africa and Europe. She attended meetings where challenges of the project were discussed. A had to address various challenges including fears over her health and safety, working with people at all levels of XYZ, and she needed to learn quickly about the complexities of the project. XYZ were keen to employ A after she finished her Masters degree.

A learnt that the impact of what organisations do on employees and customers 'on the ground' is really important to her. For A, they must gain positively from what large organisations do. In this case, this meant that all the money invested in the project would have no value unless someone benefited on the ground. A learnt that it is important to be sensitive to different environments to conduct business effectively and she also learnt the importance of listening, reflection, humility and hope:

"I saw people who after many years of war and death had nothing, but hope. I saw people who had almost lost hope, but they had not lost grip of life. They continue to live and strive to achieve a tomorrow that is a tiny little bit better than today. And for me that was coming to terms with where you are in life. I hope that this practical lesson will help me in my career and will kill the greatest enemy of success – greed in me." (A)

Scandinavian student (B) – A Scandinavian bank

When B heard that there was a work placement elective in his Masters course he:

"had no doubt that this was something [he] would find useful and beneficial".

B received "motivation, inspiration and guidance" from business skills workshops and he met people from industry who attended his course as part of the business skills and work placement teaching programme. By this stage B was fairly clear that he would like to become a management consultant. He chatted with a management consultant who attended the panel event and made contact with several financial and management consultant companies.

The situation and needs of these companies and B did not align at this time. B continued his search using information from the internet and newspapers and improved his visibility online using network sites like LinkedIn. He applied for a high rank position as a summer management trainee in an international media company based in Oslo. Although B came through four stages of the interview process successfully, at the final interview he was told that he was not sufficiently experienced or competent enough for the post.

B reflected on this. He decided he needed a job where he could build confidence and receive constructive feedback on managerial skills. He applied for a job in the financial department of a large Scandinavian bank and for a role of a group leader for an international provider of education services. He received an offer from both organisations and decided to accept the offer from a large Scandinavian bank.

This bank was established in 2000 and was the first to operate exclusively online. B's role was as a Loans Operating Officer in a securities, loans and collection department. He worked in a small team of four people who welcomed him warmly. The team worked closely with others like the Customer Support and Collection teams. B noted the professionalism of his team colleagues. He also observed that when team members can relax in each other's' company in social settings this really helps them function well in formal roles.

B learnt the importance of attention to detail in his role. He also learnt that it took some time for members of his team to trust and respect him as a one of the team. B thought that it took time for him to be taken *'seriously'* and his leadership skills were put to the test by this. B addressed this by, among other things, acting with professionalism and authenticity. As trust and friendship grew in the team, communication with him improved. He became good friends with all the members of the team, which he saw as a mark of success in addressing this challenge.

The bank had quarterly summits where management updated everyone in the company on results in the bank. Teams that had made particularly good progress were mentioned. B also attended a summer meeting of bank personnel where teams who had made most progress were awarded honours. B said that his team:

> "did not win any honour, but the department did deliver an entertainment surprise, delivered with music and humour."

B learnt a lot about himself and a work environment. He said:

> "This Work Elective experience has not only been beneficial in the experience and practical know-how I have gathered, but also for my decision-making moving forwards. At this stage in my life there are many crossroads, where I need to turn the right way. This experience has helped give me a better foundation for these important future decisions."

B learnt that he did not want to be in a purely office operations job. He wanted to work in a more dynamic working environment as a management consultant in London while able to pursue his personal interests of skiing and mountaineering.

Turkish student (C) – English language school

C obtained a work placement with an English Language School in London where she took on a number of challenges which included dealing directly with customers' enquiries; carrying out market research and preparing agreements between agents and business schools. She also had specific responsibilities for some particular markets and visited Istanbul to attend a student fair on behalf of the English School.

There were many other things C did during her placement, including organising events, marketing them with posters, preparing programmes of events and keeping students informed of activities, dealing with money, writing letters to organisations like the British Council, and putting together student packs. As a result of this, students visited the London Eye, played football matches, watched *The King's Speech* film, went to Oxford, and enjoyed barbecues. They also learned about Shakespeare and English language and culture.

Reflecting on her experience, C noted some particular challenges. For her working in a different country using a different language and coming to terms with a different management style, were particular challenges. C believed that:

> "[other] cultures [are] defined as being more conservative and traditionalist"

and are more hierarchical than UK management culture. Although she found this difficult to get used to at the start, she believed that the less hierarchal and less formal management style that she experienced in her work placement was preferable.

Another challenge was to manage time effectively and not become overcommitted to the job. At times C was working in the office until 10 pm without taking lunch breaks. She realised that this was not necessarily very productive. C reflected on this and said:

"In order to increase the quality of hours that I work and decrease the stress I started to take lunch breaks."

She realised this was an important issue for other team members too and she introduced a 'lunch agreement contract'. This meant each member of the team would take a lunch break at different times so that the helpdesk was never vacant but each team member also had lunch.

There are many things that C learnt during her work placement which included improved language skills, meeting a wide variety of people from around the world, development of a strong social network, and a better understanding of a work environment. She found that the more she put in to her work the more she learned, and she concluded her reflections saying:

"Participating in this programme has been a valuable work experience for me. It helped me to gain greater confidence and prepared me to obtain a job in the near future. As well as my professional career, the major contribution has been on my personal development. I have better communication skills and better ability to express myself. These skills are priceless..."

Albanian student (D) – A luxury cosmetic brand

D worked with a large business distribution group in Tirana, Albania working with a multi-national luxury cosmetic brand. In her role as a marketing intern with a focus on a large luxury cosmetic brand D supported a marketing manager, managed a Summer social media campaign, conducted a customer survey, worked on a marketing strategy with colleagues, helped design sale stands in shops and negotiated price levels for fees for displaying the large luxury cosmetic brand product in local stores.

In her Professional Practice module on her Masters course, D identified her key skills as:

"transmitting ideas into actions [and] communication"

and her favourite subjects were

"Marketing, Business Administration [and] Consumer Behaviour".

This meant that this work placement matched her skill set and interests well. D said:

"...I also applied [to]... a real estate agency and ... an insurance company [but even though she was] accepted at all three companies, [the large business] Group's unique exclusivity to trade world-wide famous cosmetics...made it a prime attraction for an internship because of my passion for make-up and cosmetics customers."

The business Group is one of the leading distribution groups in Albania founded in 2004, importing, marketing and distributing products of leading world brands. D faced a number of challenges and developed skills during her work experience. She said:

> "I was afraid of how my [book-based] skills would be transmitted into a real-life situation, despite all the simulations...It was challenging to me at first, because the people I worked with did not use scientific terms as much as I expected but were much more practical in their language and everyday actions."

D learnt to throw herself in to doing the tasks that needed to be done and to 'learn by doing' rather than getting worried about different use of terminology. Another challenge for D was time management, about which she said:

> "my supervisor emphasized on my first day...the importance of time management. I learnt that if I was late, the other employees would not take me seriously, therefore I learned to wake up earlier and plan for traffic, breakfast, or having a coffee on the way."

D learnt from her team the importance of efficient role allocation and to be direct with colleagues about things she did not understand, so that she could tackle her work in a time-efficient manner. She found managing social media issues a challenge too. This involved answering customers' questions online and posting new content. D understood more deeply through her work experience the importance of Facebook advertising, online experiences for customers and e-mail marketing. Also, she realised that:

> "unless used properly, they can have a wrong, undesired effect."

> "my experience with the [large business distribution] Group was rewarding and fulfilling [and that working as an] intern in a fast-paced working environment was much more fun and challenging than [she] initially perceived it would be."

However, she found it enhanced her love of marketing and working with other people to reach a common goal. She learnt the importance of being passionate in marketing products she really believed in, and how to approach a market and:

> "make sure your customers always remain happy and continue to perceive the brand positively..."

D believed that there is scope for more use to be made of social media marketing by [the multi-national luxury cosmetic brand] in Albania in the future. D also said:

> "[the business distribution] Group showed me that they care deeply about their employees and their skills, and I would love to work with them again one day if I return to Albania after my postgraduate education."

These case examples illustrate the complex learning experience that postgraduate students went through in training for, obtaining and then completing a work placement. These experiences reiterate the significance of gaining confidence, developing communication skills and understanding oneself, to work effectively in industry. However, some of the subtleties of the learning experiences from the stories of individuals are significant. For example, Student A learnt a lot about herself. In particular, she learnt about personal ethics and values (e.g. humility). However, Student B learnt about how to become part of a new team and be accepted by them, partly through socialising with them. Also, the experience of

Student B illustrated how a lot is learnt through the *process* of finding a work placement as much as during the work placement itself. So, although broad patterns can be noticed from student reflections, the true depth, breadth, and richness of such experiences can only be fully appreciated on a case by case basis. Also, in each case it is noticeable that the students valued their work placement as a very helpful personal learning experience.

Implications for business leaders, HEIs and students

The literature in this field refers to five categories of skills, competencies and knowledge that are particularly important to university students. These are:
1. Communication Skills and Teamwork
2. Professional Approach
3. Global Outlook
4. Emotional Intelligence and Character
5. Social Networking

From the patterns of learning articulated by postgraduate business and management and marketing psychology students I have worked with, the most frequently mentioned skills, competencies and knowledge they valued were: first, confidence; second: communication; and third: self-understanding. However, none of these are technological skills or competencies. There is some overlap in findings from literature and my first-hand research. However, broad patterns can hide the subtleties of what individuals learn from professional practice training at HEIs and experience in industry. This can be seen from individual case examples.

There are a number of implications of these findings for business leaders, HEIs and students for the future. For example, perhaps business leaders need to recognise that the leaders of the future need to have the communication skills, confidence and self-understanding to keep learning and adapt well to a rapidly changing technological world. These attributes are what HEIs should be seeking to nurture in students and business leaders need to value and nurture these attributes too. Also, each person needs to be developed as an individual and linked effectively to the overall output of organisations. Finally, students need to understand the significance of developing confidence, communication and self-understanding for their own employability. If they recognise the value of learning these things in HEIs before they go to industry, they should be better equipped to face the challenges they face when they begin work in industry. Also, it seems clear that professional practice and work placement programmes are a valued means of helping students learn relevant knowledge and skills for the present and future. This is an important thing for HEIs to note as a means of nurturing appropriate knowledge and skills of students for the future.

Conclusion

There are many challenges in developing the relevant knowledge and skills of postgraduate students for work in industry. However, this chapter demonstrates that international postgraduate millennial students value the development of confidence, communication skills and self-understanding when they work in industry. If postgraduate students go into industry with these attributes, skills and knowledge, arguably they will be good at continually gaining the other knowledge and skills they need to address challenges they will face in the future. One effective means of training students in these attributes is through professional training and mentoring that leads to and through work placements. This is an approach that requires careful work with each individual and some universities may regard the cost of doing this prohibitive. However, others would argue this approach gives value for money to students paying for their courses. Universities working with business and management students should focus more on developing the characteristics and skills of confidence, communication skills and self-understanding rather than focusing on technical changes in industry. This does not mean that universities should ignore the latter: this is a norm of working environments. However, when students have appropriate levels of confidence, communication skills and self-understanding they can then address the challenges of the future that come with continual innovation in technology.

References

Ali, F.A. (2016) Employability Skills and Students and Employers Perceptions: An Assessment of Levels of Employability Skills Acquired by Business Students at Ishik University, *International Journal of Social Sciences and Educational Studies*, December 2013, Vol. 3, No. 2, pp 81-93.

Bolles, R. N. (2006) What Color is Your Parachute? *A Practical Manual for Job-hunters And Career-Changers, Ten Speed Press, ISBN-13: 978-1-58008-727-8.*

Coughlan, J., Swift, S., Jamal, A. and Macredie, R.D. (2012) The Effects of Social Networking on Social Capital and Employability for Computing and Business Students, *2nd Annual International Conference on Education and E-learning (Eel 2012)*, ISSN: 2251-1814.

Crossman, J. E. and Clarke, M. (2010) International Experience and Graduate Employability: Stakeholder Perceptions on the Connection, *Higher Education*, 2010, Volume 59 pp 599-613.

Dalton, R., Crawford, P., Weiss, L. and Fink, W. (2018) *NACTA Journal*, Volume 62, Part 4, pp 298-307.

Garalis, A. and Strazdiene, G. (2007) Entrepreneurial Skills Development via Simulation Business Enterprise, *Social Research*, 2007, Volume 2, Part 10, pp 39-48.

Kantane, I., Sloka, B., Buligna, I., Tora, G., Busevica, R., Buligina, A., Dzelme, J. and Tora, P. (2015) Expectations of Employers on Skills, Knowledge and Attitudes of Employees, *European Integration Studies*, No. 9, pp 224-234.

Minocha, S., Hristov, D., and Leahy-Harland, S. (2018) Developing a Future-ready Global Workforce: A Case Study from a Leading UK University, *The International Journal of Management Education*, 1472-8117.

Myslivcova, S. (2013) Employability of University Graduates in the Czech Republic, *International Conference on Intellectual Capital, Knowledge Management and Organizational Learning*, Academic Conferences and Publishing International Limited.

Potgieter, I. (2012) The Relationship between Self-esteem and Employability Attributes of Postgraduate Business Management Students, *SA Journal of Human Resource Management*, Volume 10, No. 2, pp 1-15.

Schoenfield, C. (2018) Learning by Watching, Doing and 'Having a Chat': Developing Conceptual Knowledge in the UK Film and TV Industry, *Media Practice and Education*, Volume 19, Part 2, pp 188-204.

Sharp, P. J. (2011) The LIFE Technique – Creating a Personal Work Profile, *Special Issue Electronic Journal of Knowledge Management*, Vol. 9, Issue 1, ECKM Special Issue, March 2011, pp 57-72.

Sharp, P. J. (2019a) *Juxtaposition of Old and New Knowledge: Crafts; AI and Apps; an Example*, Blog article for 10th October 2019 on http://knowledgelearningpd.wordpress.com [accessed on 9th October 2019].

Sharp, P. J. (2019b) *Honesty to address the Knowledge and Skills Gap*, Blog article for 11th June 2019 on http://knowledgelearningpd.wordpress.com [accessed on 11th June 2019].

Smith, D.D. and Tyler, N.C. (2011) Effective Inclusive Education: Equipping Education Professionals with Necessary Skills and Knowledge, *Prospects*, Volume 41, pp 323-339.

Stone, J. (2010) *Medical Education,* Volume 44, pp 396-403.

Sumedrea, S. and Simona, A. (2016) Internship – Tool for Improving the Employability of Economic Science Graduates, *Bulletin of the Transilvania*, University of Brasov, Series V: Economic Sciences, Volume 9, Part 58, No. 1.

Taylor, A.R. and Hooley, T. (2014) Evaluating the Impact of Career Management Skills Module and Internship Programme within a University Business School, *British Journal of Guidance and Counselling*, 2014, Volume 42, No. 5, pp 487-499.

Tymon, A. (2013) The Student Perspective on Employability, *Studies in Higher Education*, Volume 38, No. 6, pp 841-856.

Wilton, N. (2012) The Impact of Work Placements on Skills Development and Labour Market Outcomes for Business and Management Graduates, *Studies in Higher Education*, Volume 37, No. 5, August 2012, pp 603-620.

Woolcock, N. (2018) Universities Denounced as Poor Value and Inflexible, The Times, 5th November 2018.

Since completing his PhD in Knowledge Management (KM) in 2003 **Peter Sharp** has taught, trained, coached, researched, and written widely in the fields of KM; research supervision, personal development, life coaching and creative thinking/art.

12

Bildung and the Digital Revolution

Emanuela Marchetti
Department for the Study of Culture, Media Studies, University of Southern Denmark, Odense, Denmark

Introduction

It has become common knowledge that the humanities are experiencing an identity crisis. Targeted by financial cuts and a digitisation process that is transforming all professional sectors, also called the *digital turn* (Drotner and Iversen, 2017), the humanities are struggling to defend their identity and status (Bates, 2015; Christiansen et al, 2015).

The digital turn is affecting universities on the professional and educational front. On the professional front, the digital turn is transforming the professions targeted by university education, introducing demands for digital skills. Traditionally centred on literary, philosophical, and artistic knowledge, the status of the humanities is being questioned. According to the statistics[1] humanists are struggling to find qualified jobs and they are perceived as lacking a clear-cut professional profile. As a result, humanists leave universities with precarious future prospects in comparison to graduates in sciences and business, often undergoing self-training and extra qualifications before landing stable jobs (Winterbotham, 2016). On the educational front, the digital turn has led universities to adopt digital learning platforms and new teaching practices, such as distant and hybrid learning (Bates, 2015). This in turn has challenged teachers' pedagogical competencies, forcing them to acquire new digital skills and to redefine their relationship with their students and their learning material. Moreover, the increasing popularity of on-line course platforms seem to threaten the status of face-to-face teaching for the future of higher education, suggesting that higher education itself might become obsolete.

In response to such issues, Danish universities have actively engaged in defining new curricula to strengthen the professional profile of humanists, introducing applied knowledge from the field of digital technologies, which can be defined as a form of *computational thinking* (Jacob and Warschauer, 2018), including knowledge and skills related to advanced use of digital tools for video

---

[1] Last seen 02/09/2019: https://www.dr.dk/nyheder/penge/nye-tal-oekonomer-tjener-mest-humanister-er-i-bund

editing, graphic design, text analysis, and analytics. Basic coding skills might be targeted as well, but without the theoretical knowledge on software and electronics, which is at the core of computer science or engineering educations.

Traditionally the identity of Danish universities has been grounded on the ideal of Bildung, defined as a form of research-based teaching. According to the Bildung, students learn best by engaging in research collaborations with the teachers, who are active researchers in their area of teaching (Christiansen et al, 2015; Dohn and Dolin, 2015). However, the digital turn is compromising the application of research-based practice in the humanities, as the demand for teaching digital applied knowledge is forcing teachers to stretch to areas outside their research areas. This chapter is exploring how the Bildung, intended as epistemological framework for knowledge construction, is being challenged and how it could be reconceptualised, to provide a valuable grounding for harmonising the tensions at the core of the identity crisis of the humanities.

The chapter builds on an ethnographic case-study, which I conducted while teaching a course called *Digital Methodologies*, which is aimed at providing digital applied knowledge in methods to conduct ethnographic research on the Internet. The course is addressing master students in Media Studies and it is aimed at providing digital competences, which could make them qualified to gain jobs in the communication sector

In the next section I will discuss current perspectives on the digital turn and on the identity crisis of the humanities (2). Afterwards I will introduce the methodology adopted in the empirical case-study (3), in section 4 a critical analysis of the findings from the case-study is provided and conclusions are presented in section 5.

Humanities identity crisis and the digital turn: A double bind perspective

A couple of years ago, at the final dinner of a conference, a student volunteer introduced himself saying that he had just obtained his master's degree from Media Studies with a thesis on the music industry. He then concluded with a sad remark but laughing at himself, saying: "But now I am going to be unemployed!"

It is not unusual to hear this kind of self-deprecating humour among humanists and jokes on humanists' unemployment can be found everywhere on newspapers and social media platforms. In order to understand what is happening and why the humanities have become object of jokes and social contempt, it is necessary to dig into what defines the identity of the humanities.

Traditionally the term *humanities* refers to: "Literature, language, history, philosophy, and other subjects that are not a science, or the study of these subjects"[2]. In this definition, a series of disciplines are listed and labelled in negative terms as "non-sciences", not addressing the essence of the humanities. Moreover, the humanities can be understood as: "Learning concerned with human culture, especially literature, history, art, music, and philosophy."[3] In this definition

---

[2] Last seen 13/09/2019: https://dictionary.cambridge.org/dictionary/english/humanities
[3] Last seen 13/09/2019: https://www.lexico.com/en/definition/humanity

the humanities are branded as theoretical knowledge, constituting learning goals for a group of people, teachers and students, hence suggesting that the humanities belong to schools and public institutions, excluded from innovation and economic growth. In this respect, the humanities are object of opposite perceptions:

- A positive perception, by which the humanities are identified with intellectual knowledge of high cultural and ethical value for society.
- A negative perception, by which the humanities are identified with theoretical knowledge that cannot bring substantial value to the national economy.

This negative view of the humanities seems to be corroborated by the media. It is not uncommon to read in newspaper that humanists are getting lower wages than other graduates and are associated with the highest unemployment rate: 11,0% for bachelor graduates, while master graduates are at 7,75 against 0,8% for medicine graduates[4], who are the most employed.

From a broader perspective, the identity of universities can be defined in relation to their institutional role within society and in relation to their practice. The institutional role of universities can be defined in terms of power, differentiation, and exclusion (Hall, 1996; Foucault, 1970). University graduates acquire a new identity for having participated in a specific community, which enabled them to develop a set of skills, a professional network, and to gain an official acknowledgement, their degree, granting them access to high level professions. Hence, a university degree has the power of social differentiation and exclusion (Bhabha, 1994), paving the road of graduates towards coveted professions, out of low-paid jobs and mediocrity, excluding all the others at the same time.

In terms of practice, Danish universities have identified themselves since the 19th century with the Humboldtian ideal of Bildung, which was formulated by Wilhelm von Humboldt (1767-1835), to contribute to a reform of German universities in 1809. Humboldt believed that the goal of university education should be a "cultivation through science", in German: "Bildung durch Wissenschaft", intended as a scientific collaboration between teachers and students, exploring research questions together with goal of enable students to cultivate their spirit. Humboldt called this scientific collaboration the 'seminar' and he proposed it as the ideal teaching method for universities (Christiansen et al, 2015; Dohn and Dolin, 2015; Humboldt, 2000). The Bildung is based on the assumption that students learn best when they can experience first-hand scientific inquiries and the knowledge that they are supposed to acquire (Christiansen et al, 2015; Humboldt 2000). Moreover, university teachers should be active researchers, able to share with their students ground-breaking knowledge and to engage them in critical discussions. Finally, according to the principle of freedom embodied in the Bildung, universities should be self-governing institutions as teachers, who are also active researchers, are the best qualified to establish their research agenda, teaching methods, and content. However, the Bildung is more than a teaching approach, the

---

[4] Last seen 03/09/2019: https://www.dr.dk/nyheder/penge/nye-tal-oekonomer-tjener-mest-humanister-er-i-bund

term can be translated into education or formation and it refers to a philosophy of development of the individual spirit, unifying intellect and emotions (Humboldt, 2000). In this sense, Bildung refers to a process of harmonic growth of the individual, in pursue of self-development and of a unique identity within society (Humboldt, 2000). Central aspects of the Bildung are represented by freedom and agency in exploring individual talents, and the role of institutions participating actively in supporting this exploration. So defined the Bildung is a lifelong lasting process of self-development, a concept embodied in contemporary theories of lifelong learning (Rasmussen, 2014). In this study, the Bildung is interpreted as an epistemological framework for learning, centred on a symbiotic nexus between teaching and research practice (Christiansen et al, 2015; Dohn and Dolin, 2015), but also targeting professional identity.

The application of the Bildung in universities has been challenged since the 1970's, when universities were rebranded as "engines of economic growth" and "knowledge generators" (Christiansen et al, 2015, p. 24). According to Schön (1983), the university crises of the 1970's was caused by a decline of confidence in the professions. The appearance of expressions like "lagging understandings, unsuitable remedies, and professional dilemmas" (Schön, 1983, p. 9), indicated a lack of trust in the ability of graduates to handle complex situations and societal problems. Since the start of the new millennium, the globalisation of education introduced pressure on universities through the Bologna process, to create internationally standardised curricula, to enable industries to hire the most qualified working force and graduates to access the global job market (Christiansen et al, 2015). Funding policies were simultaneously redefined around neo-liberal principles of competition, again compromising the research-teaching nexus, as senior staff was loaded with the responsibility of writing grant applications, while their research was being conducted by externally funded post-doctoral researchers, and teaching was given to little paid, less experienced assistants (Dohn and Dolin, 2015). Moreover, in Denmark financial cuts were applied to the humanities in combination to harsher admission requirements and an education cap[5], limiting the number of available places for students (Sörlin, 2018).

At the same time, the digital turn has led to introducing the need for technical skills, traditionally associated with engineering and computer sciences, also in sectors traditionally oriented towards the humanities, such as: libraries, archives, museums, media and communication, and public administration (Nardi and O'Day, 1999). Furthermore, due to financial cuts to the public sectors, these jobs have become less available, causing higher unemployment across humanists[6]. All these changes have caused humanists to land on little-paid jobs, not requiring any academic qualifications also after graduation (Lewis, 2018). To be able to access a qualified job, humanists must go through a process of self-training, passing from specialization courses to little-paid jobs and internships, often resulting in psychological burn-out and stress (Winterbotham, 2016). In this respect, the

---

[5] Last seen 13/09/2019: https://www.information.dk/indland/2018/07/humaniora-mistet-status-antallet-optagne-faldet-25-pct-paa-fem-aar
[6] Last seen 13/09/2019: https://www.dr.dk/nyheder/penge/nye-tal-oekonomer-tjener-mest-humanister-er-i-bund

combination of financial cuts and the digital turn has caused a crisis of identity for the humanities, spoiling universities of their power to provide their humanists with a suitable degree granting them access to specialised, well-paid jobs.

In order to address these issues, Danish universities have responded to the digital turn engaging in an ecological evolution (Nardi and O'Day, 1999), promoting digital skills among students and teaching staff, mainly through:

- A redefinition of their curricula towards applied digital knowledge and skills,
- A redefinition of teaching practice towards hybrid learning.

The applied digital knowledge, which has been introduced in the humanities, can be defined within the notion of computational thinking (Jacob and Warschauer, 2018), as it aims at providing humanists with advanced skills in the use of digital technologies and basis knowledge of coding, but excluding theoretical understanding of software development and electronics, which are still perceived as the domain of technical graduates. Targeted digital technologies include, for instance: Nvivo, which is used for multimodal text analysis, digital archives, Gephi, which is used for creating visualisations of quantitative and qualitative data, software and equipment for audio-video productions, to provide video editing skills required by the communication sector and to support ethnographic studies (Drotner and Iversen, 2017; Bates, 2015). As a result, teachers have been subject to increasing pressure, as they had to acquire themselves the skills that they need to pass to their students. As a result, humanities teachers had often to teach topics that are alien to their research practice, hence disrupting the application of the Bildung ideal.

At the same time, teaching practice has been disrupted by the demand of adopting digital platforms, leading to the implementation of hybrid learning practices, which require teachers to adapt to a different pedagogy, in which students engage independently with the leaning content through online and face-to-face sessions (Bates, 2015; Daniel, 2012). Moreover, the implementation of hybrid learning implies that teachers must be able to operate digital platforms such as *Moodle*, *Blackboard*, and *Fronter*, all of which I had to use during my teaching experience. Besides being able to operate these systems, teachers have also developed new communication skills to create engaging content, such as: video-lectures and tutorials, managing discussion boards, and gamified quizzes (Daniel, 2012; Bates, 2015).

These changes have produced positive results and humanists are "conquering" the private sectors, working as communication specialists and managers (Junge et al, 2012). Recent Danish statistics documented that the employment rate among humanists has increased by 52% within 2010 and 2017[7]. Research in the humanities has also evolved and the digital tools targeted by teaching are also adopted by researchers in their own empirical work, with the effect of realignment to the Bildung ideal. Moreover, courses in various digital platforms have also been addressed young researchers since the start of their career, turning them into

---

[7] Last seen 03/09/2019: https://www.magisterbladet.dk/aktuelt/2018/oktober/eksplosion-af-humanister-ansat-i-private-job

digitally competent researchers and teachers. Nonetheless, heated debates emerged, as university teachers complained that to please industries, these changes have prioritised applied knowledge from other fields at the expense of cultural values and moral integrity[8], undermining the status and unique identity of the humanities (Sörlin, 2018; Benneworth et al, 2017; Lewis, 2017).

Positive outcomes have been documented regarding the introduction of hybrid learning, allowing for flexibility and enabling shy students to express themselves more freely than in crowded classrooms (Daniel, 2016; Owston, 2013; Fisher, 2017). Policy makers were eager to support hybrid learning to save money, thinking that it would be enough for teachers to share their material online, while senior staff could focus on applications for research grants. However, research shows that unsupervised students will tend to lack the motivation to study and drop out of courses (Daniel, 2017; Salmon, 2005; Salmon et al, 2008). Lack of personal contact can make students feel isolated and elicit misunderstandings on the learning content and on assessment criteria (Dohn et al, 2015; Daniel, 2017).

Building on these reflections, I argue that the digital turn has led to systemic transformations in learning content and teaching practices, generating two intertwined *double binds* (Figure 1). According to Bateson (1972), a double bind is an unsolvable dilemma defined by opposite tensions. The first double bind refers to the tension between theoretical and applied knowledge, where theoretical knowledge embodies cultural values and represents the core identity of the humanities (dealing with literature, arts and philosophy), instead digital applied knowledge embodies economic value and it is perceived as an intruder, undermining the future identity and the status of the humanities in relation to other fields of knowledge.

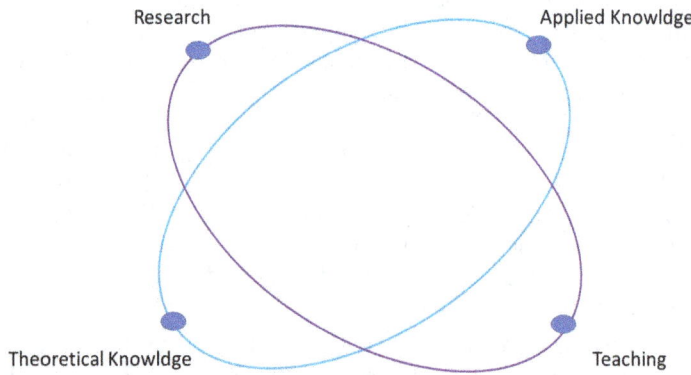

Figure 1: Intertwined double binds representing the identity crisis of the humanities

This double bind is intertwined with opposite tensions between teaching and research practice (Figure 1), which are affecting the application of the Bildung ideal. According to Christiansen et al (2015), externally funded research projects

---

[8] Last seen 03/09/2019: https://www.information.dk/indland/2019/08/humanister-glemt-vores-vaerdi-solgt-billigt?fbclid=IwAR2Edl9YB7P6dOb7X_WpXu5CfMOpik6IKCMmBP2j3gzO50TlF4itOQ1NckU

have been prioritized over teaching, in international ranking and hiring policies academics are competing based on their research output and less on their teaching portfolios. Investing in externally funded research projects and publications has, therefore, become a main concern for academics to promote their careers and for universities to gain international recognition and more funds.

Building on this analysis, I conducted an empirical study to explore how the Bildung could still play a significant role within the humanities and how it could contribute to the humanities identity crisis.

Empirical work – project-based teaching and digital humanities

The discussion presented in this chapter builds on ethnographic data gathered during fall 2018, while teaching a course for 1st semester master students in Media Studies. The course is named *Digital Methodologies* and it is aimed at forming media professionals able to engage with various software to conduct sociological inquiries. During the course, the students are introduced to methods like netnography, which is defined as ethnography conducted on online communities (Kozinets, 2015). Netnography requires the use of different digital tools, such as: Nvivo for qualitative analysis of written texts and multimedia, SPSS for quantitative analysis, analytics and Gephi for networks visualisations. The students are asked to work on a group-based semester project, where they have to apply the tools and methods learned through the course on a concrete problem domain, in this case-study the students had to work on digitisation of news. A total of 17 students participated in the study, they were divided in six groups, five groups of three students and one group of two.

The case was provided by *Der Nordschleswiger[9] (DN)*, a local newspaper based in Aabenraa, Southern Jutland (Denmark), whose mission is to provide news from Germany to the German minority in Denmark and to keep alive their cultural identity. Since in Denmark people are increasingly reading news in digital format, DN is adapting to this trend, while at the same time attempting to expand their group of readers. Issues were discussed regarding the needs of a diverse group of readers including young people, families and the elderly, who are known to struggle to adjust to digital devices (Forlizzi et al, 2004), and to reading news on the tiny, bright screens of their mobile phones (Ijiekhuamhen et al, 2016; Aroldi and Colombo, 2018). This case represented a *wicked problem* (Rittel and Weber, 1974), an ill-defined issue that can admit multiple solutions and that the students can approach from their own personal interests, exploring technological, cultural, and communication related perspectives. Moreover, it provided an opportunity for the students to experiment with different tools and methods, while collaborating with a potential employer. Following the Bildung, it was vital to grant students a certain degree of freedom in determining their research agenda and in dealing with their inquiries.

The course was structured according to the research-teaching nexus embodied in the Bildung ideal (Christiansen et al, 2015; Dohn and Dolin, 2015). The project stages provided structure to plan our lectures, to enable the students to access

---

[9] Last seen 05/09/2019: https://www.nordschleswiger.dk/de

relevant knowledge at the right time (Table 1), while supporting our respective inquiries and the students' learning process.

Table 1: Overview on the empirical work

Date	Activity	Participants and location if relevant	Methods
10 September 2018	Introduction to semester project	Students at university + one local representative for the newspaper	Ethnographic note taking
1 October 2018	Visit to the newspaper	Students and employees (especially marketing department) at the newspaper headquarter	Ethnographic note taking
9 November 2018	Literature review	Students have to deliver a literature review – defining area of research and identifying knowledge gap	Discourse analysis of the students' understanding of the problem and personal interest
November 2018	User study	Students in distant collaboration with newspaper representatives and readers	Digital methods: netnography, interviews through social media platform or phone
26 November 2018	Students' presentations – preliminary feedback and suggestions to students on their project	Students at university and 4 representatives from the newspaper	Shared discussion, note taking
December 2018	Reports delivery for exam	Students delivered their final reports	Reading – simple discourse analysis
January 2019	Reports delivery – edited – to the newspaper representatives	Improved versions of the reports were sent to the newspaper representatives	Reading – discourse analysis
February 2019	Final presentation in spring – conclusion feedback to students from teacher and newspaper representatives	Students at university + a team of 4 representatives	Video ethnography

The activities planned for the students represented an occasion for me to gather data on how the students were responding to the course, for instance while formulating their research questions and project plans in class, and while engaging with their client.

The course followed a hybrid learning approach (Bates, 2015; Salmon et al, 2008), combining face-to-face and online learning. The students had free access to learning material and were in charge of their empirical work, face-to-face sessions were used to discuss theoretical principles and to train the students in the use of the tools under supervision. In this sense, the face-to-face sessions offered the opportunity for shared discussions and peer feedback, on the issues the students encountered while reading the course material or in conducting their inquiry.

In order to gather my data, I have combined ethnographic observations and note taking of discussions held in class (Eberle and Maeder, 2016), situated interviews and video ethnography were gathered for the final presentation of the students (Pink, 2006). Moreover, I have used discourse analysis (Drotner and Iversen, 2015) on the students' drafts and videos of the students' final presentations, to analyse how they articulated their professional identity through the formulation of their research questions. In conclusion, my approach could be assimilated to organisational ethnography (Eberle and Maeder, 2016), as I have combined different methods, with the aim of understanding how students articulated their identity as humanists in the making, within the institutional frame of the humanities affected by the digital turn.

Discussion: Reconceptualising Bildung in the future of the humanities

In this study, I try to explore the role of the Bildung ideal and its reformulation, intended as research-based teaching practice, to better address the identity crisis of the humanities following the digital turn. My data suggest that a reframing of the ideal of Bildung and its research-teaching nexus can play a significant role within the humanities, incorporating perspectives of professional development, hence providing valuable room for students to explore their professional identity, in dialogue with teachers and external actors who could be potential employers (companies or institutions).

Building on the notion of social differentiation (Bhabha, 1994; Foucault, 1970), I define the identity of the humanities in relation to the knowledge and skills, which distinguish humanists from other graduates, granting them access to qualified jobs and to play a meaningful role in society. According to my study, students define their identity in relation to three dimensions:

- Personal interests,
- Professional future aspirations,
- Professional skills.

Students see their personal interests and future aspirations as intertwined and are eager to express them verbally and through their given assignments. Media Studies can be identified as an interdisciplinary field, attracting students with various interests, such as: TV and movie production, communication, marketing and design, and the social sciences. The class included a total of 17 students, six of which were female. Some students identified themselves as artists, who were searching for an education that could grant them access to stable jobs, while expressing themselves as designers or film makers. A female student claimed, with a bit of irony, that she was "fascinated by visual arts", but that she did not enrol in fine arts because she was determined to "support herself financially". Others felt that as media professionals they could be able to "canalize their artistic interests" to make a difference in society. Other students instead expressed an interest for the business side of media, wishing to become project managers and communication strategists. A last group of students admitted not to have a clear idea about their professional goals, but expressed interests for theoretical topics, like media sociology and psychology. One of the male students was a mature man, who introduced himself as a digital marketing professional, who wished to acquire new perspectives that "could be useful in his daily job" and to "catch up with the path he started years before." His presence generated curiosity in the other students, who asked questions on his practice during breaks.

Some students felt pressured by having to engage with an assigned topic, a girl said: "It is not a project I would have chosen for myself!" Other five students asked me why they had to work on that case in particular. My answer was rooted on previous experiences from the same course and I explained that working on the same case would enable them to better compare their problem formulations, helping each other in writing better reports. Moreover, I added that this case-study could represent a future professional task, enabling them to reflect on the practical implications of the course topic. Finally, I invited them to formulate a perspective that could match their personal interests, while addressing the needs of DN. As the students engaged with the project, they became able to articulate their personal interests and to transpose these into their research plans, the result was a series of projects illustrating the interdisciplinary spectrum of Media Studies. One group focused on human computer interaction addressing the elderly and their engagement with digitised news, another group focused on media sociology investigating how DN could foster a feeling of community across different age groups within the German minority. The remaining groups focused on different perspectives related to communication and marketing, two groups conducted an inquiry about how DN could redefine their communication strategy, leveraging the affordances provided by social media platforms to better reach young readers. The fifth group focused on branding and use of digital platforms as means to renew the newspaper corporate identity. Finally, the sixth group focused on event management, as a strategy to socially engage with families through local institutions, like schools and libraries.

By choosing these areas of study, the students articulated their identity in relation to personal interests and aspirations. The group who focused on media sociology made a statement of intellectual values, during our supervision meetings they asked philosophical questions about the concept of community, the desire of individuals to belong to a community, and what digital platforms and newspapers have to offer in this respect. These students were theoretically driven and provided significantly more critical perspectives in their report than other groups. They said to have chosen these topics because: "(They) are interesting and challenging!" and "We like these kinds of topics!" Hence, they expressed interest for philosophical topics, which are traditionally associated with the core identity of humanities. The group of students who focused on human computer interaction instead articulated their identity as: "We are into technologies". During meetings these students mentioned future aspirations to work as designers and IT professionals. The remaining students, who chose topics related to communication, seemed eager to work in the communication and marketing sector, which is seen as a suitable area for Media Studies graduates to find good jobs.

On the other hand, the students appeared unsure when articulating their identity in terms of professional skills. This emerged during our first lecture, when I asked the students to introduce themselves, telling their name, their previous education, and their interests within media. The students came from different educations, some continued through Media Studies, while others enrolled from literary studies, foreign languages, or sociology. A girl who graduated in English Literature, shyly said that she did not expect to use much of what she learned before. Another girl from the same education added that she was eager to get into analysing and creating multimodal texts, but that she was aware of the challenge coming from a "totally different" field. In fact, I argued that through Media Studies, these literature trained students might be advantaged when analysing the sociocultural meaning of movies, articles from magazines, and campaigns. The mature male student, who identified himself as a digital marketing professional, said that "obviously" he did not expect his professional experience to be "particularly relevant" for the course. In response, I asked him to describe his typical workday and, as I expected, he mentioned working with analytics, focus group interviews and, engagement with potential clients through social media platforms, all of which were covered by the course. Moreover, leveraging his answer I addressed the other students, saying that his experience proved that: "This course will be very relevant for your future professional life!" I concluded my remark ironically, with an emphatic preaching tone, as if I was an old-school teacher, to elicit a cheerful mood in the class.

During our visit to DN headquarter in Aabenraa, the students had to conduct interviews with employees. While preparing for the interviews, the students were nervous, they repeatedly asked for feedback on their list of questions for DN employees and sought advice on how to conduct their interviews. The visit lasted for the whole day and the students shifted from a nervous to a positive mood, when they realised that they could relate to how employees discussed their challenges and areas of uncertainty. During the break and while leaving, a few students approached me to express positive remarks: "We were lost in the start, but it was nice to see that we could relate to what they were saying!" Others added that: "It was interesting to see that they (employees) also referred to media theories!" Moreover, a few other students told me smiling: "It was nice to feel needed!" Or "That they need us!" These quotes suggest that the students felt proud to discover themselves as professionals in making, who had something to offer to a future employer.

However, during the course the students expressed again uncertainty about the value of their project, asking questions like: "Do you think that they will be able to use what we are doing?" The group of theorists were the most concerned, questioning their own choice of topic and wondering on the practical implications on their project saying: "What if they cannot use what we do?" or "Let's hope that they can use it (our study)". During supervision meetings I aimed at showing them how their analysis could provide unique perspectives, which could translate in novel approaches to engage with readers online.

The students' presentations were held in November 2018, close to the end of the course, and in February 2019 after the exam, both presentations were attended by four representatives from DN. The first presentation was intended for the students to gain formative feedback that could support them in completing their projects, the second one provided an opportunity for students and DN representatives to discuss the outcome of the project, exchanging their perspectives, hence enabling students to become aware of the professional value of the knowledge they acquired through the course. During both presentations I played the role of a conference chair, I set the frame for expectations on both sides regarding the status of the project and the aim of feedback. I facilitated the event asking questions that could lead to further discussions, but also allowing the students to independently handle their dialogue with their clients, who, on the other hand, asked relevant questions and provided constructive feedback. These presentations had also the effect to enable the students to gain recognition on the quality and relevance of their work.

Summarising, the students articulated different perspectives related to the identity crisis in the humanities, expressing doubts on their professional skills and on the relation between applied and theoretical knowledge, which were expected to embody opposite values. The students also seemed to perceive the digital skills targeted by the course as distant from their identity and hard to grasp, so that they often expressed self-doubt stating for instance: "*I am not sure on how much I will be able to learn* (referring to the tool Nvivo)!" Difficulties emerged in relation to mastering specific functions, like highlighting and visualising specific excerpts from transcripts of interviews. They also found hard to engage with the many tutorials available online, some of which were referring to older version of the tools, so they were glad to receive help during class. It has happened in previous semesters, that some students even tried to avoid using the tools, asking if it was good enough to use traditional ethnography. In general, the students asked me "how in depth" or "how well" they were supposed to know the tools, explaining that they did not expect to become able to master digital tools like "technical" graduates. These statements suggest that digital skills appeared to them as promises to future employers, eliciting a feeling of inadequacy, fearing that they might be perceived by a future employer as second rated technical professionals.

From a teaching perspective, Media Studies and the humanities are becoming increasingly interdisciplinary also because of the diversity of the students enrolled, coming from different educational and professional backgrounds. This is often presented as a challenge for universities (Christiansen et al, 2015), regarding how teaching practice can effectively address such as diverse audience. In this respect, hybrid and distant learning practices have been welcomed as valuable approaches, enabling for flexible and personalised engagement with learning material (Christiansen et al, 2015; Bates, 2015). The introduction of hybrid and distant learning proved to be another challenge for teachers, who were required to adapt to a different pedagogy, new digital platforms, and to restructure their material and teaching technique all together. The success of online learning resources has raised questions regarding the future relevance of university teaching and fear that university teachers might be delegitimated in their educational role (Dohn and Dolin, 2015). However, as exemplified by Salmon (2005) hybrid learning does not succeeds on its own, it still requires facilitation by qualified teachers, who are able to produce and gather relevant material, and to define assessment criteria, lack of leadership by the teachers can result in students' dropping out and failing (Daniel, 2017; Salmon, 2005).

In the case discussed in this chapter, my role as a teacher was to select learning material, which included texts, tools, and tutorials for the students. I also created Power Point presentations to provide the students with critical summaries and overviews of the learning material, which was quite heterogeneous. Moreover, I acted as a project manager for the students, I set the frame for the case-study, organising activities, and establishing assessment criteria. These criteria provided an evaluation framework for the students to prepare for the exam, but also for the projects' outcome, enabling our clients to fairly evaluate the students. The project provided a driving force for the students' engagement with the learning material, it provided motivation to conduct their research inquiry, to construct new knowledge of theoretical and professional value, hence exploring their professional identity. The project also set the rhythm to our lectures, as I planned my lectures following the project stages, so that the students could access relevant knowledge at the right time. In this sense the course was planned to follow the Bildung ideal, combining research and teaching within a shared inquiry on the impact of the digital turn on the communication sector to support students' learning, as discussed by Dohn and Dolin (2015). Through the course, the Bildung was applied as epistemological framework, providing room for sense making targeting theoretical knowledge, which could be applied to a wicked problem brought to us by a potential employer. In this way, we reinterpreted the Bildung addressing a concrete development project, within the contemporary media sector. Professional skills and potential employers, however, are not part of the original Bildung ideal as it was aimed at framing the pursuit of self-development (Humboldt, 2000), without concerns for the job market. In this sense, the teaching-research nexus embodied in the Bildung was reformulated, through a project-based structure including our clients and their needs. So reformulated the Bildung provided room for the students to negotiate, in collaboration with their teacher and client, how to balance their personal interests, their research agenda and their client's need, which at times appeared in conflict. The ability of juggling among these three aspects of knowledge making, in a professional environment, constitutes a learning goal for any subject, as academic professionals should be able to apply their theoretical knowledge to solve new problems in their professions (Schön, 1983). In this respect, our application of the Bildung also provided room for exploring the students' professional identities, fostering in the students "*a general level of confidence in their ability to be able to solve problem and handle problematic situations*". Hence, professional identity is understood in this study as contributing to the formation of a social identity, a principle already embodied in the original formulation of the Bildung, more specifically in relation to how humanists can contribute to society in its complex.

Starting from these insights, the ideal of Bildung still emerges as a valuable framework for the future of the humanities, but it needs a reconfiguration addressing theoretical and applied knowledge, as well as professional development. The explicit inclusion of applied knowledge within the teaching-research nexus, intertwining research-teaching-professional development, has the potential of harmonising the double binds connected to the humanities crisis, which are defined respectively by the tension between theoretical and applied knowledge, and the tension between teaching and research practice. Hence, the Bildung is being reformulated as epistemological framework for knowledge construction, resembling the hermeneutic spiral (Balzer et al, 2018), intended as a circular, iterative and incremental process of knowledge construction. As visible in Figure 2, the proposed redefinition of the Bildung ideal and of the research-teaching nexus, defines a harmonising room within an incremental process of knowledge construction, which is mediating between the opposite terms of the double binds:

- Theoretical knowledge, which represents the goal of research and teaching, and applied knowledge, which represents the application of theoretical knowledge on a concrete problem and a goal for professional development.
- Research, which represents the theoretical perspective in the process of knowledge construction, and teaching, which represents the perspective of students' learning within the same process.

In this model, the Bildung is being reconfigured introducing a perspective of professional development within its theoretical knowledge, providing an underlying structure to strengthen the research-teaching nexus and for associating theoretical and applied knowledge, hence enabling students to reflect on their identity as academics and professionals.

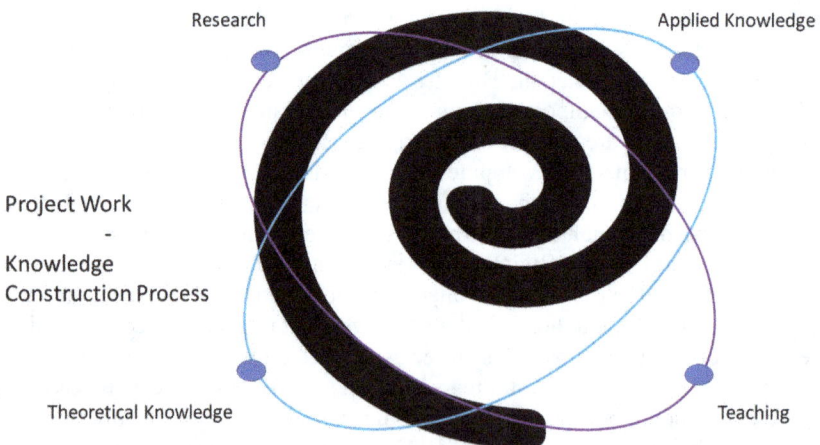

Figure 2: Proposed reconfiguration of the Bildung

This reformulation of the teaching-research nexus is already taking place in humanities, embodied in the process of redefinition of the identity of the humanities, as teachers have embraced hybrid learning and have started acquiring the digital competences needed for their students to meet the demand of future employers. Project-driven work is seen as a strategy for framing research-like processes, introducing students to research and professional practices, while fostering an understanding on the applicability of theoretical knowledge. Most of these principles are already embodied in the original ideal of Bildung, however, there is a need to reconstruct the broken research-teaching nexus and recontextualise it within professional development, to address the current crisis of the humanities.

On a general perspective, no matter which teaching and learning practices will emerge in the future, universities should strive for engaging students in collaborative inquiries, promoting social engagement among students and between students and future possible employers. Moreover, the humanities have evolved, increasingly including digital platforms and related methodologies in research practice, contributing even more to reconstructing the ideal of Bildung in the humanities. Therefore, I see future universities as keeping their leading role in providing specialised knowledge to individuals of different backgrounds and experiences. However, teaching should be given a more prominent role, through investments of resources and the involvement of qualified, experienced teachers, who can successfully challenge themselves, their knowledge fields, and their students in times of crisis.

Conclusion

Traditionally the principle of Bildung, defined by Humboldt as a form of research-based teaching, has provided grounding to the identity of university education in Denmark (Dohn and Dolin, 2015). Recent developments, such as the digital turn and financial cuts, have compromised the adoption of research-based teaching in the humanities, in mainly three ways: first by diverting hours from experienced researchers from teaching to writing proposals for research grants; second by forcing teachers to stretch towards technical knowledge areas to teach their students that digital competences that are typically outside the core of the humanities; third and last by forcing teachers to become skilled in various digital learning platforms and to adopt a hybrid learning pedagogy (Bates, 2018).

These changes have produced positive results in increasing the employment rate of humanists also in the private sector. Researchers in the humanities have become technologically smarter and are currently contributing to new understandings of digital technologies and practices, moving towards a reconstruction of the Bildung. Nevertheless, challenges persist as the experience of studying in the humanities has changed and might not correspond to students' expectations. They appear insecure regarding their professional identity, underestimating how much of their core humanistic knowledge can be applied to a professional context. At the same time, the students feel inadequate when dealing with digital applied knowledge, hence, attempting to be exempt from applying it to their projects.

In this sense, the future of the humanities is still a matter of debate, in terms of not being confused as an underrated technical specialisation. Teachers and students are experiencing a critical but highly creative process, as they are daily constructing a new identity for the humanities, although still rooted on the core subjects. In order to support this process, teaching should regain a prominent role, through investments in qualified, competent teachers willing to explore new pedagogical approaches and interdisciplinary knowledge exchanges. Moreover, students should be more aware of their role in this process, engaging in a critical dialogue with their teachers and future employers, regarding their professional identity as well as the future of the humanities.

As future work I wish to continue exploring the digital turn in the humanities combining research and teaching, hence I am conducting another similar experiment with bachelor students in Media Studies teaching a course called *Media Production – WEB*, targeting knowledge and practical skills in the field of web design. In cooperation with a colleague from the technical faculty, I am introducing knowledge from the design and social sciences, in combination to tools like Adobe Experience Design, InDesign and basic coding competences in HTML, CSS and JQuery UI. My goal is to demystify the complexity of those practices, to form digitally sharp media professionals, able to effectively cooperate with their technical colleagues in the future. Moreover, I am cooperating with the technical faculty in teaching design-related subjects, trying to bridge between future coders and media professionals, showing the applicability of theoretical knowledge coming from the humanities. My ambition In this respect, is also to pave the road towards richer understandings of the relations between technical and humanistic knowledge.

References

Aroldi, P. and Colombo, F. 2016, July. The Elderly, IT and the Public Discourse. Representations of Exclusion and Inclusion. In: International Conference on Human Aspects of IT for the Aged Population, Springer, Cham, pp. 176-185

Balzer, W., Eleftheriadis, A. and Kurzawe, D., 2018. Digital humanities and hermeneutics. Philosophical Inquiry, 42(3/4), pp.103-119

Bates, A.T. 2018. Teaching in a digital age: Guidelines for designing teaching and learning. Vancouver BC: Tony Bates Associates.

Bateson, G. 1972. Steps to an Ecology of Mind. University of Chicago Press.

Benneworth, P., Gulbrandsen, M. and Hazelkorn, E., 2016. Ireland: valuing the arts and humanities in a time of crisis and beyond. In: The Impact and Future of Arts and Humanities Research. Palgrave Macmillan, London, pp. 89-115

Bhabha, H. 1994. The Other question. In: The Location of Culture. Routledge, London.

Christiansen, F. V., Harboe, T., Horst, S., Krogh, L. and Sarauw, L. L. 2015. Trends in the development of the Danish universities. Rienecker et al. Eds. University Teaching and Learning. Samfundslitteratur, pp. 17-42

Daniel, J. 2012. Making Sense of MOOCs: Musings in a Maze of Myth, Paradox and Possibility. In: Journal of Interactive Media in Education.

Daniel, J., 2016. Making sense of blended learning: Treasuring an older tradition or finding a better future. Online Learning News, Contact North-March, 2.

Dohn, N. B. and Dolin, J. 2015 Research-Based Teaching. Rienecker et al. Eds. University Teaching and Learning. Samfundslitteratur, pp. 43-64

Drotner, K. and Iversen, S. M. 2017. Digitale metoder: hvorfor, hvad, hvordan. In: Drotner, K. and Iversen, S. M. Eds. Digitale metoder. At skabe, analysere og dele data. Samfundslitteratur.

Eberle, T. S., and Maeder, C. 2016. Organizational Ethnography. In Silverman, D. 2016. Qualitative research. Sage.

Fisher, C. 2017. Padlet: An online tool for learner engagement and collaboration. Bond University.

Forlizzi, J., DiSalvo, C., and Gemperle, F. 2004. Assistive Robotics and an Ecology of Elders Living Independently in Their Homes. In: Human-Computer Interaction. Lawrence Erlbaum Associates, Inc. 19 pp. 25-59

Foucault, M. 1970. The Order of Things. Routledge, London.

Hall, S., 1996. Who needs identity? In: Questions of cultural identity, 16(2), pp.1-17.

Ijiekhuamhen, O.P., Edewor, N., Emeka-Ukwu, U. and Egreajena, D.E. 2016. Elderly people and their information needs. Library Philosophy and Practice.

Jacob, S.R. and Warschauer, M., 2018. Computational thinking and literacy. Journal of Computer Science Integration, 1(1)

Junge, M., Nygård, S. L., and Ramsløv, K. 2012. Baggrundsrapport. Humanisterne på vej mod nye arbejdsmarkeder. DEA.

Lewis, C.S., 2017. Crisis rhetoric, stigma play: The contested status of humanities majors on an elite university campus. Symbolic Interaction, 40(3), pp.378-395

Nardi, B.A. and O'Day, V., 1999. Information ecologies: Using technology with heart. MIT Press.

Kozinets, R.V., 2015. Netnography. The international encyclopedia of digital communication and society, pp.1-8.

Owston, R., 2013. Blended learning policy and implementation: Introduction to the special issue. Internet and Higher Education, 18, pp.1–3

Pink, S., 2013. Doing visual ethnography. Sage.

Rittel, H.W. and Webber, M.M. 1974. Wicked problems. Man-made Futures, 26(1), pp.272-280

Rasmussen, P., 2014. Lifelong learning policy in two national contexts. International Journal of Lifelong Education, 33(3), pp.326-342.

Salmon, G. 2005. Flying not flapping: a strategic framework for e-learning and pedagogical innovation in higher education institutions. In: Research in Learning Technology, Sage, 13(3), pp. 201–218

Salmon, G., Jones. S., and Armellini, A. 2008. Building institutional capability in e-learning design, ALT-J Research in Learning Technology, 16(2), pp. 95-109

Schön, D. 1983. The Reflective Practitioner. How Professionals Think in Action. Routledge.

Von Humboldt, W., 2000. Theory of Bildung. Teaching as a reflective practice: The German Didaktik tradition, pp.57-61.

Winterbotham, N. 2006. Learning, Leadership and Applied Research. In: The Responsive Museum. Working with Audiences in the Twenty-First Century. Lang, C., Reeve, J. and Woollard, V. Ed. Routledge.

Emanuela Marchetti is assistant professor at the Department for the Study of Culture, University of Southern Denmark, Campus Odense. Her research focuses on playful learning, e-learning, computational thinking and assistive technology for elderly care.

13
Learning Designs and Systems in the University of the Future

Anthony 'Skip' Basiel
Queen Mary University of London, UK

Introduction

We are living through the greatest time in history to be a learner (Alexander, 2013), with the availability of so many high-quality free materials online. But, at the same time, the institutions most affiliated with knowledge and learning are facing crisis (Harris, 2018). Rising costs of operating traditional face-to-face higher education institutions and a declining student enrolment are impacting on what models of future universities will emerge (NSCRC 2019).

Illich (1970) forecasted a 'deschooling of society' almost half a century ago. He saw the paradox of the education system in that as the cost increases, so does its self-destructive nature. While universities package formal instruction, often in a 'drill-the-skill' format, which is acknowledged with a certification, he recognised that most learning actually occurs out of school. We don't need to funnel all formal education programmes through teachers.

An alternative to traditional university structure is a networked service approach to offer learning resources outside of the classroom. Informal learning locations, or 'pop-ups' (visual.ly 2012), can be in libraries or even coffee shops. In these banks of skills exchange, teachers serve to model the skillset. They become more than professional administrators or pedagogues and take on the role of learning initiators or education leaders.

A 'points reward system' can be used so that teachers can get learning opportunities by other experts. This 'skill exchange model' is a peer-matching network that promotes collaboration through building a local community of learners. The extent of effective participation can be used as a criterion to evaluate this possible new university model by measuring the impact of the learning on the individual or their professional organisation.

The next section of this chapter examines the HE futurists view. Dawson (2019) suggests that, 'the unbundling of research, education, content, and certification means that new business models and ways of engaging students will be at the heart of a prosperous future for universities.'

The University of the Future

Emerging themes from Higher Education (HE) Futurists

One current model for many traditional face-to-face Higher Education Institutions is built on criterion-based assessment design (Green, S. 2002). This education system model seeks to provide certification for the demonstration of mastery of skills/knowledge by validation through a written, presentation or other media verification assessment. A top-down, content-driven, teacher-led system starts with learning objectives that guide the student to read text, perform scaffolding reinforcement activities and often conduct a formative self-assessment quiz. How does this model match the needs of our future society?

An industrial learning society is where mass production is secured through mass education. The traditional transmission style of instructional design is, at best, sufficient for the skills of the 20th century. The skills and learning requirements of the 21st (and beyond) citizens are changing.

The following topics are identified from a thematic analysis of a selection of HE futurists:

- How jobs and employment may change in the future?
- What skills may be needed in the future?
- How future economics may impact on HE?
- How could declining university enrolment affect the HE model?
- How could blended learning technologies and pedagogies change for future HE?
- How could informal and organisational learning grow into the future of HE?
- What elements could comprise the future Higher Education model?

One measure of the value of HE in our society is the potential impact it can have on employability. Hiemstra (2013) highlights how in the past, a college degree meant a better chance of being employed than just having a high school diploma. The average person entering the workforce in 2030 can expect to reboot their career six times throughout their working life (Frey T 2016).

Jobs of the future will be those that focus on intellectual capitalism, not commodity capitalism according to Kaku (2017). We are shifting from an industrial, production model to a knowledge-based economy where intellectual capital can grow from our new, HE systems.

So, what skills and capabilities will be needed in the future? In a keynote presentation, Dawson (2019) suggests:

- *Expert thinking* – the ability to solve new problems that cannot be solved by rules,"
- *Complex communication* – the ability not only to transmit information, but to convey a particular interpretation of information to others in jobs like teaching, selling, and negotiation.

Snyder (2019) says, '*we have identified two classes of skill groups that are rising in demand and salary: non-routine cognitive analytic skills and non-routine cognitive interactive skills. Kaku (2017) goes on to emphasise that these soft skills* at ease with technologies are some of the most important talents undergrad students should be mastering today for the future of tomorrow'.

In her TEDx talk, Jana (2019) provides more detail about the nature of these 'soft skills'. By shifting from our current focus on core or 'IQ' subject matter (e.g. English, Maths, etc.) to a 'QI' skill set, the focus is on the application of knowledge, and less on the facts of the subject matter. Here 21st Century skills include:

- *QI Key Skills* – The curriculum looks at resources and techniques to promote a positive life force for the individual.
- *QI skills: Me* – Self-awareness is a critical skill to provide context. Drucker (1999) saw the 21st Century as the age of the self-manager.
- *QI skills: We* – Along with 'Me' skills, future employees need to work in teams, in person and online. People/negotiation skills are critical. We need to read other people, develop our social/emotional intelligence and strengthen our empathy capabilities. According to Gates (2015), negotiation skills will be critically fundamental.
- *QI skills: What if skills* – Our current university curriculum focuses on 'fixed solutions' from the information provided in the syllabus. Next generation leaners will need to develop skills to answer, 'How it could be?' Creativity is the most important skill of tomorrow (Jana, P. 2019). Piaget (1936), in his theory of cognitive development, saw traditional school learners match what is already known to what could be. Our future creative university learners will need to consider the 'What If' factor.
- *QI skills: Why Skills* - ME + WE. To become creative learners, we need to master the capability to ask good questions. Asking WHY has been trained out of learning, in many cases, due to a criterion-based assessment model which measures fixed responses. Future universities will be environments that incubate and foster creative 'why' thinkers that can collaborate to find innovative solutions that AI interventions cannot accommodate.
- *QI skills: Wiggle* - The problem with current traditional school systems is that they want passive students who sit quietly in the classroom. Sure, there is a move to increase learner interactivity through blended discussions e.g. face-to-face seminar followed by an online text forum, but there is little physical action or 'doing' as Schank (1995) highlights. Physical and intellectual engagement can lead to innovation (e.g. corporate 'walking meetings).
- *QI skills: Will Skills* – Finally, the future university can help students become stronger learners by developing motivation, a passion for learning and perseverance. This can be illustrated in two general categories:
- *Extrinsic* – external rewards e.g. financial commissions in the corporate sector
- *Intrinsic* – internal praise, staff recognition, gamification reward systems

These motivation techniques can be used in a blended fashion. They do not have to be implemented in isolation. The Hult Prize (2019) is an example from Hult/Ashridge International Business School demonstrating how an extrinsic award system can be built into the HE curriculum. Teams of students address global sustainability issues for corporations to find real-world solutions to our long-term concerns. The challenge solutions are researched and presented to business experts in an attempt to win a $1m prize from the Clinton Foundation.

An example of intrinsic motivation used by many American universities is 'the Dean's List'. This is a select group of students picked by the campus Dean as outstanding leaders within the academic community. They do not have to be the best in academic grades but demonstrate that they possess the capability to have a positive impact on their cohort. Like Student Representatives, members of the Dean's List can act as a voice for the community and show that the university management listens and acts to support learners.

- *QI skills: Wobble* – Jana (2019) recommends that we, ''Fail early and often.' We should not just seek positive milestones but learn how to recover from failures. Could Popper's (1959) 'falsification' approach support 'wobble' skill development? The learner/researcher does not seek to prove a hypothesis, but rather, identify where the system may fail. In this way a prevention strategy can be developed so the critical incident is stopped before it even occurs. Flanagan (1954) discusses a related methodology known as a CIT (Critical Incident Technique). Again, barriers or obstacles are identified, rather than seeking best practice. The future university will need a Social / Creative space to 'shake up things but remain standing'.

Knowledge decay, according to Snyder (2019) is the result of rapid change in information or regulations. One of the implications of this rising pace of knowledge decay is that future HE students must strive to become specialists. If we are not knowledge specialists, then we are being left behind. He sees a future of 'teacherless education'. Traditional top-down teaching (e.g. sage on the stage) requires experts. Teacherless education uses experts to create the material but doesn't require the teacher to be present each time it's presented. According to Cairns and Alshahrani (2014 p. 27), 'Some see blended learning as the inevitable educational model with variations (of) no schools and totally online systems.'

An epistemological shift can be to move from a teacher-led university, to a Web 2.0 (Downes, S 2005) 'student-as-researcher' model. Cairns and Alshahrani (2014) even suggest a Web 3.0 model of artificial intelligence chatterbots with real-time frequently asked question support.

Learners can also create the resources to support the future university curriculum. Basiel (2017) provides an example using online formative quizzes that can be generated by students who provide the correct multiple-choice questions, answers and the reference sources for feedback responses. The students generate the 'quiz pool' resource.

Global economics can also impact on our future HE system. In 1932 Ronald Coase wrote a paper titled 'The Nature of the Firm' (Coase, 1932), for which he won the Nobel Prize for Economics over 60 years later. Organisations exist because of transaction costs. As we have become connected transaction costs have fallen, creating what we can think of as a 'modular economy', in which value is created in smaller and smaller inter-connected modules (Nesta 2019a). On the other hand, Dawson (2019) explains (see Figure 1) that mature industrial economies will not only have to create a new generation of high value, technology-based products and services; they will also have to transform their workplace organisations – i.e. invent new social technologies – to permit the creation of millions of new high-value-added jobs that exploit the productive potential of applied information technology.

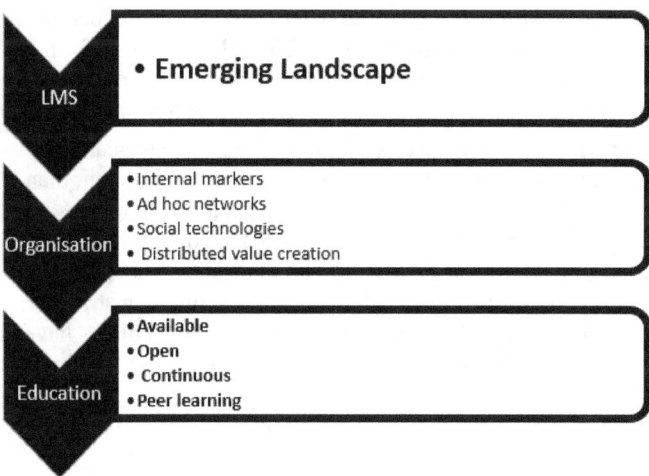

Figure 1: Workplace and Higher Education (Dawson 2019)

The World Economic Forum predicts that 2/3 of future jobs don't even exist at the time of this writing (WEF 2019). Kaku (2019) sees us working towards a 'perfect capitalism', where the consumer knows everything about a product and will have infinite knowledge of supply and demand via his/her mobile smartphone and biotech, such as contact lenses. The soft skills and capabilities combined with creative thinking discussed earlier can guide the university graduates towards new employment opportunities.

Will future universities become job recruitment centres? In a survey of 1,000 Australian students, three-quarters said that universities had a responsibility to help them find employment, according to Ross (2019). In the article Professor Sachs believes that 'a sort of a contractual relationship needs to be developed between the student, the university and the professional partner organisations' to encourage career networking potential.

Bryan Alexander (2013) identifies a threat to current Higher Education Institutions (HEIs). In 2013 there was declining enrolment in traditional face-to-face universities. Part of the reason was a decreasing birth rate which would mean fewer 18-year olds entering the academy. Additionally, fewer international or immigrant students were registering. Snyder (2019) states this may be due to less than 25% of children globally not attending school at all. What actions can HEIs develop to address these economic trends to ensure a sustainable strategy?

Blended learning technologies and instructional designs have the potential to globally provide Higher Education organisations the tools and methodologies for a sustainable future. Snyder (2019) sees a hyper-connected world where education is shifting from a teacher-centric schooling pedagogy to a learning and teaching model where 'place' matters, but in a different way. Dawson (2019) speculates that large bureaucratic higher education institutions may be replaced by smaller, private organisations or '*edupreneurs*' (2019) where blended learning innovation can happen more quickly. This blended learning design is supported through 'groupware' as a means of communicating and collaborating (e.g. WhatsApp, Office 365 Team). Learning is a possible outcome of sharing experience and knowledge through project collaboration. Webinar design is one form of this technology enhanced learning environment using real-time video, text, white boards, voting, etc. as well as recording of events and reflective text forums.

Education and technology have been intertwined since the early days of higher education, but the content, says McLuhan (1977), is less important than the media used to transmit it. Media has evolved from oral traditions to images and hand-written language, then onto print format. Media has evolved from the telegraph to the internet, from analogue mass media to global digital social media. Education, he argues, can't be print bound, since the 'web' is not linear in structure. Digital media, such as television (with online/phone voting) and webinars have the ability to affect human thought and nature in a tactile modality by supporting an action learning design. McLuhan (1977) sees us heading towards a 'global village'. The next generation university can support this global community through blended technologies.

Education is on the verge of a major transformation and artificial intelligence-based (teacherless) learning systems may quickly be taking centre stage (Frey T 2016). "In the future, where knowledge is everywhere and accessed instantaneously, and where robotics and AI can perform a variety of functions once held by humans, intellectual capital will be valued over commodity capital", says Kaku (2017).

The AI systems will learn about the stakeholder's profile to establish gaps in the intellectual understanding and key skill sets. The learning and human resources can then be provided to develop the competencies needed by scheduling appropriate learning/training opportunities. This sequence, according to Frey (2016), can be repeated until the learner has successfully demonstrated mastery of the learning objectives or successfully completed the task or solved the problem. Alexander (2019) sees assessment methodologies for these learning and training events changing. Instead of abstract learning objectives tacked onto a content-driven instructional design, future universities may assess learning mastery through real-world problem applications to support a shift to a growing [digital creative] knowledge economy where the AI system can provide data, but the students develop as collaborative innovators to build tomorrow's world.

According to Snyder (2019), the future university will need a keener sense of the real world to be market driven. Higher education has to become better at allowing the marketplace, especially business, to guide its innovations. This kind of marketplace collaboration can be supported by web video communication as webinars and blended research and development conferences. An example of this model is the Learning and Skills Group (LSG 2019) monthly webinar events to support thousands of its blended professional network members.

Learning and Skills Group (LSG) Webinars

This LSG Webinar explored the future of digital learning from a business sector perspective. As seen in figure 2, the text discussion that occurred while Alan Hiddleston (2019) of D2L presented his slides highlighted the nature of 'soft skills' in future as a key issue.

Figure 2: LSG Webinar Tag Cloud

Organisations will need to, not only, train 'hard skills' (e.g. physical operations, computer programming, etc.), but 'people' skills such as negotiation for better employee management. Future universities will work closer with industry to provide expertise in the development of professional 'people' skills.

Snyder (2019) sees a shift to more informal learning opportunities for preparing future university students for employment. The 70:20:10 learning model (iSpring 2018) was developed by Morgan McCall, Robert Eichinger, and Michael Lombardo at the Center for Creative Leadership in the mid-1990s. They surveyed almost 200 executives about their learning philosophy. The unexpected results caused a notable shift in the organisational learning/training world.

The survey results stated that learning comes from a variety of sources:
- 70% from challenging assignments in team projects and informal collaboration opportunities;
- 20% from developmental (social) relationships such as working with mentors;
- 10% from formal training in a (blended) classroom or eLearning course.

Universities of the future will also find a paradigm shift to adopt more informal *learning. Tacit* knowledge gained through real-world problem-solving experiences may take place in a face-to-face context at work or mediated through a variety of technologies. Social media can also be used to share tacit knowledge. One of the best examples of employee-generated training resources, which can be applied to a higher education context, is the British Telecom (BT 2009) 'Dare-to-Share' project. In this investigation BT employees made short informal videos of how they solved an office problem. They became the evangelist promoting the resource for colleagues to use, thus creating a culture of learning within the organisation.

What will the future university and workplace relationship look like? Dawson (2019) argues that the future of education is open, available, and continuous and takes place through peer learning. Jay Cross (2019), one of the leaders of informal learning, describes this as workflow learning that is, learning that is embedded in the flow of work.

It is no longer possible to predict the educational needs of business 6-7 years in advance, the time it takes for traditional colleges to start producing talent in a new field. Frey (2016) suggests that micro-colleges may be an alternative to our current 3-year university curriculum structure. Micro-colleges are simply immersive forms of post-secondary education done in short periods of time. Modular knowledge provides resources in a specific context, in which a question is asked, a problem confronted. When an obstacle is encountered the solution is sought in the form of a specific module of learning needed to solve that particular problem. This context specific module is acquired 'just in time'. The 'learning module' may be in any number of forms: a video, an article, or an individual who knows what you need to know or who has previously solved the problem. This kind of informal learning is about networks, about access, about critical thinking and problem solving. Because it is contextual it is more meaningful and more useful. This professional social networked learning approach may be supported through massive open online courses (MOOC 2019). The pedagogic design of these free learning resources will need to evolve to provide more informal 'people' skills to encourage creativity.

Mind the gap

Reflecting on the themes of various education Futurists, there is a gap in an important role that higher education provides society, academic humanitarian and scientific research. University research and development (R&D) centres make 'a contribution to knowledge' which can impact every discipline. Next-generation R&D will find a growing epistemological shift to a social constructivists view. Theorists such as Vygotsky, Brunner, et al. (Steffe, L. 1995) believe that knowledge is more of a personal construct. Meaning making comes from our own thinking and experiences. Knowledge, the constructivists argue, does not exist 'out there', but comes from the minds of the researchers/learners. Understanding is a result of prior knowledge and then asking, *'What if?'*

How will the role of future university researcher adapt with a more informal learning structure? Links to a commercial focus with research may impact on methodology. Goldacre (2019) warns us about the threats of 'bad science'. Can future university research centres maintain an unbiased, objective perspective? Or, is the fate of the practitioner-researcher to be influenced by the corporation funding the study?

Virtual teams and supporting collaborative project management systems (PM, 2019) will be needed to attain blue sky and applied research objectives. Since the role of the university lecturer could move away from the didactic instructor, students will need to be more autonomous as research practitioners using a variety of groupware tools. Artificial Intelligence (AI) will provide the engines for big data quants analysis, while breakthroughs in qualitative research will include improved video auto-transcription for interviews and focus groups. The days of spending hours typing out handwritten notes will be long gone. Research may, therefore, remain a core part of future university models.

This section of the chapter looks at case studies which have 'snap-shot elements' of future university models and designs:

Hult/Ashridge International Business School: Masters and MBA Innovation

There are several postgraduate curriculum innovations in this Hult Case study which contributed to them winning the 2014 AMBA Award:

- A shift to a soft skills focus
- Peer feedback
- Business simulations
- Masters Programmes: Team presentation assessment with partnered corporations
- Strong careers support model
- Hult Prize (2019)
- Alumni networking

According to Mukul Kumar (2019), Hult's Chief Innovation Officer, the shift to more of a 'human skills' focus, along with digital and business capabilities, provides future university learners the opportunity to know, apply and make decisions for productive employability in next-generation industry. This is a path to build professional confidence. Peer feedback through mobile phone applications is one technique to improve communication and analytical skills.

Business simulations are digital environments that provide settings where the learner's knowledge can be applied by working with a team. One assessment model used with the postgraduates sees teams of students-as-researchers going into global organisations to address real-world issues. Presentations are made to company managers with solutions that are backed by evidence.

The Careers Team provide professional networking opportunities through guest speaker talks with members from industry and graduate careers exhibitions. The Hult Prize (2019), previously mentioned, is an international contest between university teams to have a chance to win a $1 million prize by providing unique solutions to global sustainability challenges. University Alumni are a strong networking resource after graduation. Through blended meetings and the use of mobile apps to identify the location of Alumni members, graduates can continue to build links to a global learning community.

Adobe Captivate Prime

Adobe has conducted an interesting study to justify the addition of social learning features in their learning management system (LMS), Captivate Prime (2019),

The University of the Future

which is also a learning records system (xAPI). This platform allows the learning environment and stakeholders to connect to 'the internet of things' meaning data from any internet connected device can inform learners to solve problems. This could be very useful if a research project team wanted to have an informal brainstorming session about a topic but needed supporting data. For example, eco-scientists could get sensor data about air pollution measurements from smart clothing worn by a sample group of research participants.

Figure 3 shows examples of social learning in an organisation. The stakeholder's meaning making may come from subject experts, mentors, or members in a community of practice. Collaboration may be through forums, blogs, wikis, etc. Interestingly, most social learning was done through real-time communication. This data supports next section of the chapter proposing the value of webinar variations.

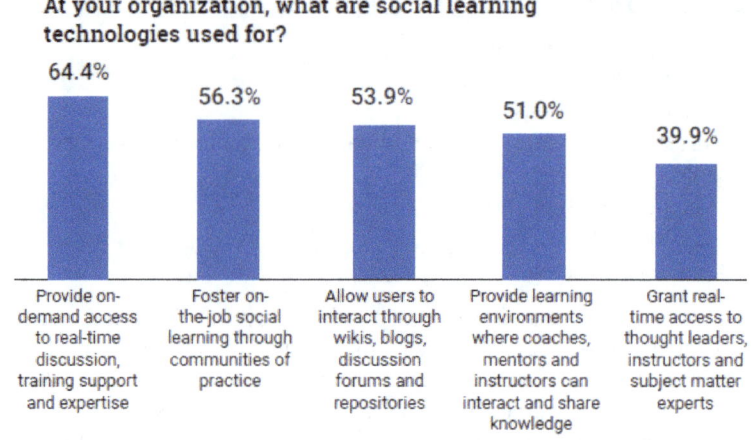

Figure 3: Adobe Social Learning Survey

The next figure shows that the type of content for social learning technologies leans towards the soft skills areas previously identified as a focus for the curriculum of next-generation universities. Through social learning employees and university students can learn through social technologies as they progress from the initial induction stage to 'lifelong learning careers' while strengthening their confidence and leadership capability.

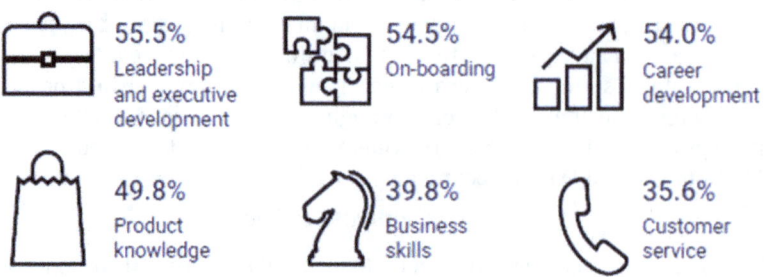

Figure 4: Social Learning Technologies

The Adobe survey entitled, 'State of Social Learning in the Enterprise' conducted by the Chief Learning Officer had some key findings to inform the nature of social learning for our future higher educators and learners:

- A majority of organisations surveyed (61.3%) currently use social learning technologies.
- The top drivers for using social learning technologies are to create and support a culture of learning and encourage collaboration at the organisation.
- Nearly half of all organisations (48.4%) that use social learning technologies for employees also use them for their customer communities.
- The top challenge to implementing successful social learning programs (and eLearning systems in general) is a lack of employee adoption (54.3%).
- Top outcomes realised through social learning include learner compliance efficiency, employee retention and greater collaboration among cross-functional groups.

Faculty are the employees of a university. Through this technology and learning design it will be possible to promote a learning culture within the higher education institution. This informal social approach to learning can be used with the university students as well.

The Adobe research summarises these conclusions; an organisation can increase internal communication and collaborative social learning to help individuals and organisations achieve their goals. Social learning technologies can help to create and support a culture of learning for teams and organisations and encourage collaboration and innovation by promoting creative thinking. By adopting social learning technologies, organisations and teams can promote learning across the enterprise while at the same time facilitating greater collaboration and sharing of ideas across geographically dispersed stakeholders. Technology can be a main factor to drive higher adoption of social learning. User-generated content and curation can enable scale without compromising quality, and that can allow higher education organisations to leverage subject-matter experts from disparate geographical areas to share their expertise with peers and eventually create a culture of collaboration.

A Possible Solution: Webinars of the future

In this section of the chapter webinar design and technologies are explored. A critical review of the systems and associated tools for webinars compares features. Instructional designs for webinars are analysed to demonstrate levels of interactivity. Finally, immersive webinars for the future are proposed offering a unique 'Fishbowl Discussion' model.

The PAP (Pre-At-Post) Model

The Pre-stage of a learning event is where 'ice-breaker' activities or 'taster' questions are offered to encourage motivation and interest from the learners. The At-stage is where the teaching or webinar presentation occurs. And, the Post-stage contains follow-up actions to keep the dialogue going and build the network through a virtual community.

Once evaluated, the PAP model can be cloned to future webinars depending on the audience profile. If the face-to-face (f2f)/online participants are similar, it may be possible to replicate the instructional design and resources.

Along with the PAP model for an individual webinar or lesson, this design applies to the curriculum of the programme over the semester of an academic year for the entire length of the degree. In this context, Pre-enrolment activity is directed at the prospective new recruits, while Post-actions are aimed at Alumni.

Related to the PAP Model is the 'flipped classroom' model (2019) which sees the content 'front-end' delivered. Students are given the majority of the content to read before the face-to-face in-class activities. In this way, the purpose of the At-event is to apply the Pre-event knowledge gained. This model requires autonomous learners who must do the prerequisite reading, or the applied lesson fails and must become a traditional lecture. Table 1 table gives a brief summary of webinar features with a PAP timeline:

Table 1: Summary of Webinar Features

Before	During	After
Prepare & Invite	Run & Interact	Analyse & Share
Webinar timeline	New Room	On-demand webinars
Sub accounts	Facebook & YouTube Live	Webinar & attendee statistics
Multi-user	Webinar room	Webinar recording
Custom branding	Audio & video	Webinar storage
Address book	Presentation	Thank-you page
Customized invitations	Whiteboard	Social media sharing
Registration page	Audio modes	Performance rating
Profile page	Screen sharing	
Waiting room with agenda	Polls & surveys	
Webinar timeline	Simultaneous chat translation	
Sub accounts	Moderated (Q&A) and private chat	
Multi-user	Toll-free phone numbers	
Custom branding	Mobile application	
	Online meetings	
	Call to action	

Next generation immersive webinars

According to Stelingyte (2017), live holographic streaming engines can change the industry by bringing real-time 3D VR/AR experiences to users. A recent VR

Learning Designs and Systems in the University of the Future

Intelligence survey showed that a lack of engaging content can hold the industry back. On the other hand, content creators need better distribution of VR/AR headsets. Immersive webinars have the potential to provide learner-generated content from an 'inside-out' perspective, but at the time of this writing, more research and development work is needed to make mainstream immersive holographic learning environments affordable for near-future HE learners.

One possible solution towards immersive webinars is to develop a hybrid model of current 2D webinar technology and 360° web video used in conjunction with mobile smartphones. This blended technology could support a 'Socratic fishbowl' discussion learning design. DATL (2019) sees the ultimate goal of the Socratic Method is to increase understanding through inquiry. Obtaining an enhanced freedom to think through discarding pre-existing bad ideas is the penultimate objective of the classic Socratic discussion. The only person who cannot think, is the one who thinks they already know all the answers. Through the deconstruction of existing ideas, the classic style of the Socratic discourse frees people to think about basic principles and ideas with an enhanced sense of necessity and clarity.

The starting proposition of this learning model states that there is no point in getting deeply into complicated theories of particular applications of a concept until one can answer a much simpler question. The Classic Socratic approach functions to tear down existing ideas of the concept. This works by exposing unknown or unacknowledged ambiguity and complexity, which makes the respondent realise they have more thinking to do. The 'Socratic Effect' provides the respondent with the opportunity to rethink the idea after having their previously existing understanding discarded with their full agreement on the basis of their own answers to questions. The 'unconference' (2019) fishbowl discussion can promote the 'Socratic Effect' which is outlined in figure 5.

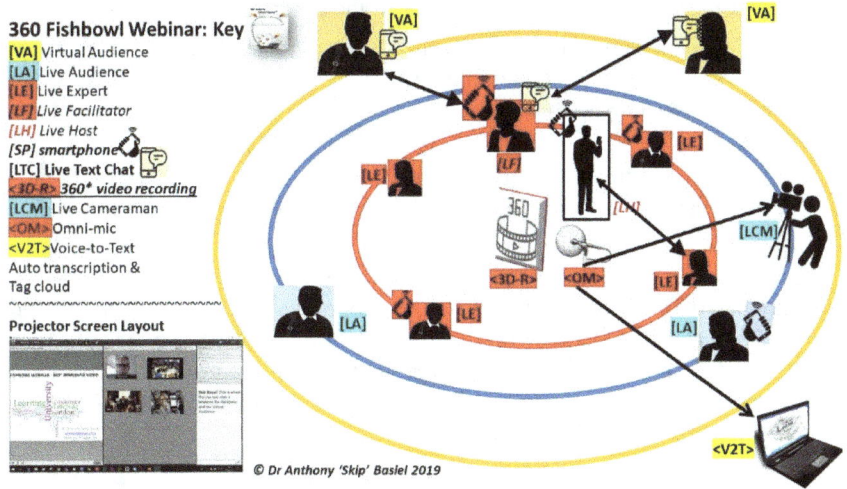

Figure 5: 360° Immersive Fishbowl Webinar Summary

The 360° Fishbowl Webinar Model

This immersive blended learning model is knitting together 360° video, mobile smartphone video conferencing, a local digital video camera, voice-to-text software for auto-transcription and a webinar host platform. The face-to-face 'fishbowl discussion' has a small central group of Local Experts [LE] sitting in an inner (red) circle with a Live Host [LH] using their mobile phone as a video camera/microphone to interview the Experts. The Host swaps the video camera from viewing themselves, when acting as Master of Ceremony, to showing the Expert speaking.

A 'Meta-Film' approach (Basiel and Howarth 2017) sees the unconference inner-and-outer circle actors [LA] using their mobile phones to record events from their perspective. These videos can be shared in social media platforms to promote the conference and develop an online community of learners.

In the centre of the circle there are two capture devices:
1. 360° video camera <3D-R>– This device records the introduction first, before the live event. Next, the fishbowl discussion is recorded.
2. Omni mic <OM> – This device is used for two outputs. First, it is the main audio input for the Live Camera Man [LCM] who produces the main screen of the event. Additionally, the audio is fed into a live voice-to-text transcription <V2T>. That text is used to create a tag cloud summary graphic of the transcript. Text captured from the event can be used as the database for an AI chatterbot dynamic FAQ resource.

The event Live Facilitator [LF] is a key player in the model. They sit in the inner circle and act as moderator for the Host and remote audience virtual [VA] members. This interaction is mediated silently, at first, by live text chat [LTC] discussion. As the Live Facilitator finds questions to add to the discussion, they give the VA member video access and turn off their [LF] self-video.

The projector screen layout diagram (in the bottom left corner in Figure 5) suggests how the event may look online to the virtual audience [VA] and projected at the live event on a big screen so the face-to-face actors can see the video of the entire group.

The event can use the interactive webinar elements such as whiteboard mind maps, voting, surveys, polling, etc. Evaluation of the event success is measured through online surveys and interviews.

Further research and development projects are proposed to test this blended learning innovation. Through this interactive mix of technology and live/recorded curriculum elements evidence can be collected to test the proposition that the immersive 360° fishbowl discussion design model can promote and support the collaborative engagement needed for the creative brainstorming problem-solving challenges future HE pupils will face.

Conclusions

Through a literature review of higher education futurists and primary data analysis from emails, phone calls and case study observations, this chapter has examined the elements of current university pedagogy and technology to inform the nature of under-and-postgraduate learning in the near future.

From a pedagogic perspective, a paradigm shift from our traditional instructional design is expected. Top-down, teacher-led assessment-driven curriculum models will be replaced. The new learning drivers will come from the needs of employers and social economics. The result will see a move from face-to-face teaching to blended and eLearning approaches. Informal learning through tacit experiences will afford professional social networked learning opportunities. The curriculum will come from real-world problems with learner-generated content. Individuals will still conduct research, but there will be more of a focus on virtual team collaboration. Appropriate supporting technology is needed for the next generation university students.

Current Higher Education Institutions use technology to focus on content dissemination. LMSs are used to access multimedia information. But, if the 'media is the message' as McLuhan (1977) suggests, what technology enhanced learning systems can promote and support 'people skills' to encourage problem solving capabilities?

Mobile interactive (immersive) webinars informed by artificial intelligence data have the potential to be the future higher education learning space. University organisations can provide professional social network contacts through guest speakers, career support and Alumni affiliates.

Sutton and Basiel (2014) see a convergence of technology in the future to wearable immersive systems accessed by motion or voice input. This chapter recommends to the publisher that they apply these predictions to the live academic conference branch of the organisation. Each chapter author can be invited to do a webinar on their topic which is then presented live at a blended format academic conference series.

The next generation of this book won't be on (dead tree format) paper, or as pixels on a screen, but rather provided to you the reader in a blended new media format to involve all of our senses and perceptions. You, the reader, will be the author, and higher education learning will never be the same again.

References

(all websites visited in May 2019)

Adobe Captivate Prime (2019) State of Social Learning in the Enterprise Chief Learning Officer / Adobe Systems Ltd.
https://www.adobe.com/uk/products/captivateprime.html

Alexander B (2013) https://bryanalexander.org/uncategorized/peak-education-2013/
Alexander B (2019) - https://twitter.com/BryanAlexander
http://futureofeducation.us/

Basiel & Howarth (2017), 'Active Learning Through a 'Meta-Film' Approach'
https://drive.google.com/open?id=0B5KEPSFKjo5OZUljMWpWNWN5RGc
Sample video: https://youtu.be/TQXk2sHItmk

Basiel A. (2007), p. 30 - ePedagogy for Virtual Learning Environments,
https://drive.google.com/file/d/0B5KEPSFKjo5OeWxIeGhYdWZOMzA/view

Basiel A (2018) Guest Speaker Proposal
https://drive.google.com/open?id=10YLxnPZeP94QAZsaMTlswM6C8883r3cv

Basiel, (2003) - Venturi L, Global Rich Pictures, http://www.indire.it/content/index.php?action=read&id=346

Basiel, Anthony (2007) A European perspective of work based learning: lessons from a CEDEFOP (European Centre for the Development of Vocational Training)study visit. In: UALL Work Based Learning Conference, 5-6 July 2007, Middlesex University, Trent Park.

British Telecom (BT 2009) 'Dare-to-Share' https://youtu.be/gtVYkEdGtfo

Cairns, L & Alshahrani, K (2014), 'Online Learning: Models and Impact in the 21st Century' - 'Teaching and Learning Online: New Models of Learning for a Connected World', Routledge Press.

Cbinsights (2019) https://www.cbinsights.com/research-ar-vr-webinar-sept

Coase, R (1936), 'The Nature of the Firm', https://doi.org/10.1111/j.1468-0335.1937.tb00002.x DATL (2019) https://sites.google.com/a/dcsdk12.org/etil-academycadre/fishbowl-socratic-seminar

Dawson R (2019) https://rossdawson.com/keynote-speaker/keynote-speaking-topics/keynote-speaking- topics-the-future-of-universities-and-education

Downes S. (2005), 'E-Learning 2.0' – National Research Council of Canada https://elearnmag.acm.org/archive.cfm?aid=1104968

Drucker, P (1999), 'Managing Oneself', Harvard Business Review, SBN-13: 978-1422123126 ISBN- 10: 142212312X

Edupreneur (2019) https://courses.edupreneuracademy.org/lesson/lesson-1-what-is-an-edupreneur

Erasmus (2019) https://ec.europa.eu/programmes/erasmus-plus/ https://ec.europa.eu/programmes/erasmus- plus/contact_en

Flanagan J (1954) https://books.apa.org/pubs/databases/psycinfo/cit-article.pdf

Flipped classroom model (2019) https://www.heacademy.ac.uk/knowledge-hub/flipped-learning-0 Frey T (2016), Cracking the Code for the Future of Education, https://futuristspeaker.com/future-of-education/cracking-the-code-for-the-future-of-education/

Gates, S. (2015) The Negotiation Book https://www.thegappartnership.com/The-Negotiation-Book Goldacre, B. (2019) 'Bad Science' Website: https://www.badscience.net/YouTube: http://www.ted.com/talks/ben_goldacre_battling_bad_science.html

Green, S. (2002) https://www.cambridgeassessment.org.uk/Images/109693-criterion-referenced-assessment- as-a-guide-to-learning-the-importance-of-progression-and-reliability.pdf

Harris, A. (2018) https://www.theatlantic.com/education/archive/2018/06/heres-how-higher-education- dies/561995/

Hiddleston, A. (2019) The future of digital learning experiences https://st3.ning.com/topology/rest/1.0/file/get/2660818966?profile=original

Hiemstra G. (2013) Education: https://www.futurist.com/2013/05/17/the-future-of-higher-education/ Hult International Business School: AMBA MBA Curriculum Innovation Award (2014)

https://www.hult.edu/blog/hult-wins-ambas-2014-mba-innovation-award/ Hult Prize (2019) http://www.hultprize.org/about/

Illich, I. (1970) – 'Deschooling Society' Penguin Books, Ltd.

iSpring (2018) 70:20:10 Learning Model https://www.ispringsolutions.com/blog/70-20-10-learning- model?utm_source=linkedin&utm_medium=social&utm_campaign=70-20-10-learning-model

Jana Laura (2019) TEDx Talk: Skills Every Child Will Need to Succeed in 21st century https://youtu.be/z_1Zv_ECy0g

Jay Cross (2019) - https://www.dontwasteyourtime.co.uk/tag/jay-cross/

Kaku M (2017) EDUCASE Keynote - https://www.ecampusnews.com/2017/11/07/michio-kaku-higher-ed- skills/

Kumar, M. (2019) https://www.linkedin.com/in/mukul-kumar-79415b/?originalSubdomain=uk Learning and Skills Group (2019) https://learningandskillsgroup.ning.com/forum/topics/the-future-of-digital-learning-experiences-alan-hiddleston-d2l

McLuhan, M. (1977), Marshall McLuhan 1977 - Full Lecture John Hopkins University on Global Village and the Tetrad https://youtu.be/PugVfJS1zCE

MOOC (2019) http://mooc.org/

Nesta (2019a) https://www.nesta.org.uk/ Ofsted's Draft Inspection Framework https://www.nesta.org.uk/blog/moving-towards-holistic-assessment-education-quality/

Nesta (2019) https://www.nesta.org.uk/education/

NSCRC (2019) https://nscresearchcenter.org/?s=enrollment+statistics+ Piaget, J (1936) https://www.simplypsychology.org/piaget.html

PM (2019) projectmanagement.com http://www.projectmanagement.com

Popper, K (1959) The Logic of Scientific Discovery, translation of Logik der Forschung, London: Hutchinson http://strangebeautiful.com/other-texts/popper-logic-scientific-discovery.pdf

Ross, J (2019) 'Students 'want universities to find them jobs', Times Higher Education, https://www.timeshighereducation.com/news/students-want-universities-find-jobs-them

Schank, Roger C. (1995) What We Learn When We Learn by Doing. (Technical Report No. 60).
Northwestern University, Institute for Learning Sciences. http://cogprints.org/637/1/LearnbyDoing_Schank.html

Snyder D (2019) http://www.the-futurist.com Snyder Family Enterprise (2010) http://www.the- futurist.com/future_watch.htm

Snyder D (2006) Longer, Fuller, Further Education - The Coming Metamorphosis of the University - http://www.the-futurist.com/from_higher_ed.htm

Steffe, L. (1995), Constructivism in Education Hillsdale, NJ: Lawrence Erlbaum, 1995. – 575 p.ISBN 0- 8058-1095-1 (hardback)0-8058-1096-X (paperback)

Stelingyte, I. (2017) https://www.brighttalk.com/webcast/13939/257137/vr-ar-live-holographic-streaming

Sutton and Basiel (2014), 'Endpiece' - 'Teaching and Learning Online: New Models of Learning for a Connected World', Routledge Press.

Unconference (2019) http://unconference.net/unconference-methods-fish-bowl-dialogue/

WEF (2019) https://www.weforum.org/

Anthony 'Skip' Basiel, an innovative life-long learner in *e*Pedagogy, is currently researching learning technology designs for immersive 360° fishbowl webinars. Gamification and computer simulations are also areas of interest.

14

Future-Proofing a Region's Knowledge Economy

Gareth Huw Davies[1], Naomi Joyce[2] and David Bolton[1]
[1]School of Management, Swansea University, Wales, UK
[2]School of Medicine, Swansea University, Wales, UK

Introduction

The origins of the modern university as places of enquiry and repositories of knowledge, as well as their role in training, are traced back to medieval Europe (Perkin, 2007). In the centuries since passed, the emergence of the mass participation form of education and competitive research communities are now subject to forces that are political and economic, both global and local (McCaffery, 2018). It was in later years that the UK sector started to emerge, and in 1828 Wales became home to a university when St David's College received its Royal Charter. Initially focused on religious education, it was joined by institutions including Swansea University, the focus of this Chapter, founded with greater focus on supporting industry and commerce.

More recently, at the turn of the last century, the future university role was described as shifting from '*ivory tower to entrepreneurial paradigm*' by Etzkowitz, Webster et al., (2000). This was described as involving a transition to a 'triple helix' paradigm or engagement between academia, industry and government (Leydesdorff and Etzkowitz, 1998; Etzkowitz and Leydesdorff, 2000). There was some apprehension expressed that this apparent evolution in focus may not be purely beneficial, risking crowding out longer-term and more speculative endeavours (Geuna, 2001). Nevertheless, despite this shift the contribution of universities to technical innovation had been long-established with academic endeavours supporting technological progress (Nelson, 1986).

More recently, the contribution of universities to national and regional economies has been further studied by academics (Wolfe, 2005; Huggins, Jones et al. 2008; Power and Malmberg, 2008) and considered by governments (Lambert 2003; WAG, 2004a) and other global stakeholders (EU, 2003; Yusuf and Nabeshima, 2006). This interest includes specifically the context of Wales, a nation within the United Kingdom and a peripheral region of the European Union (Abbey et al., 2008; Huggins et al., 2008; Pugh, 2017). The Welsh Government Knowledge Economy Nexus review (WAG, 2004a) succinctly describes contributions of universities to the economy as;

- *Direct Wealth Contribution* as businesses themselves, often as major regional employers with highly skilled workforces
- *Graduate Output*, supporting knowledge-based activity through the knowledge and skills of their alumni
- *Knowledge transfer and commercialisation,* bringing existing and new knowledge from the university into industry for economic and wider social benefit

These descriptors bear alignment to the university 'missions' of creating knowledge through research and imparting it to students via learning and teaching, along with a specific agenda of economic development (Etzkowitz et al., 2000). Subsequent consideration by Laredo (2007), presented three 'functions' rather than 'missions' with linkages to localities relating to activities including industry-focused research.

In parallel, significant increase in university participation aligned with growing interest in institutions' contribution to entrepreneurship, as a larger proportion of the working population pass through higher education. Describing the concept of the 'entrepreneurial university' Gibb and Hannon (2006) emphasise the opportunity for universities to work in partnership with their regions to deliver '*desirable entrepreneurship outcomes*', a sentiment embraced by the Welsh Government (WAG, 2010).

The relationship between institutions and their regions has involved continued consideration of managing (or perhaps balancing) both local relevance and global perspective. This has increasingly emphasised contribution to universities' localities (Charles 2003) with research undertaken to understand the relationship between different types of university and their local contexts (Hewitt-Dundas, 2012; Guerrero et al., 2015). This is particularly pertinent in Wales, with diversity amongst its universities including both research-focused and teaching-led institutions of recent and longer-established heritage.

Interest in universities' local context has often been aimed to replicate the benefits of cluster development for regional economic development. This has been described in contexts of Regional Innovation Systems (Lundvall, 1992; Cooke, 1997; Uranga et al., 1997; Cooke, 2001) and Smart Specialisations (Foray et al., 2009, Morgan, 2013). Harnessing the potential of universities to support such development has been examined by policy-makers (DTI, 2001; EU, 2010), and received significant consideration from academia (Malmberg et al., 1996). This interest has featured consistently in Welsh Government policies, incorporating concepts from clusters through to Smart Specialisation (WAG, 2004a; WAG, 2004b; WAG, 2010; WG, 2014)

However, even well-quoted examples of the university role in cluster development have led to questions regarding the direct nature of any university effect upon cluster development (Casper and Karamanos, 2003; Martin and Sunley, 2003; Power and Malmberg, 2008). This may suggest that universities alone are an unlikely sole panacea for deep-rooted socio-economic challenges such as those faced by parts of Wales. Set in the above context, a useful concept for consideration of the university role is offered by Youtie and Shapira (2008), describing how universities have progressed from storing, through to creating, and more recently, brokering knowledge.

The imperative for many UK research-intensive universities is to perform well against the Research Excellence Framework (REF) (Martin, 2011; Stern, 2016), with a focus upon 'creation' of knowledge. However, increasing REF consideration of research 'Impact' brings further attention to effective brokerage of knowledge to those who will exploit it. More recently, the translation of UK academic output into societal benefit is receiving further consideration through the emerging Knowledge Exchange Framework (KEF), including via university roles in activities of 'Commercialisation' and 'Problem-solving' (for/with partners). In this KEF context, analysis has also shown a typology of institutions (Ulrichsen, 2018), related to their local economic & industrial contexts.

Work relating to KEF has already given focus to Technology Transfer (HEFCE, 2016), noting an importance of ecosystems, and recognition that there is no single approach which will work for all institutions. Technology transfer activity has grown significantly in the US since passing of the 1980 Bayh-Dole Act (Mowery et al., 2001; Shane, 2004), with a similar uplift amongst UK institutions occurring a decade later during the 1990s (Lambert, 2003). Technology Transfer's role in economic development has been demonstrated by Tornatzky (2000) and reviewed by governments including those of the UK (Lambert, 2003) and Wales (WAG, 2004a; WG, 2018). The next section briefly presents key underpinning aspects of this University-Industry engagement mechanism to provide the context for the ILS *Infrastructure* and AgorIP *Activity* cases examined in this chapter.

Technology transfer

As introduced in the prior section, Technology Transfer exists in a broader context of University-Industry interaction mechanisms. While some observers (Perkmann and Walsh, 2007) suggest that University-Industry relationships were distinct from Technology Transfer, others emphasise their interconnection (Dechenaux et al., 2011). Technology transfer features a Technology Transfer Office (TTO) facilitating steps from discovery and Intellectual Property Rights capture/protection through to the negotiation of agreements with technology recipients, as presented below by (Siegel et al., 2004).

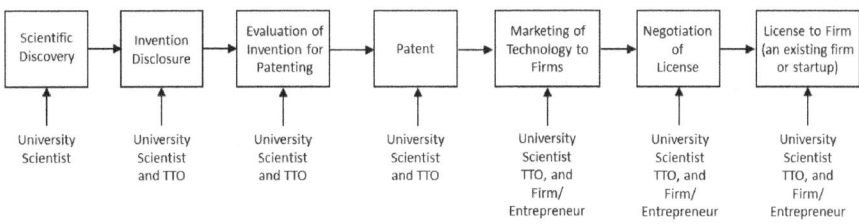

Figure 1: Technology Transfer Process – Linear (Siegel, Waldman et al. 2004)

As presented above, and within more complex Alternative Models (Bradley et al., 2013), the Technology Transfer Office plays a central role within the process. A lack of appropriate skills or experience within TTOs has been emphasised as a key performance challenge for organisations engaged in Technology Transfer (Siegel et al., 2003; Decter et al., 2007; Hülsbeck et al., 2013).

Alongside TTO skills, other factors relating to the effectiveness of TTO operations have received examination, including the proximity of partners and a critical mass of activity (Audretsch and Lehmann, 2005). Development of profile/reputation through a scale of activity is described by Macho-Stadler et al. (2007), however Siegel, et al. (2003) suggest potential decreasing returns with an increased scale. Within the Welsh context, both government (WAG, 2004a) and key practitioners (Gibson, 2007) have noted a lack of impactful and sustainable scale of activity within individual institutions.

In terms of technology transfer process output, licensing or investment into spin-out ventures are considered as principle results, in both the original linear (Siegel et al., 2004) or more recent complex models (Bradley et al., 2013). Selection of paths leading to these outcomes is in itself an area of discussion, including by Wright et al. (2006) describing a preference by venture capitalists to invest in university spin-outs once they have been developed (Ferguson and Olofsson, 2004).

As described above, the Technology Transfer process is complex and does not occur in isolation. The regional absorptive capacity and the capability of its universities are both critical factors in this perspective (Huggins and Johnston, 2009). The next section explores this context for the case of south west Wales, describing challenges that relate to many other post-industrial regions.

The environment: South West Wales

Wales is a peripheral region to the west of Europe, a semi-autonomous nation within the United Kingdom. The nation presents many of the socio-economic challenges associated with numerous post-industrial regions. For Wales, these challenges are most notable in its south west, where long-term decline of heavy industries has not been matched by economic renewal.

South west Wales, described as the Swansea Bay City Region (SBCR) consists of the Local Authorities (municipalities) of the City and County of Swansea, Neath Port Talbot County Borough, Carmarthenshire County, and Pembrokeshire County, encompassing 688,000 residents, 302,000 jobs and 22,000 businesses (SBCR, 2013). It presents much of the diversity seen across Wales, stretching from the rural west of St Davids to the heavy industry of Port Talbot, home to the largest UK steelworks.

As the crucible of the industrial revolution through the coal and steel industries, the region has been defined by its industrial legacy (Mathias, 2013). Since its role in defining global industrialisation, the region has struggled in transitioning to a knowledge-led economy. Reasons include persistently low levels of Business Expenditure on Research & Development (Edmonds, 2000; Mom et al., 2012), and weak local levels of endogenous entrepreneurship and business growth (Cooke and Clifton, 2005).

Following major contraction of heavy industries during the 1970s/80s, economic development policy in Wales focused on attracting inward investment with a 'build it and they will come' approach, described as a 'field of dreams' by Cooke and Clifton (2005). The approach brought success attracting 15-20% of inward-UK Foreign Direct Investment (FDI) (Wales population ~5% of UK) during 1983-93 (Braczyk et al., 1998; Salvador and Harding, 2006). However, FDI opportunities declined during the 1990s with the emergence of competitor regions such as China and India (Chen, 1996) and a slowing UK economy (Young et al., 1994). Some overseas-managed manufacturing branch plants subsequently relocated from Wales to regions with lower costs, with observers noting weaknesses in the 'embeddedness' of such investments (Phelps et al., 2003). In parallel, an imbalance of economic development efforts in Wales was identified, suggesting insufficient attention was being given to indigenous enterprise and clusters (Cooke and Clifton, 2005).

In response, the then recently devolved Welsh Assembly Government (WAG) took responsibility for economic development policy, shifting focus towards growth of high value-add sectors (WAG, 2003; WG, 2013). Continued weakness in the regional economy was demonstrated by much of Wales continuing to qualify for the highest levels of EU Regional Aid (Figure 2 below). This weakness also involved limited private sector R&D, resulting in much focus being given to the role universities could play in development of knowledge-based economic activity (WAG, 2004a).

Weakness in the private sector also included low levels of indigenous entrepreneurship, resulting in further emphasis on the role of universities in venture creation (WAG, 2003). However, relying upon Welsh universities to support expansion of knowledge-based enterprise drew questions, not least with the then historic rate of new venture formation by Welsh HEIs lagging in comparison with the wider UK (Brooksbank and Thomas, 2001). This concern over existing performance was echoed regarding the capacity of Welsh HEIs to deliver against future ambitions (Gibson, 2007), a view supported at that time by Wales ranking 10th out of 12 UK regions for the proportion of research-active academic staff within its universities (NAW, 2006).

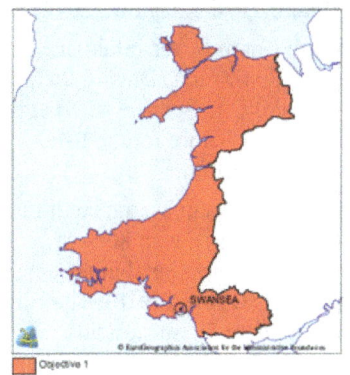
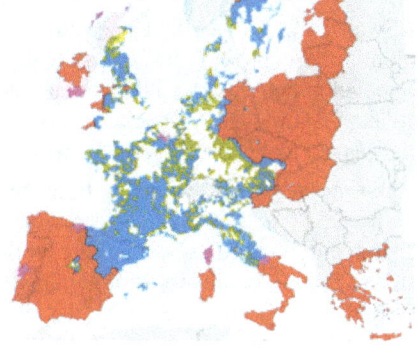

Objective One region in Wales   Objective One regions in the EU

Figure 2: 'Objective One' regions in Wales and EU (WEFO)

To support the aim of increasing University-derived enterprise, Brooksbank and Thomas (2001) recommended the development of incubation facilities and on-campus industrial collaboration environments. This was however potentially limited as an approach, considering that existing 'critical mass' of local high technology employment can be regarded as an important precondition for knowledge transfer and substantial local economic effects (Varga, 2000).

Despite the aforementioned historic weakness, recent performance has seen notable improvements in the scale of new enterprise emerging from Welsh HEIs (Huggins et al., 2008) with spin-out survival rates ahead of other UK regions (HEFCW). This has led to continuing WG interest in innovation policy involving universities, not least in formation and support of knowledge-based enterprise (WG, 2014).

The institution: Swansea University

Originally established in 1920 as the University College of Swansea within the federal University of Wales, the institution became fully independent as Swansea University in 2007. Rated as a Top 30 UK institution for research excellence (HEFCE, 2014), Swansea has a student body of over 20,000 across two campuses in the city.

From the inaugural address of the institution's first Principal, the relationship with industry was embedded, with Davies (2018) quoting the *'views of the industrial founders of the University who championed the role of the university in promoting regional competitive advantage through commercialising scientific research'*. The institution became part of the Federal University of Wales, with particular strengths in materials science and engineering, reflecting its industrial heritage.

Recent years have seen the significant expansion of the University, much of it with a focus on industry engagement. A significant part of this growth has been enabled by WG policy support (WAG, 2003; WG, 2014) and EU investment (WEFO, 2007; WEFO, 2014). This has contributed to address the capacity challenges for knowledge-based activity in Wales noted over preceding years (Brooksbank and Thomas, 2001; Cooke, 2004b; Huggins and Kitagawa, 2012).

Swansea University's Science and Innovation Bay Campus was established as a £450m initiative to embrace the triple helix model for innovation (Davies, 2018). The development followed the creation of the Institute of Life Science (ILS) at the Singleton Campus providing collaborative research infrastructure for the Life Sciences & Health sectors, which are the focus of a later section.

During the period leading up to the opening of the Bay Campus, the institution rose from 52nd to 26th in UK research rankings (HEFCE, 2014), with 80% of research output rated as being either world-leading or of international importance, much of it underpinned by strong industrial engagement (Davies, 2018). The Bay Campus development aligns with the identified requirement for successful knowledge and technology transfer of research intensity (Hewitt-Dundas, 2012) and quality (Jensen, et al., 2003).

Swansea University is certainly not alone in the region. It has important neighbours in the aforementioned local teaching-led University of Wales Trinity St David, and to the east the 'Russell Group' (research-intensive) Cardiff University. Linkages between Swansea University and these neighbour institutions through initiatives such as *Accelerate* (Life Sciences & Health) and *SPECIFIC* (Low

Carbon Built Environment) demonstrate engagement within the broader Wales-wide Innovation System.

Collectively, there now exists within the region significant academic and associated industrial research capability, as recently described in the South Wales Crucible Science and Innovation Audit for UK Government (SIA) (SU, 2018). These capabilities align with the Smart Specialisations (Foray et al., 2009) identified in Wales by the EU Commission (EU, 2017) and other key commentators (Morgan, 2013).

The next phase of Swansea University's development is centred on its activity beyond the two campuses, including the Swansea Bay City Region *Internet Coast* City Deal which aims to support a restructuring of the regional economy towards high-growth high-GVA sectors. Built upon Smart Specialisations, the Internet Coast Programme has been developed around four '*Internet Themes*' containing eleven projects with the following stated ambitions;

- *Internet of Health & Wellbeing*: to support commercialisation of Intellectual Property from the Health Service along with indigenous and inward-investing Life Sciences & healthcare activities.
- *Internet of Energy*: to create renewable energy technology for homes and buildings as part of a developing cluster around SPECIFIC photovoltaic technology.
- *Internet of Economic Acceleration*: to develop Internet and Communications Technology-driven services and infrastructure, along with major initiatives embedded in urban regeneration projects.
- *Smart Manufacturing*: to support product and process innovation in the regionally and UK-wide strategically important steel sector, along with efforts to develop Industry 4.0 practice in south west Wales manufacturing.

The Internet Themes reflect sectors targeted in WG strategies (WAG, 2009; WG, 2013), though are fewer and align more explicitly with identified Smart Specialisations (EU, 2017), including the SPECIFIC Energy capability noted by Morgan (2013). Internet technologies including the emergent 5G standard and can be considered along the lines of 'General Purpose Technology' supporting innovation across these sectors. In this context, the complexity of the innovation process is increased, with universities playing a role with 'co-specialised assets' (Foray et al., 2009) in the endeavour to support structural change in the sub-regional economy (Foray, 2014).

Building upon initiatives such as the Institute of Life Science (ILS), Swansea University has aimed to become a Knowledge Hub of the nature described by Youtie and Shapira (2008), working to develop infrastructure and activity in support of regional development, based on the above specialisations. The next sections explore the initiatives of ILS and AgorIP from perspectives of developing *Infrastructure* and *Activity*.

Emergence of open innovation at ILS

The ILS is a partnership between Swansea University's Medical School, Swansea Bay University Health Board, Welsh Government (WG) and the private sector with the purpose of supporting Life Sciences and Health research and innovation. ILS presents a major effort to develop a cluster initially identified by UK Government in 2001 (DTI, 2001), and subsequently noted as one of Wales' Smart Specialisations (EU, 2017).

Initially noted by Abbey et al. (2008a) as part of a sub-regional innovation system, its contribution to the region (Davies et al., 2018a) and its broader context (RLP, 2013) have received attention, including its role in forming linkages with regional health boards (ARCH, 2017).

The ILS infrastructure has been realised in two phases (2004-09 and 2009-15), creating research facilities with initial revenue support for industry collaboration and business development activities. The rationale for the significant £40m+ investment involving EU Structural Funds (WEFO, 2014) has been to help redress the imbalance in regional science spending, as noted by Cooke (2004). The ILS sector focus aligns with insight to the opportunities identified in a review of the wider bio-sciences value chain and the role of incubators by Cooke et al. (2006). Their work suggested the possibility of 'constructed advantage' involving efforts to commercialise research output and develop linkages by leveraging research infrastructure where other assets are weak or absent.

Since 2004, the ILS initiative has developed into a set of facilities, primarily at the Swansea University Singleton Campus adjacent to one of the region's main hospitals, though with an increasing level of activity at the nearby Morriston major hospital site. ILS facilities include biomedical laboratories for industrial collaboration, a dedicated clinical research facility, a medical imaging research suite, and a life sciences business incubator. Supported by a business engagement team to assist incubator tenants and develop external linkages, ILS is currently involved with the pan-Wales Accelerate initiative.

The ILS business incubator itself can be described as an example of a hybrid of the 'Low Selective' and 'Supportive' incubator environments described by Clarysse et al. (2005) with a diverse mix of 'lifestyle' and high-growth businesses.

A survey undertaken of companies engaged with ILS provided insight as to how the infrastructure was utilised (RLP, 2013). Research collaboration being cited as the most common nature of linkage is perhaps unsurprising given the ILS function as a research organisation (Mian, 1996), though does not feature for all enterprises engaged. The same survey also found half of the respondents had received support in developing a formal link with another enterprise in the region (for example establishing a joint venture). A similar proportion of the firms involved with ILS had also been established by serial entrepreneurs. These findings suggest the infrastructure supports both the development and embeddedness of the local cluster.

The RLP survey also provides insight to the ILS infrastructure role in supporting both start-up and existing companies (Figure. 3 below). An unsurprising bias towards new firms for early stage support was found, though with an uptake of other assistance broadly consistent across new and existing firms (it should though be noted that the small sample size of 72 precludes any deeper analysis). The findings align with those of the ILS2 end-project evaluation, which noted the importance of the sector-specific facilities and expertise in supporting industry engagements (TECC, 2015). The majority of firms reported engagement with ILS scientific expertise and facilities, supporting consideration of the ILS as being sector-specific R&D infrastructure, rather than as generic business development/finance support. This reflects the nature of its presentation in pan-Wales strategies by Welsh Government (WG, 2014) and subsequent EU Structural Funds Programmes (WEFO, 2014).

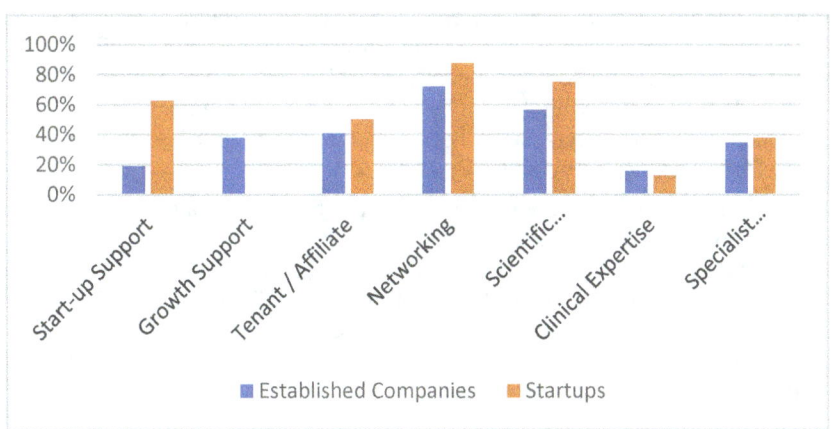

Figure 3: ILS Support uptake by engaged existing enterprises and start-ups

The linkages described above suggest ILS activity is involved in development of the cluster, subsequently shown to support job creation (Figure 4) (Davies et al., 2018a).

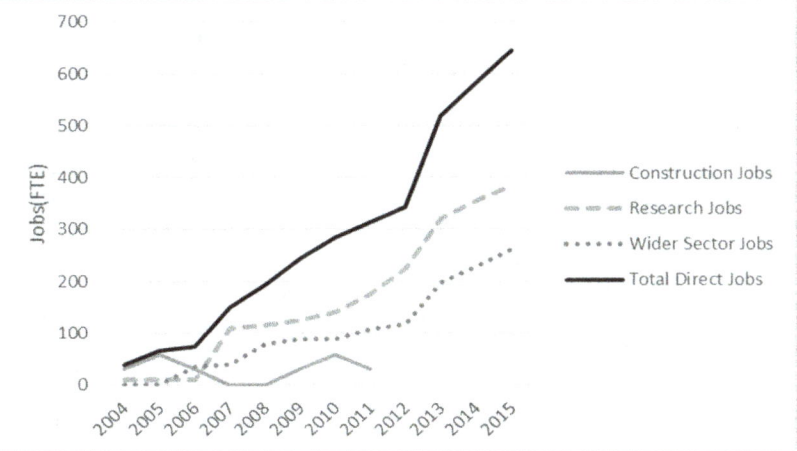

Figure 4: ILS cumulative employment growth by job type (Davies et al. 2018)

Of particular note is how this employment is distributed throughout the cluster. For example, as shown by Davies et al. (2015), two ILS collaborations created 56 jobs in the partner companies, while an additional 70 jobs were realised at a third-party manufacturing site. This example involves collaboration between ILS firms and others located elsewhere in the sub-regional innovation system described by Abbey et al. (2008). The collaborations also involved local clinical trials and professional services support, demonstrating wider cluster working and embeddedness of the innovation activity. Such examples reinforce the complexity, and non-linearity of knowledge and technology transfer activities described by Bradley et al. (2013), Bramwell and Wolfe (2008) and Hewitt-Dundas (2012).

The infrastructure dimension of ILS and its support of job creation is of particular interest for south west Wales, and a meaningful contribution to the Welsh Life Sciences sector (WG, 2013). Incubator initiatives in the region have previously had mixed success and reception (Cooke, 2004b, Abbey et al., 2008). However, ILS resonated with the call by Morgan (2013) for more effective consideration of smart specialisation, of which Life Sciences & Health is an accepted Welsh example (EU, 2017).

The ability of infrastructure to support job creation in such a high value-add sector is also an important strategic factor for the region as it aims to develop ~2,000 jobs across the region over the next 15 years (SU, 2017). The ILS experience to date and its planned 'regionalisation' highlights the complexity of activity with collaborators requiring different types of support, and at different times, with each pathway unique to the activity in question. This leads to the question of how *Activity* can then be delivered to support this collaboration, which is explored in the next section through consideration of the AgorIP initiative.

AgorIP

AgorIP, based at Swansea University, (Agor being Welsh language for 'Open') is a pan-Wales initiative to establish a shared/open TTO, developed in partnership between academia, health service, Welsh Government and industry for commercialisation of Intellectual Property (IP) from university and clinical (primarily Health Board) research. It aims to help respond to the Welsh Government call for '*a more integrated and holistic support system for commercialisation*' (WAG, 2004a), aligned with Wales' Smart Specialisations (EU, 2017).

The AgorIP TTO operates on a case-by-case basis, providing support tailored to each opportunity. The target outcome for opportunities is described as arrival at a point of 'investor-readiness' or other successful dissemination amongst potential users (SU, 2016). The outcome of the process (Figure 5) may be licensing of IP to an existing enterprise, formation of a spin-out, or creation of an open source offering. It is stated that this is delivered through an approach of co-investment from other initiatives/organisations to encourage risk sharing and resource efficiency.

AgorIP describes its approach as being 'Open Access Open Innovation' involving 'zero-waste' whereby all opportunities are progressed in some manner (SU, 2016) to extract value from all assets. The Open Innovation philosophy also opens the service pan-Wales, being agnostic to innovation source and destination, so long as benefit is captured within the region of interest, in line with the requirements of its primary funders (WEFO, 2014). The AgorIP process involves all disclosures being progressed through to one of the following four outcomes, or

returned to the inventor(s) for further development prior to potential reconsideration;
- *Soft Start*: Creating a spin-out to support development of the IP, with the purpose of attracting co-investment and exploring for market opportunity
- *Hard Start*: Creating a spin-out with co-investment in place at the outset, in order to pursue a defined market opportunity
- *Licence*: Providing IP rights to identified, like already-involved, partner(s) for their exploitation in return for a royalty
- *Open Source*: Making the IP available to the broadest possible range of users without conferring any particular advantage or receiving direct financial benefit

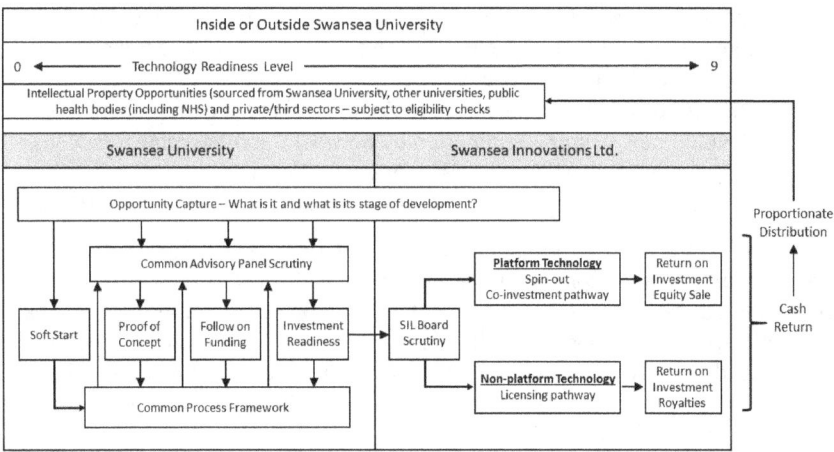

Figure 5: AgorIP Technology Transfer Process

As of March 2018, the AgorIP project had been underway for 27 months. At this point, a portfolio of 261 opportunities had been developed across sectors including Life Sciences & Health, Information and Communications Technology and Renewable Energy generation and management. These sectors have been targeted by the initiative, being identified as Welsh smart specialisations (SU, 2016, Commission, 2017).

As opportunities take time to develop and mature, this portfolio predominantly relates to opportunities in the earlier stages of commercialisation rather than outcomes. At the time of the study, 27 opportunities from the initial portfolio had resulted in spin-out companies supported by external investment, while a further 12 opportunities resulted in licensing arrangements with existing enterprises. This mix of transfer mechanisms utilised implies there is no particular favouring of either spin-out or licence as a form of output. This presents positively against potential bias described by D'Este and Patel (2007) of patenting and spin-out activities attracting disproportionate levels of attention by the technology transfer process.

The AgorIP project activity to date also targets structural and operational changes to commercialisation activity amongst the partners (SU, 2016) including;

- Harmonisation of IP policies between Swansea University and University Health Boards of Abertawe Bro Morgannwg and Hywel Dda. This involves creating alignment, or where possible, common terms of engagement amongst partners. This action responds to the UK-specific challenges identified by Decter et al. (2007) of variation between organisation policies presenting a challenge in realising industry engagement.
- Integration with delivery of knowledge transfer mechanisms such as consultancy arrangements in both university and health boards. Integrated with Swansea Innovations (a university consultancy/commercial vehicle) and health board R&D departments respectively, this aims to protect against potential overemphasis on patenting and spin-out activity, of the manner described by D'Este and Patel (2007). The initiative thereby intends to avoid internal competition between knowledge transfer and commercialisation pathways.
- The use of intensive mentoring including surrogate entrepreneurs to develop new ventures, supported by networks across sector fora. This reflects the suggestion from Wright et al. (2006) as to how weak entrepreneurial focus and skills amongst researchers can be addressed.

The AgorIP initiative has already been subject to discussion (Davies et al., 2017; Davies et al., 2018b), along with interest from policy-makers in Welsh (HEFCW, 2017) and UK (RSM, 2018) Governments. Common across these observers have been references to the open and collaborative nature of the activity, though noting it is still rather early to be looking for success. The role of universities and health boards in Wales working together to deliver innovation for patient benefit has become increasingly central in Welsh Government Policy (WG, 2018). Working across organisations as both sources and recipients of technology certainly shows elements of Open Innovation (Chesbrough, 2003), along with the more complex technology transfer dynamics suggested by Bradley et al. (2013) in their Alternative Model of Technology Transfer. It is the capacity for multiple pathways and partner configurations which presents the flexibility required to support the diversity of collaborations described earlier in relation to the ILS infrastructure.

Conclusion and policy implications

The deep longstanding relationship between Swansea University and industry stems from its initial roots formed a century ago. The institution's context of a region suffering post-industrial decline presents a reference for other regions considering the role a university can play in addressing the challenges of transitioning to a knowledge-led economy.

The interactions of Swansea University with its region and across Wales through *Activity* such as AgorIP and *Infrastructure* of ILS present aspects of Open Innovation and Smart Specialisation theory in practice. However, for both practitioners and policy-makers a core conclusion is to reinforce the long-standing observation that organisations engaged in technology-based innovation with limited capabilities must collaborate to succeed (Teece, 1986). Consideration of initiatives started 15 or more years ago also emphasises that while universities evolve over timescales measured in decades and generations, the future is a constantly moving horizon. The increasing focus of REF and KEF upon 'Impact' has recently provided added impetus to demonstrating relevance of university activity, though are themselves exercises undertaken during cycles of many years. The examples within this chapter have demonstrated this issue of development timescales, presenting work approaching two decades of endeavour since identification of the original Welsh Life Sciences 'mini-clusters' (DTI, 2001).

Individual projects, innovations and companies may evolve increasingly quickly, though universities are strategic organisations for regional ecosystems, particularly where they play a disproportionately important role. The initiatives described have shown it is possible to address capacity and deal flow challenges, such as those noted in south west Wales (Gibson, 2007), and to give focus to opportunities for smart specialisation (Morgan, 2013). In parallel, they aim to support the non-linear and collaborative nature of University-Industry interaction and commercialisation. While they present a response to particular challenges of south west Wales, and the specific context of its universities and regional industrial base, they present potential insight for other regions.

This chapter demonstrates how, despite enormous contextual changes and challenges, a university role can remain one of enlarging the world of knowledge to the benefit of the community it serves through effective collaboration with industry.

References

Abbey, J., Davies, G. & Mainwaring, L. 2008. Vorsprung durch Technium: Towards a system of Innovation in South-west Wales. *Regional Studies,* 42, 281-293.

ARCH. 2017. *A Regional Collaboration for Health* [Online]. Online. [Accessed 10th April 2017].

Audrestsch, D. B. & Lehmann, E. E. 2005. Does the Knowledge Spillover Theory of Entrepreneurship hold for regions? *Research Policy,* 34, 1191-1202.

Braczyk, H.-J., Cooke, P. N. & Heidenreich, M. 1998. Regional innovation systems: the role of governances in a globalized world, Psychology Press.

Bradley, S. R., Hayter, C. S. & Link, A. N. 2013. Models and methods of university technology transfer. *Foundations and Trends in Entrepreneurship,* 9, 571-650.

Bramwell, A. & Wolfe, D. A. 2008. Universities and regional economic development: The entrepreneurial University of Waterloo. *Research policy,* 37, 1175-1187.

Brooksbank, D. & Thomas, B. 2001. An assessment of higher education spin-off enterprises in Wales. *Industry and Higher Education,* 15, 415-420.

Casper, S. & Karamamos, A. 2003. Commercializing science in Europe: the Cambridge biotechnology cluster. *European Planning Studies,* 11, 805-822.

Charles, D. 2003. Universities and territorial development: reshaping the regional role of UK universities. *Local Economy,* 18, 7-20.

Chen, C.-H. 1996. Regional determinants of foreign direct investment in mainland China. *Journal of economic studies,* 23, 18-30.

Chesbrough, H. 2003. Open innovation. Boston: Harvard Business School Press.

Clarysse, B., Wright, M., Lockett, A., Van De Velde, E. & Vohora, A. 2005. Spinning out new ventures: a typology of incubation strategies from European research institutions. *Journal of Business venturing,* 20, 183-216.

Commission, EU. 2017. *Wales Smart Specialisations* [Online]. Available: http://s3platform.jrc.ec.europa.eu/regions/UKL/tags/UKL [Accessed 10th April 2017].

Cooke, P. 2001. Regional Innovation Systems, Clusters, and the Knowledge Economy. *Industrial and Corporate Change,* 10, 945-974.

Cooke, P. 2004a. Life sciences clusters and regional science policy. *Urban studies,* 41, 1113-1131.

Cooke, P. 2004b. The regional innovation system in Wales, London, Routledge.

Cooke, P. & Clifton, N. 2005. Visionary, precautionary and constrained 'varieties of devolution'in the economic governance of the devolved UK territories. *Regional Studies,* 39, 437-451.

Cooke, P., Kaufmann, D., Levin, C. & Wilson, R. 2006. The biosciences knowledge value chain and comparative incubation models. *The Journal of Technology Transfer,* 31, 115-129.

Cooke, P., Uranga, M. G. & Etxebarria, G. 1997. Regional innovation systems: Institutional and organisational dimensions. *Research policy,* 26, 475-491.

D'este, P. & Patel, P. 2007. University–industry linkages in the UK: What are the factors underlying the variety of interactions with industry? *Research policy,* 36, 1295-1313.

Davies, G., Clement, R., Huxtable-Thomas, L., Roderick, S., Johnson, G., Perkins, B., & Gregory, J. 2018a. Life Sciences & Health in south west Wales: A Sub-regional Innovation System *In:* James, J., Preece, J. & Valdes-Cotera, R. (eds.) *Entrepreneurial Learning City Regions.* Springer.

Davies, G., Huxtable-Thomas, L., Roderick, S. & Mair, C. R. 2015 Models of Life Sciences Start-ups: Don't throw the incubator out with the bathwater. *University-Industry Interaction 2015.* Berlin.

Davies, G., Roderick, S. & Williams, M. 2017. A Sub-Regional Innovation Ecosystem? Life Sciences & Health in the Swansea Bay City Region. *12th European Conference on Innovation and Entrpreneurship.* Paris.

Davies, G. H., Roderick, S. & Huxtable-Thomas, L. 2018b. Social commerce Open Innovation in healthcare management: an exploration from a novel technology transfer approach. *Journal of Strategic Marketing,* 1-12.

Davies, I. 2018. The Impact of a Research-led Entrepreneurial University on a Regional Economy: Swansea University's Science and Innovation Campus. *Entrepreneurial Learning City Regions.* Springer.

Dechenaux, E., Thursby, J. & Thursby, M. 2011. Inventor moral hazard in university licensing: The role of contracts. *Research Policy,* 40, 94-104.

Decter, M., Bennett, D. & Leseure, M. 2007. University to business technology transfer—UK and USA comparisons. *Technovation,* 27, 145-155.

DTI 2001. Business Clusters in the UK - a first assessment. Department for Trade and Industry, UK Government (ed.).

Edmonds, T. 2000. Regional Competitiveness & the Role of the Knowledge Economy. House of Commons Library (ed.). Online.

Etzkowitz, H. & Leydesdorff, L. 2000. The dynamics of innovation: from National Systems and "Mode 2" to a Triple Helix of university–industry–government relations. *Research Policy,* 29, 109-123.

Etzkowitz, H., Webster, A., Gebhardt, C. & Terra, B. R. C. 2000. The future of the university and the university of the future: evolution of ivory tower to entrepreneurial paradigm. *Research policy,* 29, 313-330.

EU 2003. The Role of Universities in the Europe of Knowledge: Communication from the Commission. European Commission (ed.). Online.

EU 2010. Clusters and clustering policy: a guide for regional and local policy makers. Committee of the Regions, European Commission (ed.). INNO Germany AG.

EU. 2017. *Wales Smart Specialisations* [Online]. Available: http://s3platform.jrc.ec.europa.eu/regions/UKL/tags/UKL [Accessed 10th April 2017].

Ferguson, R. & Olofsson, C. 2004. Science Parks and the Development of NTBFs-- Location, Survival and Growth. *Journal of Technology Transfer,* 29, 5-17.

Foray, D. 2014. Smart specialisation: opportunities and challenges for regional innovation policy, Routledge.

Foray, D., David, P. A. & Hall, B. 2009. Smart specialisation–the concept. *Knowledge economists policy brief,* 9, 100.

Geuna, A. 2001. The changing rationale for European university research funding: are there negative unintended consequences? *Journal of economic issues,* 35, 607-632.

Gibb, A. & Hannon, P. 2006. Towards the entrepreneurial university. *International Journal of Entrepreneurship Education,* 4, 73-110.

Gibson S 2007. Commercialisation in Wales - A Report by the Independent Task and Finish Group.

Guerrero, M., Cunningham, J. A. & Urbano, D. 2015. Economic impact of entrepreneurial universities' activities: An exploratory study of the United Kingdom. *Research Policy,* 44, 748-764.

HEFCE 2014. Research Excellence Framework 2014: The results. Higher Education Funding Council for England (ed.).

HEFCE 2016. University Knowledge Exchange (KE) Framework: good practice in technology transfer. Online: Higher Education Funding Council for England.

HEFCW 2013. OHigher Education - Business and Community Interaction (HE-BCI) Survey: Outcomes for Wales 2011/12. Higher Education Funding Council For Wales (ed.).

HEFCW 2017. Innovation Nation. Higher Education Funding Council for Wales (ed.).

Hewitt-Dundas, N. 2012. Research intensity and knowledge transfer activity in UK universities. *Research Policy,* 41, 262-275.

Huggins, R. & Johnston, A. 2009. The economic and innovation contribution of universities: a regional perspective. *Environment and Planning C: Government and Policy,* 27, 1088-1106.

Huggins, R., Jones, M. & Upton, S. 2008. Universities as drivers of knowledge-based regional development: a triple helix analysis of Wales. *International Journal of Innovation and Regional Development,* 1, 24-47.

Huggins, R. & Kitagawa, F. 2012. Regional Policy and University Knowledge Transfer: Perspectives from Devolved Regions in the UK. *Regional Studies,* 46, 817-832.

Hülsbeck, M., Lehmann, E. E. & Starnecker, A. 2013. Performance of technology transfer offices in Germany. *The Journal of Technology Transfer,* 38, 199-215.

Jensen, R. A., Thursby, J. G. & Thursby, M. C. 2003. Disclosure and licensing of University inventions: 'The best we can do with the s** t we get to work with'. *International Journal of Industrial Organization,* 21, 1271-1300.

Lambert, R. 2003. Lambert Review of Business-University Collaboration: Final Report. *In:* TREASURY, H. (ed.). HMSO.

Laredo, P. 2007. Revisiting the third mission of universities: toward a renewed categorization of university activities? *Higher education policy,* 20, 441-456.

Leydesdorff, L. & Etzkowitz, H. 1998. The triple helix as a model for innovation studies. *Science and public policy,* 25, 195-203.

Lundvall, B.-Å. 1992. National Systems of Innovation: Towards a Theory of Innovation and Interactive Learning, Pinter, London.

Macho-Stadler, I., Pérez-Castrillo, D. & Veugelers, R. 2007. Licensing of university inventions: The role of a technology transfer office. *International Journal of Industrial Organization,* 25, 483-510.

Malmberg, A., Sölvell, Ö. & Zander, I. 1996. Spatial Clustering, Local Accumulation of Knowledge and Firm Competitiveness. *Geografiska Annaler. Series B, Human Geography,* 78, 85-97.

Martin, B. R. 2011. The Research Excellence Framework and the 'impact agenda': are we creating a Frankenstein monster? *Research evaluation,* 20, 247-254.

Martin, R. & Sunley, P. 2003. Deconstructing clusters: chaotic concept or policy panacea? *Journal of Economic Geography,* 3, 5-35.

Mathias, P. 2013. *The first industrial nation: The economic history of Britain 1700–1914,* Routledge.

McCaffrey, P. 2018. *The higher education manager's handbook: effective leadership and management in universities and colleges,* Routledge.

Mian, S. A. 1996. Assessing value-added contributions of university technology business incubators to tenant firms. *Research policy,* 25, 325-335.

Mom, T. J. M., Oshri, I. & Volberda, H. W. 2012. The skills base of technology transfer professionals. *Technology Analysis & Strategic Management,* 24, 871-891.

Morgan, K. 2013. The regional state in the era of Smart Specialisation. *Ekonomiaz,* 83, 103-126.

Mowery, D. C., Nelson, R. R., Sampat, B. N. & Ziedonis, A. A. 2001. The growth of patenting and licensing by U.S. universities: an assessment of the effects of the Bayh–Dole act of 1980. *Research Policy,* 30, 99-119.

NAW 2006. Review of Science Policy in Wales. Enterprise Committee, National Assembly for Wales (ed.). Welsh Government Cathays Library: National Assembly for Wales.

Nelson, R. R. 1986. Institutions supporting technical advance in industry. *The American Economic Review,* 76, 186-189.

Perkin, H. 2007. History of universities. *International handbook of higher education.* Springer.

Perkmann, M. & Walsh, K. 2007. University–industry relationships and open innovation: Towards a research agenda. *International Journal of Management Reviews,* 9, 259-280.

Phelps, N. A., Mackinnon, D., Stone, I. & Braidford, P. 2003. Embedding the multinationals? Institutions and the development of overseas manufacturing affiliates in Wales and North East England. *Regional Studies,* 37, 27-40.

Power, D. & Malmberg, A. 2008. The contribution of universities to innovation and economic development: in what sense a regional problem? *Cambridge journal of regions, economy and society,* 1, 233-245.

Pugh, R. 2017. Universities and economic development in lagging regions:'Triple helix'policy in Wales. *Regional Studies,* 51, 982-993.

RLP 2013. Life Science Skills for Life. Regional Learning and Skills Partnership for South Wales and Central Wales (ed.).

RSM 2018. A Report for the Department of Business, Energy, and Industrial Strategy (BEIS), Research into issues around the commercialisation of university IP. (ed.). Online.

Salvador, E. & Harding, R. 2006. Innovation policy at the regional level: the case of Wales. *International Journal of Foresight and Innovation Policy,* 2, 304-326.

SBCR 2013. Swansea Bay City Region Economic Regeneration Strategy. *In:* BOARD, Swansea Bay City Region (ed.). Online.

Shane, S. 2004. Encouraging university entrepreneurship? The effect of the Bayh-Dole Act on university patenting in the United States. *Journal of Business Venturing,* 19, 127-151.

Siegel, D. S., Waldman, D. & Link, A. 2003. Assessing the impact of organizational practices on the relative productivity of university technology transfer offices: an exploratory study. *Research policy,* 32, 27-48.

Siegel, D. S., Waldman, D. A., Atwater, L. E. & Link, A. N. 2004. Toward a model of the effective transfer of scientific knowledge from academicians to practitioners: qualitative evidence from the commercialization of university technologies. *Journal of engineering and technology management,* 21, 115-142.

Stern, N. 2016. Building on success and learning from experience: an independent review of the Research Excellence Framework.
SU 2016. AgorIP Business Plan. Swansea University.
SU 2017. Internet Coast: Phase 1: City Deal Proposal Impact Appraisal. *V1.26*. School of Management: Swansea University.
SU 2018. South Wales Crucible: Initial Report. Swansea University.
TECC 2015. ILS2 End-Project Evaluation. TRILEIN, The European Consulting Company (ed.).
Teece, D. J. 1986. Profiting from technological innovation: Implications for integration, collaboration, licensing and public policy. *Research policy,* 15**,** 285-305.
Tornatzky, L. G. 2000. Building state economies by promoting university-industry technology transfer, National Governors' Association.
Ulrichsen, T. 2018. Knowledge Exchange Framework Metrics: A Cluster Analysis of Higher Education Institutions: A technical Report for Research England. Online: Research England.
Varga, A. 2000. Local academic knowledge transfers and the concentration of economic activity. *Journal of Regional Science,* 40**,** 289-309.
WAG 2003. Wales for Innovation. Welsh Assembly Government.
WAG 2004a. Knowledge Economy Nexus: Role of Higher Education in Wales. Welsh Asembly Government (ed.).
WAG 2004b. A Winning Wales; The National Economic Development Strategy of the Welsh Assembly Government. Welsh Assembly Government.
WAG 2009. Science for Wales: A strategic agenda for science and innovation in Wales.
WAG 2010. Economic Renewal: a new direction. Welsh Assmbly Government (ed.). Crown Copyright.
WEFO 2007. Approved Projects, 2000-2006 West Wales & Valleys Operational Programme. *In:* Welsh European Funding Office. (ed.). Online.
WEFO 2014. The Economic Prioritisation Framework for Welsh European Funds: Version 2. Welsh European Funding Office (ed.). gov.wales.
WG 2012. 2000-2006 Structural Funds Synthesis Report. Welsh European Funding Office (ed.). Web.
WG 2013. Sectors Delivery Plan. *In:* Department for Business, Enterprise and Transport, Welsh Government (ed.).
WG 2014. Innovation Wales. Welsh Government (ed.).
WG 2018a. Healthier Wales. Department for Health and Social Care, (ed.). Online: Welsh Government, Crown Copyright.
WG 2018b. Review of Government Funded Research and Innovation in Wales, Welsh Government. (ed.). Online.
Wolfe, D. A. 2005. The role of universities in regional development and cluster formation. *Creating knowledge, strengthening nations: The changing role of higher education*, 167-94.
Wright, M., Lockett, A., Clarysse, B. & Binks, M. 2006. University spin-out companies and venture capital. *Research Policy,* 35**,** 481-501.
Young, S., Hood, N. & Peters, E. 1994. Multinational enterprises and regional economic development. *Regional studies,* 28**,** 657-677.
Youtie, J. & Shapira, P. 2008. Building an innovation hub: A case study of the transformation of university roles in regional technological and economic development. *Research policy,* 37**,** 1188-1204.
Yusuf, S. & Nabeshima, K. 2006. *How universities promote economic growth*, The World Bank.

The University of the Future

 **Gareth Davies** is an Associate Professor in Swansea University's School of Management, with research interests in innovation and regional economic development. His practitioner interests include the AgorIP commercialisation platform and associated initiatives.

 **Naomi Joyce** is a Senior Lecturer in Innovation & Engagement at Swansea University Medical School overseeing a number of regional innovation projects and partnerships including the Healthcare Technology Centre based at the Institute of Life Science.

 **David Bolton** is a Fellow and Director of both CMI and EEUK. Having spent many years in the business support field his focus is on academic development and enterprise skills and entrepreneurship into relevant curricula.

15

Knowledge Gaps: Future of Universities in Low and Middle Income Countries

Cees Th. Smit Sibinga[1], Maruff Oladejo[2], Isaac Kajja[3], Arwa Z. Al-Riyami[4]
[1]IQM Consulting, Zuidhorn & University of Groningen, Netherlands
[2]University of Lagos, Nigeria
[3]Makerere University, Kampala, Uganda
[4]Department of Hematology, Sultan Qaboos University Hospital, Muscat, Oman

Introduction

The word *university* originates from the Latin *universitas magistrorum et scholarium*, which simply means "community of teachers and scholars". While antecedents had existed in Asia and Africa, the modern university system has its roots in the European medieval university, which was created in Italy and evolved from cathedral schools for the clergy and nobility during the High Middle Ages, 1000-1250 CE (Haskins 1898).

Today, the word means 'an institution of higher education offering tuition in mainly non-vocational subjects and typically having the power to confer degrees', with the earlier emphasis on its corporate organization considered as applying historically to Medieval universities. An important idea in the definition of a university is the notion of academic freedom. On September 18, 1988, marking the 900th anniversary of Bologna's foundation of the university, 430 university rectors signed the *Magna Charta Universitatum*. The number of universities signing the *Magna Charta Universitatum* continues to grow, coming from all parts of the world, public and private, specific and general.

How universities developed

The university is generally regarded as a formal institution that has its origin in the Medieval Christian tradition (Rüegg 1992,p. xix-xx). European higher education took place for centuries in cathedral schools or monastic schools (*scholae monasticae*), in which monks and nuns taught classes. Evidence of these immediate forerunners of the later university at many places dates back to the 6th century (Riché 1978, p. 126-27, 282-98).

All over Europe, rulers and city governments began to create universities to satisfy a European thirst for knowledge, and the belief that society would benefit from the scholarly expertise generated from these institutions. Princes and leaders of city governments perceived the potential benefits of developing scholarly expertise with the ability to address difficult problems and achieve desired goals. The emergence of humanism was essential to this understanding of the possible utility of universities as well as the revival of interest in knowledge gained from ancient Greek texts (Grendler 2004). Young men proceeded to university when they had completed their study of the trivium – the preparatory arts of grammar, rhetoric and dialectic or logic – and the quadrivium: arithmetic, geometry, music, and astronomy.

During the Renaissance period, approximately late 15th to mid-18th century (Enlightenment), the universities of Europe would see a tremendous amount of growth, productivity and innovative research. At the end of the Middle Ages, about 400 years after the first European university was founded, there were 29 universities spread throughout Europe. In the 15th century, twenty-eight new universities were created, with another eighteen added between 1500 and 1625 (Grendler 2004). This pace continued until by the end of the 18th Century, there were approximately 143 universities in Europe, with the highest concentrations in the German Empire (34), Italian countries (26), France (25), and Spain (23) – this was close to a 500% increase over the number of universities toward the end of the Middle Ages (Frijthoff 1996, p. 65).

By the 18th Century during the Enlightenment, universities began to publish their own scientific research journals and by the 19th Century, the German and the French university models had arisen. The German, or Humboldtian model, was conceived by Wilhelm von Humboldt and based on Friedrich Schleiermacher's ideas pertaining to the importance of freedom, seminars, and laboratories in universities. The French university model involved strict discipline and control over every aspect and detail of the university, knowledge, research and science.

Until the 19th Century, religion played a significant role in university curricula; however, the role of religion in research universities decreased in the 19th Century, and by the end of the 19th Century, the German university model had spread around the world. Universities concentrated on science in the 19th and 20th Centuries and became increasingly accessible to the masses. In the United States, the Johns Hopkins University in Baltimore was the first to adopt the (German) research university model; this pioneered the adoption by most other American universities. In Britain, the move from Industrial Revolution to modernity in the first half of the 20st century saw the arrival of new civic universities with an emphasis on science and engineering, a movement initiated in 1960 by Sir Keith Murray (chairman of the University Grants Committee) and Sir Samuel Curran, with the formation of the University of Strathclyde, Scotland; The Royal College, founded in 1796, gained University Status, receiving its Royal Charter to become The University of Strathclyde in 1964, merging with the Scottish College of Commerce at the same time (University of Strathclyde 2019).

Dawning light in the colonial world and beyond

The British, like the French and earlier the Spanish (Latin America), also established during the first decades of the 20st century universities worldwide in their commonwealth colonies. Higher education became available to the masses not only in Europe. That paved the way to the development of academic culture and life in the colonized parts of the world, the later post-colonial newly independent states, now largely belonging to the low and middle income countries.

The Robbins Report on universities in the United Kingdom (1963) concluded that such institutions should have four main objectives

"essential to any properly balanced system: instruction in skills; the promotion of the general powers of the mind so as to produce not mere specialists but rather cultivated 'Renaissance' men and women; to maintain research in balance with teaching, since teaching should not be separated from the advancement of learning and the search for truth; and to transmit a common culture and common standards of citizenship" (Anderson 2010).

During that period of time – post World War II – a rapid decolonialization took place with the creation of dozens of newly independent states particularly in Asia and Africa, and with the collapse of the Soviet republic also in Europe and Central Asia. However, with the withdrawal of the colonial rulers also their cultural and social infrastructure largely disappeared or was willingly destroyed and eradicated by the new nation.

Evidently, development of a society needs an environment and climate to allow step by step improvement based on the 1948 principles of the Universal Human Rights (United Nations 2015). The key Universal Human Rights are in safety, justice, nourishment, shelter, health, absence of poverty and education. These principles together with equality form the fundament for development, to which evidently economy and being self-supporting are paramount supportive elements. Most newly independent countries started from scratch in need of financial and technical support to establish an acceptable economic climate to survive. Investments were dominated by economy and military defence, where poverty increased, and access to essential nourishment, health care and education were largely unaffordable and only accessible for the well to do upper layer of society. These people could also afford advanced education abroad.

The current knowledge gaps

The concept of knowledge gap is of recent origin; in fact, it came with a hypothesis. In 1970, three researchers from the University of Minnesota namely Phillip J. Tichenor; Associate Professor of Journalism and Mass Communication, George A. Donohue; Professor of Sociology, and Clarice N. Olien, Instructor in Sociology were the first proponents of the knowledge gap hypothesis (Tichenor, Donohue & Olien 1970). According to them, the knowledge gap hypothesis explains that knowledge, like other forms of wealth, is often differentially distributed throughout a social system. Specifically, these scholars hypothesized that 'as the infusion of mass media information into a social system increases, segments of the population with higher socioeconomic status tend to acquire this information at a faster rate than the lower status segments, so that the gap in knowledge between these segments tends to increase rather than decrease.

Since the publication of World Bank's 1998/ 99 World Development Report on Knowledge and Development (World Bank 1999), narrowing the knowledge gap between and within countries has preoccupied several international development agencies as well as some national governments. According to Evers (2003), the international knowledge gap is usually defined in terms of the technological knowledge achieved in the Organisation for Economic Cooperation and Development (OECD) countries, in particular the USA (Evers 2003). The meaning of knowledge is never clearly defined, but from the discussion on the knowledge gap we can deduce that education, expenditure for research and development, and Information and Communication Technologies (ICTs) infrastructure are seen as the crucial variables.

Hardly can we talk of knowledge gap, especially between developed and developing countries of the world without making refence to digital divide. This is because sometimes the concept of a digital divide is used to relate to the technological aspect of the knowledge gap (OECD 2001). According to OECD the term 'digital divide' refers to the gap between individuals, households, businesses and geographic areas at different socio-economic levels with regard to their opportunities to access information and communication technologies (ICTs) and their use of the Internet, which reflects differences among and within countries (OECD 2001).

The big changes and challenges

European universities established the intellectual and academic traditions of university education worldwide; by the end of the 19th Century, the German Humboldtian university model was established in Europe, the US, and Japan. In the Americas (north, middle and south), first the Spanish, then the British, and then the French founded universities in the lands they had conquered early in the 16th Century, intended to professionally educate their colonists and propagate monotheistic religion to establish a formal, administrative rule of their Americas colonies. Likewise the British in Canada, Australia, and the Cape Colony, Japan, the Near East, and Africa all had universities based on European models in the late 19th Century. Those universities disseminated Western European science and technology educated and trained the local population (foremost the local elite) to develop their country's resources. Although most universities promoted the social, political, economic, and cultural aims of the imperial rulers, some promoted revolutionary development of the colonial societies.

In the 20th Century, urbanization and industrialization made a university education available to the mass population. But over the centuries, the basic structure and research purposes of the universities have remained constant; they *are among the least changed of institutions'*. What changed was the societal infrastructure and culture.

However, in the early 21st Century, concerns were raised over the increasing managerialization, commercialization, standardization and digitalization of universities worldwide. Neo-liberal management models have in this sense been critiqued for creating corporate universities where power is transferred from faculty to managers, economic justifications dominate, and the familiar 'bottom line' eclipses pedagogical or intellectual concerns (Berg & Seeber 2016). Understanding a different dimension and management of time, pedagogical pleasure, vocation, and collegiality have been cited as possible ways of alleviating such problems. Additionally, education is also affected by the fast tsunami of digitalization, with a turbulent change in education and examination approaches and styles, e.g., e- and blended learning, flipped classroom where tablets and laptops are increasingly replacing books and other written sources of knowledge. The institution of the Nobel prizes at the beginning of the 20th Century (established 1895 and awarded for the first time in 1901) (Nobel Prize 2019) twisted science towards harsh competition, leading to the ranking by audits of universities, scrutinizing education and research systems and traditions of all existing universities, whether public or private.

United Nations, UNDP ranking and the development goals

In 1948 the United Nations endorsed the Universal Declaration of Human Rights; article 26 spells out the fundamental right to education stating that higher education shall be equally accessible to all on the basis of merit (United Nations 2015). The United Nations Development Programme (UNDP) Human Development Index (HDI) is a statistic composite index of life expectancy, education, and per capita income indicators used to calculate the HDI categorizing countries in four groups – low, medium, high and very high (Human Development Index 2019).

The 2018 ranking of indexes (Human Development Index 2018) shows for the low human development countries (n=38) a range from 0.354 (Niger) to 0.546 (Solomon Islands); for the medium human development countries (n=39) from 0.556 (Cameroon) to 0.699 (Philippines); for the high human development countries (n=53) from 0.700 (Republic of Moldova) to 0.798 (Islamic Republic of Iran); and for the very high human development countries (n=59) from 0.800 (Kazakhstan) to 0.953 (Norway).

One of the indices of the UNDP Human Development Index system is education and in particular the years spent in education per individual, and the percentage of youngsters in the age categories for elementary, secondary and tertiary education. In general, that means that the higher the HDI, the more years spent in education and the larger the percentage of youngsters exposed to the education levels. In other words, the higher the knowledge level, the smaller the knowledge gap. The very high HDI serves as the reference for the other three groups.

The 2018 UNDP HDI Statistical Update (Human Development Index 2018) shows an education achievement respectively for very high and low HDI countries of 12.2 and 4.7 years exposure; and 71% vs 9% of the eligible tertiary education age group of youngsters! This obviously contributes to the knowledge gap observed by the UN and many other organizations and institutions in the world. Despite the existence of universities for higher education in every country, whether low or very high HDI, the level of knowledge is not really comparable. That raises the question 'How come?'

Over time multiple factors have contributed to the rise of the 'excellence and world class' university discourses that have systematically failed to offer a clear definition but have nonetheless succeeded in creating a global competition for quality assurance mechanisms and performance monitoring. Among these factors, some of the most important include: the rapid massification, managerialization, commercialization, standardization, digitalization and expansion of higher education as well as globalization and student mobility (Torabian 2018). The question also is, whether and to what extent university rankings are relevant if they continue to assume their perpetual inability to depict the real quality of universities and their activities (teaching, curricular contents, level of science and research, citation index and competency and capacity of teaching staff) and to reflect and measure sustainability in the near and further future? The need to convey reliable information about the provision of education and research (be it alpha, bèta or gamma) to a larger and a more heterogeneous body of students; the shift in the perceptions of the definition and the role of higher education from public good to tradeable service in a global neoliberal free market; the consequent public funding cutbacks, budget shortages and the advancement of public accountability schemes; rising competition among universities to attract fee-paying international students/consumers and the dramatic changes in attitude and focus of the new generations of students are issues of considerable importance. Much relates, however, to the curriculum and performance quality of primary and secondary education offered. The higher the degree of final education, the more important is the baseline education and knowledge acquisition at primary, high schools and colleges. Consequently, this will have a major impact on the future of higher and academic education.

The newly independent post-colonial countries also developed, but the starting levels and pace were far less advanced, illustrating the observed education and knowledge gaps (elementary, secondary, academic; education cadre; students, education tools). Additionally, academic and higher vocational institutes from the advanced world increasingly create joint commercialized ventures with similar institutes in the low- and medium HDI part of the world, as well as satellite campuses in selected higher medium income countries such as the United Arab Emirates, Qatar, Kingdom of Saudi Arabia, India and Peoples Republic of China.

Higher education and sustainable development

In preparation for the new millennium, the UN developed a global programme for all Member States focused on eight major problems, which included poverty, economy and health care, environment, literacy, etc. called the Millennium Development Goals 2000-2015 (MDG) (Millennium Development Goals 2019). Although during the years of implementation not all goals were approached satisfactorily and a number of distinct shortcomings and challenges were identified, the UN decided in 2012 to continue the programme. Which they called the Sustainable Development Goals 2016-2030 (SDG) with 17 goals (Sustainable Development Goals 2019). Goal number 4 focuses on quality education stating *'Ensure inclusive and equitable education and promote lifelong learning opportunities for all.'* The sub-goal 4.1 reads *'By 2030, ensure that all girls and boys complete free, equitable and quality primary and secondary education leading to relevant and effective learning outcomes'*, and sub-goal 4.3 reads *'By 2030, ensure equal access for all women and men to affordable and quality technical, vocational and tertiary education, including university'*. This acknowledges the obvious role of universities in the social and economic development of societies and obliges governments to implement quality primary and secondary education as well as affordable and quality tertiary education. The key point is in the desired quality of the education based on standards of curricula, competency and credibility of educators and accessibility for all youngsters, boys and girls, men and women.

With this several initiatives have been created emphasising the role of higher education in the implementation of the 2030 Agenda for Sustainable Development. One such significant initiative is the UN Higher Education Sustainability Initiative (HESI) (HESI 2019) that was created in the overture to the United Nations Conference on Sustainable Development in 2012. HESI created a special partnership between UNESCO, the UN Environment Programme, the United Nations University, UN-Habitat, the UN Conference on Trade and Development, the UN Institute for Training and Research, the UN Department of Economics and Social Affairs and the UN Global Compact Principles for Responsible Management Education. HESI seeks to provide a unique interface among participating universities to share and promote Agenda 2030 in their teaching, research, campus practices, networking and social impact, facilitating the voluntary commitments of more than 300 higher education institutions spread out over the world.

Juliette Torabian, a senior international adviser in education and sustainable development, notes other important initiatives, positioning higher education institutions as key drivers of sustainable development, including (Torabian 2018):

- *The UN Sustainability Tracking, Assessment and Rating System (STARS) (Stars 2019), which provides a self-reporting framework for colleges and universities to measure their sustainability performance, created by the Association for the Advancement of Sustainability in Higher Education.*

- *The UN Higher Education and Research for Sustainable Development (HESD) (Higher Education and Research for Sustainable Development 2019) led by the International Association of Universities, which promotes sustainability among its 650 member institutions across 130 countries.*

- *The SDG Accord launched by the Environmental Association for Universities and Colleges (EAUC) (EAUC 2019), which attracted more than 600 signatories from over 60 countries pursuing collective and powerful engagement in sustainable development.*

The impact on the future of higher education

It is obvious that at the root of higher/tertiary education is the quality and accessibility of the fundamental human right to a basic education, i.e. primary and secondary. The data presented in the 2018 HDI Statistical Update Human Development Index (2018) reveals the reality and provides a direction to a solution; governance and leadership responsibility for proper and well-planned implementation of these SDG programmes, which includes the availability of appropriate education tools. The reported knowledge gap and developmental arrears first need to be made up and will determine the future of those universities suffering from the arrear and debatable quality of education, curricular content and competency of education and scientific cadre (teachers, researchers and professors) as well as the paucity of research and scientific development work resulting in limited peer reviewed publications and PhD laureates. That requires a governmental vision and a long-term policy and strategy.

Evidently there are exceptions, as illustrated by The World Economic Forum based on the five factors deemed by the Times Higher Education Supplement as essential to the success of a university (World Economic Forum, Jones 2015):

- teaching (30%);
- research (30%);
- citations (30%);

but also

- income from industry (2.5%);
- international outlook of staff, students and research (7.5%).

Additionally, adequate funding, community involvement and flexible government guidance through a higher education and science advisory council, play a paramount role.

Such universities can be identified in China (23 in the top 100), Taiwan (19 in the top 100), India (11 the top 100), Turkey (8 in the top 100), Russian Federation (7 in the top 100), South Africa (5 in the top 100) and Brazil (4 in the top 100). This illustrates that looking beyond the universities into the mature economies, a very different and fascinating picture emerges. However, the main problem is in those economies that belong to the low and lower medium HDI, are home to around 70% of the global population. For these countries a dedicated and strong governance structure responsible for the entire education chain from primary to tertiary on a continuous and sustainable principle should be recognized as a prime fundament. Proper and long-term investment in education and knowledge is a guarantee for rewarding development of a nation.

A complicating factor, however, is in the dynamics of the developments in the advanced world which are causing a widening of the existing gaps rather than a narrowing. This, together with an inadequate and malfunctioning socio-economic infrastructure, and absence of a stimulating environment and attractive research climate, has a serious impact on future university operations in low and middle income countries. Nevertheless, students, education and research staff, and their respective tertiary institutions under development will not escape the impact of modern approaches and systems (social media and digitalization), which may contribute to faster developments and a brighter future for academic life.

References

Anderson, R. (2010). *The 'Idea of a University' today. History & Policy.* United Kingdom: History & Policy. Archived from the original on 27 November 2010.

Berg M. & Seeber, B. 2016. The Slow Professor: Challenging the Culture of Speed in the Academy. Toronto: Toronto University Press (passim)

EAUC. 2019. https://www.eauc.org.uk/

Evers, H. 2003. Malaysian knowledge society and the global knowledge gap. *Asian Journal of Social Science*, 31(3), 383-397

Frijhoff, W. 1996 Patterns. In. Ridder-Symoens, h de (Ed.), Universities in early modern Europe, 1500-1800, A history of the university in Europe. Cambridge [England]: Cambridge University Press, p. 65.

Grendler, PF. 2004. The universities of the Renaissance and Reformation. *Renaissance Quarterly*, 57, pp. 1-3.

Haskins, C. H. 1898. The Life of Medieval Students as Illustrated by their Letters. *The American Historical Review.* **3** (2): 203–229. doi:10.2307/1832500

HESI. 2019. https://sustainabledevelopment.un.org/sdinaction/hesi (retrieved 01 July 2019)

Higher Education and Research for Sustainable Development. 2019.https://sustainabledevelopment.un.org/partnership/?p=11748 (retrieved 01 July 2019)

Human Development Index. 2018. http://hdr.undp.org/sites/default/files/2018_human_development_statistical_update.pdf (retrieved 01 July 2019)

Human Development Index. 2019. https://en.wikipedia.org/wiki/Human_Development_Index

Millennium Development Goals. 2019. https://www.un.org/millenniumgoals/ (retrieved 01 July 2019)

Nobel Prize 2019. https://en.wikipedia.org/wiki/Nobel_Prize (retrieved 01 July 2019)

OECD 2001. Understanding the digital divide. Paris: OECD

Riché, P., 1978. Education and Culture in the Barbarian West: From the Sixth through the Eighth Century, Columbia: University of South Carolina Press, ISBN 0-87249-376-8, pp. 126-7, 282-98

Rüegg, W: 1992. Foreword. The University as a European Institution, in: *A History of the University in Europe. Vol. 1: Universities in the Middle Ages*, Cambridge University Press, ISBN 0-521-36105-2, pp. xix-xx

STARS. 2019. https://www.aashe.org/wp-content/uploads/2017/04/STARS-flyer.pdf (retrieved 01 July2019)

Sustainable Development Goals. 2019. https://en.wikipedia.org/wiki/Sustainable_Development_Goals (retrieved 01 July 2019)

Tichenor, P.A.; Donohue, G.A.; Olien, C.N. 1970. "Mass media flow and differential growth in knowledge". *Public Opinion Quarterly*. 34 (2): 159–170. doi:10.1086/267786.

Torabian, J. 2018. Are global rankings relevant to sustainable development? *University World News Global Edition.* https://www.universityworldnews.com (retrieved 01 July 2019)

United Nations. 2015. https://www.un.org/en/udhrbook/pdf/udhr_booklet_en_web.pdf (illustrated by Yacin Ait Kaci) (retrieved 01 July 2019)

University of Strathclyde 2019. https://en.wikipedia.org/wiki/University_of_Strathclyde

World Bank. 1998. World Development Report 1998/1999 : Knowledge for Development. New York: Oxford University Press. © World Bank. Accessible at https://openknowledge.worldbank.org/handle/10986/5981 License: CC BY 3.0 IGO.

World Economic Forum. Jones, M. (2015) Where is the best university in the developing world? https://www.weforum.org/agenda2015/06/where-is-the-best-university-in-the-world/ (retrieved 01 July 2019)

Cees Th. Smit Sibinga MD. PhD, FRCPEdin, FRCPath is emeritus Professor of International Development of Transfusion Medicine at the University of Groningen, Director of IQM Consulting, The Netherlands and Expert Advisor of WHO.

The University of the Future

 **Maruff Oladejo** has a PhD in Educational Management from the University of Ibadan, Nigeria. He specializes in Educational Policy, Planning, and Economics of Education. He currently lectures in the Department of Educational Management at University of Lagos, Nigeria.

 **Isaac Kajja, MD** has a PhD from University of Groningen, The Netherlands. He has specialized in Orthopaedics and Transfusion Medicine and is Associate Professor of Orthopaedics and Chair of the Department of Orthopaedics of Makerere University, Kampala, Uganda.

 **Arwa Z. Al-Riyami, BSc, MD, FRCPc** is a Senior Consultant Haematopathologist at the Sultan Qaboos University Hospital in Sultanate of Oman. She is the program director of the haematolopathology residency program at the Oman Medical Speciality Board.

16

Decarbonisation Roadmap for Universities of the Future

William Horan, Rachel Shawe, Richard Moles, Bernadette O'Regan
University of Limerick, Ireland

Introduction

Human development patterns have resulted in alteration of the environment on a global scale (Steffen et al., 2011; Giljum et al., 2014; Sachs, 2015; Grinspoon et al., 2016; Brunner and Rechberger, 2017; IPCC, 2018; Steffen et al., 2018). Total anthropogenic metabolism (input, output and stock of materials and energy needed to satisfy all human needs) has increased greatly from prehistoric times, with a great acceleration from 1950, due to growth in human population, but also due to increased material throughput per capita (Steffen et al., 2011; Brunner and Rechberger, 2017). Given that anthropogenic activities are putting strain on our supporting biospheres ability to perpetuate human systems; urgent action is needed to avoid major threats posed to ecosystem functions (Meadows et al., 2004; Rockstrom et al., 2009; Haum and Loose, 2015).

Higher Education Institutions (HEI) have considerable influence in shaping the mental models of society's future workforce and leaders, while also playing a significant role in societal transitions toward sustainable human development patterns (Lozano, 2011; Dyer and Dyer, 2017). As educators of future generations, fHEIs have a duty to act more sustainably and more importantly to act as leverage points in the broader societal transition towards sustainability (Dyer and Dyer, 2017). Updating of mental models relating to the feasibility of sustainability solutions may be achieved through education, outreach and demonstration of sustainability solutions, with an intention to induce widespread societal replication and translation of solutions through iterative feedback.

From a global perspective the environmental impacts related to higher education are relatively small compared to other sectors (Derrick, 2013; Lang and Kennnedy, 2016). However, the difference between education and other sectors is that the education sector views itself as playing a transformative role in global change (Derrick, 2013). Such a perspective identifies Higher Education Institutions (HEI) as institutions that need to undergo change to become more sustainable, while also being potential change agents due to distinct roles and functions within society (Stephens et al., 2008). Numerous ways in which a HEI can become more sustainable include changes in education, governance, campus operations, research and outreach, as current values and assumptions concerning these areas are considered by many authors to be unsustainable in the long term (Valasquez et al., 2006; Yarime and Tanaka, 2012; Disterheft, 2015). Efforts in influencing wider societal transitions among HEIs include "experimenting with campus-based social innovations that integrate infrastructure, operations, curriculum, research and funding while communicating new ways of thinking within and outside of the campus community" (Eatmon et al., 2016). Given that HEI campuses have negative environmental impacts associated with their operations, the logical step for campuses, to facilitate society's transition towards sustainability, is by reducing their material and energy demands (Ferrer-Balas et al., 2008).

In relation to experimentation and demonstration of sustainability solutions, HEIs have been identified as ideal testing grounds, as they may be viewed as a microcosm of society or regarded as small cities due to their size, diverse population and the numerous complex activities and operations occurring on their campuses and the associated direct and indirect environmental impacts (Alshuwaikhat and Abubaker, 2008; Jain et al., 2017). Many of the challenges that society faces are reflected at HEI level, for example, lowering material throughput of growing systems with full time equivalent of HEI students expected to increase by 50,000 over the period 2014-2028 (Department of Education and Skills, 2015). Given global growth of student numbers on campuses and the associated increase in material throughput of campuses, they serve as a useful testing ground to inform carbon reduction strategies for similarly growing populations in wider society.

There is an emerging literature surrounding scenario development relating to decarbonisation of the higher education sector internationally. HEIs in the United Kingdom (UK) have carbon reduction targets set by the UK government to reduce scope 1 and 2 emissions (on-site emissions) by 34% by 2020 and 80% by 2050 based on 1990 baseline (HEFCE, 2010). Targets were also set against a 2005 baseline for a 43% reduction by 2020 and 83% by 2050 where 1990 data was not available (HEFCE, 2010). The Higher Education Funding Council of England have suggested possible initiatives to meet these targets, specific carbon management plans produced by individual HEIs have projected emission reduction scenarios to meet these targets. Examples of carbon reduction initiatives to justify these projections include energy efficiency measures, installation of renewable energy sources on-campus, behaviour change campaigns, carbon offsetting and sale of surplus buildings.

The University of California (UC) System has pledged a sector wide scope 1 and 2 decarbonisation target of being carbon neutral by 2025 on its 10 campuses (Meier et al., 2018). The three main avenues of decarbonisation according to UCs carbon reduction plan include energy efficiency, alternative fuels and electrification (Victor et al., 2018). Similar to the UK, individual UC campuses produce climate action plans to identify carbon reduction potential options specific to their campus. These include on-site renewable energy generation, remaining energy efficiency measures, renewable electricity procurement, replacing vehicle fleets with alternative fuelled vehicles and carbon offsets. As the 63% of the UC system's carbon emissions come from the onsite combustion of natural gas, the largest share of UCs emissions, the recommended option is to replace this natural gas with biogas. For example, UC Berkley's action plan suggest using biogas to replace 50% to 100% of natural gas to aid meeting the 2025 carbon neutral target by 45% and 91% respectively. The technically feasibility of biogas production on this scale is currently unproven which limits the usefulness of these projections.

Drawing on best practice in the international literature this current study has focused on reducing scope 1 and 2 carbon emission as HEIs have the most direct control over these emissions. This paper outlines a roadmap to inform how universities can reduce their carbon emissions, with an illustrative application to Ireland's growing higher education sector. Projections were at a sectorial level but informed by the individual profiles of each HEI campus and therefore may be disaggregated down to individual campuses. This study only focused on proven technologies with no assumptions relating to future technological advances in terms of efficiency to limit uncertainty. The impact of decarbonisation technologies at Irish HEIs scope 1 and 2 emissions identified by (Horan et al., 2019) included building integrated PV, building integrated wind turbines, carport PV systems. Additional measures such as replacing oil boilers with biomass boilers and replacing campus fleet vehicle with electric vehicles were also considered. Implementation of the measures identified have the potential to reduce total on-site carbon emissions by 25% (Figure 1).

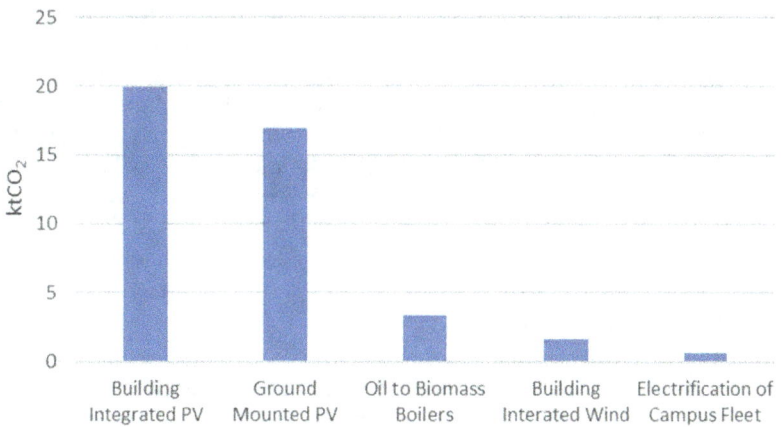

Figure 1: Carbon reduction potential of Irish HEI sector at 2016 steady state

Energy efficiency potentials were not investigated due to lack of appropriate data relating to Display Energy Certificates (DEC) ratings at Irish HEIs and lack of data disaggregation relating to current progress being due to energy efficiency retrofit or better building standards. For this reason, energy efficiency trends due to the National Energy Efficiency Action Plan NEEAP 2017-2020 (SEAI, 2018) were extrapolated to 2030 rather than quantification of individual energy efficiency measures.

University Sector Decarbonisation Roadmap to 2030 (Scope 1 and 2)

Growth Rate of Campuses: Gross Internal Area and Student Numbers

The efficiency metric used by HEIs in measuring progress towards their target of 33% improvement in energy efficiency was either Total Primary Energy Requirement (TPER) per Gross Internal Area (GIA) or TPER per student numbers (SEAI, 2018). Six out of seven universities used the per area efficiency metric while six out of fourteen institutes of technology used this metric. The GIA of HEIs that did not report their progress using the per unit area efficiency metric was calculated using the correlation between GIA and TFC of the HEIs that did for both 2009 and 2016. The growth rate of GIA between 2009 and 2016 was calculated from the estimated difference in GIA for both years. Between 2009 and 2016 the GIA of the HEI sector grew by 457,094 m2 or 21%. By extrapolating this trend into the future, the HEI sector's GIA has the potential to grow by a further 261,196m2 or 10% by 2020 and 914,188m2 or 34% by 2030 relative to 2016 figures.

In reporting progress by using the per student efficiency metric for the HEI sector, the SEAI data did not explicitly show whether student numbers were total student numbers (including part-time and remote students) or full time equivalent (FTE) students. In the international literature there are established correlations between HEI environmental impacts and FTE. Therefor FTE was utilised in this study. Student numbers of 2009 and 2016 were collected from the HEA enrolment database. Projections of future student numbers for the sector were based on the same rates of growth as the baseline scenario identified for third level fulltime student enrolments carried out by Department of Education and Skills for the period 2015-2029 (DES, 2015). Estimated future FTE student numbers were 177,223 for 2020 and 201,690 for 2030.

Based on the academic literature (Klien-Banai and Theis, 2011; Sonetti et al., 2016) and correlations between energy use, GIA and FTE students from Irish HEIs (Figure 2), it is clear that the relationship between GIA and energy use is the more strongly correlated. For this reason, future projections of energy use and therefore the sector's carbon emissions are based on GIA projections for the sector.

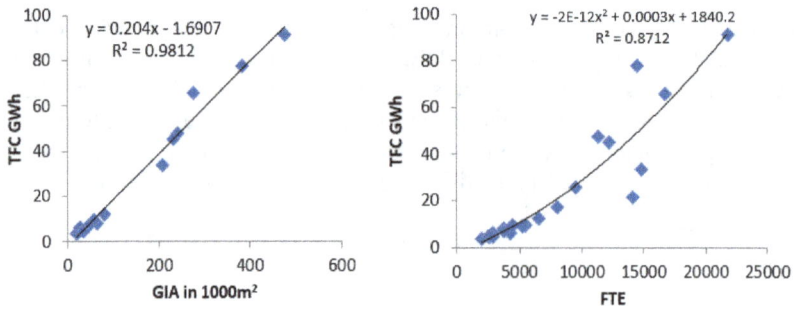

Figure 2: Relationships between total final consumption, gross internal area (left) and fulltime equivalent students (right)

Projected Energy Intensity per Gross Internal Area

Projected energy intensity per GIA of Irish HEIs was established based on extrapolation of 2009 and 2016 trends. For the period 2009-2016 there was a 10% improvement in energy intensity if measured in TFC/m2. This was the result of either energy efficiency measures on existing buildings or more efficient new buildings required by changing building standards. While (SEAI, 2018) data showed energy savings from energy efficiency projects per year of each HEI, expressed as TPER, it did not state whether these saving, were electrical or thermal energy savings which limits their usefulness in establishing the TFC or carbon savings (expressed as TPER or TFC) of these measures. For this reason, it could not be established how much of the improvement in energy efficiency was the result of retrofitting or new building regulations. By extrapolating trends relating to total TFC/m2 into the future, the HE sector is projected to be 178 kWh/m2 by 2020 and 147 kWh/m2 by 2030. Based on trends between 2009 and 2016, future improvements in energy use per m2 could be established for both electricity and thermal energy use which allow for meaningful absolute energy projections (Figure 3).

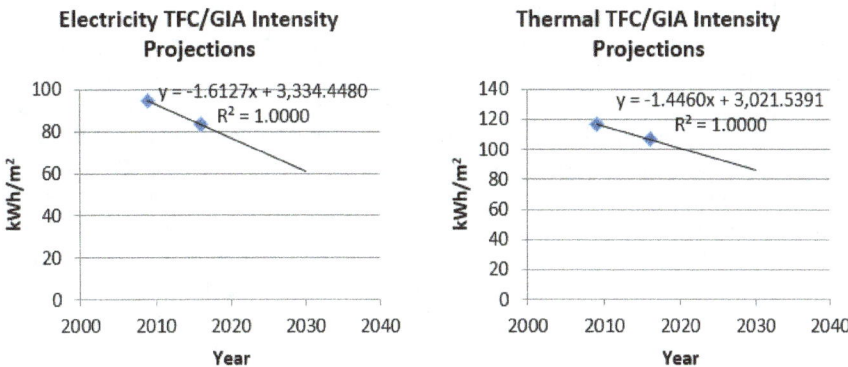

Figure 3: Projections of electricity and thermal energy intensity per gross internal area

Absolute Energy Projections

Based on projected growth rate in GIA and energy intensity improvements the absolute energy consumption of the HE sector was projected (Figure 4). Scenarios are: (1) no improvement in energy efficiency improvement post 2016 and (2) extrapolating current progress of the National Energy Efficiency Action Plan (NEEAP).

Carbon Intensity of National Grid

Projections of the carbon intensity of the national grid were established to account for potential reductions in carbon emissions from purchased electricity at Irish HEIs up to 2030. Historical trends (SEAI, relating to grid electricity emissions factors for the period 2010-16 were extrapolated to 2030. National grid intensity was projected to be 425.2 gCO2/kWh by 2020 and 331.0 gCO2/kWh by 2030.

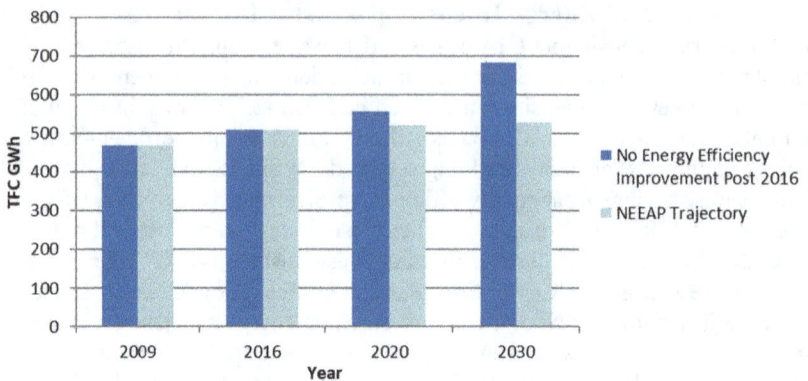

Figure 4: Projections of TFC for the HEI sector in relation to scenarios

Carbon Reduction Potential Projections

The carbon emissions of the HE sector were estimated by multiplying the absolute energy projections by their relevant Emission Factors relating to electricity and thermal energy. As thermal energy use is only broken down by source for 2016 (SEAI, 2018) it was assumed that future breakdown of thermal energy sources is of the same proportions as 2016, that is natural gas (95.00%) heating oil (4.48%) and renewables (0.42%). The carbon savings relating to onsite PV and wind generation (Horan et al., 2019) were established by multiplying the energy output of these measures by the grid Emission Factor for that year. The carbon savings from switching from heating oil to biomass boilers were estimated by assuming that the heating oil carbon emissions for a given year were converted to zero. The absolute carbon emissions for the Irish HE sector were estimated according to 3 scenarios namely (1) no improvement in energy efficiency improvement post 2016 (2) extrapolating current progress of the NEEAP (3) the NEEAP trajectory which assumed additional measures of onsite PV, onsite wind, electrification of campus fleet and switching from heating oil to biomass for heating.

The absolute carbon emissions projections for the Irish HEI sector by 2030 was estimated an 8% increase in emissions (13,067 tCO2) for the no improvement in energy efficiency scenario, a 17% decrease in emissions (28,959 tCO2) for the NEEAP trajectory scenario and a 36% decrease (59,027 tCO2) for the with measures scenario relative to the 2009 baseline (Figure 5).

Decarbonisation Roadmap for Universities of the Future

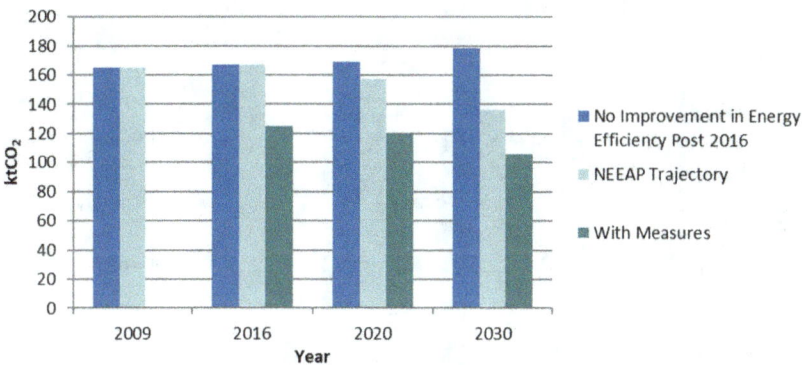

Figure 5: Dynamic scenarios of carbon reductions

The projected carbon emission saving if measures were fully implemented by the year 2016, 2020 and 2030 relative to the NEEAP trajectory were estimated (Figure 6). The carbon reduction potential of onsite electricity generation from renewables decreased overtime due to the falling carbon intensity of the electricity grid. The carbon savings from switching from heating oil to biomass boilers increased marginally overtime due to an increase in oil boilers over time by extrapolating the trend between 2009 and 2016.

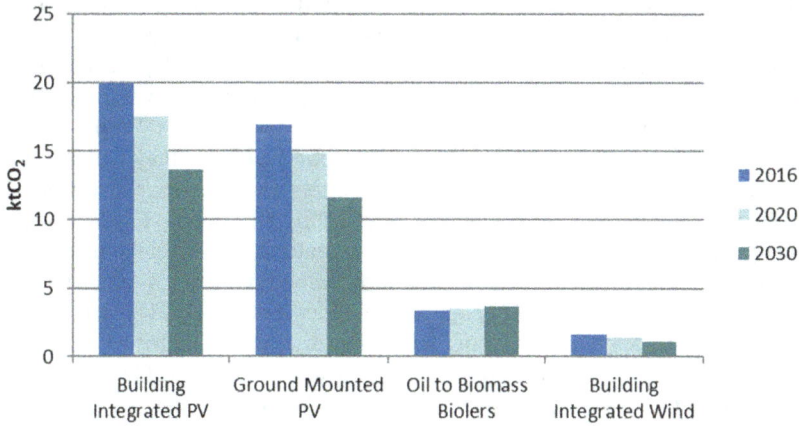

Figure 6: Potential carbon savings if measures implemented by year 2016, 2020, 2030

If progress was measured in tonnes carbon dioxide per FTE student (Figure 7) the improvement in energy efficiency relative to the 2009 baseline was 27% for the no improvement in energy efficiency scenario, 44% for the NEEAP trajectory scenario and 57% for the with measures scenario by 2030.

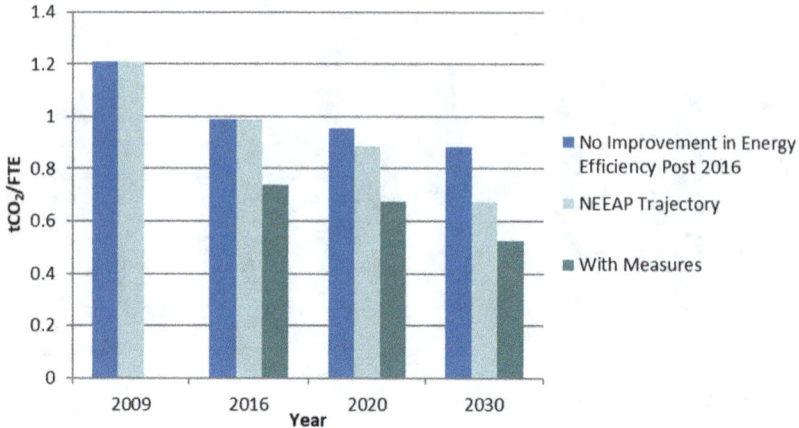

Figure 7: Carbon intensity per full time student equivalent

Discussion and Conclusions

A roadmap outlining the combined technological decarbonisation potential of carbon reduction measures for the Irish higher education sector was projected to reduce absolute carbon emissions for the Irish HEI sector by 36% (59,027 tCO2) by 2030, relative to 2009 baseline figures. Measured using the efficiency metric of carbon emissions per fulltime student equivalent, the improvement relative to 2009 was projected to be 57% by 2030. These projections highlight what is technologically feasible in terms of carbon reductions for Irish HEI campuses on-site. It was also found that for HEIs to have the greatest impact in facilitating national decarbonisation transitions, the earlier they take action by deploying decarbonisation technologies the greater the carbon emissions they will offset. This would be due to improvements in the national grids carbon intensity over time reducing the amount of carbon that may be offset by HEI action. Given growth of student numbers and the associated increase in material throughput on campuses, they serve as a useful testing ground to inform carbon reduction strategies for similarly growing community populations in wider society. By HEIs capitalising on the decarbonisation potentials of their campuses they would be demonstrating best practice and increase learning rates associated with deployed technologies relevant to informing wider societal transitions. The methods employed in this study have the potential to be replicated by higher education sectors in other countries to inform localised decarbonisation action plans.

Acknowledgments

This study was funded by the Sustainability Pillar of the Environmental Protection Agency (EPA) Research Programme 2014-2020 (2015-SE-MS-3).

References

Alshuwaikhat, H. M., and Abubakar, I. (2008) 'An integrated approach to achieving campus sustainability: assessment of the current campus environmental management practices', *Journal of Cleaner Production*, 16, 1777-1785.

Brunner, P.H. and Rechberger, H. (2017) *Handbook of Material Flow Analysis*, 2nd ed., Boca Raton: CRC Press.
Department of Education and Skills (DES) (2015) *Projections of demand for full time third level education 2015-2029*, Department of Education and Skills, Dublin available: https://www.education.ie/en/Publications/Statistics/Statistical-Reports/Projections-of-demand-for-full-time-Third-Level-Education-2015-2029.pdf [accessed 20 Dec 2016].
Derrick, S. (2013) 'Time and sustainability metrics in higher education', in Caeiro, S., Filho, W.L., Jabbour, C., and Azeiteiro, U.M., eds, *Sustainability Assessment Tools in Higher Education Institutions*, Cham: Springer.
Disterheft, A., Caeiro, S.S., Leal Filho, W., and Azeiteiro, U.M. (2015) 'The INDICARE-model-measuring and caring about participation in higher education's sustainability assessment', *Ecological Indicators*, 63, 172-186.
Dyer, G. and Dyer, M. (2017), 'Strategic leadership for sustainability by higher education: the American College & University Presidents' Climate Commitment'. *Journal of Cleaner Production*, 140,111-116.
Eatmon, T.D., Krill, H.E. and Rynes, J.J. (2016) 'Food production as a niche innovation in higher education' in Leal Filho, W. and Zint, M., eds, *The Contribution of Social Sciences to Sustainable Development at Universities*, London: Springer, 145-160.
Ferrer-Balas, D., Adachi, J., Banas, S., Davidson, C.I., Hoshikoshi, A., Mishra, A., Motodoa, Y., Onga, M., and Ostwald, M. (2008) 'An international comparative analysis of sustainability transformation across seven universities', *International Journal of Sustainability in Higher Education*, 9(3), 295-316.
Giljum, S., Dittrich, M., Lieber, M. and Lutter, S. (2014) 'Global patterns of material flows and their socio-economic and environmental implications: A MFA study on all countries world-wide from 1980-2009', *Resources*, 3, 319-339.
Grinspoon, D. (2016) *Earth in Human Hands: Shaping Our Planet's Future*, New York: Grand Central Publishing.
Haum, R. and Loose C.J. (2015) P*lanetary guardrails as policy guidance for sustainable development*, Sustainable Development Knowledge Platform, available: https://sustainabledevelopment.un.org/content/documents/616161-%20Haum%20and%20Loose%20-%20Planetary%20Guardrails%20as%20Policy%20Guidance%20for%20Sustainable%20Development.pdf [Last accessed 08/03/2018].
Higher Education Funding Council for England (HEFCE) (2010) *Carbon reduction target and strategy for higher education in England*, Bristol: Higher Education Funding Council for England, available: http://webarchive.nationalarchives.gov.uk/20180322111302/http://www.hefce.ac.uk/pubs/year/2010/201001/ [accessed 7 Nov 2018].
Horan, W., Shawe, R., Moles, R. and O'Regan, B. (2019) 'Development and evaluation of a method to estimate the potential of decarbonisation technologies deployment at higher education campuses', *Sustainable Cities and Society*, 101464.
IPCC (2018) *Global warming of 1.5°C Summary for Policy Makers*, Geneva: Intergovernmental Panel on Climate Change.
Jain, S., Agarwal, A., Jani, V., Sinhal, S., Sharma, P. and Jalan, R. (2017) 'Assessment of carbon neutrality and sustainability in educational campus (CaNSEC): a general framework', *Ecological Indicators*, 76, 131-143.
Klein-Banai, C. and Theis, T.L. (2011) 'Quantitative analysis of factors affecting greenhouse gas emissions at institutions of higher education', *Journal of Cleaner Production*, 48, 29-38.
Lang, T. and Kennedy, C. (2016) 'Assessing the global operational footprint of higher education with environmentally extended global multiregional input-output models', *Journal of Industrial Ecology*, 20(3), 462-471.

Lozano, R. (2011) 'The state of sustainability reporting at universities', *International Journal of Sustainability in Higher Education*, 12(1), 67-78.

Meadows, D., Randers, J. and Meadows, D. (2004) *The Limits to Growth: The 30-year Update*, London: Earthscan Ltd.

Meier, A., Davis, S.J., Victor, D.G., Brown, K., McNeilly, L., Modera, M., Pass, R.Z., Sager, J., Weil, D., Auston, D., Abdulla, A., Bockmiller, F., Brase, W., Brouwer, J., Diamond, C., Dowey, E., Elliott, J., Eng, R., Kaffka, S., Kappel, C.V., Kloss, M., Mezić, I., Morejohn, J., Phillips, D., Ritzinger, E., Weissman, S. and Williams, J. (2018) *University of California Strategies for Decarbonization: Replacing Natural Gas*, available: https://www.nceas.ucsb.edu/files/research/projects/UC-TomKat-Replacing-Natural-Gas-Report_2018.pdf [accessed on 7 Nov 2018].

Rockström, J., Steffen, W., Noone, K., Persson, A., Stuart III Chapin, F., Lambin, E., Lenton, T.M., Scheffer, M., Folke, C., Schellnhuber, H.J., Nykvist, B., de Wit, C.A., Hughes, T., van der Leeuw, S., Rodhe, H., Sörlin, S., Snyder, P.K., Costanza, R., Svedin, U., Falkenmark, M., Karlberg, L., Corell, R.W., Fabry, V.J., Hansen, J., Walker, B., Liverman, D., Richardson, K., Crutzen, P. and Foley, J. (2009) 'Planetary boundaries: exploring the safe operating space for humanity', *Ecology and Society*, 14(2), 32. http://www.ecologyandsociety.org/vol14/iss2/art32/ [Last Accessed 08/03/2018].

Sachs, J. (2015) *The Age of Sustainable Development*, New York: Columbia University Press.

SEAI (2018) *Organisational- Level Energy Data*, available: https://psmr.seai.ie/Public# [accessed on 29 Jun 2018].

SEAI (2017) Energy in Ireland 1990-2016, available: https://www.seai.ie/resources/publications/Energy-in-Ireland-1990-2016-Full-report.pdf [accessed on 30 Jun 2018]

Sonetti, G., Lombardi, P., Chelleri, L. (2016) 'True Green and Sustainable University Campuses? Toward a Clusters Approach', *Sustainability*, 8(1), 83, doi: https://doi.org/10.3390/su8010083.

Stephens, J.C., Hernandez, M.E., Román, M., Graham, A.C., and Scholz, R.W. (2008) 'Higher education as a change agent for sustainability in different cultures and contexts', *International Journal of Sustainability in Higher Education*, 9(3), 317–338.

Steffen, W., Grinevald, J., Crutzen, P. and McNeill, J. (2011) 'The Anthropocene: a conceptual and historical perspective', *Philosophical Translations of the Royal Society*, 369, 842-867.

Streffen, W., Rockström, J., Richardson, K., Lenton, T.M., Folke, C., Liverman, D., Summerhayes, C.P., Barnosky, A.D., Cornell, S.E., Crucifix, M., Donges, J.F., Fetzer, I., Lade, S.J., Scheffer, M., Winkelmann, R. and Schellnhuber, H.J. (2018) 'Trajectories of the Earth System in the Anthropocene', *Proceedings of the National Academy of Sciences of the United States of America*, 115(33), 8252-8259.

Victor, D.G., Abdulla, A., Austin, D., Brase, W., Brouwer, J., Brown, K., Davis, S.J., Kappel, C.V., Meier, A., Modera, M., Pass, R.Z., Phillips, D., Sager, J., Weil, D., TomKat Natural Gas Exit Strategies Working Group (2018) 'Turning Paris into reality at the University of California', *Nature Climate Change*, 8, 183-185.

Velazquez, L., Munguia, N., Platt, A., and Taddei, J. (2006) 'Sustainable university: what can be the matter?', *Journal of Cleaner Production*, 14(9), 810–819.

Yarime, M., and Tanaka, Y. (2012) 'The Issues and Methodologies in Sustainability Assessment Tools for Higher Education Institutions: A Review of Recent Trends and Future Challenges', *Journal of Education for Sustainable Development*, 6(1), 63–77.

Decarbonisation Roadmap for Universities of the Future

 **William Horan** is a researcher at the University of Limerick focusing on higher education decarbonisation, integrated assessment and community sustainability transitions. The title of his PhD thesis is 'The Role of Irish Higher Education Institutions in National Decarbonization Transitions'.

 **Rachel Shawe** is a researcher at the University of Limerick and specialist in higher education sustainability outreach, education and research. She is also involved with Leave No Trace Ireland which promotes responsible outdoor recreation through education, research and partnerships.

 **Bernadette O'Regan** is Senior Lector in Environmental Science at the University of Limerick and expert in systems dynamics modelling, systematic environmental science, environmental impact assessment and conservation ecology.

 **Richard Moles** is Professor Emeritus of Environmental Science at the University of Limerick and expert in climate change mitigation and adaptation, decarbonisation, community action, and conservation ecology.

17

Higher Education in a Post-Conflict Society

Dima Moain Dayoub
English Language Teaching Department, Higher Institute of Languages, Tishreen University, Lattakia, Syria

Present-day universities: A phase in the development trajectory

In the not-too-distant past, only four Syrian state universities provided higher education, for free, to Syrian students from all regions. The open-door policy has been the most prominent feature of these universities: the sole criterion for enrolment is the student's marks in the final Baccalaureate exams. At the turn of this century, the national higher education system has been redefined in many respects including policy (enrolment criteria, tuition fees, target student) and classroom-related dynamics such as attendance and interaction. Driven by concepts of modernization, "relevance and quality assurance", Syrian universities started to witness nationwide reforms that can be summed up by the diversifications of specializations, modernization of curricula and update of laws, among other aspects of reform.

Reform strides were nevertheless disrupted by new imposed realities: damage to the national higher education infrastructure, brain drain, and demographic shifts (Mourtada, 2019, pp. 355-357). The conflict has undone years of progress, prompting immediate remedial measures, adding new objectives and modifying others. The concept of a university in Syria was/is bound to evolve to accommodate the diversity of students' needs, capacities, and individual circumstances and to keep up with local and global imperatives such as modernization, inclusion, outreach and recently, post-conflict national reconstruction.

Paid access to higher education has simultaneously multiplied higher education access opportunities and increased financial returns. Horizontal expansion in higher education came in response to the rising numbers of students, compounded by capacity limitations faced by the four state universities - Damascus University, Aleppo University, Tishreen University (in Lattakia) and AlBaath Univesity (in Homs). To ease enrolment pressure, four more state universities were launched, one of which is completely virtual. The Syrian Virtual University was founded according to a legislative decree in 2002. In parallel, since 2001, private universities have proliferated, exclusively in remote rural or developing areas, partly as a way to revive the countryside and to contribute to economic and social welfare. Open learning programmes also run on traditional campuses at weekends to avoid competing for universities' resources during the week. They attract a certain category of prospective students. Broadening the routes to higher education is also evident in introduction of "parallel education". Parallel education has enabled a limited number of students who did not achieve entry requirements to apply for admission into regular programmes, for fees that remain less than those of private universities.

Another critical change agent in the goals and missions of higher education institutions has been the advent of technology. Over the last ten years, portable smart phones and consoles have become pervasive. Younger generations, the Syrian digital natives who are currently university students, have acquired technological and other skills through digital gameplay and the extensive use of mobile devices and consoles in informal settings. Additionally, technological tools have created inroads into otherwise inaccessible valuable resources for independent, portable and social learning. While this carries the potential of empowering the Syrian student and lecturer alike, it also brings about new roles and responsibilities. Digital transformation has profoundly influenced higher education at three levels: learning, research and development, and administrative services (Sebaaly, 2019, pp. 171-174). Syrian higher education was no exception. Yet, the impact of technology varies across Syrian universities: its most notable manifestation is the Syrian Virtual University (SVU). It is not an overstatement to refer to the Syrian Virtual University as a pioneering project, not only owing to the fact that it emerged when the technological infrastructure and cultural attitude towards a novel learning model were yet to mature, but also because it was the first completely virtual university in the Middle East.

What follows will cast light on the case of Syrian universities in the phase of post-conflict reconstruction, taking as a constant frame of reference the three contexts of higher education – state, private, and virtual – at which I have been a lecturer. Threaded with this is a vision of tomorrow's university as delineated by pressing needs.

Widening access to higher education

Virtual routes to universities: The Syrian Virtual University

Technology-enabled routes to higher education have transcended significant obstacles such as geographical distance and time confinements. The affordance of flexibility and adaptability to various lifestyles and circumstances is essential to promoting life-long learning and optimizing access and inclusion.

The SVU's slogan "beyond the boundaries of time and space" reflects the core affordance of virtual education. The university has targeted those heavily committed to family and work. In this sense, widening access means promoting lifelong continued learning. Importantly too, the SVU has served as a safer alternative for those students could not attend bricks-and-mortar universities in some regions during and after the crisis in Syria. It has created a shared academic space for students who are geographically dispersed inside and outside Syria, promoting thereby a sense of community. Widening access in this sense means bypassing the obstacles physical distances. Put simply, the university has brought higher education to students rather than students to higher education institutions.

Removing physical, geographical and temporal barriers in the pursuit of higher education is one of the SVU's distinctive affordances.

Until the SVU's establishment, it was hardly conceivable that a completely virtual university would be viable in Syria, especially given the then-mediocre national Internet infrastructure and uncertain cultural receptivity. Nearly two decades later, not only has the Syrian Virtual University taken off, but it has also gained reputation and recognition nationally and regionally. This was translated into an expansion of its academic programmes and infrastructure coupled by a rise in the number of enrolled students, which reached 30,000 in 2018, according to Ajami, the current SVU provost, and Haidar (2018, p. 28).

What sets the Syrian Virtual University apart from other national and regional educational technology initiatives is that technology is the "matrix" and "principal enabler" (Kuutti, 1996, p. 35) of the whole teaching-learning activity, not simply a complementary tool. The SVU is literally a virtual campus comprised of the following underlying systems: the information system (SVUIS) where students manage online registration, profile and class selection, the learning management system (LMS) Moodle where students access course materials and upload assignments, the virtual classroom system *WebDemo* where live scheduled meetings take place, and the assessment management system (Ajami and Haidar, 2018, p. 28). Yet, this virtual infrastructure is complemented by physical self-access centres that mainly function as authorized exam centres. Although the SVU has gained credibility for being state accredited, monitoring online exams has ensured integrity, adding further rigor to the culturally alien concept of virtual education. Although the number of students is highly likely to have outgrown available resources, the telecentres have alleviated disparities in access. Students who have poor access or simply encounter technological problems at home can still use the university's computers where programmes are installed and a technical support team available. Finally, the centres serve as social spaces for the SVU community, which helps diminish the potential sense of isolation that characterizes distance learning. According to the SVU's website, there are 18 national and 10 international telecentres located in Lebanon, Egypt, Turkey, Kuwait, Saudi Arabia, Jordan, Oman, the United Arab Emirates, Bahrain, Iraq, and Germany. This reflects the ambitious outreach objective embedded in the SVU policy. It is "*the growing need for higher education, the large number of people who could not access it, and innovations with the potential to make it more accessible*" that laid the foundations of Harvard (Christensen and Eyring, 2012, p. 52). Today, this premise still resonates and justifies the emergence and endurance of Syrian universities in general, and the SVU in particular.

Enhanced access to classes and academic materials

In modern higher education scenarios, the notion of attendance needs to reflect choice and belonging. It should not be synonymous with turning up to physical classes at fixed times. Rather, attendance should be synonymous with engagement and commitment, in- or out-of- class. Virtual education has indeed extended traditional notions of attendance beyond real-time class timings.

In the SVU, attending live virtual classes is enhanced by extensive out-of-class attendance alternatives. Synchronous meetings at scheduled times form an integral part of the SVU tuition as they maintain structure and social presence, making the transition to virtual learning less abrupt. Optional attendance of these sessions, however, aims to instil a new ethos of autonomy, choice and decision-making.

WebDemo affords the automatic recording of live virtual lectures and the SVU policy requires immediate uploads of sessions at the end of each meeting. Recorded sessions are of paramount importance as they become re-accessible for self-paced reinforcement of understanding or simply available to those students who missed the live sessions. The fact that live classes can be re-accessed also creates a climate of accountability, transparency and quality evaluation by tutors and managers alike. Tape-recording lectures is a widespread frowned-upon phenomenon in classical universities: it reinforces the image of the lecturer as the prime source of information and emphasizes an entrenched exam-oriented mindset. Besides, the quality of recordings is most often compromised since it takes place in large lecture theatres or classrooms with background noise. Businesses, mostly unprofessional, transcribe lectures and sell lecture notes, often of low-quality, to students who are mainly concerned with passing exams. In comparison, the SVU has enabled a more effective tool of re-accessing live lectures than the commodification of lecturers' input.

Figure 1 is a screenshot of a recorded session, from the tutor's view. A viewer where tutors can share the require academic material replaces the traditional board. Textual interactions, which are mainly responses to a tutor's questions, are typed in the keyboard chat. Audio interactions take place when a tutor enables a student's microphone. Recorded sessions save interactions in their multimodality: textual, audio and visual.

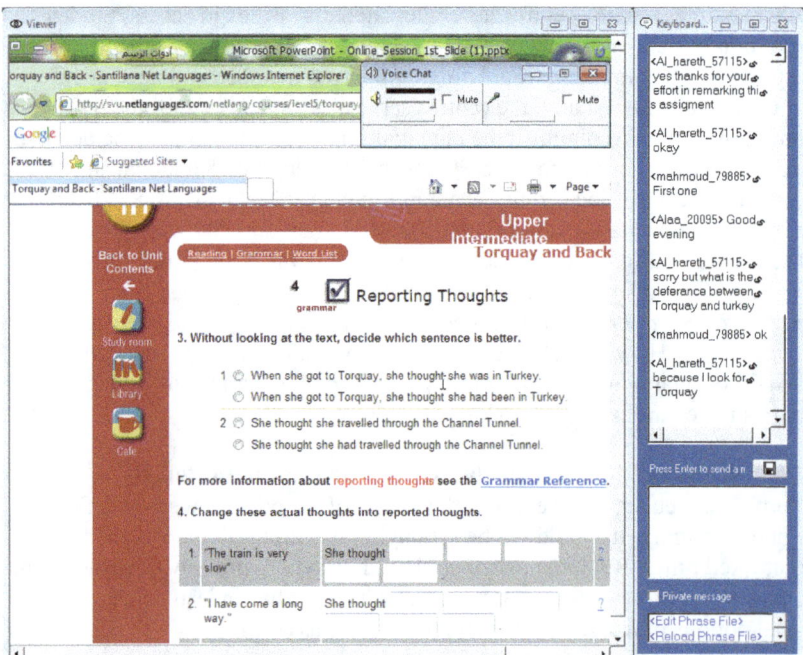

Figure 1: Screenshot of a recorded SVU live class

According to the SVU's policy, attendance is not mandatory and turning up to only 30 percent of live sessions entitles students to take final exams. In the light of the then-prevalent war-imposed realities such as frequent power cuts and interruptions in students' lives and studies, tutors were even advised not to take attendance strictly; that is, to promote a culture of voluntary attendance and to reward active participation and commitment to online sessions. It may be worth adding that lenient attendance regulations are not synonymous with reduced interactivity. Rather, the nature of teaching at the SVU is more extensive and intense. It is not bound to live sessions but involves asynchronous interaction with students via email and Moodle, out-of-class scaffold, assessment of students' academic progress, and attention to technological issues (Sebaaly, 2018, p. 176). Throughout the academic term, students' progress is closely monitored as tutors provide thorough feedback on three assignments and a project. Not surprisingly, the criteria for evaluating SVU tutor performance varies from traditional evaluation criteria. In their study, Ajami and Haidar conclude that there is no relationship between the "number of attendees" in an online session and students' evaluation of their online lecturers. They add that the SVU is more of a "self-learning system" where the availability of recorded online sessions, tutors' organizational skills on Moodle, and the clarity of assignment grading criteria all positively impact students' evaluation in the same manner as interaction in online sessions does (2018, p. 44).

Having said that, in live virtual classes, active attendance becomes especially relevant in the absence of face-to-face contact and meta-language. Building rapport becomes feasible since class size no longer matters in so far as potential noise and disruptive behavior are concerned. Noise is filtered as learners do not share the same physical space. That a student is logged in to a live virtual class does not necessarily mean that they are actively engaged. Tutors have devised strategies to encourage active attendance such as personalizing interaction using students' names, eliciting and acknowledge responses and contributions. Such personalized in-class interaction has also helped build and consolidate rapport with students. Virtual class management in the SVU takes on totally new dimensions and lecturers have to unlearn some strategies and practices and learn others. As Lanzara (2016, p. 14) puts it,

> *the emergence of new skills cannot happen without simultaneously unlearning or forgetting previous behavioral patterns that are often deeply engrained and will not be easily relinquished. In a process of innovation, therefore, we may observe both making and breaking systems and patterns of action, destructuring as well as restructuring.*

Overall, new notions of identity and belonging are nurtured in the Syrian Virtual University, and so is a new concept of participation based on a genuine incentive to learn. Despite the relaxed attendance policy, attendance in some classes was impressive and active as it stemmed from intrinsic motivation. The presence of a tutor seems to create structure and sustain the social dimension, but does not assume the centre of the learning process. In fact, establishing rapport with the SVU students is an imperative and a byproduct of *WebDemo* and its embedded interaction dynamics.

The potential of blended learning

Introducing hybrid or blended instruction that marries the strengths of online and face-to-face experiences can be the way forward for current open learning and traditional programmes. Blended instruction affords the benefits of "periodic classroom-based instruction" and continued informal learning at home at the same time (Christensen & Eyring, 2012, p.51). Some academics might be reluctant to embrace online tuition or might find in its adoption a threat of redundancy and competition. Blended learning, however, can be utilized to enhance, not eliminate, existing teaching models (Sebaaly, 2018, p. 176). Unlike the provision of totally online tuition that requires recruiting experts and developing infrastructure from scratch, traditional universities have the advantage of readily equipped computer laboratories and staff, which makes the integration of some online modules more affordable.

In Syria, open learning programmes are available to students who do not achieve the required grades for admission into regular programmes. However, many students opt for these programmes due to attendance difficulties such as residence in remote areas, heavy workloads and/or family commitments. Even though such programmes run at weekends as they use the same resources, facilities and buildings of traditional universities, attendance remains challenging and many students rely on buying lecture notes prepared by unprofessional businesses. A blended higher education model can counter current challenges faced by Syrian students in general: It gives them flexibility and choice regarding the timings of some lectures, helps them cut down on travel expenses, provides them credible materials and lecture notes in digital formats, and expands the limited infrastructure capacity of traditional universities.

Widening access: Differentiated higher education modes of delivery

Paid access

Paid access to higher education programmes in Syria has not emerged as a substitute for free access, but rather as an expansive inclusive measure. Access remains nearly free for those students who meet the requirements of entry into state universities. Another source of profit should nevertheless come from research and its applications in real-life. Partnerships with private funding bodies to sponsor significant research initiatives, even at state universities, can significantly help implement a research-based culture to higher education.

The competitive quality of digital universities is usually seen in terms of cost-effectiveness (Christensen & Eyring, 2012, p. 51; Zwaan, 2017, p. 143). However, this does not apply to the SVU because although tuition fees are more affordable than those of Syrian private universities, the SVU is still the only fee-paying state university. Strategically speaking, virtual higher education in Syria is meant as a remedial alternative rather than a disruptive technology that threatens the status of traditional universities. Even culturally speaking, tuition-free universities are considered more prestigious, not in terms of the quality of teaching, but due to the fact that enrolment requires higher grades and so they are always associated with higher-achieving students. At the same time, a paradox was created since fee-paying alternatives such as private universities, parallel education, virtual education, and open learning programmes all have their own criteria for enrolment that are usually less demanding in terms of marks than those of state universities. Some academic programme offerings such as medical sciences, computer science and art are similar to those in traditional universities. Others, including hospital administration and occupational therapy, are new.

Reviving remote and rural areas

In theory, private universities are meant to alleviate pressure from state universities; in reality, the pressure was intensified in some respects. The complementary mission is manifest in the geographical distribution of the Syrian private universities. The list of universities on the Syrian Ministry of Higher Education's official site includes 22 private universities, established over a span of 18 years, extending from Damascus countryside to Aleppo countryside, Homs countryside, Idlib, Qamishli, Der Izzur, Dera'a, and the coastal countryside. Such focus on isolated rural or remote areas has the potential of revival and economic prosperity. Most students travel from surrounding and nearby cities to universities' physical campuses or rent locally, thereby reviving the area's systems of transportation, estate agencies and restaurants. Economical boosts also come from creating work opportunities for locals who can apply for administrative vacancies.

The need for qualitative expansion

The Syrian higher education system has already witnessed the initiation of the Syrian Virtual University, the proliferation of private universities, the expansion of traditional ones through open learning programmes and parallel education. Despite that, this horizontal expansion in the structure of higher education was not paralleled by an enhancement of the existing cornerstones. Conversely, private universities have competed for, even exhausted, existing human assets in state universities. Higher pay packages have attracted a considerable number of faculty members. Academics are permitted to teach up to 8 hours at private universities, exclusively at weekends. This has adversely impacted commitment to research by consuming academics' energy in teaching, and in travelling to private university campuses. Further, feeling the weight of working overtime, many staff members have taken leaves from state universities to work full-time in private ones. As a result, the former concept of brain drain has been compounded by the new phenomenon of internal brain drain. Likewise, newly established state universities, the SVU and open learning programmes have all largely relied on faculty from established universities to compensate for the shortage of academics.

The impact of technology outside higher education boundaries

Heightened opportunities of non-formal learning

The SVU is an example of how technology has robustly propelled change in higher education in Syria. The impact of technology on higher education is not, however, limited to virtual education. There is evidence of non-formal serendipitous learning triggered by a plethora of technological resources and technology-enabled social forums. For instance, digital games, in their multiple genres (adventure, simulation, role play, serious educational games), were perceived to be a potentially rich source of language learning for Syrian university students and staff (Dayoub,

2019). This lends support to the role of interactive technologies and edutainment in non-formal learning, even at the tertiary level. Likewise, social technologies have served as a developmental platform, according to a small-scale study involving postgraduate students in two Masters programmes at the Higher Institute of Languages, Tishreen University. The study reveals that students have resorted to social media to express and develop their professional identities despite regularly meeting face-to-face in traditional classes. They have voluntarily created Facebook pages and groups to interact, share academic resources and news, discuss assignments, publish exam results, signal out useful grants sites, and follow professional pages. In summary, they have found in social networks an arena to strengthen their sense of belonging to the local and wider academic circles (Dayoub, 2018).

The ubiquity of digital information: Promises and perils

Formally speaking, in Syrian universities, the submission of research-based assignments, projects and dissertations is a requirement in many departments. Yet, there are only a handful of academic libraries and resources are often outdated. The Web as a virtual library and an arena for knowledge exchange has, to some extent, resolved this paradox. The classical concept of university teaching materials has indeed been challenged by pools of digital resources available to mass audiences globally (Zwaan, 2017, p. 143). The ubiquity of digital information has defied the entrenched notion of the lecturer as a sage on the stage and the sole provider of knowledge. Indeed, this unparalleled flow of information has offered unlimited learning resources: MOOCs (Massive Open Online Courses), open-source educational resources and other multimodal materials such as YouTube videos, among others. Open access initiatives such as the MIT OpenCourseWare were envisioned to be the information foundation of an emerging global "meta-university". The latter is described as a *"transcendent, accessible, empowering, dynamic, communally constructed framework of open materials and platforms on which much of higher education worldwide can be constructed or enhanced"* (Vest, 2006, p. 30). By empowering is meant scaffolding informal learning and formal higher education institutions world-wide. Indeed, open-access materials have provided invaluable aid and helped flatten hierarchies of access, at least to some extent. For example, in English for Specific (Medical) Purposes classes in Syria, utilizing a professionally made medical animation that illustrates the muscles of the heart or parts of the brain in native English concretizes abstract knowledge and enables unmediated exposure to native English pronunciation of medical terms. More sophisticated are immersive technologies such as virtual and augmented realities that promise access to physically inaccessible virtual learning environments. Especially in developing countries, harnessing such technologies to promote leaning and research can broaden the horizons of student experiences.

On the other hand, despite the availability of credible academic content, authoring digital content does not necessarily conform to traditional publishing criteria. Academically speaking, questions are raised regarding "quality control" including the cost of distributing and maintaining sophisticated academic materials for free (Vest, 2006, p. 28). Other concerns voiced relate to issues of *"navigation, structure, interactivity, complexity, security, stability, and time wasted by undisciplined or confused users"* (Fahy, 2008, p. 182). Today, ownership of smart phones that are equipped with intuitive media production tools is on the rise. The Internet is replete with generic publishing forums with no publishing regulations. While this may be ideal for cultural inclusion and participation, it is challenging in terms of the quality and quantity of published information.

This raises the question of how to move from accessibility to information to accessibility to knowledge. Incorporating modules that substantially focus on developing Syrian students' research skills is a key requirement for future higher education in Syria. Among the skills that could ensure research integrity are digital information literacy, multilingualism, and critical and higher-order thinking skills.

Relevance

Key 21st century skills and subjects: Digital information literacy
Although the World Wide Web is a vast virtual library, it is one without a librarian and with changing notions of authorship and credibility. Therefore, a key 21st-century skill is digital information literacy, both in its generic transferrable sense and in its subject-specific context-specific sense or "source criticism". The first can be acquired and applied across disciplines; the latter is longer-term and more complex. Source criticism calls for subject-matter expertise, context sensitivity, cultural awareness, and adherence to research ethics and procedures (Johannessen, 2017, pp. 89-94). Importantly, information literacy includes handling multimodal information given "the emergence of post-typographic forms of text production, contribution, and reception" (Koltay, 2011, p. 211).

The process of locating and retrieving relevant online information requires training. Students need to develop their self-critical skills; that is, to employ neutral rather than attitude-laden search keywords, to discern high quality peer-reviewed academic sources, and to rely on "*academic databases over search engines*" (Johannessen, 2017, p. 103). The wealth of online information and the dearth of training in sound academic practice is one of the profound concerns facing Syrian universities, like elsewhere. The trend towards enhancing academic practice in Syrian universities is accelerating, yet the actualization of this objective is still tentative. Having said that, without re-evaluating current assessment systems that focus heavily on final exam results, the importance of academic and research skills cannot be brought to the fore.

Enhanced digital presence: Multilingualism and interdisciplinarity
Another significant hindrance to access is monolingualism. Many state-of-the-art resources are authored in languages other than Arabic. In order to maximally benefit from such digital information, researchers need to be versed in the target content languages, mainly English. Some initiatives to voluntarily translate scientific, literary and academic articles such as the Facebook page *The Syrian Researchers* الباحثون السوريون have attracted more than 2.2 million likes. The popularity of this page reflects mounting interest in accessing and making accessible available research. Yet, for the digital divide be further reduced Syrian universities need to become digitally visible by producing, not just consuming, quality digital content. It may be worth noting that most faculty members hold

doctorate degrees from international universities including Britain, France, Germany, and Russia, among others. In other words, they have the language and content knowledge necessary to publish and enhance the digital presence of Syrian universities. In practice, release time and interdisciplinary collaboration is needed for such tasks. In the meantime, endeavours to disseminate open access locally produced resources have emerged: The SVUpedia is an example. SVUpedia enables access to some course textbooks, outstanding papers in different Masters programmes, published papers by SVU students and alumni, and training programmes, as Figure 2 illustrates.

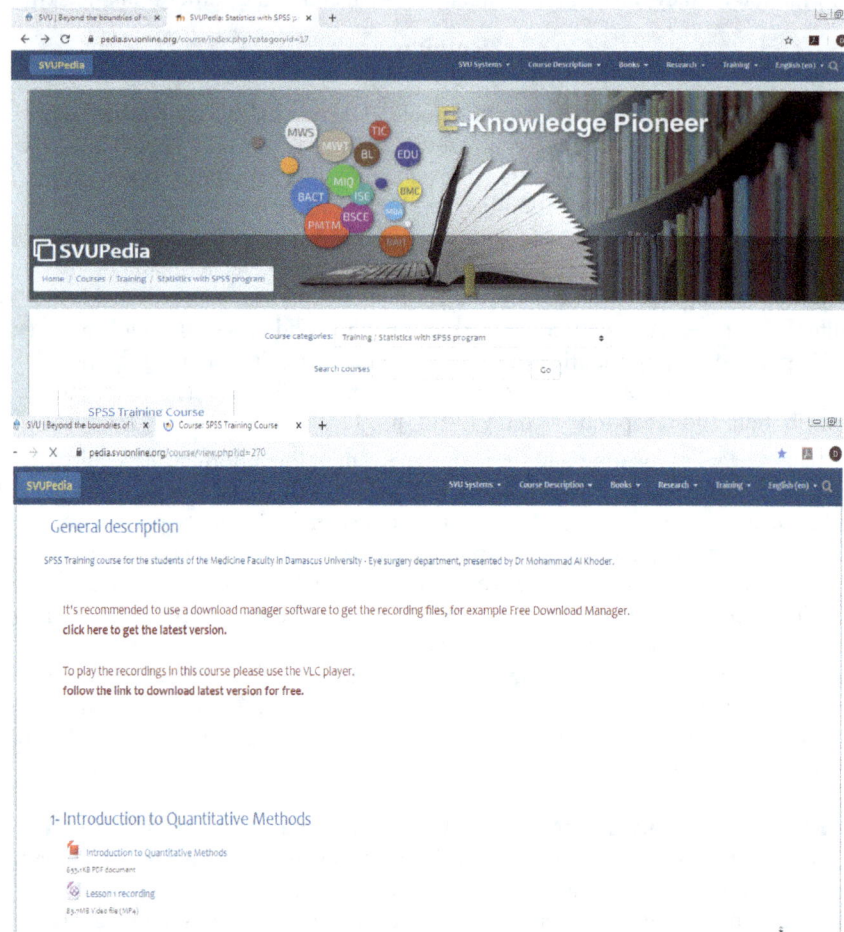

Figure 2: Example of SVUpedia open-access training materials

Taking into account that the production of digital content is not necessarily only textual but also multimodal, the task becomes two-fold: providing content that is academically credible or research-based and crafting appropriate in-built interactivity at the same time. The dilemma is that subject matter experts (SMEs) are not all trained to produce multimedia-rich content. Mastery of advanced specialized skills is a pre-requisite for making sophisticated content that is adaptive, challenging, entertaining, culturally appropriate, stimulating of critical thinking and compatible with end user's computer systems. Suleiman and Ajami (2014) define interactive electronic content in terms of its subscription to desired learning outcomes, embedded opportunities for experimentation, potential to deepen subject knowledge, provision of meaningful feedback, compatibility with the learners' intellectual levels and cultural considerations. Only local production of digital content can address these context-specific dimensions. The potential of interdisciplinary teamwork appears to be a worthwhile approach to material development in the future. There are endeavours to upgrade staff skills in Syrian universities through the Department of Continued Education, yet these remain sporadic and basic. Alternatively, specialized advanced courses can be made available to faculty members in relevant departments as part of their professional development.

Higher order and critical-thinking skills

The modernization task that higher education has undertaken is not limited to harnessing digital resources in a productive academic manner. Its magnitude becomes more tangible when considering that "*applications of modern technology such as artificial intelligence, machine learning, cloud computing, cybersecurity, big data analytics, internet of things, robotics, smart manufacturing, 3D printing, simulation, virtual and augmented reality*" are predicted to automate and replace the human workforce. With this in mind, developing higher-order skills is the key to a "future-proof graduate" (Sebaaly, 2019, pp. 168-171).

When passing exams is an overriding concern, universities will remain engines of reproducing the status quo: patterns of thinking and behaviour that stand in sharp contrast with higher-order thinking skills. The widely common rote learning culture fails to trigger the learners' mind and obstructs the next phase of higher education development. Replicating lecture notes and using available literature verbatim without referencing are common problems in Syrian universities. Universally, plagiarism is the plight evident in many academic papers and perpetuated by such factors as massification of higher education, heavy faculty workloads and easy access to online information and unclear plagiarism penalties (Singh & Remenyi, 2016). An exam-oriented mentality is detrimental to critical thinking, defined as "*a type of thinking that remains too advanced, too nuanced, and too creative to be emulated by machine intelligence or AI [artificial intelligence]*" (Sebaaly, 2019, p. 169). The aim of future universities is not a graduate that can emulate machines, but one whose skills cannot be emulated by machines and whose competencies cannot be made redundant and stagnant. Specifying and cultivating the skills and competencies needed for globally sustainable and nationally meaningful careers should be the ground for developing new curricula, modules and assessment systems. Future universities need to transform rigid course structures and curricula into vibrant platforms and networks of knowledge resources. Assessment should stimulate and fuel higher-order skills.

Specializations inspired by societal and developmental relevance
Introducing new specializations into the Syrian higher education system has recently been driven by market demands. The SVU, for instance, rationalizes its mission and selection of programmes on the grounds of responsiveness to market demands locally and regionally:

[The] SVU's objective is to meet the market needs nationally and regionally. SVU is working to provide a modern learning, training and research system in academic and vocational fields to enable the learner and the trainee to engage effectively and directly in the labor market by developing their skills and regional needs in science and technology.

While this is crucial for knowledge advancement, employment opportunities and economic growth; post-conflict reconstruction must also inform decision making in this regard. Mourtada (2019) underlines the fact that focus on majors such as medicine and engineering in the national reconstruction phase is undeniably pertinent. Physical recovery from the consequences of the war in Syria requires qualified prosthetics specialists, post-traumatic stress disorder specialists, rehabilitation centres, school counsellors, civil engineers and electrical engineers, among others. However, it is rightly contended that the underemphasized social sciences and communal research are equally important.

If reconstruction is to be meaningful then universities have to be involved in conducting studies, doing research, and preparing graduates in all disciplines, not only to alleviate the pain of post-war conditions, but also to suggest approaches, plans and a vision that would prevent, or at least reduce, the possibility of future conflicts. Understanding the significance of empowering universities to improve their output in social sciences and humanities makes them more relevant in post-conflict contexts. (2019, p.358)

Emphasizing the role of human sciences does not necessarily mean introducing new specializations. In fact, students of humanities and social sciences far outnumber those enrolled into scientific majors. It could simply mean focus, orientation and guidance by, for example, encouraging projects and dissertations in this direction. The target of social sciences should be geared towards tackling communal problems in a practical way that adds tangible value to society.

It may be worth noting that universities have hosted students who relocated from other regions during the crisis. Additionally, students were allowed to temporarily attend a safer state university when their original universities were disrupted, destroyed or directly affected by the crisis. This cross-regional integration also has the potential of building inter-communal cohesion and enriching universities' communities of staff and students alike.

The vision of the future university

No uniform concept of a university encompasses the spectrum of diverse and emerging individual and societal needs and conditions in Syria single-handedly. Responsiveness to such needs means the continuity of differentiated higher education contexts, free and paid, virtual and traditional, while adhering to the main mission of increasing access and participation. The overarching objective of these contexts is meeting global imperatives and academic quality. The university of the future is the university of today in a constant strive to survive and harness competitive disruptions, to adapt to new givens, to renew its human capital and infrastructure, and to build on its unique assets and past experiences. The ultimate aim is to enhance the relevance of the university in response to societal needs and human development.

An ideal model of the future Syrian university is one that prioritizes innovative interdisciplinary, locally meaningful, internationally competitive research. To achieve this, the horizontal expansion in the structure of the Syrian higher education must run in parallel with vertical in-depth consolidation of the pillars of universities by enhancing research facilities and resources, making new staff appointments and enabling release time for research assignments. This is a real challenge in the light of current economic sanctions, i.e., the new brain drain challenge encountered by state universities.

Additionally, open and regular learning programmes can be upgraded through the digitization of curricula and the adoption of blended learning. As such, universities can capitalize on the best of the real and virtual worlds. Syrian universities were originally founded on the premise of the "open-door" policy in the sense that the door is open to high-achieving Baccalaureate students for free. Ideally, the future university is one with no boundaries and no walls, one that promotes an "open-access" policy in the sense of curtailing transportation costs, bypassing physical space limitations, and facilitating students' free and convenient access to vibrant and stimulating academic materials. The notion of attendance will be re-visited to reflect commitment and intrinsic incentive. The traditional concept of formal assessment will be replaced by the trend to equip students with skills that have real-life and future relevance.

Today's university students are digital natives, the Google generation, in an era where technological innovations such as deep fakes, artificial intelligence and immersive technologies have blurred the boundaries of information, misinformation and knowledge. Since information modalities, dissemination and presentation are constantly changing, a parallel change should aim at developing the competencies needed to achieve academic integrity and meet future employability requirements. Among the most relevant skills that students will need to cultivate are digital information literacy skills, and critical thinking and higher-order skills. Equally important is emphasizing universities' digital presence by producing credible content, both in English and in Arabic. Universities of the future will harness the overwhelming and constant flow of information, fully utilize the powerful educational potential of technological innovations and push the frontiers of research, in its applied rather than abstract sense.

References

Ajami, Kh. and Haidar, O. (2018) "Applying Students Evaluation of Teaching (SET) in Virtual Learning Environment (Case Study: Syrian Virtual Learning)", International Journal of Teaching and Education, Vol. VI, No. 2, pp., 24-45.

Christensen, C. and Eyring, H. J. (2012) "The Innovative University: Changing the DNA of Higher Education", Forum for the Future of Higher Education, pp., 47-53.

Dayoub, D. (2018) "The Mediation of FaceBook in Identity Expression in the Case of Postgraduate Students of MA Programmes in English Language Teaching at the Higher Institute of Languages at Tishreen University", Tishreen University Journal for Research and Scientific Studies: Arts and Humanities Series, Vol. 40, No., 5, pp., 633-644.

Dayoub, D. (2019) "Vernacular Digital Games as English Language Learning Tools: An Exploratory Study in the Syrian Context", Tishreen University Journal for Research and Scientific Studies: Arts and Humanities Series, Vol. 41, No., 2, pp., 791- 804.

Fahy, P. J. (2008) "Characteristics of Interactive Online Learning Media", in Anderson T (ed.), The Theory and Practice of Online Learning, 2nd edition, Edmonton, AU press, pp. 167-199.

Johannessen, H. (2017) "Teaching Source Criticism to Students in Higher Education: A Practical Approach", in Ingvaldsen S, and Oberg D, (eds.), Media and Information Literacy in Higher Education: Educating the Educators, Chandos Publishing, Cambridge.

Koltay, T. (2011) "The Media and the Literacies: Media Literacy, Information Literacy, Digital Literacy", Mind, Culture & Society, Vol. 33, No. 2, pp., 211-221.

Kuutti, K. (1996) "Activity Theory as a Potential Framework for Human-Computer Interaction Research", in Nardi B, (ed.), Context and Consciousness: Activity Theory and Human-Computer Interaction, Cambridge, MA, The MIT Press, pp. 17-44.

Lanzara, G. (2016) Shifting Practices: Reflections of Technology, Practice, and Innovation, the MIT Press, Cambridge, MA.

Mourtada, H. (2019) "Higher-Education Relevance in Postwar Syria", in Badran A, Baydoun E and Hillman J R, (eds.), Major Challenges Facing Higher Education in the Arab World: Quality Assurance and Relevance, Springer Nature, Switzerland, pp. 353-361.

Sebaaly, M. (2019) "Digital Transformation and Quality, Efficiency, and Flexibility in Arab Universities", in Badran A, Baydoun E and Hillman J R, (eds.), Major Challenges Facing Higher Education in the Arab World: Quality Assurance and Relevance, Springer Nature, Switzerland, pp. 167-177.

Singh, S. and Remenyi, D. (2016) "Plagiarism and Ghostwriting: The Rise in Academic Misconduct", South African Journal of Science, Vol. 112, No. 5/6, pp. 1-7.

Suleiman, M. and Ajami Kh. (2014) "Evaluating Interactive Learning Content in an eLearning Environment", eLearn magazine, June, viewed 12 June, 2019, <https://elearnmag.acm.org/archive.cfm?aid=2632550>

The Syrian Ministry of Higher Education (2018), viewed 25 June, 2019, <http://www.mohe.gov.sy/mohe/index.php/>.

The Syrian Virtual University (2017), viewed 20 June, 2019, <https://www.svuonline.org/>.

Vest, C. M. (2006) "Pen Content and the Emerging Global Meta University," Educause Review, pp. 18-30.

Zwaan, B. V. D. (2017) Higher Education in 2040: a Global Approach, AUP, Amsterdam, viewed 10 June, 2019, < https://www.jstor.org/stable/j.ctvfp63n9.16 >.

Dima Moain Dayoub is an associate professor of Educational Technology and ELT and the head of the English Language Teaching Department at the Higher Institute of languages, Tishreen university, Syria, where she teaches *Integrating Technology into Language Learning and Teaching* and *Academic Research* to Masters students. She holds a Ph.D. from the University of Manchester and was awarded an Erasmus+ Teaching Mobility scholarship at the University of Barcelona and the Media and Digital Literacy Academy scholarship at the Lebanese American University in Beirut.

Epilogue

Making sense of the different information and opinions acquired during the preparation of this book has been a fascinating experience. The range of ideas relating to how universities might evolve in the future indicates how strongly the need for further development of the idea of the University is felt in some quarters. Perhaps the single most lasting realisation which has come out of this book production exercise is that a university cannot be complacent about it's position in society and that it continually needs to be sensitive as to how society is developing and be able to respond to its requirements. This view will not be welcomed by everyone and modernisation can be traumatic. Some will say that a university has to defend tradition. An example of this is that although as far as we are aware no university is still teaching in Latin some are operating their graduating ceremonies in that peculiar language. It is not clear what the value of this is.

Tradition is deeply embedded in universities. The titles used by senior office bearers, such as Chancellor and Dean reflect that. More importantly the operational structure of Faculties and then Departments or Schools often make any attempt at central leadership difficult. And then there is the question of academic freedom. Academic freedom, which has been described as an overreaction to the repressive attitude taken toward Galileo Galilei, is still held to be precious by many universities. There is some considerable value in academic freedom, but this principle can make changes and innovation in the university environment quite difficult. On the other hand, if the university is not to become a living museum it must deliver in order to satisfy the needs of the present.

Here, an attempt will be made to distil some of these ideas into a small number of what might be regarded as central issues. These could be used by both prospective students in choosing a university and by university administrators in deciding how to prioritise development in their own institutions.

The three fundamentals

But before these ideas are discussed there are four issues which need to be addressed.

A university is by its very nature always a work-in-progress and it is incumbent upon any university to continually reinvent itself in order to reflect the needs of the society for which it functions.

The range of institutions which describe themselves as universities is so diverse that it is quite misleading to think that there is one model of a university. Furthermore, this range is likely to increase in the future as new ideas of how to deliver higher education are explored. As university funding continues to change and as the demand for higher education grows so will the number of institutions offering higher education vary in a wide variety of ways.

The student experience will be vastly different. There is virtually nothing in common with the university experience the student will receive when attending a small ancient university in comparison to what will be experienced during the course of a degree from a large distance learning institution.

Prospective students need to become much more aware of what different higher educational options offer and which of these will be most suitable to their personal circumstances. Before applying to attend a university a prospective student needs to undertake considerable research with regards to what the University is offering and what type of result the acquisition of a degree from that university will produce. On the one hand the prospective student also needs to understand the marketplace with regards to the supply of higher education while at the same time being aware of how this education will help him or her develop personally and what opportunities graduates from the institution are likely to be offered. Although league tables of universities' performance may be of some help in this regard, the research required needs to be conducted at least to some extent with empirical evidence by the prospective student engaging in discussions with faculty, current students, alumni as well as prospective employers. This will put pressure on universities to be more transparent as to what they are offering and how they present the value package a prospective student could look forward to.

In a sense the last idea, which is the most important from the point of view of any prospective student is well described by the old Latin aphorism *caveat emptor*. Assumptions about university education which are made without adequate empirical evidence are highly suspect and universities need to encourage prospective students to be able to articulate why they want to attend university and why the university they have chosen is the right one for their needs.

Summary of the current environment the university faces

So many different ideas have been produced by the contributors to this book that any attempt to summarise them must inevitably fall short. The following 12 points are some of those which may have the most impact on how we think about and understand the way universities operates and which directly influence how they will evolve in the future.

1. Many, if not most universities have become large multiproduct, multiprocess and multi-outcome global organisations. They should be no longer seen, as they have been in the past, as simple public service institutions created in order to educate the youth of the more privileged parts of our society. They have accepted the neo-liberal view of the need to satisfy the requirements of the marketplace.
2. There will be increasing pressure for universities to liaise or collaborate with prospective employers of their students. This will result in new types of degrees, new formats of delivery, and a greater emphasis on preparing students to have a fuller understanding of the organisational life which may lie ahead of them.
3. Government funding, on which many universities have relied in the past and are currently reliant, is likely to become increasingly difficult in the forthcoming years and this will put additional strain on the University both from an academic and administrative point of view. Delivering education is highly expensive.

Epilogue

4. Although a university education is not suitable for everyone, for those who require a degree it can be a completely life changing experience which opens many doors both on a career level and the personal level. It is unlikely that the demand for university education will do anything other than increase exponentially over the forthcoming years.
5. Although there are examples of private universities offering less-expensive degrees than the established institutions it is most probable that the cost of university education will increase substantially, and it will become harder for individuals to justify the substantial outlay that is required to obtain a degree. In addition to the fees and living costs the issue of opportunity costs will become increasingly important. Thus privatisation will bring with it an increase in bogus degrees offered by predatory institutions.
6. The balance between research and teaching will become an increasingly contentious issue as value for money becomes an issue especially for fee paying students who will continue to question the value for money they are receiving.
7. The fact that lecturing is an ineffective way of transmitting knowledge is increasingly accepted and universities need to innovate in a number of different ways. A greater emphasis on modern pedagogical thinking is now required and expertise alone in the subject matter or degree content is not adequate to be regarded as a valuable member of the University faculty.
8. Being able to stimulate students' interest and inspire them to want to learn is every bit as important as having an in-depth knowledge of the subject which is being presented.
9. There is a pressing need to address a number of ethical issues some of which are to do with plagiarism and ghost-writing which are undermining academic integrity and need to be urgently prevented. Other concerns relate to admission and to the evaluation of the results of learning achieved by the students.
10. Continued research into pedagogy is critical in as far as it will be possible to utilise current technologies such as AI to facilitate student and faculty learning. To handle the new pedagogy, the physical structure of the university will need to change. Most campuses are still populated largely by traditional lecture theatres and libraries, but are underinvested in flexible study classrooms, and lack effective facilities for distance and hybrid course delivery and access to electronic sources of content and communication to meet the needs of today's technologically savvy student. Technology-enabled informal group study/workspace is also a challenge.
11. There will be further interest to increase the sustainability of the physical operation of the university.
12. Universities in some parts of the world will be pressured to examine governance, programs and curriculum to acknowledge the Western colonial influences on approaches and content and introduce elements of indigenous culture and community.

The University of the Future

Although much will change for the university over the next decade the general ethos which proclaims the importance of acquiring and using knowledge will remain at the heart of the institution. This can be summarised by saying that the ultimate responsibility of the university is to inspire students so they assume the core value which places their personal intellectual development high on their list of priorities. This involves recognising that one's education is never complete and that one's cognitive capacity is something that has to be both cultivated and cherished. Whatever role an individual plays in society and whatever level he or she reaches there is always something more that he or she may learn. It is this dimension of knowledge and education which makes involvement with a university an exciting experience.

Index

Age of Data, i, xi, 105, 109, 110
Age of Reason, 109, 110
AI, ix, xi, 3, 11, 18, 19, 22, 23, 27, 105, 108, 110, 112, 116, 118, 126, 164, 185, 188, 191, 196, 251, 257
antithesis, 70
Artificial Intelligence, ix, 18, 22, 27, 126, 191
attrition rate, 2
auto-didacticism, 65
badges, 9, 11
benchmark, 126, 146
best-in-the-world, 84
bias, 81, 115, 116, 117, 118, 208, 211
Bildung, i, xiii, 165, 166, 167, 168, 169, 170, 171, 173, 177, 178, 179, 181
Blended learning, 181, 187, 246
borderless, unequal world, 35
brave new world, 85, 86
bricks-and-mortar universities, 242
career development, 69
career prospects, 49, 92
case room, 99
caveat emptor, 256
certification, 92, 115, 124, 183, 184
channel capacity, 115, 116, 117
Chief Learning Officer, 193, 197
class barriers, 1, 8
Cloud Campus, 61
cluster development, 202
cognitive flexibility, 19
collaboration, 28, 36, 47, 50, 56, 58, 99, 126, 128, 129, 130, 154, 167, 172, 177, 180, 183, 188, 189, 193, 197, 205, 208, 209, 210, 213, 217, 250
colonial influences, 257
Common sense, 8, 9
competence, 73, 75, 79, 115, 148
Complex communication, 184
computational learning, 114, 117
confidence, xiii, 18, 48, 79, 80, 156, 158, 160, 161, 162, 168, 177, 191, 192
consumer sovereignty, 3
contested territory, 68
cost, 2, 3, 5, 20, 22, 27, 38, 59, 84, 85, 95, 98, 108, 151, 163, 183, 246, 248, 257
critical perspectives, 174
cultural sclerosis, 3
Culture shift, 17

curiosity, 18, 19, 26, 58, 84, 174
Decarbonisation, ii, xv, 229, 232
decolonisation, xi, 82, 83
deep learning, 74, 89, 110
democratic society, 66
digital books, 18
digital equity, 30
Digital Methodologies, 166, 171
digital revolution, 31, 107
digital skills, xiii, 165, 169, 176
digital turn, xiii, 165, 166, 168, 169, 170, 173, 177, 179, 180
discourse, 49, 59, 71, 172, 173, 195
double bind, 166, 170, 178
downside to education, 80
ecosystem, 135, 136, 137, 138, 229
edupreneurs, 188
effective teaching, 91, 94
e-Learning, 40, 81
elite education, ix, 1, 5, 9
empiricism, 109
entrepreneurial university, 130, 136, 138, 202, 215
entrepreneurship, 11, 56, 58, 102, 103, 127, 130, 140, 148, 152, 202, 204, 205, 216, 218
environmental degradation, 135, 142
epistemological shift, 186, 190
ethical challenges, 73
ethical issues, 257
Ethics, i, xii, 121
examinations, xi, 1, 76, 77, 86, 95
Expert thinking, 184
F Factor, 126, 138, 140
falsifiable claims, 109
Formal degrees, 17, 26
Fourth Industrial Revolution, 19, 32, 41, 42
fraudulent, 84
funded research projects, 170
Future of Jobs, 23, 33, 42
Future Proofed University, i, viii, 1
future-proof graduate, 251
German research model, 91
gig economy, 20, 21, 22, 26, 142
GII, 136
good university education, 48
governance, ix, xii, 5, 31, 33, 47, 55, 56, 121, 122, 124, 130, 131, 214, 225, 226, 229, 257

green economy, 131, 132, 133
groups, 3, 6, 12, 20, 32, 49, 72, 73, 76, 96, 99, 143, 144, 155, 156, 160, 171, 174, 184, 191, 193, 223, 248
groupthink, 116
hard skills, 189
HDI, xiv, 223, 224, 225, 226
HESI, xii, 121, 134, 225, 227
higher education, vii, viii, ix, xiii, xiv, xv, 1, 2, 3, 4, 5, 8, 12, 13, 14, 29, 30, 31, 32, 33, 34, 35, 36, 37, 38, 39, 40, 41, 42, 43, 45, 55, 56, 59, 65, 66, 68, 84, 86, 92, 101, 102, 105, 106, 107, 110, 111, 112, 122, 125, 126, 127, 130, 135, 139, 140, 148, 151, 154,165, 181, 183, 188, 190, 193, 196, 197, 202, 213, 216, 217, 219, 223, 224, 225, 226, 229, 230, 231, 236, 237, 239, 241, 242, 243, 246, 247, 248, 249, 251, 252, 253, 255, 256
Hult Prize, 185, 191, 198
humanities, xiii, 37, 69, 70, 73, 165, 166, 167, 168, 169, 170, 171, 173, 174, 176, 177, 178, 179, 180, 181, 252
hybrid learning approach, 173
ILS, 203, 206, 207, 208, 209, 210, 212
indigenous culture, 257
Industry 4.0, 126, 133, 207
Information Age, 110
information-driven creativity, 112
intellectual capabilities, 45
intense specialisation, 87
interest in learning, 68
international experience, 153
internships, xi, 78, 97, 153, 168
IPCC, 133, 138, 229, 237
jam-packed, 73
KSA, 127
learning community, 96, 191
Learning modalities, 113
lecture, xi, 3, 18, 69, 71, 72, 73, 82, 86, 94, 95, 96, 98, 99, 105, 133, 138, 144, 175, 194, 244, 246, 251, 257
lecturing-to-the-average, 72
left behind, 24, 80, 186
machine learning, xi, 57, 105, 109, 113, 251
Magna Charta Universitatum, 122, 219
managerialism, 83, 135
managers of the future, 142
market economy, 83
marketisation, 128, 134, 135

massification, viii, 4, 8, 9, 12, 31, 71, 76, 85, 125, 127, 223, 251
mature and experienced academics, 34
mega-universities, 87
Mickey Mouse, 125
Millennium Development Goals, 224, 227
mindset, 20, 21, 26, 27, 34, 38, 48, 80, 124, 126, 135, 139, 244
Mobile interactive, 197
MOOC, 124, 190, 199
moral integrity, 170
motivation, 47, 69, 72, 97, 116, 154, 156, 158, 170, 177, 185, 186, 193, 245
Mr Memory, 74
multiple choice tests, 76
narrative forms, 144
Neo-liberal, 222
neutral education, 81
noneconomic, 32
non-traditional formats, 100
ODeL, 36
OECD, 30, 35, 40, 222, 227
Open Distance e-Learning, 36
Open source, 122
outcomes, xi, 17, 30, 56, 59, 61, 65, 86, 94, 95, 96, 97, 112, 113, 115, 117, 121, 133, 139, 170, 193, 202, 204, 210, 211, 224, 251
Outreach, 50, 51
Overseas recruitment, 2
Oxbridge, 2, 91
Pan Commonwealth Forum, 37
PAP, 193, 194
parallel education, 242, 246, 247
pedagogy, xi, xii, xiv, 31, 34, 57, 58, 73, 82, 83, 85, 89, 93, 100, 102, 133, 144, 147, 169, 176, 179, 188, 197, 257
PGCHE, 127
placements, xiii, 97, 125, 154, 155, 156, 163
Plagiarism, 254
Plasticity, 115
platform, 3, 30, 33, 51, 142, 172, 192, 196, 218, 248
popular media, xii, 141, 143, 144, 147
post-colonial, xv, 221, 224
Post-Conflict Society, ii, xv, 241
power of universities, 100, 137
powers of reasoning, 67
Pragmatists, 82
primary university models, 91

Index

private universities, 84, 241, 246, 247, 257
professional goals, 174
professional training, 72, 163
professoriate, 5, 12, 91, 92, 93
public library, ix, 10
Quality assurance, 10
quality of teaching, 92, 246
range of institutions, 255
Reason-based learning, 114
reconstruction, xv, 179, 241, 242, 252
Redbrick universities, 1
Reflective Reports, 156
research and teaching, 37, 55, 93, 101, 177, 178, 180, 257
research perspectives, 95
risk, xv, 3, 4, 6, 9, 21, 24, 25, 26, 40, 56, 96, 97, 115, 132, 138, 210
Robbins Report, 221
robotics, ix, 19, 22, 23, 24, 27, 188, 251
role-playing, 97
Russell Group, 130, 206
sage on the stage, 83, 95, 186, 248
SDG, xii, 30, 31, 36, 124, 126, 131, 134, 224, 225
self-development, 168, 177
self-reflection, 97
self-understanding, xiii, 122, 156, 162
simulational learning, 114, 117
Smart Campus, 57, 58, 62
smart learning, x, 57, 58, 59, 60, 61, 62, 63
Smart University, i, v, x, 55, 56, 57, 61, 62, 63
social process, 67, 71, 81
socio-economic challenges, 202, 204
specific learning needs, 125
spot, 76
standard courses, 112
STEAM, 49, 50, 53
Student engagement, 95, 144
student experience, 6, 7, 30, 84, 95, 97, 98, 100, 248, 255
student-centric learning, 95, 96, 97, 98
SULITEST, 125, 139
sustainability, x, xii, xv, 13, 29, 30, 31, 32, 37, 38, 56, 61, 121, 125, 126, 129, 130, 132, 133, 139, 141, 142, 143, 147, 148, 186, 191, 224, 225, 229, 230, 236, 237, 238, 239, 257
Sustainable Development Goals, xii, 42, 124, 134, 135, 137, 139, 224, 227

SVUpedia, 250
syllabi, 73, 88
synergies, 16
synthesis, 70
talk and chalk, 83
Teaching or learning, 95
teaching practice, 30, 33, 165, 169, 170, 173, 176
technology transfer, 204, 206, 210, 211, 212, 213, 214, 215, 216, 217
TEDx, 185, 198
tensions, 16, 40, 122, 134, 137, 166, 170
tertiary education, xiv, 11, 57, 61, 66, 69, 75, 84, 91, 223, 224, 225
theoretical learning, 114, 115
thesis, 70, 93, 166, 239
training, xi, xiii, 1, 19, 23, 45, 46, 47, 48, 59, 60, 62, 65, 67, 72, 77, 81, 87, 93, 100, 106, 107, 110, 112, 127, 133, 142, 151, 152, 155, 157, 161, 162, 163, 165, 168, 188, 189, 190, 201, 249, 250, 252
transformative, 29, 32, 105, 112, 130, 229
triple helix, 201, 206, 215
truth-seekers, xii, 131
Two Cultures, 69, 70
types of knowledge assets, 113
UNESCO, 29, 30, 31, 41, 42, 46, 47, 52, 58, 63, 225
Universal Human Rights, 221
university alliances, 8, 10
university performance, xi, 83
Virtual class management, 245
virtual reality, 19, 112, 117
Virtual teams, 190
von Humboldt, 55, 63, 167, 220
WebDemo, 243, 244, 245
Webinar, xiv, 188, 189, 194, 195, 196
what-if, 117
what-is, 50, 53, 67, 117, 198
wicked problem, 171, 177
Wi-Fi, 61
work-in-progress, 255
workload, 40, 41, 93, 96
work-ready, xi, 77, 78, 79, 85, 88
Work-Savvy, 79
World Bank, 217, 221, 227
World Economic Forum, 19, 23, 28, 32, 33, 42, 187, 226, 227
World Wide Web, 111, 249

www.ingramcontent.com/pod-product-compliance
Lightning Source LLC
Chambersburg PA
CBHW070242230426
43664CB00014B/2387